GAY SUNSHINE INTERVIEWS
Volume 1

This Book Donated to CLGS by

The Rev. Dr. Louis Weil

GAY SUNSHINE

A JOURNAL OF GAY LIBERATION

Lou Harrison, 1965

This Issue
INTERVIEWS
with
Lou Harrison
&
John Rechy

John Rechy, 1967

NUMBER 23

Gay Sunshine Interviews

Volume 1

EDITED BY WINSTON LEYLAND

Gay Sunshine Press
San Francisco
1978

The following interviews appeared originally in *Gay Sunshine* journal (abbreviated as GS in this listing). William Burroughs (Interview I): GS 21 (Spring 1974); Charles Henri Ford: GS 24 (Spring 1975); Jean Genet: GS 35 (Winter 1978); Allen Ginsberg: GS 16 (January 1973), GS 17 (March 1973); John Giorno: GS 24 (Spring 1975); Lou Harrison: GS 23 (November-December 1974); Christopher Isherwood (Interview I): GS 19 (September-October 1973); Harold Norse: GS 18 (June-July 1973); Peter Orlovsky: GS 25 (Summer 1975); John Rechy: GS 23 (November-December 1974); Gore Vidal (Interview II): GS 26/27 (Winter 1975/76); Tennessee Williams: GS 33/34 (Summer-Fall 1977).

Gay Sunshine Interviews Volume 1: Copyright © 1978 by Winston Leyland (for Gay Sunshine Press, Inc.). All rights reserved.

Gay Sunshine Interviews: Burroughs, Ford, Giorno, Harrison, Isherwood (Interview I), Norse, Orlovsky, Rechy, Vidal (Interview II), Tennessee Williams, Genet (English translation), copyright © 1973, 1974, 1975, 1976, 1977, 1978 by Winston Leyland (for Gay Sunshine Press, Inc.).

Allen Ginsberg Interview: copyright © 1973, 1974 by Allen Young. Reprinted with permission. Gore Vidal (Interview II): copyright © 1974 by John Mitzel and Steven Abbott. Reprinted with permission from the book *Myra and Gore* (Manifest Destiny Books). Jean Genet Interview (French version): copyright © 1977 by Hubert Fichte. Photograph of Jean Genet by Jerry Bauer. Reprinted by permission of Grove Press, Inc.

First edition 1978.

Cover design by Ed Aulerich.
Frontispiece: cover of *Gay Sunshine* 23 (1975).

Library of Congress Cataloging in Publication Data:

Main entry under title:

Gay Sunshine interviews. Volume 1

   1. Artists—Interviews. 2. Homosexuals—Interviews.
I. Leyland, Winston, 1940–
NX163.G39   809 [B]   78-8722
ISBN 0-917342-60-7 (hardcover)
ISBN 0-917342-61-5 (pbk.)

Gay Sunshine Press
P. O. Box 40397
San Francisco, CA 94140

CONTENTS

Introduction 7

WILLIAM BURROUGHS 9
    Interviewed by (I) *Laurence Collinson and Roger Baker;*
    (II) *John Giorno*

CHARLES HENRI FORD 35
    Interviewed by Ira Cohen

JEAN GENET 67
    Interviewed by Hubert Fichte

ALLEN GINSBERG 95
    Interviewed by Allen Young

JOHN GIORNO 129
    Interviewed by Winston Leyland

LOU HARRISON 163
    Interviewed by Winston Leyland

CHRISTOPHER ISHERWOOD 189
    Interviewed by (I) *Winston Leyland;* (II) *Roger Austen*

HAROLD NORSE 207
    Interviewed by Winston Leyland

PETER ORLOVSKY 239
    Interviewed by Winston Leyland and Charley Shively

JOHN RECHY 251
    Interviewed by Winston Leyland

GORE VIDAL 269
    Interviewed by (I) *John Mitzel and Steven Abbott;*
    (II) *Steven Abbott and Thom Willenbecher*

TENNESSEE WILLIAMS 309
    Interviewed by George Whitmore

Biography of Winston Leyland 326

INTRODUCTION

In JANUARY 1973 *Gay Sunshine*, the San Francisco–based cultural/literary journal which I edit, initiated its now celebrated series of interviews. Since that time we have published twenty-two in-depth interviews with gay artists: eleven poets, five novelists, two playwrights, two composers, one underground film star/poet, and one poet/librettist.

Although many literary magazines have featured interviews in the past few years, none of them, in my opinion, have been truly satisfactory. For instance, those in the *Paris Review* are much too dry and academic, and the artist *as person* is rarely considered. The *Gay Sunshine* interviews, however, have a very different focus. As general editor of the series (and interviewer in nine cases), I have been personally responsible for the form they have taken. Along with other interviewers, I have emphasized the cultural *and* the personal, engendering from the artists reflections and insights into the connections between sexuality and creativity as well as in-depth discussions of literary techniques. The interviews in Volume 1 with Ginsberg, Rechy, Norse, and Giorno are especially successful in this respect.

The interviews in the two volumes demonstrate the existence of a definite gay sensibility in the arts. Its modern genesis is to be found in the work of writers such as Walt Whitman, Oscar Wilde, John Addington Symonds, Edward Carpenter, and Constantine Cavafy. The current gay liberation movement, which received its impetus from the Stonewall demonstrations of 1969 in New York City, was especially catalytic for this gay sensibility. The rise and spread of post-Stonewall gay consciousness has had a deep effect on many writers, freeing them from societal or self-imposed retraints. To give a concrete example: homosexual themes have been present in the poems of Allen Ginsberg and Harold Norse for several decades. But since 1969 both writers have written and published many more overtly gay poems (see the two gay anthologies *Angels of the Lyre* and *Orgasms of Light* for some of these). Several of the interviews in the present anthology document the impact of gay liberation on literature and the arts.

In his review of this anthology Jacob Stockinger writes:

"Held by its fascination and prevalence, we forget that the interview is a recent form of communication. Although chronicles, diaries, letters, and other forms of literal and figurative memorabilia survive from past ages, the interview is largely an invention of our own. And at its best it is a valuable one indeed for its capacity both to entertain and to instruct. It seems such a straightforward, uncomplicated exchange of information. And yet the interview is really quite paradoxical. It tries to make a public figure more privately accessible by destroying the distance needed to sustain admiration; it aims to serve both our contemporary taste and the historical perspective; and it indulges our need for frivolity even while providing serious psychological, sociological, historical, and cultural data. Successful interviews do all this, and perhaps one thing more: indirectly, they help us to interview ourselves.

"The axis of every interview in this collection is, of course, gay sexuality. Many will wonder whether that is a sufficient basis for interviewing prominent personalities, for there is only so much one can say about being gay. One of the ironies to emerge—if it was not expected in the first place—is that even the finest of artists do not differ very much from the rest of us in their sexuality; they differ from us in their art. Yet the need to question such persons from a gay perspective is a necessary one, given the previous reticence of earlier interviewers and even of some of the same men interviewed. It is just this situation which makes the publication of the collected *Gay Sunshine Interviews* an important event in the contemporary culture scene."

Volume 1 comprises fifteen interviews with twelve artists (Burroughs, Isherwood, and Vidal are interviewed twice). Twelve interviews appeared originally in the pages of *Gay Sunshine* journal between 1973 and 1978. Two interviews (Isherwood's second and Vidal's first) were done under different auspices and are reprinted here with permission (see copyright page for details). The second Burroughs interview is previously unpublished.

I would like to thank all the interviewees for so generously giving their time and energy to this project. It is, I believe, a crucial volume for understanding and evaluating gay artistic sensibility and a seminal contribution to the ongoing Gay Cultural Renaissance.

WINSTON LEYLAND

San Francisco
Spring 1978

PHOTO BY PETER BARRY CHOWKA, 1977

WILLIAM S. BURROUGHS

WILLIAM S. BURROUGHS was born in St. Louis in 1914 and graduated from Harvard in 1936. He has worked as a newspaper reporter, private detective, exterminator, and for the past twenty years as a full-time writer. He was a narcotics addict from age 30 to age 45, and he wrote about this experience in his book *Junkie,* published in 1953 under the pseudonym William Lee (unexpurgated edition in 1977 under the title *Junky*). Burroughs' best-known work is the novel *Naked Lunch* (1959), a grim and horrifying depiction of the addict's existence with surrealistic portrayals of the drug experience. His other novels include: *The Soft Machine* (1961), *The Ticket that Exploded* (1962), *Dead Fingers Talk* (1963), *Nova Express* (1964), *The Wild Boys* (1971), and *Exterminator* (1973). Other books include *The Job* (1969; interviews), *The Last Words of Dutch Schulz: A Fiction in the Form of a Film Script* (1975), *The Book of Breething* (1975), and the autobiographical accounts *Port of Saints* (limited edition, 1973) and *Cobble Stone Gardens* (1976). *Yage Letters* (1963) reproduces his correspondence with Allen Ginsberg on the mescaline-like drug *yage.*

Burroughs' themes are totalitarianism, corporation capitalism, medical and psychiatric tyranny, homosexuality, war, and addiction; his dark vision pictures a universe ruled by unrestrained technological power groups.

TWO INTERVIEWS are printed here: Interview I was taped in London, England, in early 1973 by Australian writer Laurence Collinson and English journalist Roger Baker. It originally appeared in *Gay Sunshine* 21 (Spring 1974). Interview II was taped in New York City in spring 1977 by poet John Giorno (see biographical note on p. 130). It is published here for the first time. See also the Ginsberg and Norse interviews elsewhere in this anthology for more on Burroughs.

I

Laurence Collinson and Roger Baker interview
WILLIAM S. BURROUGHS

INTERVIEWER: Could you tell us something about you own past and present sexual encounters?

BURROUGHS: I've lived for many years in Mexico and in North Africa. And there the scene was I usually had one boy friend for quite a long time. I had one for a year, two years—something like that. If I have a boyfriend who is satisfactory, I don't feel like anything else. Not a question of love or being faithful or anything of that sort. It was just enough. So while I was in Tangier where there were lots of boys available, I had about ten or, at most, fifteen different people over a period of five years.

INTERVIEWER: Was this also happening during your junkie period?

BURROUGHS: No. Nobody is sexy on junk. No sex at all.

INTERVIEWER: And when you say "boy," do you mean an actual boy?

BURROUGHS: More properly a youth. Most of my boys have been between the ages of 18 and 25; a few younger.

INTERVIEWER: Nowadays, do you do something similar, or do you have a settled partner?

BURROUGHS: Oh yes, I've had several boys while I've been in London, always much younger than myself.

Apparently Japan is the ideal place for older men. I've talked to people who have lived there for years, and they say it really is the place for men over a certain age, because they have a sort of respect for older men you don't find in the West. Tangier, Morocco, is a sort of Mecca for the English. I've known lots of Englishmen stuck in some little town in the country where they have to toe the line, and they go to Tangier for vacation. Then they're insatiable. Sex always has to be paid for. You keep the boys, buy them clothes—things like that. The whole thing is that the boys don't have any money.

You know, homosexuality is a worldwide economic fact. In poor countries—like Morocco and parts of Italy—it's one of the big industries, one of the main ways in which a young boy can get somewhere. If he's lucky and gets a rich lover, he can then go on and get rich himself. Naturally, the homosexual is taking advantage of the fact that people are poor. But in view of the situation that exists, why not? It's not in my power to change the economy of Morocco or other poor countries.

INTERVIEWER: But is it not possible to have a relationship with a young man of that age without considering the economic factor?

BURROUGHS: It's quite possible in an affluent society and does occur. But in Morocco we have a boy who is working at hard and dull work which will bring him seven dollars a week. He can earn five dollars in ten minutes through sex. If I was young and poor, I'd certainly turn a few tricks rather than work in a factory all day. I had a number of jobs during the war and most jobs are absolutely unbearable. I could only stick them for a week. It's just unbelievably awful: you sit there and do some absolutely meaningless and uncomfortable thing for eight hours; and worse still is the white-collar work, like being a filing clerk. That was the dullest job I ever had in my life. I fucked up their whole office system. The only job I was ever able to keep for any length of time was as an exterminator—cockroaches and bugs. I'd work in my own time and usually finish in two hours. The rest was easy, walking around, talking to people. I'd go see ten different apartments in a day.

INTERVIEWER: Is this possibly why there's so much pest imagery in your work?

BURROUGHS: Yeah. I had that job for eight months. The only job I enjoyed.

INTERVIEWER: Do you regard writing as a job?

BURROUGHS: Very definitely a job. There's the whole business side; it's a job that's hard to make a living at. For example, if I were as well known in any other field as I am in writing, I'd be making five times as much money, at least. Some times I feel that I might have done something else. Hell, if I were a plumber I'd be making three times as much money as I am at writing—in the States at least.

My first book was *Junkie*. I wrote it when I was thirty-five. The next book after that was *The Yage Letters*. There was quite a long period when I was doing very little, because I was using junk so heavily—not conducive to writing. After I took the apomorphine cure and got back to Tangier, in 1956, that's when I really started writing full time. And from then on I've really done very little else.

INTERVIEWER: Can you live in Tangier on very little these days?

BURROUGHS: Prices are going up there as everywhere else. It's three or four times as expensive now as it was in 1956 but still much cheaper than London. It's cheaper if you cook in, get someone in to do the shopping and cook. For five dollars a day you'll get a lunch for five with enough left over for dinner for two or three. Arab style cooking, of course.

INTERVIEWER: Is the Arab world's concept of a homosexual quite the same as in the Western world?

BURROUGHS: No, it's quite different.

INTERVIEWER: We are trying to present ourselves as individuals, whereas to the Arab homosexuality is more of a genital thing and doesn't really spill over into their concept of the family, the home...

BURROUGHS: It's much more casual. It is common for married Arabs to have homosexual affairs, but these are casual. They don't have a word for loyalty.

INTERVIEWER: Do they have homosexual relationships on a permanent or semi-permanent basis?

BURROUGHS: Yes, I guess they do, though I can't think of many.

INTERVIEWER: Are their relationships mainly with boys or with older men?

BURROUGHS: Mostly with boys. It is considered quite normal for someone to like women and boys.

INTERVIEWER: Allen Ginsberg says you've become a hero figure, or guru, of the gay liberation movement. Do you feel this is so?

BURROUGHS: My participation has been in writing so far. I haven't taken part in demonstrations, but I feel they are useful. Naturally I'm all for gay civil rights—it goes without saying.

INTERVIEWER: Do you think there is any real future in a movement that is not a revolutionary one—for everyone, not just gays?

BURROUGHS: I don't like to seem pessimistic, but it's my feeling that no revolutionary movement in the West has any real chance of success. There are a number of reasons for this. For one thing, the industrial process has gone too far. After a certain point of industrialization, a revolution from the bottom—that is, from the streets, the barricades—is completely impractical. Even Mexico has reached that stage. This simply means that the people who are in a position of power can hold down ninety-nine percent of the population by sheer force if they have to, if they have the weapons to do it. In the old days anyone could go down to his basement and make his own weapons, a spear, a bow and arrow, a crude gun. But he can't make automatic weapons. He can't make tanks, planes. He can't make heavy weapons. The only viable weapons for a revolution now are biological and chemical weapons.

INTERVIEWER: What about the revolution in Cuba?

BURROUGHS: Cuba was, of course, a country that had not reached that stage of industrialization; there are such countries in South America. There are now more CIA men than guerrillas in South America, swarming all over each country, to be sure that revolution doesn't happen, and infiltrating the guerrilla groups and operating the government forces there.

INTERVIEWER: There was a lot of controversy in gay circles here and in the States about the Cuban revolution and the oppression of gays in Cuba. Ginsberg was kicked out because he was homosexual.

BURROUGHS: Well, the whole military structure of the West naturally brings about a situation where it is essential for Marxist countries also to have a military establishment. That's what the whole cold war is about—the strength of the conservatives in both camps.

INTERVIEWER: What sort of biological weapons do you envisage?

BURROUGHS: Well, biological and chemical weapons are, of course, chemicals, gases, and germs, or bugs. They need not be indiscriminate. It is within the range of biochemistry now to create selective pestilences that would attack, say, only whites, only colored, only females. Certain groups are much more liable to certain diseases than others anyway.

INTERVIEWER: In your books and interviews you express very strong anti-establishment feelings. Do you feel that Gay Liberation has anything to contribute to—using your own terms—the overthrow of *Them* by *Us*?

BURROUGHS: Well, yes I do. I don't think a political revolution as such is possible in the West at the present time. That could only be possible in a completely chaotic state, say if we started a war. Drop five atom bombs on the United States and the chaos would be unbelievable. In a situation like that, perhaps.... But there is also the possibility of a cultural revolution that would make changes—that fact that young people growing up now are going to be the people of the future. That is the real area of hope; it lies with the new generation. They're just not making those old-style conservatives any more. In another thirty years many of them will have passed away. And I don't think there's an unlimited supply coming on to take their place.

I think that Gay Liberation, the breakdown of censorship and so on, are very important cultural factors. And this includes the fact that many young people today just accept that some people are gay. Forty years ago, when I was in college, there was no acceptance at all. You just shut up about it. People might *know*, but never mention it. You got the situation of these queens saying, "Nobody knows anything about *me*." Well, they did. You didn't talk about it, and the idea of claiming it as a right was out of the question. But now Allen Ginsberg gets up before an audience of college students and talks about how he jacked off Peter Orlovsky last night, and they all cheer. Forty years ago they'd have been ridden out on a rail. So that is a terrific change.

INTERVIEWER: Your own books deal with homosexual experience and are widely read and accepted.

BURROUGHS: Indeed. And Genet's *Notre Dame des Fleurs* was a best seller.

INTERVIEWER: Can we talk a little about your interest in Scientology? Many ex-Communists took it up as a new religion. I found Scientology pamphlets almost incomprehensible. It was only reading what you have written about the reactive mind that made any sense whatever to me.

BURROUGHS: Scientology *is* a religion. They call it a religion. When I found out that it was a religion, I quit. I'm not interested in religions.

The whole thing in Scientology is this instrument called the E-meter, which is actually more or less a biofeedback. A lot of ordering after a certain stage; when you are ordering yourself, all you are doing is seeing your reaction to whatever it is. Suppose you had an encephalograph that shows you your reactions when you consider certain material. This is exactly what the E-meter does, but they will not admit that this is a biofeedback.

INTERVIEWER: They attach some mystic importance to it. I held the cans as if I were going through some peculiar embarrassing joke. But the way you write about it, it had some significance.

BURROUGHS: I think it has. You see, it is passing a small charge of electricity through the brain and through the body and by repetitive emphasis is directing the current towards certain brain areas, and is also a form of electric brain stimulation; and we know that electric brain stimulation can accomplish almost anything. Did you see the article in the *Observer* about Professor Delgado, the one that stops the bull? He's got electrodes in the bull's scalp, in the bull's brain. He presses a button and the bull charges. He presses a button and the bull stops. They've done this with people; they can make them frightened, or sexually excited, or produce any emotional reaction simply by pressing a button.

INTERVIEWER: Do you still hold to what you wrote about the reactive mind?

BURROUGHS: Ron Hubbard's concept of the reactive mind I don't hold with at all. Of course, it's partly what Freud called the unconscious.

INTERVIEWER: The concept of the two contradicting messages—that seems to make a lot of sense. The contradiction makes people powerless.

BURROUGHS: Well, there's no question about that. What anxiety is, is contradictory signals. That's what causes the feeling of shakiness and powerlessness; you are getting simultaneous signals that are contradictory. The lines of communication within the body are from bodily processes to the back brain which is the emotional center, and then to the front brain. The cat wakes up; it's hungry. The hunger is communicated to the back brain, then its front brain goes into operation to find some food. You can never give a front brain order to the back brain and to the body, and the more you try the worse it gets. I mean, if someone's hand starts shaking and he tries to pull himself together, as they say, he can't because that's not the way in which communication works; you are simply calling the wrong line.

INTERVIEWER: Have you any further thoughts on gay liberation?

[*Burroughs responded by reading his essay published in* The Gay Liberation Book (1973). *In 1974, after this interview had already appeared,* Gay Sunshine *published a revised and expanded version of that essay, under the title "Sexual Conditioning" (*Issue no. 23, p. 25*), accompanied by a photo of Burroughs taken at the benefit reading he did for* Gay Sunshine *in November 1974. This revised essay is now published here for the first time in book form. —Ed.*]

SEXUAL MORALITY in the Western world is based on the Bible and especially on the teachings of St. Paul which presume to impose one arbitrary and dogmatic standard of sexual behavior on all people everywhere and forever. The teachings of St. Paul are now dead and unworkable. Dead since the pill has separated sexual pleasure from reproduction. Dead since overpopulation has made reproduction something to be curtailed rather than encouraged. Dead since experiments have shown that sexual desire is a matter of stimulating certain brain areas and that such stimulation is *purely arbitrary*. Admittedly homosexuals can be conditioned to react sexually to a woman, or to an old boot for that matter. In fact both homo- and heterosexual experimental subjects *have been* conditioned to react sexually to a boot—to an old boot. You can save a lot of money that way.

In the same way heterosexual males can be conditioned to react sexually to other men. Who is to say that one is more desirable than the other? The latter-day apologists of St. Paul who call themselves psychiatrists have little to recommend them but their bad statistics. Psychiatrists say they need more money and more personnel to deal with the ever-growing problem of mental illness, and the more money and personnel channeled into this bottomless pit, the higher the statistics on mental illness climb. It is indeed an ever-growing problem at this rate. Personally I think that mental illness is largely a psychiatric invention.

On December 3, 1973, the American Psychiatric Association decided that homosexuality would no longer be considered a mental deviation. Well, if they have more mental patients now than they can handle, it would seem to be a step in the right direction to remove homosexuals from this category. But the decision has caused a storm of protest. One psychiatrist compared the decision to "a psychiatric Watergate which we hope won't be our Waterloo...." They just don't like to see any prospective patients escaping; it could start a mass walkout. Doctor Charles Socarides, associate clinical professor of psychiatry at the Albert Einstein Clinic, staunchly opposes the new APA approach: "The APA has done what all civilizations have trembled to do ... tamper with the biologic role between the sexes." Fancy that! And in a letter to *Playboy* in June of 1970, Dr. Socarides says, "Five hundred millions years of evolution have established the male/female standard as *the* functionally healthy pattern of human sexual fulfillment."

Just a minute here, Doctor—the human species is not more than one million years old according to the earliest human remains so far discovered. Other species have had a longer run. Three hundred million years have established a big mouth that can bite almost anything off and a gut that can digest it as a functionally healthy pattern for sharks. One hundred thirty million years more or less established large size as functionally healthy for dinosaurs. What may be functionally healthy at one time is not necessarily so under altered conditions, as the bones of discontinued models bear silent witness. But sharks, dinosaurs, and psychiatrists don't want to change.

The sexual revolution is now moving into the electronic stage. Recent experiments in electric brain stimulation indicate that sexual excitement and orgasm can be produced at push-button control or push-button *choice,* depending on who is pushing the buttons control. Buttons to the people. None of these bits of technology are in the future. The knowledge and most of the hardware exist today. In terms of human sexuality what could it mean? It could mean you can plug in anything you want.

Experiments in autonomic shaping have demonstrated that subjects can learn to control these responses and reproduce them at will, once they learn where the neural buttons are located. Just decide what you want and your local sex-adjustment center will match your brain waves and provide a suitable mate of whatever sex, real or imaginary, while you wait. It is now possible to provide every man and woman with the best sex kicks he or she can tolerate without blowing a fuse.

Any candidate running on that ticket should poll a lot of votes and bring a lot of issues right out into the open.

* * *

... What is sexually exciting to someone is essentially a film.... I was asked to write an article on what is sexy, but I never quite got it together, though I made some notes. [*Burroughs then proceeded to read out loud from his notes on what people find sexy.*] "What is sexy to an individual human creature? An old film, a film usually laid down in early childhood on a reception screen. Take for example this story, rather typical, passed along to me by the usual means, a street pick-up: This highly placed civil servant paid boys to don uniforms and treat him like a boy in reform school. They were, in fact, given a very precise script for certain words, like 'You little bastard.' You see, he always wanted to be a Borstal boy, not an old school tie.*

"He is tied to that little piece of film as the only way he can achieve ejacula-

---

*Borstal is the British reform school institution; an "old school tie" is the upper-class public school institution. —Ed.

tion. He may be sick of it, disgusted by it, may even laugh at it—but not while it is going on. Anybody ever explain why sex and laughter are incompatible? Who can laugh and come at the same time? I've only seen one boy who could do this and his name was Ali. He called me 'Master'—he was being ironical, of course, for he was the master. He disappeared before I could learn his secret. I feel sure the highly placed civil servant did not have any secret. In his case the film was, and is, a dreary slavery. It may be much wider and include a whole shifting gamut of scripts, but it's still a film.

"The whole question of what is, and is not sexy, and the question of so-called normalcy, have been placed in an entirely new light by recent discoveries in the area of electric brain stimulation. Stimulate the sex centers of the brain and anything in sight is sexy—even a psychiatrist. There was an eleven-year-old boy who became very amorous toward the psychiatrist under electric brain stimulation. In fact, subjects have been conditioned to react sexually to an old boot.

"Now, back to our film analogy. That piece of film is quite literally wired to the sex centers of the brain. With electric brain stimulation we should be able to plug into another film. So here's the man with his boot—turn off the current and it's just an old boot. Enter the psychiatrist with a naked bunny girl. He turns on the current full blast and the man is cured. Or is he? Well, let's leave the current off. He examines the naked girl critically: beautiful! he feels some sexual excitement, but—um—you know, put your clothes on, dear and you'll be sexier. Dodges sideways and brings up a knee to his groin, and his slight sexual excitement evaporates.

"Well, what happens if all the old films of prohibition and excitement were removed from a person. What would his sexuality be without those films? I don't know. Let's see. Speaking for myself, the one thing I find sexy is creation, to create on paper a sexy person—sexy to me, that is. And if it is a real creation, it will be interesting to other readers as well. I do not share Genet's sexual tastes, but his petty pimps and thieves are creations made with love and consummate artistry, and I will say that any writer who has not masturbated with his own characters will not be able to make them live on paper. If the writer tries to write a character who'll be sexy to the reader but not to him, it will not live on paper; it'll simply be a piece of someone else's film. I don't think people realize to what extent our previous ideas about sex have been really annulled by these discoveries. The knowledge is now available and one could literally reprogram someone."

INTERVIEWER: To what end?

BURROUGHS: The question is: is he satisfied with his film? If he is, there's no reason to alter it. If he's not, well, I don't think many people are.

INTERVIEWER: A lot of people cling to the film because it's the only thing they know.

BURROUGHS: It's the only thing they've got. Tell me why they can't get it off...

INTERVIEWER: You either let them stay with it, or try and break them from the habit into something more satisfying.

BURROUGHS: As I said, at least into a film that has a wider range and could give them more satisfaction.

INTERVIEWER: Would you like to have your film changed?

BURROUGHS: Well, not my sexual program necessarily. But there are certainly some things I'd like to change. I think all of us to a certain extent have been crippled by early conditioning, and there are always traces of that in me that I'd be glad to get rid of.

INTERVIEWER: Very hard to get rid of. It would require immense practice.

BURROUGHS: Yes, but quite possible if a state of society existed in which patterns were not forced on the child. But we are certainly a long way from that. The whole family structure—I mean whatever sort of hangups the parents have, they will pass on to their children.

INTERVIEWER: What are your feelings about matriarchal/patriarchal societies?

BURROUGHS: I think there are lots of things that need to be said that haven't been said. One of them is the assumption that homosexuality is disapproved of in a patriarchal society. This is not true at all. The only patriarchal society that I know exists today is the Arab, and of course they're tolerant. America's certainly no patriarchal society, neither is England. To whose advantage is it that homosexuality should be disapproved of? It is to the advantage of the female sex, no question about that.

I've just noticed in *The Gay Liberation Book,* and I've heard it from other sources, partly from Reich, that the patriarchal society was anti-sexual in general. I say the opposite—all *matriarchal* societies are anti-sexual in general and specifically anti-homosexual. It's to the advantage of women. They want to get married, for Christ's sake. So the more of a damper there's put on sex in general and the harder it is to get it outside marriage, the better chance they have—no question of that.

INTERVIEWER: But is the female urge to get married natural, or is it part of the social structure? Why should women want, above all things, to get married?

BURROUGHS: That's the point, of course, that the women's lib people are always making. It's conditioned by a lot of factors in the West. They want to get married so they're settled financially, so they have security. Certainly the whole social structure in the West is molded in that direction.

INTERVIEWER: In your earlier work, especially in *The Job,* you prophesy many of the ideas that are now commonplace in gay liberation and women's liberation circles, particularly about the nuclear family and the role of the father and the mother who are crippling the child.

BURROUGHS: There is no doubt that this is what the family does. R. D. Laing and David Cooper have gone into all that extensively and I think very much to the purpose. But no one has come up with a really viable substitute for the biologic family. It's partly economic.

INTERVIEWER: But it's essential to the economy that the biological family continue.

BURROUGHS: Exactly, exactly!

INTERVIEWER: Once you get people acting on their own initiative then wham goes civilization as we know it.

BURROUGHS: A good thing, too, probably. But to return to the effect of gay militancy. A factor many of them don't seem to have taken into consideration is the huge, top-heavy concentrations of people in urban centers. How many millions of people have to work just to get food into the shops, into restaurants, to create power etc. and keep all those people alive. Now if everybody dropped out and did their thing, then millions of people would be starving overnight. So if you think in terms of a political situation, whatever your political program is, you are going to have to keep those people on that job doing the same thing. Or get somebody else to do it—right? But so many of the modern militants don't seem to think in those terms. The Marxists did. They had very definite ideas about what they were going to do about food distribution etc. And if you're going to have to keep everybody doing just about the same thing they're doing now, there isn't going to be a helluva lot of difference. It doesn't make much difference to the individual whether the means of production is state-owned or individually owned.

INTERVIEWER: In a sense I think it does. I feel more antipathy towards the idea of my working bringing profits to an individual than to the state. I feel it's wrong for a particular person to exploit me.

BURROUGHS: All right. You are, say, a factory manager in Russia. There's not a helluva lot of difference between that and the same job in a company owned by an individual. You probably wouldn't make so much money in a state-owned factory. Your position wouldn't really be changed, and who cares whether the railroads are, for example, owned by the state or by individuals. Many are owned by the state in Europe—doesn't make any difference to the individual who works there or to the individual who travels on the railroads. I just don't see that as any solution. It wouldn't make any changes in the lives of most individuals.

INTERVIEWER: But by transferring many enterprises to state control, a government can to some extent rationalize them. For example, housing in Russia is much less expensive than it is here.

BURROUGHS: There's that factor, of course. The capitalist economic system is supposed to do many things. You know, we've been brought up to the idea that a good product will be produced and will find buyers. Well, that's not true at all, because of the lobbying of vested interests. The real estate lobby has prevented any cheap housing in the States. Every time anyone has come out with a really cheap practical prefabricated house, he gets frozen out by the real estate lobby. It's not in their interest to produce houses that are cheaper, houses that will last.

Of course, overpopulation is one of *the* biggest problems here in Britain. Say twenty million people could support themselves reasonably well. Now there are about sixty million. That, of course, means the cycle of more and more pollution, and less and less food to feed more and more. And it's going to take progressively more and more money to buy less and less, because there *is* less and less. The end of money will come when no amount of money will buy anything. It would be quite possible to calculate when this will occur. The whole value of money is in other people not having it. If everyone had money, it would have no value, which is also why people in positions of wealth and power can't make too many concessions. You would say: well, why don't they shut the militants up by legalizing marijuana and giving them sex—sex centers where they can go and get a satisfactory sex partner, as often as they want. Because if they did, money and power would lose their value. Money and power only have value if someone else doesn't have it.

INTERVIEWER: Are you opposed to the use of amphetamines?

BURROUGHS: I think it's terrible stuff. I hate it myself. I hate the sensation. It depends on how much, of course. When you get people taking a lot of it, it destroys their appetite. It's very bad for their health in any large quantity. A very small quantity, though, is easily absorbed and shouldn't cause any problem at all.

I think apomorphine would be tremendously useful if it could be in general use, helpful to people who are insecure in their own personalities. And if they started experimenting with it, synthesizing it, they could develop much more powerful varieties and no doubt could eliminate the nausea factor. Nausea isn't necessarily a major factor. Dr. Dent pointed out that there is no need for anyone to be sick to have the benefits of apomorphine. He'd regulate the dose and find out the dose that would produce vomiting; then he would start dropping it until he got the highest dose people could tolerate without vomiting. People vary considerably in their reaction. Some can only take a fortieth of a grain, others up to a tenth. People who can take more are very rare. An injection of a tenth will almost always produce vomiting. It is a drug that has no exhilarating or narcotic effects, unless you are in a state of acute anxiety or metabolic disturbance. Then the removal of those states can have an exhilarating effect. It seems to me to be the most useful drug in curing alcoholism and drug addiction.

INTERVIEWER: Do you mind talking about work in progress?

BURROUGHS: Yes, while in progress. I've just *completed* a novel called *Exterminator!* published in New York in spring, 1973. I'm not doing anything in particular just now. I've also just completed assembling and describing my archives for sale to a university or to an individual collector. That took five months. I had Barry Miles, who is an expert. He worked on Ginsberg's archives. The catalogue alone has four hundred pages.

Exterminator! is very much a continuation of *The Wild Boys.* Always when I write a book there are a lot of manuscript pages left over. I always have a lot left over from previous books. And it's largely that material that went into this new book; *The Wild Boys* is a sort of homosexual *Peter Pan.*

INTERVIEWER: The imagery in your books of boys screwing each other and great spurts of come going all over the room strikes me as romantic . . .

BURROUGHS: It is romantic. Of course, sodomy is much more widespread among oriental people and the Arabs, and also in Mexico and South America. It's regarded as the rational thing for people to do together, rather than sucking. In fact, the Arabs feel that cocksucking is a terrible, dirty thing to do. They don't approve of it at all. It's the cultural pattern. I found this to be true in Arab countries and in South America.

I feel that something that should be investigated are ways of increasing sexual enjoyment. One of these is certainly Reich's orgone accumulator. These could be greatly potentiated by using magnetic iron, an experiment I haven't made. Magnetic iron, instead of just sheet metal, would pass a whole magnetic field through the body. But there's no question that the orgone accumulator, even in its present state, does enhance sexuality. On my lecture tour and in my writing, I'd like to get people actually experimenting with some of these things, like the orgone accumulator, because I think they could turn up something. Reich's experiments are very easy to perform. Orgone boxes are very simple to build— just a wooden framework, a box big enough for you to sit in, with a small opening for ventilation; or you can have them big enough for two people and completely lined with sheet metal. I've also seen them made with steel wool, but I don't like that; it's a mesh and the mesh peels and you are always getting in there and some piece of wire sticks into you. You stay in for half an hour, fifteen minutes a day. Someone did build one for me, but it was such a huge object I had to get rid of it.

Reich observed that cancer was almost always a disease of sexual decline and therefore something that potentiated sexuality could be anti-cancerous. In his book *The Cancer Biopath,* Reich says that cancer is essentially a disease of sexual suppression and deprivation. If I had the money, I'd certainly set up an experiment with some of these things. But I just don't have it. Undoubtedly something does happen to you. You feel healthier and sexier from using them regularly.

II

John Giorno interviews
WILLIAM S. BURROUGHS

BURROUGHS: I was speaking about the so-called gay community, which is not actually a community since there are people in it with disparate interests and so on. But it's very important that they get out of the whole defensive protest position which they're still in, and no wonder, we've had such phenomena as Anita Bryant, the Miss America down in Florida who's doing the crusade against homosexuality. So really, they're continuing a circle because they realize that suddenly they may be the big scapegoat. They're scared as hell that suddenly we'll have a fascist state and all gays will be thrown in concentration camps. I think that they have the same sort of hysterical reactive attitude which you find in any kind of persecuted group. Like the Jews, a persecuted minority. It's all very well to say that they should get out of their position of defense, but it's going to be difficult because as we have seen in actual practice these things can happen.

GIORNO: I agree with you. That state of protest becomes a state of aggression that's totally binding.

BURROUGHS: But it's also interesting in that it brings down the very thing that they fear. Like the Jewish Defense League trying to ally themselves with the most reactionary elements, bringing down on themselves the very thing they fear—the panic reaction is always met by a larger reaction.

GIORNO: The fear of loss is loss.

BURROUGHS: Yeah.

GIORNO: There must be some position one should take in a non-aggressive, non-hysterical dealing with the anti-gay thing occurring in the world.

BURROUGHS: And the defensive doctrinaire attitude that gays are more sensitive and better than other people, that gay writers are more profound, I think this is shallow and inadequate.

GIORNO: Do you think of yourself as a gay writer?

BURROUGHS: No. I don't know what that means. I'm obviously a homosexual writer with hardly a woman in his books.

GIORNO: Do you consciously have that sexual division? Because the way I work and feel, what makes me a gay or homosexual writer is working with images of desire. I do not for one minute think that homosexuality is any different from any other kind of sexuality or desire.

BURROUGHS: I'm inclined to think it is.

GIORNO: How so?

BURROUGHS: Well it's a different object. Someone who's attracted to a candlestick may not be attracted to a boot or an old tin can, it's a different object.

GIORNO: That's the point. It's a different object, but in totally accomplished sexuality there is no man or woman in the space of their sexuality, just as there should not be two men. There's some kind of other dance and if it's done properly there's energy—some kind of energy.

BURROUGHS: I have no quarrel with that. It's energy.

The question arises as to who is really down on homosexual practices and precisely why. We know that a lot has come from the Christian religion. Not from Christ himself, he was probably a faggot, but from St. Paul. Talking about man and man lying with each other and doing that which is inconvenient. And as Anita Bryant is saying down there, "It's an abomination." An abomination from the Bible. Quoting the Bible or any long book out of context you can prove absolutely anything. Like snake handlers, "Pick ye up serpents," and actually rattlers from Florida wiped out a whole nest of snake handlers. Well the moral is the abysmal ignorance of this fucking lower-church Protestant thing. They're lunatics, absolute lunatics, dangerous lunatics—"Kill a queer for Christ." Can "Kill a Jew for Jesus" be far behind? And she's got fifty thousand signatures.

Now, since we've been forced into the same position as the Jews perhaps we should enact the same strategy. We should try to get our own state like Israel.

GIORNO: But don't you think there's some other space? The reason why everything now for gays in the Western world is so good is because of you and Allen, years ago, doing this thing which expanded and expanded. I agree with you about the aggression that comes with being a politically active gay, but there's another non-aggressive way of doing it in a very active fashion, you know what I mean?

BURROUGHS: Of course my dear, and this has been going on for thousands of years. Gays have been living in relative security.

GIORNO: There's never been a battle—that's totally correct!—there's never been a battle in the world except in our minds.

BURROUGHS: Well I wouldn't say that either.

GIORNO: It's the mind projecting it in space.

BURROUGHS: Not at all. Of course it could be managed that way. But the more extreme it gets on any side, the thing escalates. From mild anti-Semitism to death camps.

GIORNO: William, what do you think of communities like the West Village where ninety percent of it is gay?

BURROUGHS: Well. It's the thing now. I believe that gays should be allowed to live in an all-gay community. This would be a very healthy thing. There could be a gay laundry and a gay restaurant and a gay everything. If this could extend through our society, where a person associated with only the people he wanted to associate with, this would be a great source of harmony. There may be blacks who with good reason may not ever want to see another white person as long as they live. Well that's fine. There's no reason why they shouldn't arrange it, have an all-black community. This is a very important idea, the right of a person to live in a community of people he relates to and who relate to him. He doesn't always have to be faced by some hostility from someone who has a different idea.

GIORNO: So in other words, a ghetto is really a sublime place.

BURROUGHS: In a sense yes. There's also the question: if you're happy and secure in a ghetto situation, you may not be aware in time of dangers brewing from the outside.

GIORNO: Unless you have a good secret service and a very powerful state. Gay State!

BURROUGHS: We'll have the best secret service in the world.

GIORNO: Would you model it after the CIA? British Foreign Service?

BURROUGHS: If I modeled it after anything I really think it would be the CIA. I really think they are the best secret service in the world. For all its mistakes, the British never get caught with their pants down, but they don't attempt as much, they don't go as far. The CIA is more in touch with present times.

GIORNO: Do you think the CIA has been affected by all the bad publicity? Do you think it has affected its operability?

BURROUGHS: Not seriously.

GIORNO: Is the Gay State a real geographic place too?

BURROUGHS: It would have to be.

GIORNO: What would be the policy regarding heterosexuals?

BURROUGHS: Well there wouldn't be any policy. Heterosexuals would be welcome in the Gay State so long as they don't engage in any subversive political activity.

GIORNO: And that is what the secret service is for. To make sure that that's the case.

BURROUGHS: And also to protect us against our enemies outside of our state. Now you can see we're getting into a very interesting philosophical area, whereby we are saying that as long as one enemy to our sacred community draws breath, we are not safe. Because god knows he might organize an anti-queer crusade. But queers are taking over our kids with dope. They are.

GIORNO: Do you believe every gay should have a gun?

BURROUGHS: No. That's not what I'm saying at all. What I'm saying is the lunacy on which we've all been brought up. The fact that there's terrible people, out there, across the river, in this country or that country. And there ain't no compromise. We've got to kill them all. And this has been going on for thousands of years. This stems from a very ancient reputable philosophical concept, known as Dualism, and this is the Manichaean philosophy—the fight between Good and Evil. In Christian terms, good is sure to win. But in the Manichaean terms it was a fight that was up for grabs. In the spirit of our society, what is evil is anything that fucks me up, what's good is anything that helps me and improves me. Simple as that. So this whole irreconcilable conflict of interests is obviously the terminal insanity of the Dualistic universe. Good or Bad, white or black, gives rise to the stupidist terms like "There ain't room for both of us in this town." There ain't room for me and Anita Bryant in the same town. Suck your orange. Obviously this is the most primitive kind of thinking that dates back to the origin of the species, territorial rights. But it goes through the whole society. If anybody's got something they took it from somebody else, like we took America from the Indians.

GIORNO: But isn't that the basic nature of the world of desire? It doesn't have to be Jews or gays, it could be anybody.

BURROUGHS: It's the nature of rivalry and time. Out of thousands of streetcorner punks maybe ten or fifteen get in the Mafia, get to be a hit man. The most sought-after job in a slum environment is being a hit man for the Mafia. Talk about a travesty of civilization. People falling all over themselves to be an abject hit man.

GIORNO: It's like going to Hollywood and being a star.

BURROUGHS: And the Mafia only has room for about fifteen hit men a year.

GIORNO: It's really the Super Bowl.

BURROUGHS: We don't need many of these fuckers. We have all we need now, people are being encouraged to leave the industry.

In a Manichaean universe the forces of Good and Bad are absolutely equal, which leads to a stalemate or an anti-matter explosion. In the hope of averting such a confrontation the Christians always assumed that they were right and were going to win. They couldn't believe they could possibly lose. With the illusion that they are going to win, the Christians are at a great disadvantage in the struggle, being rooted in stupidity.

GIORNO: But don't you think, William, that the dynamics of the situation you describe are based on illusion?

BURROUGHS: Well remember everything is illusion. But illusions try to make themselves as real as possible, naturally, in order to gain currency.

GIORNO: How do you say we deal with these illusions?

BURROUGHS: I don't have any panacea. If you really accept the doers of Good and Evil you come to realize that the actual power of each of them must be the same. Because every time Evil gets a big push, it gives an equal push to the other side.

GIORNO: It's just like fucking, isn't it?

BURROUGHS: And the Christians say, "We're going to win because we're right." Obviously they have no objective orientation at all. There's a possibility that what we call Good and Evil is really matter and anti-matter and when they get together for a final confrontation the whole shit-house will go up. We'll have a black hole.

GIORNO: A black hole I would think is just part of the same dynamics.

BURROUGHS: We poets and artists have to think about our work, and that's the important thing.

Ask me a question. Like, "Mr. Burroughs, do you think, if it were in your power, would you make heterosexual activities as illegal as homosexual activities are now? Do you think that you would have it in your heart to do this? Mr. Burroughs?"

GIORNO: That's a great question, William.

BURROUGHS: Ain't that a great question? And shove the mike right in your face.

GIORNO: Well what do you say?

BURROUGHS: I go all mealy-mouthed, like any old politician. "I believe in more of everything, more life, more happiness, more everything for all people on this great planet earth, men, women, Jews, kikes, queers, every fucking thing that crawls around on this earth, and that is my sincere feeling. It's unthinkable that I would harm any person at all or do wrong to any man, unless there was some smart son-of-a-bitch starting some trouble, huh? Yeah! So that's the way I feel about this whole thing. Under no circumstances, no matter how much power I had, would I abuse that power to harm any decent fucker, any decent person, any decent WASP. I will tell you that if I had to use that power to prevent certain forces from taking over and corrupting and degrading everything that we Americans hold dear, I would not hesitate. I would not hesitate to use that power even if the whole fucking universe blew up!"

GIORNO: Right on!

BURROUGHS: Right on! Yeah. Like the senator said, "I would not hesitate to use the cobalt bomb against Russia."

So this is the impasse of a dualistic universe. Everyone says, I would not hesitate, I would not hesitate, I would not hesitate, to use to use to use, the most extreme the most extreme the most extreme BOOM! Maybe it's just as well, what the hell....

...John and I were talking about readings and professionalism, and quite a bit about the basis of the American Dream, which is money. And then John says we've got to record something for this interview, and I said to him I haven't been thinking about homosexuality for the last past half hour, or conversing on it.

GIORNO: We were conversing about money. Money! Power!

BURROUGHS: Yes, exactly. So I think this follows what I was saying about gays getting out of a defensive prickly position where they've got to be gay twenty-four hours a day. You can relax and think about other subjects. Because after all, how much time does sex actually take in anybody's life? And once gays can be gay and do what they want the whole matter shrinks down to a small percentage of time.

GIORNO: Do you see any difference between heterosexual and homosexual, beside the difference that one like a woman and one likes a man?

BURROUGHS: Well you can have a heterosexual man who spends half an hour three times a week, or whatever the hell how much time he spends, and then you can have heterosexual men who are obsessed with sex, and it takes all their time.

GIORNO: There's this thing called desire which is a basic unexplained energy, which is basically great, but is like a poison for most people, heterosexual or homosexual. And it's just desire, the grasping of something.

BURROUGHS: It's stupidity to be obsessed with any subject. I remember this man, it was from Krafft-Ebing, this man was a masochist, and I remember this phrase: "And mad with sensuality I rushed all through Central Europe." So he must have been neglecting his business. After all, sex has to be kept in some sort of limits.

GIORNO: There's no difference between gay and heterosexual men, except style. Like long hair and macho. The idea is that desire totally captures people and locks them into a grid, a stranglehold. It doesn't matter what the object is, it's desire.

BURROUGHS: Historically, a Victorian out of the nineteenth century could be flagrantly gay, like there was a don at Oxford who had six or seven boys living with him. But no one said anything about it because you could *do* anything so long as you didn't *say* anything. And I remember one English gentleman telling me about his great-uncle or somebody, this magnificent old type who was totally obvious in his behavior, but never once did he admit to anyone that he was gay. For sixty years he kept this façade while living with six or seven English boys. Extraordinary state of mind.

GIORNO: Do you think young people, in their twenties, thirties, forties, are consumed sexually, not in a maniacal way, but with a constant mental preoccupation, particularly gays?

BURROUGHS: Well I couldn't take any sort of census. Obviously a lot of people are racing around in a public search. There's the whole bar scene, there's the whole one-night-stand scene, there's the guys who run antique stores or sell art, making it together. And the respectable people that they circulate among actually know this of course. Straight people are not as dumb as all that. "Oh really nobody knows anything about me!" "My dear, *everybody* knows about you!" So there isn't really one gay community, there's many different patterns and so forth.

GIORNO: There is something I think is totally great that's happened in a few cities in America like New York and San Francisco, and very few other cities in the world outside the United States. That is where there are giant areas where there are, say, two hundred thousand gay people living, and incredible promiscuity. Every kind of thing that's fantasized about. It's totally horrible and painful for each one of the people, they are like any ordinary person, just totally fucked up and out of their fucking neurotic mind. But externally it's just like a fantasy.

Gay supermarkets, gay apartments, endless areas, so that's rather terrific. It's an achievement over what existed in Europe. Like London in the early part of the century, or going back, where there was one hundred percent hypocrisy, which you were describing.

BURROUGHS: I think hypocrisy has its advantages. I'm sure those old characters got some very good sex from their six or seven resident Arab boys. Yes, perhaps things were better.

GIORNO: In the good old days?

BURROUGHS: Well there was certainly a better situation in those days for people getting on in years. It was on a money basis. Now every fucking punk's got money. You got no leverage anymore. Now you got to get 'em in the movies or something [*Laughter*].

GIORNO: But William, don't you think it's totally amazing that once one was young and beautiful. The whole visual trip. And then one is exactly in the weird space of being totally old and ugly?

BURROUGHS: Time hits the hardest blows.

GIORNO: And then you get rich and famous and it all works itself out because you get exactly what you want to get only in a different vein.

BURROUGHS: My dear, when you were rich in the 1890's there was no limit to the boys you could have and you didn't have to be all that rich. Two shillings and you had them coming. Now they want more more more, you have to make the boy a movie star, an assistant professor or a cardinal. Of course it's a great time for young people who are pretty and on the same level as the people they are approaching. Still some of these young people complain that they haven't got enough.

GIORNO: That's the same syndrome, the same desire syndrome. When you're young you're always broke, no matter how much money you have. You're fucked over, and that's exactly where everyone is. I mean, to hear the talking, everyone is totally broke. Unless they're very lucky somehow, but most people aren't.

BURROUGHS: Not right at all. These young punks in America never had it so good in history. They can do anything they want sexually. They can get $250 a month compete disability insurance for being absolutely good for nothing. Look through history for any young people who've had it easier than the young people in America today and you will not find one instance.

GIORNO: You're right.

BURROUGHS: And they beef and they beef and they beef. Well the more you give people the more they beef, there's no doubt about it. So the young American gay today is really very spoiled. He doesn't realize how easy he's got it. When I was twenty years old I'd never tell anyone I was gay. Your friends, your uncle, your father would turn on you. It was the most horrible thing. But at the center of the total hypocrisy, if you never *said* it, everybody knew it and didn't give a shit. It was a real double standard. You can do it, but you can't say it.

Now this is the whole dichotomy of private and public behavior. And actually the Victorian attitude is endemic among the Arabs and the Spanish, where what you do privately is one thing and what you do publicly is another.

GIORNO: Where did the Victorian attitude come from? Did it come from England or the Arabs or somewhere else?

BURROUGHS: I don't know but it's a very widespread thing. For example, in Tangiers the Arabs have this word called *hushima,* shame. Well for an Arab boy to be making money by sleeping with a British or American tourist or resident, that's not shameful.

GIORNO: It's work.

BURROUGHS: Yes, everybody knows this, and he is contributing money to support his family and they all know where the money is coming from. But to *admit* this is totally shameful. For example, for the mother of the Arab boy to meet the tourist, this would be extremely shameful. Unthinkably shameful, an acknowledgment of something that everyone knows already. So the acknowledgment is shameful but the behavior is not. This is of course the reverse of the whole Calvinist ethic.

GIORNO: But that's no different from anything that exists in this world. It doesn't matter if you're from some grand New England family, if you're living off the opium trade in the nineteenth century. If you're a Rockefeller, this unpleasantness is not disclosed.

BURROUGHS: I wonder about that.

GIORNO: The source of all money is shameful. Can you think of any of the great fortunes in America? If it's Frick, it's the coal miners; if it's somebody else, it's the steel workers; if it's not the garment workers, it's ten-year-olds slaving away; or it's some trip in Africa, in Asia. The source of all great wealth is abhorrent.

BURROUGHS: You're suggesting that about the source of all wealth large or small. A family in Tangiers has a good-looking boy. The money he brings in is keeping the family going. Now this is known not only to the family but to all the neighbors. Still for the mother to meet the tourist would be extremely shameful.

GIORNO: Has that ever happened to you?

BURROUGHS: Well yes, I was living with a young boy, and if I suggested that he should introduce me to his mother he was scandalized beyond belief.

GIORNO: You've lived in Tangiers, is that the trip?

BURROUGHS: I have, yes.

GIORNO: Then there's the whole American trip which I know you do not frequent.

BURROUGHS: Oh I'm an old-fashioned man.

GIORNO: And very proper.

BURROUGHS: Yes, I'm influenced by my European training.

GIORNO: Do you think of any preferability between Tangiers and America in terms of sexual openness?

BURROUGHS: Well of course the Tangiers that I knew is gone with the winds of change. And of course the situation in America now is very encouraging and offers a lot to young gay people who are just popping out of the watercloset

[*Laughter*]. They don't know how lucky they are, they've had so much assistance. "You're a lucky man, Mr. Smith, you don't know how highly you rate." Myself, I was brought up in another tradition. What were you asking me?

GIORNO: I was asking—you answered it. That's what I think—it's totally great in America, like being the Gay State, is really like being Connecticut. Everything is so impermanent. There may be some kind of giant backlash about to knock everyone on their asses. But for the last twenty years it's been amazing. And it's all to do with what you and Allen and a number of other people have worked on for numerous years. It's succeeded.

BURROUGHS: As for a total backlash, such a phenomenon could hardly occur without a complete disintegration of what we call society now. When the Middle Ages came in, the Greco-Roman culture crumbled away to nothing. It hasn't happened here yet.

GIORNO: At least not for fifty or a hundred years or so.

BURROUGHS: Well we don't know, certainly not in the next few years. The Hiltons and the jets are still working, all's right with the world.

I'd like to retire to a simple old-fashioned community where money still meant something, if I had some. [*Laughter*.]

GIORNO: I know that sounds good. Don't you like expensive hotels?

BURROUGHS: I like expensive hotels, the more expensive the better, but certainly not to live for any length of time.

Mr. Giorno, while I'm sticking the mike in your face, how do you feel about being West Coast Gay?

GIORNO: I think it's sweet.

BURROUGHS: Got anything else to say?

GIORNO: Not much.

BURROUGHS: Well I'm getting a jump on this—"How do you feel about being a lousy son-of-a-bitch" and then you say, "Well, I've come to deal with it." Then you rush down to the South and say, "How do you feel about being a WASP." "Well I feel like it was sorta my upbringing." Or whatever. In fact this could be a television program known as *How Do You Feel about What You Are* [*Laughter*]. Your roving reporter could jump out at all sorts of people and shove the mike right in their face: "How do you feel about being a potato-eating Irish?" Or "How do you feel about being a wop?" The first thing off their head. He jumps out of the car and says, "How do you feel about being a redneck?" And then asking a redneck what he thinks about gays, and asking gays what they think about rednecks, who would kill who first, and so on. Now you're a queer faced with Anita Bryant, what would you say to Anita Bryant? He'd bring it up that all of his kids are gay too. And so what do you say about this, Anita Bryant? What would you say to this man if you were confronted with him? And what would you say to this woman?

GIORNO: On television they had this gay guy in the studio and they telephoned Anita Bryant down in Florida. Then they had this conversation which was totally innocuous because they didn't get to Anita, they got to her husband, and they had some conversation about grammar: how do you spell gay or something. They talked for five minutes without saying anything.

BURROUGHS: The name of this program would be *Confront*.

GIORNO: That's a great title.

BURROUGHS: And watch Anita Bryant confront the champion of the gays.

GIORNO: What would you say?

BURROUGHS: Oh I'd say, "I understand, Anita Bryant, you were one time almost Miss America, but you didn't quite make the grade, did you? Well you got some questions to ask me maybe?" That's the way.

GIORNO: What do you think of equal rights for gays, the things that were being passed. About hiring.

BURROUGHS: Oh, policemen and firemen. I don't see any reason why they shouldn't be passed if they want to.

GIORNO: Do you think that's a worthy thing to pursue?

BURROUGHS: It's entirely a matter of choice. Gay people are now trying to get on the cops here with the understanding that they're gay. One of the archetypical figures of evil has been the gay Gestapo agent.

GIORNO: Which is a gay fantasy in a lot of physical sex scenes.

BURROUGHS: The archetypical Gestapo questioner was represented in the 1930's as being gay, and this was largely Communist propaganda. Now we know the whole gay thing was officially eliminated in 1934 with Roehm and the SA.

[*Pause to make drinks and roll a joint.*]

BURROUGHS: We were discussing the fact that in my experience many sophisticated heterosexuals are *not* repressed homosexuals at all. I've had them say to me that most of their emotional feelings go towards men but that they simply can't sexually make it with men. And I don't think they are any more repressed homosexuals than all gays are repressed heterosexuals.

GIORNO: It's a very common phenomenon, the man who hates women but can only make it with women. All his emotional relationships are with men. He's just stuck at a certain point. It's a very mysterious thing. Like all desire, he's arbitrarily fixed at a certain point and that's it. It's very hard to alter those points.

These points, to everyone's chagrin, are just karmic habits. You form these habits and then you go in the direction of sensuality—these habits—and increase them. So you get more attached to them because they feel so good. You know the whole syndrome: sucking and fucking and fist-fucking, any kind of sexuality and everyone has his preference. One is totally at the mercy of them, which is karmically arbitrary.

As far as I'm concerned there's two advantages in being gay. One is that it's absolutely sweet and blissful and everything one would ever want. And second, if used properly, it's like an instrument for cutting through conception, and conception has to do with structures. Which are heterosexual and homosexual.

BURROUGHS: In the Western world all the objections to homosexuality are culled from the Bible. We still have the Bible Belt with us. This absolute menace, this sociological time-bomb that could blow up the whole fucking planet.

GIORNO: It's the Bible Belt that killed Kennedy, I suppose. Is that what they mean about Texas?

BURROUGHS: I wasn't thinking that. I was thinking that if people with that mentality ever got a super atom bomb—

GIORNO: But don't they have it? Aren't those people in the Pentagon?

BURROUGHS: No, you're oversimplifying. The people in the Pentagon are not Bible at all. God knows who they are. But they're very far removed from that mentality. Not that they don't understand and *use* it, but they're not of it. It's a much more sophisticated phenomenon. The Bible Belt is the people who take orders. But as to what is actually going on on this planet, I don't think anyone has a clue. There's so many conspiracies and counterconspiracies, I don't think anyone knows at all what's going on. The important thing for an artist is just to do his work and not be concerned with all kinds of conspiracies.

What is the greatest prize that anyone can get in Western culture?

GIORNO: What is the prize?

BURROUGHS: Very simple. Freedom from fear. You get strong enough so that you're not scared of anybody.

GIORNO: So there's two ways. One is to become a Rockefeller, and the other is to become a junkie. Because heroin temporarily gets you away from the fear.

BURROUGHS: Oh just a moment. There's nobody more riddled with fear than a heroin addict because he's afraid of having his junk cut off.

GIORNO: Do you think all those millionaires like Getty, Rockefeller, or the Duponts are any more or less riddled with fear?

BURROUGHS: Well if they've got any sense. But on the objective level they've got much less to fear. Fear is people afraid of something, it isn't fear floating around in a vacuum. Now if I've got a billion dollars I don't have to be scared of nothing.

GIORNO: A moment of being totally high is no different from being rich. Getty's been dead, how long, a year, two years. If he isn't reborn he's more scared now than any junkie in the street has ever been.

BURROUGHS: I think you got a point there. They're thinking in short-range terms. Anyone who's looking for immediate safety is very much frightened and anyone who's frightened is thinking in very short terms.

GIORNO: Do you feel in your personal life that your activities are more involved with heterosexuals? People who are on the road, or who invited you to this dinner and arranged meetings or business?

BURROUGHS: I don't know, I seem to meet a fair portion of both when I'm on the road. So no I don't feel that one necessarily preponderates. The whole idea of *the* gay community is extremely misleading indeed, because I don't think that there's any reality that corresponds to that. Nor is there any gay community in the sense of any sort of organized mutual aid. Anything corresponding to the, say, Chinese tong system. It wouldn't be a bad idea to have gay tongs. You join a certain gay tong and—

GIORNO: Dues like fifteen dollars a month?

BURROUGHS: Yes, and that means if you're ever in trouble you get bailed out. If you lose your job the tong will support you. You have the support of the tong at all times.

GIORNO: Do you think we should start a gay tong?

BURROUGHS: Well I think that the whole tong principle is a very workable system. Of course a lot of gays will say, "What to I need a tong for?" High teacup queens. Well you know even in a penthouse like this—

GIORNO: In your fortress on the Bowery—

BURROUGHS: Disagreeable things could happen. You pick up the wrong kind of person. It's getting rapidly to look like some kind of a shake—...

This is an argument used frequently by anti-gay movements: that gays, like the Jews, have certain inherently disagreeble characteristics. When Hitler issued a formal order, the whole Gestapo went into action against homosexuals. The directive was that they were "kriecherisch und herrsuchtig." These are two almost untranslatable worlds with the general meaning of creeping, cringing or skulking; at the same time in a slimy way trying to dominate people. So you have these terrible characteristics of being cringing and whimpering and at the same time trying to get power over other people. And Anita Bryant with her "youth recruitment" comes down to the same proposition: that homosexuals are bad by nature like devils.

GIORNO: Is that like Nixon and Kissinger and Ford, because they're all power junkies, they're just the same way with a need for power?

BURROUGHS: No. The specific unpleasant picture of homosexuals was that they were at once servile and cringing and at the same time ready to leap on any advantage.

GIORNO: The corrupting influence being that you're taking our sons and corrupting them?

BURROUGHS: Yes, the presumption that homosexuals were a sort of *race* with certain despicable qualities inherent in their condition, just exactly like the evil Jews.

GIORNO: As if faggots' "swish" were like Yiddish Jewish or something?

BURROUGHS: Yes. It was very similar, the same sort of evocation of this theme. I was studying medicine in Vienna at the time when all this was getting started.

GIORNO: When did you study medicine in Vienna?

BURROUGHS: In 1936 for a year. I read the *Volkischer Beobachter* and saw the emergence and manipulation of these fiendish archetypes. A Jew head with a spider body. Picture of a Jew accused of some crime: "From his horrible Jew eyes speaks the crime world of the Talmud." And this image was then grafted onto the homosexual.

The concept of the homosexual as a fiendish plotter is indoctrinated into the

L.A. police—"You know what these fruits want. They want a fruit world."

GIORNO: Is this true?

BURROUGHS: The concept of unlimited license has a certain appeal to anybody homo- or heterosexual. Any group using physical power to foster the interest of that particular group without any limitations on them can become intolerable. On this planet we have groups with disparate interests and in many cases the separation has been forced on them. If someone is persecuted as a homosexual, a Jew, a black they will if given the opportunity organize to defend their interests, and there is no viable defense of one's interests that does not involve certain political and ultimately certain military objectives. And while allegedly simply protecting their interests they often tend to extend the area of that influence. Someone said that the world consisted of Hitler and lebensraum . . . life room. This is the pretext of the cold war or any war: "We are just trying to protect our interests. That's all." And there is no end to Russia and America protecting their interests.

GIORNO: Don't you think this is a basic characteristic of human nature?

BURROUGHS: It is a very basic problem.

GIORNO: So how does one cut through that?

BURROUGHS: Perhaps one doesn't. Except to say that there are people who do want to mind their own business and be left alone to do what they want to do, and there are people of another category. And there is the question as to what degree of force is necessary to protect your interests and what your interests actually are and where to stop. In self-defense you may have to take measures against someone who doesn't yet know he's going to have to take measures against you. In the words of the immortal bard, "Only fools to those villains pity who are punished ere they have done their mischief."

Before Anita Bryant opened her big orange-sucking mouth the position of gays in America was steadily improving. It was almost possible to take the whole issue casually and get on with one's business. . . .

To my way of thinking the basic difference between a shit and a decent person is very simple. A decent person wants to be left alone to mind his own business, and he is willing to let others do the same. A shit has no business of his or her own to mind, any more than a smallpox virus. How can Anita Bryant be contained? Hit her sponsors where they live—in their $$. *Total boycott on Florida oranges in any form.*

PHOTO BY IRA COHEN, KATHMANDU, 1974

CHARLES HENRI FORD

CHARLES HENRI FORD was born in Mississippi in 1910. Before he was twenty he had published his poems in a dozen literary magazines and was editing one of his own, *Blues: A Magazine of New Rhythms* (1929-1931). In 1933 he collaborated with Parker Tyler on the gay novel *The Young and Evil* (recently reprinted by Arno Press). His first book, *The Garden of Disorder* (1938), is a collection of poems with an introduction by William Carlos Williams. *The Overturned Lake* (1941) continued his experiments in surrealism in the lyric form. *Sleep in a Nest of Flames* (1949) includes a foreword by Edith Sitwell and fresh experiments—ballads, epigrams, nursery rhymes. From that time on, his work led to a new lyricism and to new material, prose poems, found poetry, and finally to collage or poster poems, *Spare Parts* (1966) and *Silver Flower Coo* (1968). His selected poems, *Flag of Ecstasy,* were published by Black Sparrow Press in 1972. His poems also appear in the two gay anthologies *Angels of the Lyre* (1975) and *Orgasms of Light* (1977), as also do those of Ira Cohen, his interviewer.

During World War II Ford edited the highly influential surrealist magazine *View* (1940-1947), where a number of young American poets were first published. He also turned his talents to painting and photograpy and had exhibits in London, Paris, and New York. In the mid-sixties he dedicated himself to filmmaking. His first full-length feature, *Johnny Minotaur,* was released in 1971 to praise from avant-garde film critics.

For twenty-three years, beginning in the early thirties, Charles Henri Ford was the lover of the Russian/American modernist painter Pavel (Pavlik) Tchelitchew (1898-1957); see Parker Tyler's detailed biography *The Divine Comedy of Pavel Tchelitchew* (1967). Ford currently makes his home in New York City, Kathmandu (Nepal), and Crete.

THE PRESENT INTERVIEW was taped in Kathmandu in July 1974 by Ira Cohen. Cohen edited the magazine *Gnaoua* in Tangiers where he lived for four years. He invented spirit photography in New York where he made the film *The Invasion of Thunderbolt Pagoda,* an experiment in opium dreaming. His recent books *Poems from the Cosmic Crypt* and *Gilded Splinters* were published in Kathmandu in 1976 and 1977 respectively. The interview originally appeared in *Gay Sunshine* 24 (Spring 1975).

Ira Cohen interviews
CHARLES HENRI FORD

COHEN: Since you are particularly well known as a surrealist, I would like to ask you what value you give to love in relation to surrealism.

FORD: I've never been obsessed with love in relation to surrealism in the sense that Breton was, and naturally surrealism can exist in any form. Surrealism as love can be surrealism after the love, not before.

COHEN: But somehow it does seem that love plays a very important role in surrealism in the work of Breton and many of the other poets, in your own work as well.

FORD: I was never conscious of it in that sense. You see, Breton was exalting the woman and I didn't identify with that either.

COHEN: Did you feel the surrealist movement was lacking in homosexual focus, that the woman was somehow an overly-ideal love?

FORD: The prime homosexual surrealist was Jean Cocteau who was rejected by the official surrealist movement.

COHEN: Do you consider that was the main rejection for his rejection?

FORD: I don't consider that was one of the main reasons but that certainly entered into it.

COHEN: Do you know why he was supposedly rejected? His work seems to have all the most beautiful and most perfect elements of surrealism, for me at least.

FORD: I feel he was a natural surrealist but surrealism was always a group, and like Cummings, Cocteau was not a joiner.

COHEN: But do you know whether or not there were actually discussions over policy, textural policy, in the same way as there was over political policy?

FORD: I think there is a prejudice against homosexuality. One of the well-known homosexual surrealists was René Crevel and he committed suicide [in 1935 — *Ed.*]. I don't think it was over his homosexuality but it was a complication between adherence to surrealism or to communism or to homosexuality; he couldn't get it all worked out.

COHEN: Did you know René Crevel?

FORD: Yes, I met him at Gertrude Stein's. And also, I would have met him through Tchelitchew because they were together a lot, great friends. Tchelitchew did several portraits of Crevel, and they were lovers.

COHEN: This was before you met Tchelitchew?

FORD: Yes, they were together as lovers before I met Tchelitchew.

COHEN: You lived for a long time with Tchelitchew, sharing an intimate life with him.

FORD: Yes, our life together began actually when he came to America in 1934. It was largely my doing, getting him to America.

COHEN: I suppose you would consider this love relationship the most important in your life?

FORD: Yes.

COHEN: And also, since he was older, he was in some way like a teacher to you?

FORD: Yes, he was mentor and guide in the domain of painting. At the same time I believe I brought inspiration to him. At one time I think I remember telling him (although I knew so little about painting, when one is young one thinks one knows everything), that painting is stagnant. And I think I caused a revolution in his own painting style, for it changed radically after he met me.

COHEN: Will you describe the difference?

FORD: His painting became much more violent and the images, the composition much more disruptive.

COHEN: Did Tchelitchew ever consider himself a surrealist?

FORD: No, he was never a surrealist. He was a neo-Romantic. This was a school name coined by Julien Levy who had the gallery in New York. And the neo-Romantics were said by Soby to paint the dreamer whereas the surrealists painted the dream.

COHEN: I would like to ask you more about your relationship with Tchelitchew, whose paintings I've always greatly admired and who was really one of the great painters of our time.

FORD: I remember your telling me you used to stand before Tchelitchew's *Cache-Cache* in the Museum of Modern Art, right?

COHEN: It was actually one of the first two or three things that ever really affected me strongly when I was very young and came for the first time to the Museum of Modern Art. Actually, I had an experience of finding a small baby in a paper bag when I was a child and it was almost traumatic for me to see that particular painting, because of the embryonic structures in the trees and so forth. How did you get him to come to America? Were you already familiar with his work?

FORD: Yes, I wrote Parker Tyler from Paris: I've discovered a genius. We had spent a winter, not living together, but seeing each other every day. It was at the time Edith Sitwell was also in Paris. She had discovered Tchelitchew and they were great friends. Anyway, we were all there together that winter in Paris. Edith complained in some letters about Tchelitchew's seeing so little of her, and without mentioning my name she blamed it on me. So we were seeing a lot of each other which took away a lot of his time from Edith. I had been trying to get him to go to America and the only way I could really get him to pull up roots was to leave. So I left on a freighter in November, 1934, and before Christmas he had arrived. That was the beginning of his American career, and he later became an American citizen.

COHEN: How long did he spend in America?

FORD: All the rest of his life. He became an American citizen in 1942. He was already in the Julien Levy gallery when he arrived. And the most important part of his career was in America.

COHEN: Where did you first meet Tchelitchew?

FORD: I was introduced to him, I think, by Telia Perlmutter. And Telia was one of the two blonde sisters that used to keep company with Cocteau and Radiguet during the days when Radiguet was in love with Telia's sister and Cocteau was in love with Radiguet. Telia introduced me to Tchelitchew at an art show in Paris.

COHEN: When you came to Paris, you came specifically with the idea of seeing Gertrude Stein?

FORD: Yes, because I edited a little magazine from Mississippi in my teens. Gertrude herself wrote some of the expatriates and they very kindly responded with manuscripts. Ezra Pound, Kay Boyle, and so on. So I had letters. Gertrude had sent me her books. So when I arrived in Paris she already knew who I was. I wrote her a note and she invited me to one of her Rue de Fleurus teas. I was to be a regular visitor there.

COHEN: Was Pavel going there at that time?

FORD: No, she had already dropped Pavlik out of jealousy of Edith Sitwell.

COHEN: He was excommunicated, in other words.

FORD: Yes. She was always dropping people. Well, as I told you, Edith Sitwell came along and took over Pavel, and Gertrude was jealous. Pavel was devoting more time in adoration of Edith than he was to dear Gertrude.

COHEN: Actually I was really trying to tease out of you this other bit of gossip you once told me about Pavel talking about Gertrude's baby.

FORD: Oh, yeah, the hump. Alice [Toklas] always had it in for Pavlik 'cause the word got to her that Pavlik had said the hump in her forehead was Gertrude Stein's baby.

COHEN: Was it?

FORD: Well, Hemingway seemed to think they were lovers.

COHEN: You don't think that Hemingway and Gertrude might have had a secret affair?

FORD: Never. Gertrude was always very platonic about her young men.

COHEN: But they were strongly attracted to each other in a dynamic way at that time?

FORD: Yes, Gertrude always had some kind of psycho-erotic rapport with her protégés.

COHEN: But someone like Hemingway, you feel, was one of her stronger relationships with her protégés?

FORD: Yes, definitely, Particularly since his writing was made famous by her.

COHEN: Most of her protégés were probably homosexual?

FORD: I wouldn't make that generality. Certainly Hemingway wasn't.

COHEN: I remember reading some stories of Hemingway's extreme animosity against any of the gay people on that scene at that time. It seemed to make him stand out in some way as a little bit gauche in that salon.

FORD: Yeah, with his big feet.

COHEN: Yeah, I remember that his big feet were remarked on by someone.

FORD: By Mrs. Bradley, in that film *When This You See Remember Me*.

COHEN: I'd like to ask you about Djuna Barnes and the time you spent with her in Tangiers when she was writing *Nightwood*.

FORD: She had finished *Nightwood* and I was typing it for her. I found a house in the Casbah, and Djuna came down from Paris and lived with me there and our daily routine was that I would go to the beach in the morning, come back and have lunch, type in the afternoon. I don't know if I finished the book before she went back to Paris or not.

COHEN: How do you feel about *Nightwood* as a book now?

FORD: I wasn't all that enthusiastic when I was typing it. I'd enjoyed her earlier novel *Rider* much more. She made her reputation on *Nightwood*. If *Nightwood* hadn't been written, she wouldn't be the great Djuna Barnes which she is today.

COHEN: Did she ever continue writing after that?

FORD: She's been working on a book for years. Since *Nightwood* she's come out with a published play which was performed in Germany.

COHEN: But that's so slight for a very important writer over such a long time of silence. How many years is that?

FORD: Well, Katherine Anne Porter was working for twenty years on *Ship of Fools*. Djuna's been working for many years on a single work besides writing poetry.

COHEN: Are you familiar at all with this work?

FORD: No, she hasn't released any of it.

COHEN: You've never seen any part of the manuscript or heard anything about it?

FORD: No. The only thing she's released has been poems, one of which was published in the *New Yorker*. I didn't see it. But I heard she was writing a lot of poetry. She used to write poetry in her early days when she was writing all the short stories. Did you ever see *A Night among the Horses and Other Stories*?

COHEN: No.

FORD: Marvelous stories. And she wrote short plays, too. And she was a friend in the old Greenwich Village days with Eugene O'Neill and they were having their plays produced at the Provincetown Playhouse. Djuna had a couple of short plays produced there before I ever left Mississippi but she told me about them and I read them.

COHEN: Paul Bowles tells me you were living in a house that was actually his house and that it was filled with jackal furs and snakeskins.

FORD: In Tangiers. I don't remember those details, though. We moved out. We lived actually in three houses in Tangiers. One Paul lent us. Then we moved into another big house with a garden where the rats got into Djuna's wardrobe trunk and ate her stockings. Then we moved into a very charming house in the Casbah.

COHEN: I know that Paul Bowles complained to me so many years afterwards that he would come to practice the piano and that he could never get into the house because you were always sleeping.

FORD: Yes, but he was arriving at seven in the morning. Who wouldn't be sleeping?

COHEN: And he was coming to practice or play the piano?

FORD: Yes, at seven in the morning.

COHEN: Every morning? Was he composing or working at the time?

FORD: Well, he was always doing something or the other, eating oranges or composing.

COHEN: When did you first meet Paul?

FORD: Probably in New York City. He's the one that recommended Tangiers so highly to me. I went there, kept in touch with Djuna; she came later.

COHEN: You loved Tangiers, didn't you?

FORD: I didn't really love it. I found it very exotic and spent one winter there, and when *The Young and Evil* came out in 1933, I left and went back to Paris. I visited Gertrude Stein on the way.

COHEN: *The Young and Evil* is the novel you wrote with Parker Tyler?

FORD: Yes, published by Obelisk Press the year before Henry Miller came out.

COHEN: Did you have any static about the book being printed because of the subject matter, the fact that it was a gay book? It was one of the first published which was known and successful in literary circles.

FORD: Yes, it was first. Kronenberger pointed that out in the *New Republic,* the only review we got in America. It appeared with blurbs on the jacket by both Gertrude Stein and Djuna Barnes. Gertrude said it created its generation as Fitzgerald in *This Side of Paradise* created his generation, which was quite a good blurb.

COHEN: How much do you consider things have changed from what that generation was to this generation now?

FORD: Well, there was a little note in *Gay Sunshine* reviewing gay literature in the last number [Summer 1974] saying that *The Young and the Evil* is still authentic for the 1970s so it doesn't date that much as a period piece. It was really avant-garde, having been written that long ago and still valid, and also got a good word from Gore Vidal in his review of all the erotic and porno books. *The Young and Evil* is the only one he had any praise for of all the Grove Press publications.

COHEN: How did you and Parker Tyler work together on the book?

FORD: That's been asked many times. I had the idea for the book. I made the plot, invented the characters. At the time I was in Mississippi and in very close correspondence with Parker. His letters were so witty and campy and I used so many of his extracts in the dialogue that I just decided I should give him credit as co-author. And I did in my chapter outline give him entire chapters to write, too.

COHEN: Did you live with Parker in New York for some time?

FORD: Yes, we lived on Grove Street at one place together. William Carlos Williams visited us there.

COHEN: Were you lovers, you and Parker?

FORD: No.

COHEN: You and Parker have been lifelong friends?

FORD: Not lifelong. Since the *Blues* days, 1930; I was in Mississippi, hadn't met Parker, had just heard about him. He was quite a figure in Greenwich Village at that time, known as the beautiful Parker Tyler. He wore his hair very long and had penciled eyebrows and mascaraed eyelashes, and used to give poetry readings.

COHEN: Parker became largely a critic in his later work, didn't he?

FORD: Yes, he was my associate editor on *View* and began to write critical articles on the movies, and that led to books on the movies. That was his specialty as a critic.

COHEN: He was also a poet, wasn't he?

FORD: Yes, Black Sparrow published his selected poems, *The Will of Eros*.

COHEN: Do you feel a common ground between Parker's poetry and your own?

FORD: No, totally different. At one point he didn't consider himself a practicing poet; he was totally into criticism.

COHEN: And you always considered yourself fundamentally a poet?

FORD: Yes, I concentrated on poetry. I didn't go into criticism, book reviews. I made a stab at playwriting and the one novel.

COHEN: Do you see all of this as an expansion of yourself as poet?

FORD: Yes, and also what I'm doing now in the sculptures. It's the sculpture of a poet.

COHEN: Can you tell me who your favorite poets are? Or the poets who most influenced you or you most admire?

FORD: Rimbaud is at the top.

COHEN: Are there any poets writing in America today in whom you are interested?

FORD: I follow Philip Lamantia's work, particularly since I discovered him when he was fifteen. I published his first poems in *View*, and got him to come from San Francisco to New York and gave him a job in the *View* office. In spite of a rivalry between Breton and me for the New York scene, I got Lamantia. I was impartial enough to invite Breton to the office one day and tell him I would like to publish a book of his [Breton's] poems in English, the first time it had ever been done. We did it with a cover by Marcel Duchamps and translations by our friend Edouard Roditi. The Duchamps cover is the Statue of Liberty with the face cut out and Breton's face substituted.

COHEN: Now that you are living in Kathmandu after having traveled and lived in so many places, can you tell me how Kathmandu affects your work or your life style?

FORD: I find a completely new inspiration here, probably because it is the East and also because Nepalese art is so radically different from Western art. So the novelty and the impact has been so tremendous that it's inspired a whole exhibition in New York in January called the Kathmandu Experience. And it's propelled me into an art form which I have never practiced before but which I think I will practice in the future, which is sculpture. What do *you* think about Kathmandu? Do you think it's influenced your recent poetry or would you have written this kind of poetry anywhere else?

COHEN: I think it's influenced all my work enormously in a very self-conscious way since I haven't thrown myself in any way in any of the more obvious lines that could be very attractive here, ranging from Buddhism to Hinduism and walking over mountains, but somehow have quietly assimilated the feeling of mentality of the whole place, this whole valley. I don't think about it.

FORD: You don't think about it, but when you do, you know there has been an influence.... I've written down these reasons in my mind, in my diary, because the reasons are very definite to me, beginning with the climate, the visual on the streets, the unparanoiac way of life.

COHEN: Shall we discuss the gay scene in Kathmandu? Is there a gay scene?

FORD: No. In Greece the first thing they think of is sex; in Nepal, it's the last thing.

COHEN: What is the first thing they think of in Nepal?

FORD: Rice rations.

COHEN: And the last thing in Greece?

FORD: Rice rations. Pilaf, according to the Turks.

COHEN: So in comparing Kathmandu to Greece, Turkey, Morocco, or New York, it has less of a gay scene?

FORD: There's no gay scene as such here.

COHEN: What do you think the reason is for the fact that there are so many statues with hard-ons in Kathmandu? Especially, death figures, skeletons in the temples.

FORD: I think most of the erections are not on skeletons on temples. They're on monsters, usually animal monsters with huge erections. Painted all colors of the rainbow. Somebody said it might be like wishful thinking. But naturally there is the adoration of the lingam, which is so prevalent.

COHEN: By the Hindus.

FORD: Well, Nepal is a Hindu kingdom. The minority of the population is Buddhist. The official religion is Hindu and all of the holidays are Hindu. The Buddhists have their own private holidays. But lingam worship is very prevalent here, and you always see huge lingams all over the place everywhere you step.

COHEN: I wanted to ask you what your own preference is today, whether for sailors or master painters or fur cups or silver storks, as a sexual preference or as a kind of life style?

FORD: Well, the Asiatics now to me are the most beautiful people in the world, maybe because I'm living among them. Because when I was living in Italy I thought the Italians were the most beautiful; and in Greece, the Greeks were the most attractive. But I find the image of the Orientals very obsessive now.

COHEN: Have you personally been able to work out a sex life in Kathmandu? Or is it not so important?

FORD: I have adapted more or less to the customs of the people, in other words, not putting sex first. And I find that the people are very erotic without being sex-obsessed. You see boys holding hands on the streets, and although it may not go any further than that, it's obviously an erotic gesture. I think a lot of eroticism can be fulfilled without touch, without penetration.

COHEN: Do you think there is any way we can prepare for the unexpected?

FORD: In sex?

COHEN: In life or in art? Create a context of the unexpected?

FORD: Oh, you want to cultivate the unexpected? To cultivate the unexpected is merely working as an artist.

COHEN: Rimbaud, whom you describe as a major influence in your poetry, was certainly so famous about his discussions about deranging the senses. This is part of this idea. There are other aspects, hallucination, vision, trance, oracles.

FORD: Yes, I don't know how far he went in the physical direction. After all, Rimbaud was a very literary person, and his derangement of the senses could have been totally conscious and underanged.

COHEN: But don't you think drugs have a definite value in this way, if not for you personally, for people you have known and observed?

FORD: For deranging the senses?

COHEN: In a positive sense. Artistically.

FORD: I have been trying in reading drug experiences to discover any value or worth in art that drugs could bring, but most of the apostles of drug-taking don't impress me as producers.

COHEN: Well, it's not just apostles. Many people like Cocteau who was an opium taker. His work could be said by anyone who takes opium to be inseparable from opium.

FORD: Most of his masterpieces were not opium-oriented.

COHEN: Do you think that we are fallen angels?

FORD: No, we're merely whirling creatures on spaceship Earth.

COHEN: You've been working as a film-maker and a photographer along with the other things—sculpture, painting.

FORD: Not in Kathmandu. I haven't had a camera in my hand. But I feel the more I live here that photography could be all-absorbing. I eliminated the idea of a slide show from my forthcoming exhibition because it wouldn't have been doing it any justice, the art of photography. I feel I've discovered here that in any art you have to absolutely mine the vein you're working in because it doesn't come all that quick. And it took me weeks, not months, to discover the vein.

COHEN: Did you ever publish a book of photographs?

FORD: No, but I've had exhibitions. I had an exhibition at the ICA in 1954 called "Thirty Images from Italy." And it will be shown now two decades later in New York at the same time as my Kathmandu Experience show. That's what led me to making moving still photography because that's what cinema is.

COHEN: Can you tell me which photographer's work you admire the most?

FORD: Well, there's only one I can name that really turns me on, Henri Cartier-Bresson. He was also a surrealist at the time I met him.

COHEN: One doesn't see much of his work in that style.

FORD: No, he went into photojournalism after he began to work for *Life*. But the young Henri and I met actually in Tangiers, and we became very close friends. I saw him in Paris. The photograph he took of me coming out of a pissoir in Paris is on the cover of my selected poems. And I was very excited about his photographs.

COHEN: You told me that you wrote one line down that you dreamt last night? You recorded it in your notebook this morning?

FORD: I'll read it to you. "On a chain of zinnias, the key for Narcissus."

COHEN: Do you want to start at the beginning of the paragraph that you read to me, the entire anecdote about Djuna Barnes?

FORD: When you arrived yesterday I had just read something from Sylvia Beach's memoir *Shakespeare and Company* and I had just copied this sentence: "Djuna Barnes, so charming, so Irish, and so gifted, came to Paris early in the twenties." And I continue to read my diary: "I met her in 1931 in New York, and we were together in Paris later that same year. She asked me to go with her on a long-desired visit to a line of cities—Munich, Vienna, Budapest—and so we went. I gave her my last hundred dollars as my share of the expenses, so she took care of all the trains and pension bills. In Munich we saw quite a bit of Putzi Hanfstaengl, who was later to become Hitler's intimate and staff member. In Djuna's Greenwich Village days she had known Putzi, who was in love with her. So many men were in love with the beautiful Barnes in those days. Laurence Vail was another."

COHEN: I wanted to ask you about Pavel Tchelitchew's erotic drawings because you know that I admire his work very much, but I never see as much of it as I would like to.

FORD: When Pavlik died he left a whole sheath of beautiful porno-erotic drawings in his will to his sister along with most of his other work that was in his Paris studio. They were later donated to the Kinsey Foundation.

COHEN: Would you describe some of the drawings to give an idea what they were like or what they represented?

FORD: Well, they were polymorphous perverse and not limited to any one sex. I have one that's an actual beauty that Pavel gave me, and it's of a Gay Nineties period, three boys dressed in nineties' clothes and hats in a hansom cab in a three-way orgy, fully clothed except for the sexual organs.

COHEN: When did you meet Tennessee Williams in the first place? Was that when he came to work for you at *View*?

FORD: He wasn't exactly working for me. He would just drop in and help stuff envelopes with the magazine. That was before his first success, *The Glass Menagerie*.

COHEN: He was a friend, in other words.

FORD: Yeah, he was a friend. He knew all the crowd, and one day he said he would like to review Marianne Moore's poems. So I said, "Tennessee, can you write?"

COHEN: You didn't even know he was a writer at that time?

FORD: No, I didn't know any of his works, but I knew he was trying...

COHEN: Did he write this review of Marianne Moore's poems?

FORD: No, because I didn't give him the book. He never came back to stuff envelopes after that. But we've stayed friends through thick and thin.

COHEN: Do you think that your work will be expanding continually, finding a stronger audience or a better context in these next years?

FORD: No, it's simpler than that. I at last have the possibility of seeing my creative work bring in some lucre.

COHEN: In other words, you can see a more popular base for your work?

FORD: No, not a more popular base. It can still be very elitist and avant-garde, but it might have a market.

COHEN: Have you ever made money from anything?

FORD: Never... You don't make money from poetry. At least I haven't. Maybe James Dickey has, or Edna St. Vincent Millay. I've written a novel, poetry, and had three art shows in Paris. They all sold, but they didn't make me rich. And the last art show I had was the poem posters in New York. I wasn't opulent even for a day on that.

COHEN: How did you bring William Burroughs and Jayne Mansfield together for that show?

FORD: There was a whole wall of posters celebrating Jayne Mansfield, and I called up Earl Blackwell of Celebrity Service, and I said, "Can't you get Jayne Mansfield here? I think she would enjoy seeing the posters."

COHEN: That was before she lost her head, I guess.

FORD: Yeah. She was quite self-contained at the exhibition. But she happened to be slightly pregnant, and wore a maternity dress, but still she was beautiful. You saw the film of the show, didn't you?

COHEN: No; I would have liked to. Do you remember if there was any conversation between Bill and Jayne? I know that you told me on the film there's a shot of the two of them meeting each other.

FORD: All they say is, "How do you do." But you do see them meet.

COHEN: Did you ever have strong contact with Bill Burroughs?

FORD: Yes, in the Beat hotel I used to see a lot of him. Sometimes he would come round and pick me up at my hotel and we'd have dinner. He always went to bed early in those days. About eight o'clock you'd see Brion Gysin and he's say, Bill is already in bed. I don't know what his intake was then. Maybe he was kicking something. Some people go to bed on junk. I remember when I was in Puerto Rico for New Year's Eve, I had a room in a little B-hotel. Actually Bill Barker and I were there together, and there was a knothole in the wall where you could see into the other room. So two Puerto Ricans came in and did the whole shoot-up thing with heroin, and then turned out the light and went to bed. That's what heroin addicts do sometimes. Just enjoy it in the dark. They nod out anyway, so why not cut the light out.

COHEN: Do you dream often?

FORD: Every night and I think they are the most boring dreams these days that I have ever had, and thank God one doesn't remember all of them.

COHEN: Can you remember any of them?

FORD: I remember them, and then I forget them. I don't even write them down. I remember Breton used to say, "Don't tell me your dreams, you'll bore me to tears." People thought because he was a surrealist he would be interested in hearing their dreams, and he definitely wasn't.

COHEN: I guess they were boring to him because he had his own dreams. And he was trying to record the chance encounters of his dreams. Doing that in his work, he probably lost interest in other people's dreams. How would you evaluate Breton? He is really the pope of surrealism, and was considered such.

FORD: Pavlik used to call him Pope Joan.

COHEN: Many people were not aligned always so officially with the surrealist movement, at least as Breton laid it down. Other people excommunicated someone like Cocteau as not really part of the movement, and yet at the same time for me Cocteau represents surrealism as well or better than anyone of the period.

FORD: Surrealism was in the air. If Breton hadn't invented surrealism as a movement, it would have existed anyway. So to me it's not as inspiring as a movement as for the individual practitioners. Some of them were very talented and some of them were geniuses.

COHEN: Do you think that authoritarianism is in any way an integral part of surrealism?

FORD: Of all, that is the least interesting part.

COHEN: I feel the same way. It's interesting, of course, because Breton said so many incredible things and was like a great figure.

FORD: Well, he was a poet; it's as simple as that.

COHEN: And he laid down so many—

FORD: Nobody's going to be interested in all his "lay downs." They're going to be interested in Breton as a poet. Even Marx is dating terribly today. You know what I mean?

COHEN: What do you think of the Gay Liberation movement?

FORD: All I know about it is what I read in the papers. I never participated. And I am as much for it as I am for Women's Lib, Black Lib, or any lib. How can one be against it?

COHEN: Certainly, a newspaper like *Gay Sunshine* never existed before this time.

FORD: No, it's got on its masthead, "A Journal of Gay Liberation." I like the word gay. When a young woman here used the word faggot, I said, "Don't use the word faggot. It's a putdown word, like calling a woman a cunt. Use the word gay."

Do you consider yourself bisexual, or have you outlived your gay experience?

COHEN: I couldn't predict anything about the next moment of my life.

FORD: When was your last gay experience? Have you had any gay experiences in Nepal?

COHEN: No, actually I haven't.

FORD: But you've had chances to have them. You told me there was a Tibetan trying to inveigle you into a dark doorway.

COHEN: That was just one of those weird nighttime scenes, probably more likely to result in my being strangled, the way it felt at that moment.

FORD: Are you excited, like Baudelaire, about seeing two women make love?

COHEN: Yeah, I think that's quite exciting. I like the idea. Are you turned on by it?

FORD: Well, I've never seen it, but sometimes I can imagine myself being a lesbian.

COHEN: Do you remember your first gay experience?

FORD: As far as I can remember my sex life began at the age of four, but I can't remember whether it was with my black nurse or a traveling man who was a customer at my father's hotel in Mississippi. I think both happened around that time, both homosexual and heterosexual.

COHEN: Did you ever love anybody?

FORD: It took me a long time to experience what I would call the ideal love. To me the ideal love has been after peak maturity and with pederastic relationships.

In other words, the older man and the younger boy. I was never very comfortable being the younger boy to the older man.

COHEN: But when you met Pavel Tchelitchew of course, that was the relationship.

FORD: That was the relationship but it somehow was influenced by his genius and by my artistic preoccupations rather than by sex because the sex thing was cut off quite early when we were living together. He tolerated my adventures with boys. The older I got the younger the boys were in relation to me, because their age sort of stayed stable as I grew older. Sixteen has always been the ideal boy.

COHEN: It doesn't matter much whether you're sixteen and a half or sixteen?

FORD: Well, fifteen and a half is better than sixteen and a half.

COHEN: During this time when you were more or less sexually active with Pavel and he was so tolerant of your actions, did he also continue his own sex life most of the time?

FORD: Well, not really. He gave so much energy to his art and in the end he used to say that he'd given up sex altogether. He was more like a monk, dedicated to his art.

COHEN: Do you feel yourself somehow that this ratio is changing in your life: that you have less interest in sex and more in your work?

FORD: No I don't. I feel that everything should be balanced, like food and exercise and sex and work. Everything should be a harmonious whole.

COHEN: For example, in your life now in Kathmandu, do you make a separation in some way between your sex life and your love life?

FORD: No, because sex has been an aesthetic experience always with me.

COHEN: Do you feel that this aesthetic experience is for you to make it aesthetic, I mean it's more in the eye of the beholder so to speak?

FORD: Yes. It's like the quality of life, if you're creating a life style that's an aesthetic, your occupation.

COHEN: Do you love the aesthetic in the subway?

FORD: Well, it could be an aesthetic vision that you want to make if you happen to see him in the subway.

COHEN: Speaking of subways, I know that you read Alfred Chester's book *The Exquisite Corpse* and that you liked the book, isn't that so?

FORD: Yeah.

COHEN: And talked about it. I thought of it many many times. It seems to me that it's the most neglected book of recent years especially on the subject of homosexuality. I don't see it as having even any peer.

FORD: I think it'll be rediscovered, if it ever was fully discovered.

COHEN: Do you think it would necessarily be a must on any gay reading list?

FORD: It would be over the heads of most people and most people would prefer reading *Last Exit to Brooklyn*.

COHEN: Why do you feel that would be true?

FORD: Because the style of *The Exquisite Corpse* is very involved and the plot is very obscure and it's more like a surrealist poem than a narrative. How big an audience is there for that? Let's face it. Très limité.

Do you feel depleted in the balls today?

COHEN: No, but I feel a little exhausted in general.

FORD: Do you feel that way after sex, too, sometimes?

COHEN: So exhausted? Sometimes I feel tired out, but usually it can give me energy. Don't you get energy?

FORD: Psychic energy, of course. One thing I've discovered about sex in Nepal is that one doesn't have to have the orgasm. And that is the Hindu way, isn't it? The erection without culmination?

COHEN: You mean, withholding the semen?

FORD: Yes, so as not to climax. And I've done that now since it's in the Buddhist and Hindu precepts, religious precepts. I've done that deliberately when having sex, and I find the satisfaction is not decreased and one does not feel deprived. One feels just as though one had complete satisfaction without the reaction, the kind of debility you sometimes feel after the climax. In other words, sex can be just as beautiful and satisfying without climaxing.

COHEN: Well, is this giving you more energy?

FORD: Yes, it's giving me more psychic and physical energy because you don't have the depression which comes after orgasm.

COHEN: It doesn't cause you any physical pain?

FORD: No. It's not coitus interruptus I'm talking about. It's just not going for the orgasm. In other words, having an erection for a longer time, much more erotic play without pushing it to the orgasm. Then when it's over, the play comes to an end, then it's just as though you had total satisfaction without orgasm.

COHEN: Is that true also of your partner?

FORD: Sometimes the partner will have an orgasm and I won't; particularly if he has one first, then I stop. 'Cause I know a lot of people don't like to go on with sex when they've had the orgasm.

COHEN: Do you find with the Nepalese that they want to re-experience orgasm or that they also somehow accept the sanctity of not having an orgasm?

FORD: They accept it because it's in the whole religious philosophy: erection without orgasm. Certainly, it's prevalent in the Hindu religion among the Saddhus. They sit with erections but they don't want an orgasm.

COHEN: Well, you know there are certain sects of Saddhus where part of the initiation involves breaking a certain nerve in the penis so that it's impossible ever to have an erection.

FORD: You can have much more sex life that way, if you don't always require an orgasm.

COHEN: Would you say that this is the most intense new experience that you've had sexually in Kathmandu, relating to this particular idea of withholding orgasm?

FORD: No, it's just added to my sexual knowledge.

COHEN: I wanted to ask you, what is the best way to enter another body?

FORD: With spittle. Vaseline is very demodé.

COHEN: As compared with the Kathmandu teaching that you withhold orgasm to gain energy, what did the Greeks teach you?

FORD: Instant eroticism and no preliminaries, and that's where you begin by immediately taking off your clothes.

COHEN: You think New York or America has something to teach in that respect?

FORD: Only something to unteach. It's too roundabout, too neurotic and circulatory. They have to drink most of the time to get rid of the inhibitions to go to bed.

COHEN: How do you envision being in New York?

FORD: I never have sex in New York. Maybe once in a while I see a young hustler on Forty-second Street. Last time there was a half-Indian boy there I took back. But I never go to the baths, never go to the gay bars, so I'm not really in a milieu where sex comes naturally.

COHEN: So you think that in spite of all the so-called changes in America, and talk about sexual revolution and bisexuality, gay liberation, you feel it's still pretty contorted and not successful?

FORD: I don't know, maybe for others it's been a great liberation but sex is still kind of sick in New York, as far as I can see. Lots of drinking and lots of cruising and lots of hustling. It doesn't have the naturalness that sex in Greece has.

COHEN: Do you plan to make another movie, Charles?

FORD: Making *Johnny Minotaur* was a one-shot movie. I mean, Jean Genet made one. That was it. Let somebody else make them.

COHEN: Didn't you have something to do with bringing the movie *Chant d'Amour* to America?

FORD: No, Grove Press brought it to America, but it was billed with *Johnny Minotaur* and it was the first public showing, 'cause it was the only film that went to the Supreme Court for a decision, and the Supreme Court said obscene. And in billing it with my film *Johnny Minotaur* for the first theatrical exhibition, Grove Press was defying the Supreme Court. Well, by that time porno had made such inroads that nobody did anything about it.

COHEN: Do you feel that eroticism is indispensable to art?

FORD: Art is eroticism, but not necessarily pornography.

COHEN: Do you think you had a liberating influence on a lot of your contemporaries, kind of sexually, in terms of living freely?

FORD: [*Laughs.*] Liberating, well, one tries to liberate oneself. Any fringe benefits to others is just on the fringe.

COHEN: Have you ever taken heroin?

FORD: No, only opium and marijuana.

COHEN: What did you feel about those experiences? Did they open you up in any way?

FORD: No, they shut me down.

COHEN: Completely?

FORD: Yeah, they were just sort of sedatives. I feel I don't need sedation at this point.

COHEN: Under what conditions did you take the opium?

FORD: In Paris.

COHEN: Smoking?

FORD: Yes.

COHEN: You weren't smoking with Cocteau, were you?

FORD: No, with one of the protégés of Cocteau.

COHEN: Do you think there's another adventure after Kathmandu?

FORD: Yes, you have to go around the world full circle.

COHEN: So you think you're going to continue eastward.

FORD: Yes, definitely.

COHEN: You have the next stop planned? In the future, whenever the Kathmandu experience has completely exhausted itself?

FORD: There may be islands of Japan that haven't been totally polluted, overrun with tourists. Tourists are a form of pollution, too. One of the worst.

COHEN: I wanted to ask you about Dali. He seems to be one of the foremost figures operating out of the surrealist movement from the time you were active in starting it in America. I just wondered about your contact with Dali. Did you ever have any particularly interesting close contact with him?

FORD: Well, at one time, yes. After his Paris success, we were all in Italy together: Tchelitchew, Dali, and me. We were guests of Peter Watson, who as an art patron, a millionaire who later founded *Horizon* magazine. So, traveling together, staying together, and that was exactly the moment when Dali got news of the assassination at the hands of the firing squad of his former close friend, García Lorca. He didn't seem particularly moved.

COHEN: He didn't seem moved? Didn't that seem quite astonishing to you at the time? Or perhaps even more astonishing at this time in looking back?

FORD: Given Dali's character, it seems now natural, because he's always been very objective.

COHEN: But nevertheless it was a complete surprise.

FORD: Well, also at that time I didn't know how close they had been.

COHEN: How close were they?

FORD: They were lovers. Lorca wrote the poem *Ode to Salvador Dali* and then there's a photograph of them, in the edition I saw, taken together. And Dali, I wonder if he reminisced then about their being lovers. Anyway, he doesn't hide it.

COHEN: No, he always speaks of Lorca in glowing terms.

FORD: Yes, Lorca's reputation, of course, has grown, since that moment. So Dali came to New York, and we all were in New York after the war started in France. And I started *View* magazine. I was aligned with the surrealists and on the side of Breton. By that time Breton had excommunicated Dali, and one of the early newspaper formats of *View* gave a whole article attacking Dali. It was headlined, "Anti-Surrealist Dali." It was written by a Greek surrealist. Then we interviewed Breton. Anyway Dali was one of those people who could take everything in stride, and was more flattered than anything else by this attack, and cited it in his autobiography.

COHEN: How would you characterize Dali sexually? He's seemed to enjoy presenting himself as a sexual enigma.

FORD: Well, in that way he resembles Andy Warhol, doesn't he?

COHEN: Do you think it's true that Dali always masturbates on his paintings as he completes them?

COHEN: I don't know. Does he say that?

COHEN: I've heard this story from Bill Barker who observed Dali doing it. Dali claimed that this was the way that he celebrated the completion of his paintings, with an orgasm on the painting. . . . Have you ever been turned on by Charles Olson?

FORD: Not to the extent of copying down one of his verses.

COHEN: You said that founding a school is an idea alien to you.

FORD: No, I said I can't see why Olson founded a school. Why he had so much impact and people deriving from him. It's not the sort of poetry I would derive from. I don't quite relate to his influence, which I know has been profound.

COHEN: One thing I've always been impressed with is the way you were right on the scene. We talked about Paris and Gertrude Stein. I know in New York you always were right there with whatever was happening.

FORD: It's all been accidental, too. When I got back to New York in 1962, I had been gone exactly ten years. Marie Mencken and Willard Maas were giving a party out in their Brooklyn penthouse. I'd known them before I left. So I arrived one evening with Andy Warhol. That was before the big publicity for pop art. But Marie already knew what was happening. Frank O'Hara was there, Kenneth Koch was there. Andy was very impressed with them because he was completely unknown. But Marie knew what was coming, so she said, "Oh, Charles, you just come back, just like you haven't been away for ten years, and you just pick up where you left off, coming in with Andy Warhol." And she rushed over to kiss

Andy on both cheeks, and he fled, and she started chasing him around the dining room table. I don't know if she ever caught him or not. By that time I was talking to Frank O'Hara, who said how much he liked *View*.

COHEN: I know of your friendships with young poets, such as Gerard Malanga.

FORD: That was a total accident. I met him at Willard's that same night. Later on, Gerard was reading his poetry, and I took Andy Warhol to his reading, down at the New School for Social Research. After the reading, I got Andy and Gerard together at the bar around the corner. Andy had just lost his silk-screening assistant, and Gerard was looking for part-time work to keep him in Wagner College. So that's the first time they'd met and Andy hired him on the spot. That's the beginning of their relationship. Catalysm is usually accidental.

COHEN: You do have some special kind of feeling for youth and what's happening in the present. You've been close friends in some way with people like Jack Smith, Irving Rosenthal, or Gerard Malanga that I've also known in all the same ways. Of course, I have an interest in things, people, personalities that aren't around to meet anymore. But I don't feel any separation in generation from you.

FORD: Hearing you mention people that are not around anymore, my selected poems, *Flag of Ecstasy* [Black Sparrow Press, 1972] is dedicated to twenty-two people, one for each trump in the Tarot; none of them are around anymore, such as Gertrude Stein, Edith Sitwell. Beautiful people who have meant something to me personally and in my artistic development. Some of them are known, some of them are unknown. So it reads like a whole *Who's Who* of a past couple of decades of avant-garde art. In the book you gave me yesterday, I was pleased to see that Gertrude Stein hasn't peaked in their opinion. They consider her one of the three most important poets of America. Did you read the preface?

COHEN: If you consider Gertrude Stein so important, would you consider any particular work of hers memorable?

FORD: No, it's like saying Van Gogh never painted a masterpiece. It's his whole body of work that's a masterpiece; the same with Gertrude Stein.

COHEN: I myself have certain reservations. I can see her genius in everything, her stylistic importance, but I'm almost irritated by the fact that I can never find anything more than a few lines here or there that have a personal significance to me, and there is nothing that I would want to write down. When there is something, I really value it, and usually it's something very simple, and usually something which carries very good advice with it. I think that was one of her best qualities, being able to give good advice to people. Did she ever give you any special advice?

FORD: Not that I remember. I don't think I ever got any directives like that from her. When I was coming back from Morocco, I telegraphed her and asked her if I could visit her. She was in south France. She cabled back, yes, I'll receive you if you come alone. She didn't want me to bring any friends along.

COHEN: Was she anticipating anyone in particular?

FORD: Yes, Carmita, this girl she knew I was with down in Tangiers.

COHEN: She and Alice were very monogamous, I mean, unpromiscuous?

FORD: Yes, I think they led a very normal life.

COHEN: Was it interesting to be there?

FORD: Yes, on account of the food. My God, if there had been bad food, nobody would have stayed. Can you imagine a more improbable quartet for a lunch which I organized at my studio in the Dakota—Irving Rosenthal, Jack Smith, and W. H. Auden?

COHEN: What happened?

FORD: Irving immediately started talking about the cocksucking poem that Auden had written and asking why he didn't want to acknowledge it.

COHEN: What did Auden have to say? It certainly has appeared in print ten thousand times since it appeared in Ed Sanders' *Fuck You*. . . . Did anything else interesting happen?

FORD: Well, Irving began the lunch by taking his napkin and polishing the silverware, as though the servants had neglected to do it. And Jack took out a string of pearls and pretended to be eating them. So they were completely out of Wystan's milieu.

COHEN: When did you first know that you were an artist, Charles, or have a clear idea of how you were going to spend your life?

FORD: When I sent my first contributions to the children's page.

COHEN: How old were you?

FORD: Ten. Drawings, poems, and short stories.

COHEN: And they were printed?

FORD: Yeah.

COHEN: Do you still have copies of those?

FORD: No. They were printed in the *Commercial Appeal* of Memphis, Tennessee. That's the paper that was read in all three states like Arkansas, Mississippi, and Tennessee.

COHEN: When did you first have an idea of your own sexual definition?

FORD: I was seduced also when I was ten years old by an older man. But I didn't take it as my sexual definition because I was still excited by little girls. So it was really not until I reached adolescence and I read Oscar Wilde and I knew there was a whole other sexual side.

COHEN: Did you have a clear idea? Sometimes people go through many years of torture.

FORD: No. The minute I knew it, that's what I wanted to do. so I immediately went out and picked up a Mexican taxi driver in San Antonio, Texas.

COHEN: You never felt any great guilt about your sexual life?

FORD: Never. It was something that energized me. I knew many homosexuals that felt this, too. There's so many types of homosexuals one can't identify with at all.

COHEN: Up until recent years, I would characterize most homosexuals as being "Closetqueens."

FORD: To me, that didn't even enter as a possibility. Actually, homosexuality was flaunted in *The Young and Evil*, which was a precursor of many frankly-dealing books.

COHEN: Did many people you knew in the thirties feel shocked by your flaunting of it in this book?

FORD: Mary McCarthy told me she felt shocked when she read it, but then now she's less shockable.

COHEN: You remember the interview with Christopher Isherwood in *Gay Sunshine* [no. 19] which I thought was very frank and open. I remember that he was saying, too, that he was never able to deal with it openly, and he was concealing characters, changing. It's sort of ironic that Sally Bowles was actually based on the name of Paul Bowles. Do you think that Christopher and Paul had any relationship? One always pays for the dishonesties one perpetrates.

FORD: I suppose you pay with uncomfortableness in the presence of others, but I've always been inclined to think I should be accepted as I am. I never had the slightest compunction about hiding it.

COHEN: Don't you feel there's the same kind of honesty in your work? If you were to write your autobiography or memoirs...

FORD: Oh, sure, I write them every day. Just as in this interview, especially since it's for *Gay Sunshine.*

COHEN: Somehow I have a feeling that people today, instead of concealing homosexuality, have a tendency to exaggerate it, especially people who might not truly be homosexual.

FORD: You mean like Mick Jagger? Some people say that his impersonation of a bisexual doesn't ring true. He's certainly an attractive person.

COHEN: It's true that's probably equally attracted to men and women, wouldn't you say?

FORD: No, I wouldn't say. He gives me the impression of being pleased to attract both sexes without really being attracted to both sexes.

COHEN: My own feeling about someone like Jagger is that he is very likely sexless.

FORD: Well, he's very narcissistic. He gives you the impression. That's what makes him attractive. What about David Bowie? Is he supposed to be gay?

COHEN: All these glitter rock stars usually come together with a look-alike wife. Maybe it's just preparation for the space age.

FORD: Well, a lot of them are spaced out before the age gets there.

COHEN: You have noticed there is a tendency to celebrate one's bisexuality or homosexuality?

FORD: I'm all for it.

COHEN: I think one of the important things about it is that it makes it easier for people to be honest about who they are and what they're doing.

FORD: Yes. Too bad when people are made to feel neurotic about their sex habits.

COHEN: You never received any heavy static about your sexual identity from your family or in any professional way?

FORD: No, 'cause I left home at an early age and went to New York where I immediately fell in with the homosexual milieu, and then in Paris there was the example of Cocteau and his lovers. Cocteau being a marvelous poet, artist, playwright, successful in every way and a known homosexual. Same with Gide. That sort of climate, literary and artistic, did not exist in America. That was what was so attractive about Paris. So I immediately identified with that and accepted that as the way things should be.

COHEN: So you really picked up your life style...

FORD: From Paris. Stuffy New York literary people, what could you get from them? *Saturday Review of Literature*, who needs it? *Harper's*, are you kidding? I never made any effort to make a literary career in America because I was bored by the people I met, read, or heard about. So therefore, my reputation as a poet was never cultivated. Because you have to be in all that clique—mutual aid and mutual admiration, before you're even published.

COHEN: In order to be free of this social falsehood and to maintain your own artistic integrity it was necessary to make that move to Paris.

FORD: Yes, I guess it was, in retrospect. I never made any conscious decision. I just did what I wanted to do. It had nothing to do with means or money, just desire.

COHEN: Do you think Kathmandu can represent for you today what Paris represented for you years ago? In the same way you came to Paris as a young man and were so influenced by the life style and were able to find your identity in that life style? Do you feel Kathmandu is offering you the same thing in some relative way today?

FORD: No, it's totally different. Rather than receiving from the environment, it's the environment that's receiving from me here. In other words, I'm mining artistic productions out of my self rather than receiving. I'm more on the producing end now, rather than the receiving, although what I'm fed by the visions of Kathmandu produces these products. But I wasn't particularly productive in Paris. I was merely experiencing the environment, the milieu, and the creations of others. Now I feel the most important thing in my life is to create myself. That's why I can come away from the large creative centers like New York. I would say that New York now is the equivalent of Paris insofar as there are so many different thousands of artistic productions going and everything, the cultural thing giving you inspiration, the vibrations of others, the whole electric circus. So I come here really more or less to isolate myself, to work, to go back where it's happening. I wouldn't say that Paris is as exciting now as New York.

It was a whole new period for me, New York in 1962. The whole pop scene to which I immediately related was just beginning to bud. In Paris I wasn't in on any of the movements. I just got the aftermath. Surrealism had already peaked, although it was still going on and still being renewed. But I wasn't in on the beginning of anything there like I was in New York in '62 at the beginning of the pop thing. And I was very energized by that and I produced two books: *Spare Parts* and *Silver Flower Coo*.

In New York there was Warhol, Oldenberg, the two main ones there. Rauschenberg and Jasper Johns had already been precursors. Just like there were Dada precursors of surrealism, there were certain precursors of pop. But the real identity of pop happened with Warhol and Oldenberg. I would say they were the two that registered the most. Oldenberg is still registering in a big way with his sculpture. Andy himself said that pop art is completely over now and he thought it was just a fad anyway. It was probably just his way of self-deprecation.

COHEN: I think it's more true of pop art than surrealism.

FORD: Yes.

COHEN: You pointed out that all great art has qualities of surrealism.

FORD: That's why I enjoyed pop art while it was happening. For me it was another manifestation of the surrealists, and very close to Duchamps who was definitely a surrealist after being a dadaist.

COHEN: How do you feel about the relationship between surrealism and homosexuality?

FORD: Breton was always screaming about total liberation. I should think that includes homosexuality.

COHEN: For me, I think that one of the most pernicious things about the current movement is in this desire to normalize, to put gay relations on the most hideous level of bourgeois heterosexual relations.

FORD: To level off and be accepted by the community and all that.

COHEN: Finally, we have gay couples living out in the suburbs in the same way that heterosexual couples do.

FORD: That's the ideal of a lot of homosexuals—and a lot of them do live that way.

COHEN: I think that everyone is entitled to do what they want, but I would personally like to see most people pushed toward constant confrontation with the revolutionary or whatever is most free. So once committing oneself to something, it's very difficult to turn back.

FORD: That's called momentum. You got to slow down before you can stop.

COHEN: Don't you feel continually driven to a sense of perfection in everything you do?

FORD: Yes, I guess I would call myself a perfectionist. Wouldn't you call yourself one, too?

COHEN: Yes, I think so. In spiritual doctrines, one of the things that is often underlined is the idea that whatever you do, you do it perfectly.

FORD: Perfect is one of your favorite words.

COHEN: So is imperfect, actually. Often in the end I define a fine perfection as imperfection.

FORD: In the anthology you gave me, that's one of the points they bring up: about a fact and its opposite or a feeling and its opposite, that's all one thing. That everything should be encompassing.

COHEN: Haven't you found that many times in your work, whether it's in a painting or a photograph, that it's the mistake that is, that comes out the best, for example. I mean the imperfect one, the photograph where the lighting was wrong, and something happened and somehow there was that perfect accident.

FORD: Yes, the element of chance can be very beautiful.

COHEN: You have recently been doing sculpture and will be taking them to New York for your forthcoming show in New York ["The Kathmandu Experience," January 1975]. This is the first experiment in the area for you.

FORD: It'll look primitive in retrospect. That's as it should be. But I feel really as excited as I did when I took the *View* office. I feel like I've got a whole new project ahead of me.

COHEN: All these sculptures have been made in just the last two months?

FORD: Yeah. They started coming out. It's taught me a lot about how to work, too, because you don't do anything cold. You have to work your vein. You mine jewels or you mine coal. You work it. It's just not given to you right away.

COHEN: I always had that same image in my mind. I always felt I had to go down into the emerald pit one more time when I was making the slides of New York.

FORD: Yeah, on any project like that, the inspiration comes *in* the work, like some people say appetite comes in the eating. Then you look back and you see you couldn't do another one right there cold even though it's your own work; you'd have to get into it.

COHEN: But you think that you might start making the sculptures much larger?

FORD: Yes, definitely, because I'm not actually having to work on them. I'm the designer. So that makes the possibilities infinite because somebody else is executing your designs while you're having other ideas.

COHEN: Is there just one person doing this work, or are there several?

FORD: Several. And when I get into the different materials, like in America I hope to be experimenting with glass and plastic.

COHEN: Sculpture at the moment is the main thing that you've been working with. And these people who are sanding down the wood and working with it so intimately in direct physical contact with their hands and everything else, do they comment on the erotic fantasy that's so implicit in these sculptures?

FORD: Well the younger the workers are the more they see it; the boys immediately saw the whole thing.

COHEN: What do they say?

FORD: Well they just smile. They enjoy it, as though they were looking at an erotic book. The older men just take it.

COHEN: Do they like to touch these sculptures and to feel the different parts of it?

FORD: Yes. They're titillating. That's been the reaction of most people in the studio, that they want to touch....

COHEN: I think you should encourage people to touch the sculptures in the show in New York. Usually it's the opposite, you know.

FORD: They get more polished.

COHEN: And if so it'll be a wonderful scene if somebody actually can't take their hands off one....

Your relationship with Pavel lasted for a long time. What would you say it was that held you for such a long time? Did you want to break away many times?

FORD: Yes I did. And at those times his dependence on me held me. Because he was somewhat like you in that respect; he was very dependent on the person he was living with and attached to. He was almost like a child in that respect.

COHEN: But you must also have been dependent on Pavel.

FORD: Well, in the beginning I was dependent on him financially, but he was making all the money and I was merely taking care of various things. He would say, "Why don't you go out and get a job?" and I would say, "Who would cook for you? And be your secretary, chauffeur, and general companion?" When it was in later stages, he had a lot of friends who were always complaining of me.

COHEN: What would they complain about?

FORD: That I was being kept and should be working, and all that.

COHEN: Well, it sounds like you were working pretty hard if you were taking care of all these other things.

FORD: Of course I was. It used to upset my mother, that I was devoting my life to this Russian artist.

COHEN: What was it that disturbed her?

FORD: Not doing enough for my own career. One of her favorite expressions was "in a big way," and I wasn't really doing anything in a big way. I wrote a book of poetry that wouldn't sell, four hundred copies. She saw that Pavel depended on me and she thought I was just enslaved.

COHEN: But there is no question in your mind about whether you would do it all over again today?

FORD: No, I wouldn't do it all over again today. I would like to lead a totally different life. I hate the idea of repeating. I always like to move on to something new. And I feel that way about countries as well. My first experience in Europe was France, and then I went on to Italy, and then there was a ten-year Greek period, and now it's Asia. So I feel that I don't want to repeat those experiences. I don't know where I'll go from Asia.

COHEN: When you were living in Greece, did you share a life with any one person over an extended period of time?

FORD: No, it's impossible to have a menage with any Greek. Various boys came along with whom I thought I could make a life in the way I did with the Italians, but the Greeks are not that way. They're very unadaptable to homosexual menages unless they're completely homosexual, and I don't fall in love usually with homosexuals.

COHEN: You find the Italians very different in that respect?

FORD: Yes, they're very adaptable and malleable and they can adapt to any milieu, any circumstance.

COHEN: So, really, how have you spent your years? I know that you lived with Pavel for many years, and you've told me that you lived with Parker Tyler though you weren't really lovers as much as very very good friends. I know now you are living with Indra, and the time that you lived in Greece you had many lovers.

FORD: But not living with anybody. I lived with Djuna Barnes for a while in Paris.

COHEN: About how long was that actually?

FORD: Well it was short, a year altogether. It began with our autumn exodus to Middle Europe, returning to Paris for the winter where she had an apartment. I lived in the servants' room above the apartment, two flights up, which we furnished together with blue wallpaper and blue bedcovers.

COHEN: Could you characterize in some way the difference of how you felt living with Djuna, let's say, as opposed to living with Pavel or in any other relationship?

FORD: Well with both of them I felt they were the great celebrated artists who'd fallen in love with the quiet, little-known poet. And naturally that had its degree of flattery for me.

COHEN: In both cases you were turned on largely by the fact—

FORD: By the attention of these people whom I admired, who were already famous. Djuna told me one day, "You're nobody." And then she was discussing with somebody whether I should be saved from the gutter, whether I was just a type of street boy of Montparnasse.

COHEN: Didn't it bug you sometimes to hear that?

FORD: Well I just laughed, because after all I'd edited *Blues* and, although I'd never published a book, I'd been called the best young poet in America.

COHEN: Well, was it more like a put-on?

FORD: No, I think they were serious, but I couldn't take that attitude seriously. When you're very young you see the pretentiousness of a lot of older people, no matter how famous they are.

COHEN: Well, do you think their main attraction was really their success, or their knowledge?

FORD: Their success, their knowledge, combined with their attractiveness to me. Djuna was very beautiful, Pavlik was very dynamic and handsome, and I can only say it was like anybody being flattered when Cocteau would fall in love with somebody. Cocteau would take him up, and that would be the new protégé of

Cocteau. I felt somewhat the same way. Anyway, seventeen years later, I come back, and I'm still introduced as the protégé of Djuna Barnes! Which was, which I thought very funny. She wrote a short story about me which was never published, and she was just the greatest.

COHEN: What was the story?

FORD: I forget the title of it; something about a little boy. And she described our relationship, and my mother. I wish I had a copy of it.

COHEN: It seems that Djuna actually has left many things unpublished. She's not an artist who has consciously pushed her career.

FORD: That's true. Djuna's a recluse and intransigent, and truth-speaking, non-flattering, non-careerist. Well, she hit the top when T. S. Eliot wrote the preface.

COHEN: There are lines from *Nightwood* that echo in my mind still after all these years. Like, "an eland chapleted with orange-blossoms [and bridal veil] coming down,"—describing someone walking down a staircase—"one [a] hoof raised in the economy of fear." I think it's actually a line that Eliot mentions in the introduction as well. But there are many scenes with this mad doctor and I remember especially "Bow Down." That was her original title for the whole book before she changed it to *Nightwood*. Does the girl in the book actually make, make it with a dog at the end of the book?

FORD: It's ambiguous.

COHEN: I had the feeling from just the little bit that you've mentioned about Djuna that there's probably an enormous treasure of unpublished material clinging to her somewhere in suitcases and trunks and bureau drawers that would be quite fantastic if they will all come out someday. Are you thinking of writing your memoirs?

FORD: I write them every day. I've kept a diary since I was a child, but the first time that I started keeping the adult diary was the year after *View* magazine closed. *View* closed in '47, so the first day of the year of 1948 I began a diary which I continue to keep regularly as a major work. When Pavlik used to reproach me that I hadn't written my masterpiece, I used to reply that the diary was my masterpiece.

COHEN: Do you still feel that?

FORD: Well, Parker Tyler confirmed that ten years later. When he read the manuscript, he said, "This is your masterpiece." He helped me edit it and I call it "Water from a Bucket," a quote from Goethe, saying that something that he wrote had no plan or system, just like water from a bucket. Now I have the main version in my house in Crete which I'm going to retype and submit to another publisher. The ten-year diary is from the first of January 1948 until the end of 1957, which is the year that Tchelitchew died. After that I've kept, on and off, a diary. I did a street diary in Athens, which I didn't even make a transcription of; it's all in the University of Texas archive.

COHEN: What do you mean, "street diary"?

FORD: I kept a notebook with me at all times and wrote wherever I was, usually when I was on the streets in Greece. I even developed the technique of writing while walking as though it were a camera instead of a diary.

COHEN: That can be difficult, I know. Did you even try writing in a taxicab?

FORD: I guess I wrote everywhere I was. Anyway I concentrated on certain experiences, too. Very much. The Athens street diary would make a book in itself. It already has a title. But I never typed it up. Half of the "Water from a Bucket" is typed.

COHEN: How is it you let it go into an archive collection?

FORD: But it is still my property. It's available to me whenever I want to publish it. They're still trying to catalogue my archives: letters from Gertrude Stein, Djuna Barnes, Edith Sitwell. And then scattered letters from literary people, including one from H. L. Mencken, who read *The Young and Evil*.

COHEN: Parker and Djuna and Pavel are the key people in your life, and now Indra occupies part of center stage in your life here in Kathmandu.

FORD: Yes, the new act is with Indra.

COHEN: He's certainly very different from all the other people that you've mentioned.

FORD: He's different, but he's kind of the ideal that I was looking for in all these Italians and Greeks and never found.

COHEN: But this is the first time in a way that you're mentioning a person as central in your life that isn't a person for whom you had a very strong artistic affinity.

FORD: No, I had another one, the young Italian. After Pavlik died I immediately pursued my interest in this young Italian whom I knew first when he had not yet reached fourteen. His father died and I sort of became responsible for him. I took him to Paris, sent him to school there: he studied mime with Marcel Marceau, he learnt French, and then he went to acting school in Rome when we were living in Rome, and the result was he got several movie parts. He was in pictures directed by Marcel Carné and Réné Clément and was given auditions for Visconti and is now pursuing his TV career. When I was in New York last October, he telephoned me from Los Angeles saying he was out there on a screen test. So he's one I put in orbit, a totally simple boy who had left school at age eleven.

COHEN: What would you say is the real basis for a successful relationship in living with someone? I mean all these different experiences as varied as they were seem to have worked out and been successful for you.

FORD: Well there's been no formula, just as you really can't have a formula for works of art. You just go to the next creation. I feel that Indra's one of the works of art of life. A work in progress, a very definitely creative project. It's always been a question of life in art. As well as art in life.

COHEN: I think it's part of your reputation, as far as I've always known it. I've heard other people envy your basic success and I know that many many well-known artists have come to you and even asked you for advice on how to [*Both laugh*] maintain a successful relationship or just even how to pick someone up successfully.

FORD: Oh, you're thinking of the *sexual* relationship? Kimon Friar got that flash too, when he said that I didn't let the sexual life interfere with my life as an artist, that I have combined the two. It's not that conscious with me; what comes out is what comes out, like writing a poem.

COHEN: Well so many people have a streak of masochism, and that can be disastrous. I don't think that you have that.

FORD: I'd never doubt that. I'm much more inclined to sadism, which is actually supposed to be the more creative of the two emotions. A sculptor, when he's hacking away, is supposed to be very sadistic in a sublimated way.

COHEN: Have you ever given any broad scope of expression to sadistic impulses?

FORD: No, only perhaps psychologically. Turning the screw in a certain situation.

COHEN: What would you say is most characteristic of the Nepalese? I notice that Indra seems so remarkable for his innocence. Is it *that* that you feel particularly turned on by?

FORD: Yes. The innocent has a charm of its own.

COHEN: Do you think there's any danger that he can lose this innocence when you take him abroad?

FORD: No, because some people are born with their natures which are either easily corrupted or incorruptible.

COHEN: Do you feel that you've managed to maintain your own innocence?

FORD: Yes. Yes, I'm still just a Southern child. A long way from home. There's nothing more vicious than children, either. I mean, you can be innocent and still be vicious. Some of the greatest criminals were very innocent too.

COHEN: I have the impression you're getting ready for a date later, that you want me to get out of here by a certain time. Do you have a date tonight?

FORD: I told a boy I'd be around about six-thirty, but he's told me to come around before and hasn't been there, so I'll probably give him a last chance.

COHEN: Oh. What do you think you're gonna do? Where would you go?

FORD: Bring him back here.

COHEN: That sounds the best. Often I've heard you say in talking about someone, well, this person is not my type. Can you tell me what is your type?

FORD: I seem to have a recurrent type. Even in Indra I find traces of an Italian protégé of mine, and then there are vestiges of a long-ago love of mine who is Mexican, and my type seems to be towards the almond-eyed.

COHEN: But you have very definite standards of physical beauty that turn *you* on.

FORD: It would have to be hairless and almond-eyed. So I guess that lets you out.

COHEN: Hmm. Well, I could shave.

FORD: You could put some tape on your eyes too like Leonore Fini used to do. Why don't you do that tomorrow? Shave and come with taped eyes.

COHEN: Then we could finish the interview on a more personal level, perhaps.

FORD: See what happens...

COHEN: Do you identify yourself as an Aquarian?

FORD: I always say I'm an Aquarian, and this is the Aquarian Age and I can do no wrong, we can do no wrong.

COHEN: I think you are typical Aquarian in your role of having made films, directing a magazine, launching people into orbit, finding all of these involvements as opposed to someone who wouldn't have any interest in doing any of those things.

FORD: Pavlik must have meant that when he said that I change people's fates. He looked upon me as a kind of fate-figurement. People I come in contact with, their fates are somehow altered. He made a distinction between fate and fortune...

You told me that Pegasus relates to Aquarius.

COHEN: It seems that it is particularly an Aquarian symbol, and it struck me in some lines from your poem on Baudelaire which I can't recall exactly.

FORD: Yes. "A wingless horse heard the story one day, of a horse with wings, and flew away."

COHEN: The nature of your poetry seems to be summed up in those lines, and in essence, your own life style.

FORD: It seems to evoke the power of imagination, that's all, in a concrete image, which is something one always tries to do in poetry.

COHEN: In the last analysis, it really is imagination which will sustain us, don't you think?

FORD: Well, the motto of *View* was, "By the imagination we live." But still, I don't know if I would use it again as a motto.

PHOTO BY JERRY BAUER

JEAN GENET

JEAN GENET was born in Paris in 1910. An illegitimate child who never knew his parents, he was abandoned to the Assistance Publique. At the age of ten he was sent to a reformatory for theft and he spent the next thirty years in and out of many of the most notorious prisons in Europe. After his tenth conviction for theft in France he was condemned to life imprisonment, but he was granted a pardon, primarily through the efforts of important French literary figures, including Gide, Sartre, and Cocteau. Between 1940 and 1948 he wrote several autobiographical prose narratives dealing with homosexuality and crime, including *Our Lady of the Flowers* (tr. 1963), *Miracle of the Rose* (tr. 1965), and *The Thief's Journal* (tr. 1964). Genet's first two plays, *The Maids* (1948) and *Deathwatch* (1949), established his reputation as a dramatist concerned with theater as ritual or ceremony. Considered classic examples of the theater of the absurd, his dramas portray a world of outcasts in revolt against everything that renders man helpless, subservient, and alone. Among Genet's later works are *The Balcony* (1957, tr. 1960), *The Blacks* (1959, tr. 1960), *The Screens* (1961, tr. 1972), *Funeral Rites* (tr. 1969), and *Querelle* (tr. 1974). See also his *Poèmes* (1948) and *Reflections on the Theatre* (1972), and Jean Paul Sartre's study *Saint Genet* (1952).

THIS INTERVIEW was conducted by Hubert Fichte in December 1975 and originally appeared (in German) in the magazines *Die Zeit* and *Him/Applaus*. Hubert Fichte was born in Germany in 1935 and has, among other things, been employed as an actor and as a shepherd. His first publications are fairly conventional but subsequent works contain a unique mixture of autobiography, fiction, and documentary material. Fichte is best known for the following books: *Der Aufbruch nach Turku* (1963); *Das Waisenhaus* (1965), for which he was awarded the Hermann Hesse Prize; *Die Palette* (1968); *Detlevs Imitationen "Gruenspan"* 1971); *Versuch ueber die Pubertaet* (1975); *Xango* (1976); and *Mein Lesebuch* (1976). His most recent books are the result of trips to South America and the Caribbean. See his essay "The Razor Blade and the Hermaphrodite" published in *Gay Sunshine* 33/34 (Summer/Fall 1977), pp. 12-13. The interview was translated from the French by Richard Mills, Kristiane Zappel, and Rhodes Barnett, with special thanks to Fabienne Valarchez. It appeared in *Gay Sunshine* 35 (Winter 1978) and is reprinted with permission of Hubert Fichte.

Hubert Fichte interviews
JEAN GENET

FICHTE: Yesterday you told me about a demonstration in which you participated.

GENET: No, I did not participate in it; there was a demonstration yesterday which reunited members of the CGT, the CFDT, and the CGC [French labor federations —*Trans.*] and the three opposition parties, that is the Communist Party, the Socialist Party, and the Leftists. Officially this demonstration took place to protest against the government's economic policy. But actually it was provoked by the arrest of several union members and ordinary soldiers accused of demoralizing the army, and who now risk going on trial before the courts where the sentences could be from five to twenty years' imprisonment.

FICHTE: Then the demonstration was directed at Giscard d'Estaing?

GENET: At the minister of defense and above all at the minister of the interior.

FICHTE: Aren't you a member of one of the parties which demonstrated there?

GENET: No, not at all, I am not a member of any party.

FICHTE: Until recently it was said that you don't have a permanent address, that you live in small hotels...

GENET: That's unintentional, I happen to have my passport with me. Here's my address, you can read it.

FICHTE: It's Gallimard's address [Genet's French publisher —*Ed.*].

GENET: I don't have any other, it's my official address.

FICHTE: Living without a permanent address or an apartment makes it difficult to have friends, you can't invite people over, you can't cook.

GENET: I don't like to cook.

FICHTE: You're always the one who's invited.

GENET: So what? Of course there are problems, but at the same time it makes irresponsibility possible. Socially I am not responsible for anything, and it also allows for instant commitment, for on-the-spot decisions. When Bobby Seale was arrested, Bobby Seale was the head of the Panthers, the Panthers paid me a visit in Paris and asked me what I could do for Bobby Seale, it was in the morning and I said: "The simplest thing is to go to the United States and check out the situation." They asked me: "When?" and I said: "Tomorrow."—"So soon?"—And I noticed that the Panthers were taken aback. They are used to moving fast and I moved faster than they did, and for the simple reason that I was living in a hotel. I had one small suitcase. Would I have been able to do that if I had had an apartment? Would I have been able to move so quickly if I had had friends?

FICHTE: Are you afraid of being entrapped by a kind of bourgeois luxury which you cannot afford on the basis of your success?

GENET: Ah! that's very silly of course. No, I don't think so since I don't admire bourgeois luxury at all. It would have to demonstrate the qualities of a Renaissance castle. Well. But my royalties do not allow me to hold court like a Borgia. I don't risk very much.

FICHTE: What fascinates you about a Borgia court?

GENET: It doesn't fascinate me, I simply think that the last manifestations of architectonic luxury occur in the Renaissance. I don't find anything after that. The eighteenth century in France doesn't grab me, and neither does the seventeenth century. But I don't want to say that architecture stopped after the Renaissance. I was shocked the first time I was in Versailles. The little brick palace is rather pretty, but when you enter the garden and you turn around and there you are, in front of the huge façade, well, it's shocking. I wonder why this guy, what was his name? Mansard, is that right? well, why didn't Louis the Fourteenth multiply the miles of columns even more, it's heavy, stupid, innumerable, there's no feeling in it, there are Renaissance palaces in Italy which seem to be very small, but are actually immense and very beautiful and which were inhabitable. The Hall of Mirrors, I don't know the exact proportions, but it has been done better, in Brasilia, for example.

FICHTE: You don't think that Brasilia repeats itself infinitely?

GENET: No, no, it possesses several units which form a whole, a very harmonious one. I've flown over it. I know it in the sun, in the rain, in night and day, in the wind, in the cold and in the heat and I know Brasilia from the ninth floor of the Hotel Nacional and from the street, and the funny thing is that here is this guy who is a Communist, I'm talking about Oscar Niemeyer, who created this city, he could not prevent Indian shacks from springing up all around the city. You would think these high-rise apartment buildings in Brasilia could be inhabited only by guys six feet tall, blonde or brunette, but in any case well built, more like sculptures than people, and in reality they are occupied by minor officials, ambassadors, and ministers, and not by Brazilian Indians or blacks, and nevertheless I don't know of any other city like Brasilia, which was created in entire units which are obviously harmonious. There are certain things Oscar Niemeyer did not understand; he wasn't capable of conceiving an urbanism which recognized the necessity of housing the proletariat in a humane way. The most striking building there is the Ministry of Foreign Affaris. The cathedral leaves me cold. I was in the little church in Vence built by Matisse, a little church dedicated to a guy I should detest, St. Dominic; it's quite small. You have to enter it. The utilization of space there is unbelievable; you are inside a poem.

FICHTE: Romanesque architecture has the same poetic quality.

GENET: Yes, yes, yes.

FICHTE: In Montmajour, in Solignac. Have you been in the cupola church in Solignac?

GENET: Yeah. Romanesque churches always have a cupola.

FICHTE: There are some with vaultlike arches.

GENET: They almost always have cupolas, because the Roman arch demands a cupola.

FICHTE: Would a comparison of Niemeyer's architecture with Matisse's little church lead you to the conclusion that Matisse was a revolutionary artist?

GENET: No. One has to be very careful in using the word revolutionary. It must be used deliberately. It's not easy. I wonder if the concept of revolution can be separated from the concept of violence. You have to use different faculties, different means, in order to realize what Cézanne, for example, accomplished. I think people like Cézanne, as well as the painters who followed him or the musicians who questioned the concept of tonality, were audacious, but not too audacious, since concepts like perspective in painting or the chromatic scale in music had already begun to be arranged by moods and whims. Alban Berg composed without taking himself too seriously, and then completed the work on his ideas later on. He was audacious. That is of considerable importance, but I don't think it had, as an adventure of the intellect, the same importance to them as we think it did. That may be the reason why Cézanne remained a very simple man. He did go to mass, he lived with a woman, a woman he wasn't married to. It must have hurt him that Zola, his childhood friend, didn't understand him, but I am not sure that Cézanne thought that he would have the sort of posthumous fame which he has had.

FICHTE: Yesterday you talked about Monteverdi. Is his an art which brutally breaks with tradition?

GENET: To me there is nothing more cheerful and joyful than the mass of the *Beata Vergine*.

FICHTE: You have said you are not religious, an atheist; how do you approach the *Vespro della Beata Vergine?*

GENET: Twenty years ago I read the *Iliad*, it is very very beautiful, does that mean I believe in the religion of Zeus?

FICHTE: To be honest, I don't think you are really very far from it.

GENET: The last time I was in Japan, seven or eight years ago, I saw a Japanese Nō play which touched me greatly. You know that the women's roles are played by men. At one point there is the mask of an old woman, who is the last Buddhist woman, she enters a cave and covers her face with a fan, and then she uncovers her face and it is the face of a very young girl, the first Shintoist woman. The theme was the transition from the Buddhist to the Shinto religion. Do you think that I'm a Buddhist or a Shintoist?

FICHTE: I think your work, your whole existence reveals a fascination with ritual.

GENET: There is nothing ritual in the *Iliad*.

FICHTE: There is the ritual of description in the *Iliad*, there are refrains and *topoi*, for example: "and their intestines spilled out on the ground."

GENET: No, that's a way of collapsing. I wonder if it is really an invention of Homer's, or just a way of moving along.

FICHTE: The style of Homer's narration is almost religious.

GENET: In the *Iliad,* yes, but not in the *Odyssey.*

FICHTE: Why do you like Strindberg's *Miss Julie* and why don't you like Brecht's *Galileo Galilei?*

GENET: Brecht just said a lot of nonsense, because *Galileo Galilei* just states obvious things which I would have discovered without Brecht. Strindberg, at least in *Miss Julie,* doesn't propose anything that is already evident. That's very new. It surprised me. I saw *Miss Julie* after I saw *The Dance of Death,* what's it called?

FICHTE: *Dödsdansen.*

GENET: And I also liked that a great deal. Nothing that Strindberg said could be said in any other way than poetically, whereas everything Brecht said can and has been said prosaically.

FICHTE: That's what Brecht intended. He called his theater "epic theater" and he introduced, or at least pretended to introduce, the concept of *Verfremdung,* which was exactly what Strindberg had already accomplished in his introduction to *Miss Julie.* Strindberg had already presupposed the emotionally neutral spectator, the Brechtian spectator with a cigar in his hand.

GENET: By choosing the gesture of a cigar smoker, an act of disrespect against the work of art is committed which is not permissible. The work of art does not permit such an act. I am not acquainted with the Rothschilds, but I could imagine discussing art with them while smoking a cigar. You can't go to the Louvre to see "La Marquise de la Solana" using the same cigar-smoking gesture that you use when discussing art with the Rothschilds.

FICHTE: In other words, you think that the Brechtian gesture is bourgeois and capitalistic.

GENET: It seems that way to me.

FICHTE: At least when standing before the work of art, since you're smoking a cigarillo right now.

GENET: When you smoke a cigar as a cigar smoker, when you can be defined as a cigar smoker, when I listen to Mozart's *Requiem* and the action of cigar smoking is more important than listening to the *Requiem,* then it's not only a matter of *Verfremdung,* it's also a matter of a lack of sensitivity, it's a matter of not having ears for, that is, of not being touched by the aesthetic phenomenon which constitutes the *Requiem.*

FICHTE: You speak of contemplation before the work of art.

GENET: Standing before the work of art I lose the feeling of being "myself," the feeling of my "self," more and more. But when confronted with subversive events, my "self," my "social self" grows, becoming stronger and stronger. The possibility, the freedom of contemplation becomes less and less when faced by such subversive events. One day I asked Boulez who was conducting *Daphnis and Chloe:* "To what extent do you perceive each instrument?" and he said . . . Pierre Boulez said to me: "Only about twenty-five or thirty percent," and he has one of the finest ears in existence. So to conduct an orchestra you have to be extraordinarily attentive, and when you are listening you have to be attentive too. And if your ear isn't as fine as Boulez's, then you have to concentrate so intensely that, at least for me, I can't look at more than two or three paintings in a museum or hear more than one or two pieces in a concert. And as for the rest . . . I'm too tired.

FICHTE: And reading?

GENET: Ah! it's the same thing. It took me more than two months to read *The Brothers Karamazov*. I was tired. I was in Italy, I read one page and then . . . I had to think about it for two hours. And the same thing all over again, it's unbelievable, you're exhausted.

FICHTE: Contemplation absorbs your "self" to the point of extinction?

GENET: Not to the point of extinction, not to the point of completely losing the "self," because your leg suddenly falls asleep, you come back to your "self," but there's a tendency for you to lose yourself.

FICHTE: Whereas the revolutionary act?

GENET: Ah! That's the opposite, I think, because you must act. But standing before the work of art requires you to act too. The tension you bring to the work of art is an action; if, given my modest means, I don't compose Monteverdi's *Beata Vergine* mass while listening to it, then I'm not hearing it, I'm doing nothing, I'm hearing nothing, and if I don't write *The Brothers Karamazov* when I read it, then I'm doing anything.

FICHTE: Then it's twofold?

GENET: Yes. Don't you have the impression that it's something like that?

FICHTE: Yes, but revolutionary action is also twofold.

GENET: But it's not through the same means; you risk your body with a revolutionary action, but by creating a work of art you may risk your reputation, but you don't endanger your body. If you botch a poem, if you botch a concerto or a building, well, people may mock you, or you won't have the reputation you deserve, but you aren't in physical danger. But committing a revolutionary act puts your body in danger, and therefore all revolutionary adventure too.

FICHTE: When you write, is it an action similar to recreating *The Brothers Karamazov,* is it an action similar to the contemplation of the "self," or is it rather an act similar to the concentration of the "self" through the danger brought about by a revolutionary act?

GENET: Your first formulation is more correct. I never, I have never put myself in physical danger through the act of writing, at least not seriously. I have never written anything while in this physical state which would have caused me to be put in prison, or to be prosecuted or killed.

FICHTE: But your works have disturbed and influenced a whole generation. Although this is exaggerating, I would say that there are no homosexuals in the world today who have not been directly or indirectly influenced by your work.

GENET: First off, sheer prudence forces me to be skeptical about what you are saying. You're trying to attribute an importance to me which, in my eyes, I don't have. And secondly, I think you are wrong; what I wrote did not effect the liberation of which you speak, but the other way around, it is the liberation which came about, roughly coinciding with the occupation of France by Germany and its subsequent liberation, followed by peace, etc. . . . It was this kind of liberation of the mind which permitted me to write my books.

FICHTE: I insist. Until 1968 there was a German law which forbade sexual intercourse between adult males. The Genet trial in Hamburg was decisive for the freedom to publish erotic works, etc.

GENET: Even if my books did cause a sensation, the act of writing, the simple act of writing while in prison did not nearly affect me in the sense that there is a disproportion between what you have described to me, that is, the result attained by my books, and the writing of my books; the writing itself was practically the same as if I had described a boy and girl making love, for me it was no more difficult than that. I even wonder if the methods of transmission and mechanical reproduction have an inflationary influence. Two hundred years ago, someone painting me would have ended up with a portrait. But now, when someone photographs me, the photo is printed in quantities of two hundred thousand, or even more. OK, but does that make me more important?

FICHTE: No, not more important, but more significant.

GENET: But significant in a new, a different way.

FICHTE: According to Sartre, the manuscript of the Marquis de Sade's *The 120 Days of Sodom* had no importance as long as it was kept in a crack in the wall in the Bastille, whereas it influences an entire generation when available as a paperback.

GENET: Do you think that the Marquis de Sade helped to liberate the end of the eighteenth century through his work and his way of life? I think it was the other way around. It was the growing and already existent freedom of the epoch of the Encyclopedists in the second half of the eighteenth century which made the works of Sade possible.

FICHTE: In reading your works, one discovers your admiration of the beauty of brutality, the elegance of brutality.

GENET: Yes but you know that I was thirty when I wrote my books, and now I'm sixty-five.

FICHTE: And this admiration which I find so disconcerting, this admiration of murderers, of Hitler, of the concentration camps, is now gone?

GENET: Yes and no. It is gone but has not been replaced, it is an emptiness which is rather strange for those still living. What does this fascination before brutes or murderers or Hitler mean? In more neutral terms, perhaps simpler ones too, I remind you that I had neither a father or a mother, that I was a public ward, that I did not belong to the village. I was educated in the Massif Central. And I learned it in a stupid, ridiculous way: our teacher asked us to write a short essay describing our homes; I described my home, the teacher liked my essay so much that he read it out loud. And everyone made fun of me and said: "But that's not his home, he's a foundling." And I felt so empty, so... I instantly felt like a stranger. Oh, the word isn't very strong, to "hate" France, that's nothing at all, there must be something else other than "hate," to "puke out" France... finally I... and... the fact that the French army, thirty years ago the most respected in the world, capitulated to the troops of an Austrian private delighted me. I had my revenge, even though I know very well that it wasn't I but others, a whole system, who effected it, and I also know that it was a conflict within the whites' world which astounded me from afar, but French society had finally received a blow and I couldn't but like the person who had given such a blow to French society. Then I was so totally satisfied with everything that happened, with the breadth of the punishment dealt out to France. In just a few days the French army and even the French population fell from the Maubeuge-Bâle line back to the Spanish frontier. If you have been militarily defeated to such an extent, then you have to admit that France was humiliated, and I could only adore those who had set this humiliation of France in motion. Consequently I had no choice but to join the oppressed blacks who were revolting against the whites. Perhaps I'm a black with white or pink skin, but I'm a black. I don't know my family.

FICHTE: Did the Black Panthers accept you despite your white skin?

GENET: Without hesitation. I often asked myself this question. I was alone, there were no other whites, I was with them for two months, and the police sent a summons to the Panthers saying that I had to meet with them. The Panthers told me: "It's better that you leave, because otherwise we might get in some trouble." I left. But for two months I was all alone with them. I ate with them. I asked myself: "Aren't they fed up with seeing this whitey around all the time?" Evidently not. I saw Angela Davis again three months ago. I told her: "We were very worried about you," and she told me: "But we were just as worried about you." She told me about an incident during Bobby Seale's pre-trial which I attended, when David Hilliard, who had replaced Bobby Seale, was arrested. He was about to show me a document when the police surrounded him and seized him. I noticed that he was about to speak so I shouted, I said in French: "David, David, don't say a word, shut up," I was very scared. I saw that nobody intervened; I found a lawyer and told him, he had a beard like you [Fichte —*Trans.*], you know American lawyers don't wear robes like they do in Europe, and I took him by his shoulders and told him: "Listen to me, do something... prevent this..." and he had me arrested. I was mistaken, he was the D.A. Since I didn't understand English, I couldn't do anything about it, I was arrested, but very gently; they led me out, but practically asked me to leave. I noticed the difference in treatment. I'll tell you what happened: we arrived at the courtroom in New Haven, I was together with the Panthers; there were about ten Panthers and one white, a white man sixty years old, myself, and the courtroom is very small. There were two or three rows of chairs in front of the judge, and behind them were benches and the whites were seated on the chairs and the blacks on the benches. There happened to be an empty seat in the first row, and a cop took my arm and without asking me led me to the empty seat, and I followed him because I didn't understand, and only when I looked up did I see that David Hilliard was in the back. I said: "I am going with you" and the cop... I struck his hand and said: "Let me go!" and he did, but you see, I felt the difference. And something else: when David left, he left behind a small attaché case with notes inside and there was a black who managed to get it into the hall, and then it was necessary to get it out of the courthouse. Well, to whom did they give the attaché case? To me, because they knew they would be carefully searched before leaving the courthouse, which was what happened.

FICHTE: You say that the Panthers made a poetic revolution?

GENET: Oh well! before saying that, I would like for us to agree that it is possible. There seem to be at least two kinds of communication: a rational, reflective communication, do you agree that this lighter is black?

FICHTE: Yes.

GENET: Yes. And then there's a communication which is less certain, but nevertheless obvious. Do you agree with Baudelaire's line: "Blue hair, banner of taut darkness." Do you think that is beautiful?

FICHTE: Yes.

GENET: And we're communicating. So, there are at least two forms of communication: a recognizable, controllable form, and then an uncontrollable form. The Panthers' actions demonstrated the uncontrollable kind of communication. In San Francisco I was in a taxi with a black driver and asked him: "Do you like the Panthers?" and he said: "Like them, no, admire them, yes." He was fifty years old and told me: "But my kids like them very much." Actually, he liked them too. You can't admire without loving, but he couldn't bring himself to say it, because they were associated with violence. It was said that they looted and killed, and that's true, they killed some cops, some whites. But that's less violence than the Americans used in Vietnam, Korea or elsewhere. It was a revolution on a level of emotion and sensibility, so there's no connection ... there are perhaps connections, but only very tenuous ones with the revolutions which were tried in other ways and other places.

FICHTE: The revolution which you have in mind is analogous to that of the Panthers?

GENET: No, no, the Panthers were risking a sensibility which we lack and which doesn't result from the fact that they're of African descent or that they're black, but simply because they're outcasts, for four centuries they were outcasts and they've rediscovered themselves in the word "Brother." Such fraternity isn't possible when thinking about global revolutions, that's how it seems to me. You cannot speak that way without having a lot of time ahead of you.

FICHTE: We say that there is a difference between poetic, artistic and social revolutions.

GENET: What is called a poetic or an artistic revolution is not exactly a revolution. I don't think they change the order of the world. Nor do they change your view of the world; they refine the view, complete it, they make it more complex, but they don't radically transform it like a social or a political revolution. When we speak of an artistic revolution, we need to remember that we are using a cumbersome, worn-out expression. As I told you, political revolutions rarely correspond, or I could say, never correspond to artistic revolutions. When the revolutionaries achieve a total restructuring of society, they then find themselves facing the problem of expressing their revolution in the most adequate way possible. It seems to me that all revolutionaries continue to use the most academic means of the society which they just overthrew or intended to overthrow. It's as though they are telling themselves: "We are going to prove to the regime we just overthrew that we are just as capable as they were." And then they imitate the academic traditions, they imitate the official style of painting, the official architecture, the official music. Only much later do they consider a cultural revolution, and then they appeal not only to the academic but to tradition and to the new ways of using tradition.

FICHTE: Are there no exceptions to the rule? Danton? Saint-Just?

GENET: Danton, no! I don't think that Danton approached a revolutionary expression, that is, a new way of feeling the world and expressing it. Perhaps Saint-Just. Not in his proclamations, but in the statements he made on the occasion of Louis XVI's execution. The style is still the style of the eighteenth century, but with such an impudence! The rhythm, the syntax, the grammar are all of the eighteenth century. But the syntax seems deformed, or at least transformed by the audacity of the positions he took. If you like, he expressed himself in a very violent courtly language. But even Diderot's language, and sometimes even Montesquieu's, was rather violent. In his second statement supporting the execution of Louis XVI, Saint-Just said: "The king is right, he is the legitimate sovereign, and therefore the people who revolted against the legitimate sovereign must be killed—or else the legitimate sovereign is the people and the king is an impostor, and in that case the impostor must be killed." That's quite new. No one dared to speak like that.

FICHTE: Were there any other moments of poetic or artistic revolution during the various French revolutions?

GENET: No. There was the Paris Commune. The entire population of Paris had actually seized the reins of power. And emotionally that is quite beautiful, but the only artist who served the revolution as an artist and as a revolutionary was Courbet, who is a great painter, but not a painter who revolutionized the painting of his time. Victor Hugo was very proud because a cannon bearing the name "V. Hugo" had been manufactured by the Parisian foundries. He tried to understand. And he did understand, more or less, he was even a little shocked by the breadth of the Paris Commune. But he didn't change as a writer. The Paris Commune didn't last long, it lasted such a short time that it couldn't change anything. The revolution of '48. What do we owe to it? Well, Baudelaire seems to have been on the barricades, but Baudelaire had already written the most beautiful poems in *Les Fleurs du Mal*. We do owe *L'Education Sentimentale* to the revolution of '48. But *L'Education Sentimentale* was written by Flaubert, and he was not at all in favor of the revolution. At the end of the war it seemed as though a new kind of sensibility would find its counterpart in the Soviet revolution. But in the end the Surrealists were quick to cut their ties with the Soviet Union—Aragon wrote "Moscow, the Rotten" at this time—as well as with Freud, who didn't understand anything at all. His meeting with Aragon demonstrated that he wasn't at all interested in surrealism, and that he did not see why psychoanalysis should be used solely for poetic purposes.

FICHTE: Have you ever been in the Soviet Union?

GENET: No, never.

FICHTE: But you have been invited?

GENET: No. Sartre proposed that I accompany him there; I think he thought he'd be bored to death if he went by himself; together we would have had a lot of fun, but I wasn't invited. I probably wouldn't have been given a visa.

FICHTE: Why didn't you try?

GENET: I was afraid of being bored to death too.

FICHTE: Do you see a chance for a poetic or an artistic revolution in the Cuban experiment?

GENET: No. When Castro saw modern Western literature and painting while in Europe, he saw it only through a Cuban perspective, but what he saw were already recognizable forms, academic forms; he recognized them but he didn't recognize the forms actually native to Cuba.

FICHTE: You were supposed to go to Cuba, but refused that as well?

GENET: When the cultural attaché invited me, I said: "Yes, I'd very much like to go to Cuba, but on one condition: I pay for my trip, I pay my way, and I go where I want, I live where I want," and I said: "I would like to go, if it's really the revolution I want, that is, if there aren't any more flags, because the flag is a sign of recognition, like an emblem which people rally around. It has become a theatricality which castrates, which kills, and what about the national anthem? So ask him if there's no Cuban flag and no Cuban national anthem anymore." He told me: "That's too bad, because the national anthem was composed by a black."

FICHTE: In Cuba there is a concept of death, *Patria o muerte;* what do you think about that?

GENET: It seems very important to me, because, I don't say an artist, but anyone at all assumes his real dimensions once he's dead, that is the meaning, I believe, of Mallarmé's line: "Such as in him eternity changes him." Death transforms everything, perspectives change; as long as a man is alive, he can modulate his thought; alive, he can change things, he can try to disguise his true personality by negations or affirmations, nobody really knows who he is. Once he's dead, everything changes, he's fixed, and you see him differently.

FICHTE: So to you, giving a tape-recorded interview is a little like dying, fixing fixing something?

GENET: No, it's really the other way around, in talking to you like this, I'm giving a more acceptable image of myself, an image which conforms more to what I want at the moment, in a certain sense it's hypocritical. When I am talking to you, here in front of the microphone, I am not completely sincere. I want to give a certain image of myself. And I cannot say exactly who I am and what I want, because I am like anybody at all, basically changing.

FICHTE: Do you see in the May '68 movement the possibility of your kind of revolution?

GENET: No, no, a lot has been written about May '68, and people spoke of a mimodrama, and that seems to be fairly accurate to me. A group of the students, the most up-front ones, occupied the Odéon Theater. I was in the Odéon Theater twice while it was occupied, and the first time there was a sort of violence, especially in the chanting. Look, here is the stage; the revolutionaries, the guys, the students were there on the stage. They had reconstructed—approximately—the layout of an ordinary court, that is, a big table and behind or in front of it the spokesman of the Idea and on both sides the different groups which contested or accepted the spokesman's Idea. Opposite was the public, which was seated in the boxes and the seats and more or less accepted who was the rebel or etc.... The second time I was in the Odéon in May '68, all this violence had disappeared, the words which were pronounced on the stage were accepted by the public, it can only be called the public, and these words, which were sometimes instructions, were repeated like an echo from the stage to the public, from the public to the stage, and each time a little weaker. In the end, the students had occupied a theater. What is a theater? First of all, what is power? It seems to me that power cannot do without theatricality, never; theatricality is sometimes simplified, sometimes it is changed, but there is always theatricality. Power protects itself with theatricality, as in China, in the Soviet Union, in Great Britain, in France, theatricality dominates everywhere. Giscard d'Estaing himself claims to have destroyed all theatricality, but actually he has transformed the theatricality of the Third Republic into a theatricality which is a bit more modern, Swedish or even American style; walking up the Champs Elysées on foot, things like that. There is a place in the world where theatricality does not conceal any power, and that's the theater. When an actor gets killed, well, he gets up, he takes a bow, and the next day he starts all over again getting killed, taking a bow, etc.... It's not at all dangerous. In May '68 the students occupied a theater, that is, a place from which all power has been expelled, where theatricality alone remains, unendangered. If they had occupied the Palais de Justice, first it would have been much more difficult, since the Palais de Justice is better guarded than the Odéon Theater, but then they would have to send people to prison, to pronounce judgment, that would have been the beginning of a revolution, but they didn't do it.

FICHTE: Can you tell me what your revolution would be like?

GENET: No, because I'm not sure I really want a revolution. To be honest, I don't really want it. The present situation, the present governments allow me to revolt, but the revolution would probably not allow me a personal revolt, that is, an individual revolt. But this situation, this government allows me individual revolt, I can be against it. But if it were a matter of a real revolution, perhaps I couldn't be against it. People would join in and I'm not the kind of person who joins in. My point of view is very egotistical. I would like the world, and pay attention to the way I'm saying it, I would like the world not to change so that I can be against the world.

FICHTE: Well then, what sort of revolution would be the most dangerous to you?

GENET: From what I know about it, the Chinese revolution.

FICHTE: What would it be like, this poetic revolution that you want?

GENET: First off, can I have some grapes? I was invited by two revolutionary movements, the Black Panthers and the Palestinians. Well. During our earlier conversations I told you what I could admit, reasons I could admit to; now, what is more difficult to admit is that the Panthers are black Americans, the Palestinians are Arabs, it would be difficult for me to explain why things turn out that way, but these two groups have a very strong erotic charge. I wonder if I could have belonged to revolutionary movements, even if they were as just as—I find the Panthers' movement and the Palestinians' movement to be very just—but this belonging, this sympathizing with them is at the same time dictated by the erotic charge which the Arab world in its totality or the black American world represents to me, to my sexuality. There is still another thing, the problem of game-playing. Going to America with the Panthers when the U.S. embassy had refused me a visa three times was a game, it amused me enormously, and that's a factor, that too. Even if I was doing something worthwhile, I really wanted to be provocative. I noticed, for example, that the police didn't dare to arrest me, or didn't know that I was there, and then the FBI, it's a joke, they know neither who enters nor leaves the country, or else they know and—

FICHTE: They don't give a damn.

GENET: They don't give a damn and on the other hand, there is a very old anti-convict law which states that no one who has previously been convicted may be admitted to the territory of the United States, so they transgress against their own law.

FICHTE: I can distinguish the following components in what you call a poetic revolution: eroticism, having a good time, provocation, and perhaps keeping your distance. Is that right?

GENET: Yes, I don't know if you've put them in their order of priority, but the components seem to be there. But at the same time, the will to oppose all established power, to be on the side of the weakest, because if Wallace, not Nixon but Wallace had invited me to the United States, I obviously wouldn't have gone to the United States.

FICHTE: I don't want to find contradictions in what you are saying, perhaps we understand each other because we accept contradictions.

GENET: Yes.

FICHTE: As a joke you once said you would go to Rome if the Pope invited you.

GENET: I said that on a certain occasion, I said it in connection with the Cuban invitation. I can't go to worship as all the European intellectuals have done, to worship Cuba, to worship what's-his-name, Castro, but after all, since I don't believe in the Pope, not at all, the Pope isn't important.

FICHTE: Why does the Chinese revolution trouble you?

GENET: First, because the people running the Chinese revolution found the means to liberate the immense territory of China from all foreign powers: the Japanese, the French, the English, the Germans, who else? the Americans, and this seems extremely important to me: all the whites have been chucked out; second, and that is important too, they have been able to feed eight hundred million people, they have permitted the al... I don't know how to say it, the alphabet doesn't exist, they have made the Chinese literate.

FICHTE: From a very simple point of view: I visited Chile while Allende was in power. It seemed to me that in the political posters, in the immense murals which covered entire districts, that every artist could express himself freely, each in a very different way, that the workers could express themselves freely, they painted the walls, the streets, entire districts. This was perhaps not very new but it gave a striking touch to the rather gray city of Santiago, and for me it was the beginning of a revolutionary pictorial art.

GENET: I don't really know, what you're telling me is new to me. I wasn't aware of it.

FICHTE: And the economic projects of Allende's government, do you think they were viable?

GENET: No, on the contrary, they didn't seem viable to me, taking into account the large number of strikes in the copper mines, and by the truck drivers, and the extraordinary inflation, that hardly seemed viable to me.

FICHTE: They were caused by ITT.

GENET: Well, I agree there, they were caused by the United States, by ITT, sure, but the government either foresaw them and wasn't able to prevent them, or didn't foresee them.

FICHTE: It is very difficult for me to hear you of all people say that in May '68 the students should have put other people in prison.

GENET: Or on the other hand destroy the prisons, but in any case to pass judgment.

FICHTE: In the case of Saint-Just, it's a question of asking for the death sentence. Isn't there a possibility of doing something more progressive than passing a death sentence, though in an equally bold style?

GENET: Ah! yes. The Chinese did that in the case of the former Manchu emperor, they turned him into a gardener. [Henry P'u Yi, 1906-1967; emperor 1908-1912. —Ed.]

FICHTE: And you think that's more progressive than sentencing Louis XVI to death?

GENET: No, more ironic; but in both cases, it's a matter of annihilating the idea of the sovereignty of a person. Louis XVI was very clever with his hands. He was a locksmith, you know. If the French revolution had made a good or an average locksmith out of him, that would have been just as beautiful as chopping off his head. But the forces were such at the time of the Terror in '91, '93, to make it necessary either to sentence him to death or to send him into exile. And to exile him would have been very dangerous.

FICHTE: Why is it as beautiful to turn someone into a gardener or locksmith as to chop off his head?

GENET: It is as beautiful because it's not a question of exalting death in the case of Louis XVI, it's a question of ridiculing the idea of one man placed above others.

FICHTE: Do you find an intrinsic beauty in the act of someone being decapitated?

GENET: There is a beauty in it. In the case of revolutionaries, I don't know if you can speak of beauty because they have already taken power. And you know when Pompidou refused a stay of execution to Buffet and Bontemps, the two murderers, that wasn't very beautiful. The murders caused by Pompidou, the double murder of Buffet and Bontemps, I see nothing heroic in it, nothing aesthetic, nothing at all. He gave in to a climate of opinion which demanded death, because the wife of a guard was murdered by Buffet. I don't find it admirable that he gave in to public opinion.

FICHTE: But you can admire a poor man who commits murder.

GENET: First, you must not confuse the levels. There is the literary level and the experiential level. The idea of murder can be very beautiful. The actual murder is something else. Shortly after the liberation I saw an Algerian murder a Frenchman. They were playing cards. I was standing beside them. The Algerian was twenty-four years old and didn't have any more money. He had been totally fleeced by the Frenchman. He wanted to borrow some money and try his luck one more time. They wouldn't lend him any. He drew his knife and killed. I saw the guy die. And it was very beautiful. But why was it very beautiful? Because the murder was the completion, the last consequence of a revolt, which had filled this young Algerian for a long time. It was the revolt which was beautiful, and not so much the murder itself. The danger lent him a power, yes . . . if you like, allowed a sense of conviction because of the inherent risk. The murderer had to flee, and he wasn't captured. To kill without risk, like a policeman, no, I don't find that very admirable.

FICHTE: Why have you never committed a murder yourself?

GENET: Probably because I wrote my books.

FICHTE: Are you possessed by the idea of committing murder?

GENET: Yes! But a murder without a victim. I at least have made an effort to believe that the life or death of a person is unimportant because death is unavoidable. Thus, whether it's caused by me, by normal heart failure, or by a car accident, etc. . . . it's not all that important, and nevertheless it is. Now you could ask me: have you caused the death of anyone?

FICHTE: Yes.

GENET: But I will not answer the question.

FICHTE: Involuntarily?

GENET: No, voluntarily. The question is this: have you voluntarily caused someone to die?

FICHTE: Yes.

GENET: I don't answer.

FICHTE: And that oppressed you?

GENET: No, it didn't oppress me at all.

FICHTE: How did your thinking develop, what was the path from your life to the written work?

GENET: If you will accept a rough answer, I would say that the impulse to murder has been channeled into a poetic impulse.

FICHTE: Why do you think that we love to read about cruel things, about murders and tortures, that we love to describe murders and tortures, and that in daily life we exhibit an extreme reluctance towards other people, the bodies of others, towards other people's integrity?

GENET: Can you ask the corresponding question? Why do murderers, even when they write, almost always describe themselves, their actions or their imagined actions as if they were describing the First Communion?

FICHTE: You've asked the question. I would like to come back to our remarks concerning the *Iliad*. I think it contains what I would call magic, ritual. You touched on it just now when you spoke about theatricality.

GENET: I don't agree on the question of ritual. What you said the other day, that is, the singsong repetitions of the same expressions at certain moments; that is not ritual. That is a mode of literary expression which can be used in ritual. Ritual is something else. It's the recognition of a transcendence, and it's the repetitive recognition of that transcendence, day after day, week after week, month after month, like the Panathenaea, like the rituals of... no, like any ritual, even like the rituals of the Catholic Church or the Masonic rituals. In the course of these rituals books, recitations or chants are used which are not in themselves rituals. The *Iliad* is one of those. The *Iliad* was recited officially during the Panathenaea. But the *Iliad* itself is neither ritual nor sacramental, it is a poem.

FICHTE: But that in a very ritualized world?

GENET: But everything is ritualized. There is nothing that is not ritualized, with the obvious exception of high-powered research in laboratories or—

FICHTE: Or revolution.

GENET: Yes, obviously revolution. Of course revolution, when it is taking place, because once it has taken place it becomes ritualized almost automatically. Look what happened in China with Mao, all those rituals. When you think that they counted the minutes and almost the seconds which Mao Tse-tung granted to his visitors. No.

FICHTE: I wanted to give you an example of a very particular ritualization. There are certain rites of initiation, a group composed of flagellation, betrayal of the tribe, betrayal of the family, the murder of the members of the family, urine rites, fecal rites, animal-skin rites. They are called the panther society, the crocodile society, etc. In rereading a part of your work, especially *The Miracle of the Rose,* this entire group seems to me to be in it, but not within such narrow limits. Do you think that you attained a ritual and archaic profundity?

GENET: Yes. I don't know anything, I know absolutely nothing about anthropology. What you just described are rituals of transition. Of the transition from puberty to manhood. The tribe has to be betrayed in order to rejoin the tribe. Urine must be drunk, in order to not drink it. Particularly in *The Miracle of the Rose* it is possible that I tried to discover, all on my own, unconsciously, of course, the rites of passage. This is an idea that hasn't occurred to me before. But that could explain why I did not write any more books after having left prison except *A Thief's Journal.* I had nothing else to write. The transition was behind me.

FICHTE: Therefore the complete works in '52.

GENET: That's your interpretation. It seems to me that it's close to the truth.

FICHTE: What role do you attribute to violence?

GENET: Oh! We'll have to talk about what I am not. We'll have to talk about potlatch, about the inebriety of destruction. The inebriety of destruction even among the most conscientious and intelligent of men. Remember Lenin, who promised golden pisspots to the Soviet people. In all revolutions there is a panic inebriety, more or less contained, but more or less unleashed. This inebriety manifested itself in France, in all of Europe during the peasants' revolts prior to the French revolution, and also through other means: through ritual or ritualized forms like Carnival. At certain moments the entire population wants to liberate itself, to surrender itself to the phenomenon of potlatch, to a complete destruction, to a total expenditure; it needs violence. I often go to England. From a musical point of view I greatly admire the Rolling Stones, not the other pop groups, but the Rolling Stones, yes. I've been going to England since 1948. Really, practically from one day to the next, in the moment when England lost the Commonwealth, all its dependencies, its colonial empire, England also lost its Victorian morality and it became a sort of bazaar, a festival.

FICHTE: Is violence, potlatch, also subject to rules, to ritualizations?

GENET: Of course.

FICHTE: All the violence and catastrophes in your works are drenched in rites. Shortly before he was murdered, Pasolini said that proletarian violence has undergone a fundamental change, that it now aims only for consumer goods, that today Italian proletarians murder to get a motorbike, or bourgeois clothes, and that they should be punished like the Italian neofascists. I think that this conclusion is totally false.

GENET: Yes, totally false.

FICHTE: But on the other hand, hasn't murder become totally banal, totally de-ritualized? Someone kills someone else for a dollar, or not even for that; that is a violence which is very different from the violence you have described.

GENET: But you just said the opposite of what Pasolini said. When Pasolini says or has said: "Proletarian violence has the function of preparing itself for the appropriation of consumer goods." In fact, I wonder, and you just answered that, if it is, after all, a question of expressing yourself violently, of being violent and of finding an outlet for this violence. So, as they say, it's for a dollar or a shirt. In reality it's for violence itself.

FICHTE: So for you, there's no difference between the violence of Querelle and the violence of the young baker who murdered Pasolini?

GENET: In the case of this baker, I don't know. I think he may have wanted some money, that he was shocked by the idea that Pasolini wanted to fuck him or put his hand on his ass. I don't know. Everything is possible among Italian adolescents. They can accept all sexuality and the most obvious whoring, and then, suddenly, they turn into heterosexuals. "Ah! I am a man. I don't want to be touched like that!" I don't know.

FICHTE: Do you think that the motivation claimed for a murder changes its psychic value?

GENET: Probably. Man can't live if he can't justify himself, and he always finds the means and ways to justify himself and his actions in his conscience. It is possible that the young baker sits in his cell, encouraged by his attorney, and keeps repeating to himself: "After all, I killed a millionaire, someone who had distanced himself from the masses, my cause is just." I don't know. I'm making that up.

FICHTE: It seems that Pasolini had masochistic tastes?

GENET: I don't know the details. If he wanted to be struck or whipped or beaten, it's quite possible that for the fun of it or because he was being paid for it, the boy gave the first blows, and after that he started to enjoy it. He couldn't stop himself any longer and he goes on until the guy is dead. It's possible. I don't know.

FICHTE: What do you think of my questions?

GENET: They're good, but I can't tell the whole truth. Only in art can I tell the truth.

FICHTE: What does truth mean to you?

GENET: Above all, it is a word. You use it to make people believe in your own sincerity. You say: what I am saying is the truth. I don't think I can use this word in trying to define it philosophically. Nor can I define it, as the experts do, when they talk about objective truth. Truth is obviously the result of an observation and of general observation. But these observations don't necessarily allow us to discover the truth and above all don't allow us to discover it in an immediate way. I have used my life or a part of it to test scientific conclusions.

FICHTE: Which scientific conclusions could you verify?

GENET: Practically none.

FICHTE: And which did you want to verify?

GENET: There is one which intrigues me, this one: do races exist? Does the concept of race mean anything? And are there inferior races and superior races? And if superior races exist, should they be on top, if you don't want humanity to become inferior? But are there superior races? That is a truth I would like to know.

FICHTE: Would the African black be a superior race to you?

GENET: Not superior. But I don't consider it to be inferior. Now, that requires a proof, but I can't prove it. I know professors... but after all, even the title of a professor at the Collège de France doesn't mean much; they claim that there are races and that there are inferior races, just as there are inferior individuals and superior individuals intellectually, physically, etc....

FICHTE: Is there an essential difference between sincerity in a conversation and in art, or is it simply a question of degree?

GENET: I can answer that at once: yes. There is an essential difference. In art you are solitary, you are alone, facing your self. In a conversation you speak to someone.

FICHTE: And that disturbs you?

GENET: Of course, that changes the whole perspective.

FICHTE: You don't speak to others when you write?

GENET: Never. I probably did not succeed, but that is my attitude to the French language, which I wanted to utilize in the most beautiful way possible, everything else meant nothing to me.

FICHTE: The language which you knew best, or the French language?

GENET: The language I know best, of course, but also the French language because it is the language with which I was sentenced. The courts which sentenced me did so in French.

FICHTE: And you wanted to answer them from a higher level?

GENET: Exactly. Perhaps there are other, more subterranean motivations, but I think that, in the final analysis, they don't play a large role.

FICHTE: What would they be?

GENET: Oh! You should ask a psychoanalyst and not me. Because what I think is rather unimportant.

FICHTE: When did you start on this poetic project?

GENET: It's difficult for me to think back that far, because I haven't got very many clues. I think I was twenty-nine or thirty years old. I was alone in my cell. So it was 1939. I was alone in jail, in the cell. First off, I have to say that I had not written anything other than letters to my friends, and I think these letters were very conventional, that is, formula phrases, things I'd heard, things I'd read. And then I wrote a Christmas card to a German girl friend who was living in Czechoslovakia. I bought the card in prison and the back of the card, the part meant for the message, was coarsely grained. And this texture moved me greatly. And instead of talking about Christmas, I talked about the texture of the postcard, and about the snow which it evoked. From this moment on I began to write. I think that was the trigger.

FICHTE: Which books or works had impressed you until then?

GENET: Popular novels. The novels by Paul Féval. The books we had in the prison. I don't know. Except when I was fifteen in the reformatory at Mettray, I got hold of the works by Ronsard and I was enchanted.

FICHTE: And Marcel Proust?

GENET: Well. I read *A l'Ombre des Jeunes Filles en Fleurs* while in prison, the first volume. We were in the prison yard and exchanged books secretly. It was during the war, and since I wasn't paying much attention I was one of the last and they said to me: "Here, take this one." And I saw: Marcel Proust. And I said to myself: "But that must be boring as shit." And then. Now I must ask you to believe me, even if I am not always, even if I am not always honest with you, I am this time. I read the first sentence of *A l'Ombre des Jeunes Filles en Fleurs* which introduces Monsieur de Norpois during a dinner at Proust's mother's and father's house, or in any case with the author's parents. And the sentence is very long. And when I finished the sentence, I closed the book and said: "I can be at ease now, I know I will go from one miracle to the next." The first sentence was so dense, so beautiful, that this beginning was a first big flame which proclaimed a burst of fire. And it took me the whole day to recover. And I didn't open the book again until the evening, and I did in fact go from miracle to miracle.

FICHTE: Had you already written any of your novels?

GENET: No, that is, I was writing *Our Lady of the Flowers*.

FICHTE: Are there any other works which fascinated you as much as Proust's?

GENET: Ah yes! Even more so! *The Brothers Karamazov*.

FICHTE: And Balzac?

GENET: Not so much, Anyway there's a trivial side to Balzac.

FICHTE: Stendhal?

GENET: Yes. Yes. Of course Stendhal. *The Charterhouse of Parma* and then even *The Red and the Black*. But especially *The Charterhouse of Parma*. But there is nothing like *The Brothers Karamazov*. There are so many different times. There was Sonia's time and Alyosha's time, there was Smerdyakov's time and then there was my own time as a reader. There was the time of interpretation and then there was the time preceding their appearance in the book. What was Smerdyakov doing before he was spoken of? Finally, I had to reconstitute all of that. But it was fascinating. It was very beautiful.

FICHTE: Would you allow me to make a sidetrack on the question of time?

GENET: Yes.

FICHTE: How do you experience time?

GENET: You're forcing me to answer a difficult question because for twenty or twenty-five years I've been taking Nembutal, so the whole morning I'm under the influence of Nembutal which makes you fall asleep at once . . . well, in ten minutes . . . or a quarter of an hour . . . yes. But it has side effects, a cup of coffee's not enough in the morning. The Nembutal has to stop working on the brain. Well. During the time that the Nembutal is affecting me I don't experience time. If it's a matter of performing exactly outlined actions, which, to put it briefly, I will term profane, like buying something, I do it in a very exact way, in an exactly determined time span. I don't get distracted. It's no problem. But when I want to write, I need unlimited time for myself. The other day I was rather angry with Gallimard, because I had just seen Monsieur Hugnin and I had asked for a rather large sum of money. And Claude Gallimard wanted to pay me in monthly installments, comfortable monthly installments. But I said no. "I want it all at once, today. I want to be absolutely free. Sleep when I want. Go where I want. Otherwise I do nothing. I do nothing, it's impossible. I have to be able to keep writing for two or three days at a stretch, staying in bed day and night, etc. . . . or just for an hour, etc. . . . It depends."

FICHTE: And he refused?

GENET: Oh no! I was rather uncomfortable because all my pockets were stuffed with bills.

FICHTE: What's the monthly income for a writer in France?

GENET: I don't know what other authors earn. I've never asked for details. I am not ashamed of money, and I'm not ashamed to say how much I earn. I can't say earn... writing is a bit painful... and not very pleasant. It's not work. So, earning, if you like. Last year I earned about two hundred thousand francs from my books. Which doesn't include my plays.

FICHTE: Is money important to you, the bills, the currency?

GENET: Yes, especially when they're large. I like them a lot.

FICHTE: Does money signify a gain in time or a gain in sensuality?

GENET: In time. Not in sensuality. I do not earn a lot of money. But it's enough, I can afford to be badly dressed, unwashed, to do things like that, not get my hair cut, I don't like that. Getting your hair cut is boring. It's not important if I don't get my hair cut.

FICHTE: You used to be on the wrong side of the tracks. Now you are on the other side. What do you feel now when you encounter young asocials?

GENET: Nothing, nothing at all. I don't have any feelings of guilt. When somebody asks me for some money, or even when they don't ask, I just give it to them, it's very easy and it's of no importance. The world is unjust but not because my royalties are relatively large.

FICHTE: You've described how you yourself robbed pederasts who were looking for sex. Have young men attempted to rob you?

GENET: Yes, that's happened very very very often. In Hamburg, for example. There was nothing I could do but let the two guys take the money I had in my pockets.

FICHTE: And that didn't scare you?

GENET: Ah! Not at all. Not at all. Not at all. I get upset if it's a large sum of money. That makes me angry because then I have to go back to Gallimard. But you see, I was fifty-six years old yesterday... fifty-five years...

FICHTE: Fifty-five or sixty-five?

GENET: Sixty-five. So, I was fifty-six years old when I was in Karachi. The plane arrived at one in the morning. I was all aone. The airport is twenty-five kilometers from the city. Well. There was a cop who gave me a stamp [for his visa —*Trans.*] for one month and then he called a taxi. I didn't notice that the taxi driver was all wrapped up in muslin. And another man got in beside me before I could even object. He was a money changer. He was very insistent. And it was in the middle of the night. "Where are you going to stay?" he asked me in English. I said: "At the Hotel Intercontinental." That is the biggest hotel in Karachi. I said: "I can change ten dollars." "You can't live on ten dollars in the Hotel Intercontinental." "I have friends"—which was a lie. "I have friends waiting for me at the Hotel Intercontinental." I did not want to take my money out. But it would have been easy to get rid of me after having taken everything. Anyway, I held out. And I said: "Here, that is really everything I can give." He gave me the rupees and then he got out when we arrived at the Hotel Continental. Arriving at the Hotel Continental, the ten dollars weren't enough to pay the young guy with. Then I said to the doorman... the hotel was full. It was night. Everybody was sleeping on chairs, on mats, on carpets, and I said: "Do you have a room? I would like a room at least for tonight." "No." What am I going to do? And my fifteen thousand. It was in a roll in my pants pocket and all done up with pins. In order to take out a bill, I would have to take out the whole roll. "Can you change some money for me at once?" And I took out all my French money. I was immediately given a room. Well. But the young guy, he didn't know that I had that much money and I gave him a little money to compensate him. But certainly not as much as he would have earned if he had left me fifteen kilometers outside of Karachi. Now, sometimes you have good luck: I was in Morocco. I met a young Moroccan man, twenty-four, twenty-five years old, and very poor. He came to my room every day. He stayed in my room. He didn't touch my money. He didn't touch anything. Do I admire him for that? No. I think it was a trick. But I admire him for being as cunning as that.

FICHTE: Afterward you took him with you to France?

GENET: Of course, and he was very clever, I don't regret having taken him to France; in the Arab countries and in the Third World a young boy can't help but seeing a possible victim, a man to rob, in a white who pays a little attention to him, that's to be expected.

FICHTE: What is the attitude of a young man, gifted, sensible, intelligent, who loves men, but is miserable and robs an old pederast?

GENET: I don't know anything about that; first, he can simply be hungry and the old pederast is the easiest man to rob.

FICHTE: Are you describing what you yourself have done?

GENET: But of course I've done it, I did in in Spain for example, in Spain and in France, so what?

FICHTE: And there wasn't any perspective, this perspective...

GENET: The point of view is to steal, in every case. If I went with an old pederast, I would prefer him to be weaker, it was stealing.

FICHTE: Out of necessity.

GENET: Of course, of course.

FICHTE: Betraying that sexual necessity did not shock you?

GENET: But I didn't betray any sexual necessity, I was not attracted sexually to the old men whom I robbed; what attracted me was their money; so the question was to take their money by beating them or by making them come; the goal was money.

FICHTE: Didn't it occur to you that you were helping a society which you detest by using an elderly pederast?

GENET: Oh! that would have been asking me to have a political and revolutionary consciousness fifty years ago. Fifty years, that was around the time of the split of the Tours congress, the birth of the French Communist Party; can you imagine what that could mean to a fifteen-year-old peasant who grew up in Massif Central, what could he think? That was the great epoch of Rosa Luxemburg; do you think that could have occurred to me then? It can occur nowadays.

FICHTE: When did you discover that you were attracted to men?

GENET: Very young, I was perhaps eight, not more than ten years old, very young in any case, out in the country in the Mettray reformatory where homosexuality was not, of course, approved of; but since there weren't any girls there, it was unavoidable for all the boys between fifteen and twenty-one; there wasn't any recourse but transitory homosexuality or permanent homosexuality, but in any case, to homosexuality, and that's what makes it possible for me to say that I was really happy in the reformatory.

FICHTE: And did you know that you were happy?

GENET: Yes, yes, yes, yes. In spite of all the punishments, in spite of all the insults, in spite of all the blows, in spite of the bad conditions, the work, in spite of all that I was happy.

FICHTE: Did you take into account that your behavior was different for you than for the others?

GENET: No, I don't think that I asked myself that question. Only rarely in this period of my life did I think about other people. For a long time my attitude was narcissistic. That was my happiness. It was a question of my happiness.

FICHTE: Were you an outcast?

GENET: I was. First because... but it may seem contradictory to you... in spite of the happiness I felt, very profound, very serious, at being in this reformatory, at having such passionate relationships with other boys of my own age or a little older or a little younger, I don't know... it didn't occur to me to question the system and the prison system, the social system, I knew nothing about all that. Imagine, I didn't know until I was released, until I was to be drafted, that Lindbergh had crossed the Atlantic. I didn't know that. I didn't know things like that. You are isolated, completely cut off from the world. It is a sort of monastery. Well. My revolt against the system, the prison system, was much harder and wilder than that of the toughest men there. I think that I learned very quickly to ridicule the attempts at re-education, the prayer meetings, because we prayed there, the gymnastics, the good behavior to get the flag, anyway nonsense like that.

FICHTE: Did this knowledge go as far as eroticism and the fulfillment of sexuality? Or did you accept the roles which the system forced on you in this prison universe?

GENET: No, but I've never lived by pure sexuality. It has always been accompanied by tenderness, perhaps by a very brief, rough affection, but right up to the end of my sexual life, there has always been... I never made love in a vacuum... without emotional content. It's a question of individuals, boys, individuals... but not of a role. I was attracted to a boy my own age... don't force me to define too much... I can't define love of course... but I could not make love to boys without loving them... if not... I also made love to guys to earn some money.

FICHTE: Do you have a revolutionary concept of eroticism?

GENET: Oh no. Revolutionary! No. Associating with Arabs has been... satisfying on the whole—fortunately. In general young Arabs are not ashamed... of an old body, an old face. Growing old is part, I won't say of the religion, but is part of the Islamic civilization. You grow old, you are old.

FICHTE: Has the fact that you are older changed your relationships with your Arab friends?

GENET: No. But I understand them better. When I was eighteen years old, I was in Syria, and in love with a little hairdresser... he was sixteen... I was eighteen ... and everybody in the street knew that I was in love with him and they laughed about it, anyway the men did... the women were veiled and didn't go out... but the boys, the young, the old men were amused. They told me: "So what! Go with him!" And he wasn't at all ashamed either. I know that he was sixteen. I was about eighteen and a half... I felt really good with him. Really good with his family, really good in Damascus. I was in Damascus shortly after the bombing which had been ordered after the Druse revolts, which had been ordered by General Gourot... General Gourot... that was a guy who had lost an arm and he transformed Damascus into a pile of ruins. That is, he used a cannon and had given strict orders to always go out armed and in groups of three, and you had to stay on the sidewalk. If women or old Arab men, or Syrians, passed by or crossed our path, they had to move to one side. This pattern was broken, broken by me... but only in my case, naturally. I always got out of the way of the women and I always went to the souks which are wonderful in Damascus. I went to the souks unarmed and it quickly became common knowledge because Damascus had only two hundred or two hundred fifty thousand inhabitants, and I was very very well received.

FICHTE: Is there a paternal element in your relationships with young men at this stage in your life?

GENET: Ah yes! But in spite of myself. It comes from them and not from me.

FICHTE: Would you like to give them some day-to-day security, to introduce them to art?

GENET: Oh, of course! That is a very complicated problem which you've mentioned. Today you've asked me personal questions. Now it happens that I've reached a stage in my life in which my person doesn't count for much. I don't think that I want to hide something, but it's simply boring. You've mentioned my particular problem and my particular problem doesn't exist any longer.

FICHTE: But you have projected your obsessions, your coincidences, your prejudices on the world. They have influenced the behavior of a whole generation.

GENET: Yes. But you're talking about things which took place thirty-five or forty years ago, and which have more or less been wiped out by old age and by drugs which erase everything that could be unpleasant, and leave behind the pleasant memories. You are reminding me of a primeval forest which possibly still exists, but in which I no longer live in the same way. I've pruned away the biggest branches. I've made a sort of clearing, I don't see the jungle so clearly anymore. And when you tell me: "but there were ferns and lianas where you lived."—Yes, when you tell me that, I know that it's true, but I don't know what they were like anymore and it doesn't interest me very much either. All that has faded away.

FICHTE: What is your theory about homosexuality?

GENET: I have none. I have several. Several have been proposed. None of them is satisfactory, whether it's Freud's oedipal theory, whether it's the theory proposed by geneticists, or Sartre's theory, which he proposed in one of his books, in which I reacted in a certain way, but in a free way, to the social conditions which were imposed on me. None of them satisfy me. So, I don't know. I don't have any theory about homosexuality. I don't even have a theory about undifferentiated desire. I ascertain that I'm homosexual. OK. That's no cause for alarm. How and why are idle questions. It's a little like my wanting to know why my eyes are green.

FICHTE: In any case you don't consider it to be a neurosis?

GENET: No. I even wonder if I didn't experience it as the solution to a neurosis, if my neurosis wasn't present before my homosexuality. I don't know about that either.

FICHTE: Doesn't it surprise you that all the revolutionary models we know of don't contain a theory of sexuality which is freer than the theory of the middle class?

GENET: On the whole you get the impression that revolutions are made by family men.

FICHTE: When you were accepted by the Panthers and the Palestinians, were you also accepted as a homosexual?

GENET: That's sort of funny. A black asked the questions during an American TV interview with David Hilliard. He asked David, who obviously knew it since he had read all my books, he asked him: "Do you know that Jean Genet is a homosexual?" David: "So what? Yes." "And that doesn't bother you?" "No, it would be great if all homosexuals would come twelve thousand kilometers to the defense of the Panthers."

FICHTE: That's nice and that's superfluous. Imagine a great socialist, a womanizer, Castro, for example.

GENET: His brother, Raúl Castro, is homosexual.

FICHTE: Let's suppose a good socialist, handsome, powerful, a womanizer, arrives at the Black Panthers, they're not going to pimp for him, but they'll help, they'll even go so far as to introduce him to some girls. To accept the homosexuality of Jean Genet in a revolutionary way while among the Black Panthers would have been to make it livable, concrete.

GENET: Well, David loved women. He was married but also had lovers. But I know that a black, and I don't think that he was homosexual, one evening after I spoke at Yale University, we always embraced each other, everybody kissed me and he did not kiss me like the others, he kissed me very affectionately, really, he hugged me, and he was not... he did not try to be secretive about it either. He did it in front of twenty blacks.

FICHTE: Earlier you spoke about the end of your sexual life. Your fascination, your desire did not go farther than that with the Black Panthers?

GENET: What they asked of me was really very very difficult, I went on taking Nembutal because I had to sleep. They were boys eighteen to twenty-five years old, twenty-eight years old, David was twenty-eight years old and extraordinarily active. They woke me up at two o'clock in the morning to go to a press conference; to be ready at two o'clock in the morning to answer questions at a press conference. I assure you that I did not think about making love. And then another phenomenon is that I didn't make distinctions among the Panthers, I loved all of them, the one didn't attract me more than the other. I loved the phenomenon of the Black Panthers. I was in love with it.

FICHTE: So you did not submit yourself to an erotic abstinence which you would not have accepted in the normal liberal world?

GENET: Not at all. To the extent that Bobby Seale sent me a letter asking me to write an article about homosexuality; and then the letter had either been badly translated or carelessly, anyway, I answered: "If you attack the homosexuals, I will attack the blacks." In the following week I received the newspaper, Newton wrote the article himself, in which he said that it was absolutely necessary to be on the side of the homosexuals and to defend them, that they were a minority group, and that it was necessary to accept their defense of the Panthers and likewise to defend them.

FICHTE: Are you sure that this theoretical defense would actually be practiced?

GENET: Obviously I can't prove it. No. Because the Panthers' movement is very young, I met them in '70, so they were two, the movement was two years old. They said, don't believe in God, but they wanted to get married in church, things like that.

FICHTE: I would like to come back to your literary creations. Were there other important works you read while working on your own novels?

GENET: Dostoevsky.

FICHTE: Even while in prison?

GENET: Ah yes. Ah yes. Before going to prison. I read *Memoirs from the House of the Dead,* I read *Crime and Punishment* while I was a soldier. For me, Raskolnikov was really alive, more alive than Léon Blum, for example.

FICHTE: Do you esteem Cocteau as a poet?

GENET: No, you know the poets I like. They are Baudelaire, Nerval, Rimbaud, that's all, I think.

FICHTE: Mallarmé?

GENET: Ah yes! of course, Mallarmé.

FICHTE: And also Ronsard?

GENET: No, no, no.

FICHTE: Rutebeuf?

GENET: Yes, but only occasionally, Rutebeuf. I know some verses of Mallarmé's by heart, of Baudelaire's by heart, of Nerval's by heart, of Rimbaud's by heart, but none by Rutebeuf.

FICHTE: You are working on something new, will it be a play?

GENET: I can't talk about it. I don't know what it will be.

FICHTE: Did I drive you crazy today?

GENET: No, not really. The questions you asked did not interest me like those of yesterday and the day before yesterday. Today you wanted me to talk about myself. That doesn't interest me very much.

FICHTE: Do you think that this interview gives an idea about what you are really thinking?

GENET: No.

FICHTE: What's lacking?

GENET: The truth is possible only when I am alone. Truth has nothing to do with a confession or a dialogue, I'm speaking of my truth. I've tried to answer your questions as exactly as possible. In fact, I was far from it.

FICHTE: Isn't it very hard, what you just said?

GENET: Very hard for whom?

FICHTE: For everyone who approaches you.

GENET: I can't say anything to anyone. Nothing to anyone but lies. Perhaps I tell a little of the truth when I'm all alone. I tell lies when I am with someone. What I say is inapplicable.

FICHTE: But lies have a double truth.

GENET: Ah yes. Discover the truth that they contain. Discover what I tried to hide while telling you some of these things.

PHOTO BY ELSA DORFMAN

ALLEN GINSBERG

ALLEN GINSBERG was born in Paterson, N.J., in 1926, the son of Naomi Ginsberg, Russian émigrée, and Louis, a lyric poet and schoolteacher. He left Paterson for Columbia University in 1943 and remained there about five years. During this period he developed close friendships with Jack Kerouac, William S. Burroughs, Neal Cassady, Herbert Huncke, and Lucien Carr. In 1954 he met Peter Orlovsky in San Fancisco and began an enduring love relationship. (See the interview with Orlovsky beginning on p. 239.) Especially seminal was his poem "Howl," published in the City Lights book of the same name. (See also *To Eberhart from Ginsberg: A Letter about HOWL 1956,* Penmaen Press, 1976.) Since that time he has traveled around the world participating in readings and festivals, often accompanied by Peter Orlovsky. Ginsberg teaches part-time in the Naropa Institute in Colorado.

Ginsberg's Pocket Poets City Lights editions include: *Kaddish* (1961), *Reality Sandwiches* (1963), *Planet News* (1968), *The Fall of America* (1972), *Mind Breaths* (1977). Other books by Ginsberg are: *Ankor Wat* (1968), *Airplane Dreams* (1968), *TV Baby Poems* (1968), *Iron Horse* (1972), *The Gates of Wrath: Rhymed Poems 1948-52* (1972), *Improvised Poetics* (1972), *Visions of the Great Rememberer* (1974), *First Blues* (1976). *Allen Verbatim* (1974) is a collection of his lectures on poetry, poetics, and consciousness. Ginsberg's *Journals Early Fifties Early Sixties* appeared in 1977, as did his collected correspondence with Neal Cassady under the title *As Ever*. Selected gay poems and correspondence by Ginsberg and Orlovsky are being published by Gay Sunshine Press.

THE PRESENT INTERVIEW took place at Ginsberg's farm in Cherry Valley, New York, on September 25, 1972. It originally appeared in *Gay Sunshine* 16 (January 1973) and 17 (March 1973) in a version edited by Winston Leyland. It was later issued in 1974 by Grey Fox Press as a chapbook. Allen Young, who conducted the interview, is a long-time movement activist. He is co-editor (with Karla Jay) of the anthologies *Out of the Closets: Voices of Gay Liberation* (1972) and *After You're Out* (1975). He currently lives on a farm in Orange, Massachusetts.

Allen Young interviews
ALLEN GINSBERG

YOUNG: One of the things that provoked this whole conversation between us was my reading of *The Dharma Bums* last summer. In that book the character Alvah, who is quite obviously you, is portrayed by Kerouac as heterosexual. There are a number of sexual encounters and there isn't any indication that there was any kind of homosexuality in this group of people.

GINSBERG: That was Kerouac's particular shyness. You know, I made it with Kerouac quite often. And Neal, his hero, and I were lovers, also, for many years, from 1946 on, on and off, at least I wanted to be, and we got to bed quite often, we didn't really fully . . . finally he didn't want any more sex with me, he rejected me! That's what he did! But we were still making it in the mid-1960s after having known each other in the mid-forties, so that's a pretty long, close friendship—Neal and Jack, for that matter.

YOUNG: Did Jack Kerouac identify himself as being a gay person?

GINSBERG: No, he didn't. A lot of that took place in the cottage we all held together, and then I had been living with Peter for several years. Peter, Jack, Gary [Snyder] and I and various other people were all sleeping with one or two girls that were around. Jack saw me screwing and was astounded at my virility. I guess he decided to write a novel in which I was a big, virile hero instead of a Jewish Communist fag.

YOUNG: What was your reaction to that? Did you feel that he was hiding?

GINSBERG: I didn't notice. *On the Road* has one scene in the original manuscript in a motel where Dean Moriarty screws a traveling salesman with whom they ride to Chicago in a big Cadillac; and there's a two-line description of it which fills out Cassady's character and gives it dimension. That was eliminated from the book by Malcolm Cowley in the mid-fifties, and Jack consented to that. So Jack actually did talk about it a little in his writing.

In a book that's being published now, *Visions of Cody,* there's a longer description of the same scene. It was written in 1950-51 by Kerouac and was his first book after *On the Road,* a sequel to it. It was a great experimental book, including a couple of hundred pages of taped, transcribed conversation between him and Neal, over grass at midnight in Los Gatos or San Jose, talking about life to each other, the first times they got laid, and jacking off, and running around Denver.

YOUNG: Why is it first coming out now?

GINSBERG: Kerouac always wanted it published. But the commercial publishing world wasn't ready for a book of such great looseness and strange genius and odd construction. It's more like a Gertrude Stein *Making of Americans* than it is speedy Kerouac.

YOUNG: Was it a fight for Kerouac to get his stuff published?

GINSBERG: Oh, yeah. *On the Road* was written in 1950 and was never published till '57, even though he had previously published his great book *Town and the City*. The commercial insistency was that he write something nice and simple so everybody could understand it, to explain what the beat generation was all about. So he wrote *The Dharma Bums*, to order, for his publisher, a sort of exercise in virtuosity and bodhisattva magnanimity. He wrote in short sentences that everybody could understand, describing the spiritual revolution as he saw it, using as a hero Gary Synder; actually, "Japhy Ryder" is Gary Snyder.

YOUNG: So then your portrayal as a heterosexual doesn't have anything to do with being in the closet.

GINSBERG: No. I came out of the closet at Columbia in 1946. The first person I told about it was Kerouac, 'cause I was in love with him. He was staying in my room up in the bed, and I was sleeping on a pallet on the floor. I said, "Jack, you know, I love you, and I want to sleep with you, and I really like men." And he said, "Oooooh, no..." We'd known each other maybe a year, and I hadn't said anything.

At that time Kerouac was very handsome, very beautiful, and mellow—mellow in the sense of infinitely tolerant, like Shakespeare or Tolstoy or Dostoevsky, infinitely understanding. So in a sense—there's a term that I heard Robert Duncan use for poetry and I've heard others use for relation between guru and disciple—as a slightly older person and someone who I felt had more authority, his tolerance gave me *permission* to open up and talk, you know 'cause I felt there was space for me to talk, where he was. He wasn't going to hit me. He wasn't going to reject me, really, he was going to accept my soul with all its throbbings and sweetness and worries and dark woes and sorrows and heartaches and joys and glees and mad understandings of mortality, 'cause that was the same thing he had. And actually we wound up sleeping together maybe within a year, a couple of times. I blew him, I guess. He once blew me, years later. It was sort of sweet, peaceful.

YOUNG: Did you experience any kind of a split between your hipster circle and getting involved with other gay people as you were coming out?

GINSBERG: It's in a poem ["In Society"] that I read at the Chicago Seven trial. This is a dream I had in 1947 while I was at Columbia:

> *I walked into the cocktail party*
> *room and found three or four queers*
> *talking together in queertalk.*
> *I tried to be friendly but heard*
> *myself talking to one in hiptalk.*
> *"I'm glad to see you," he said, and*
> *looked away. "Hmn," I mused. The room*
> *was small and had a double-decker*
> *bed in it, and cooking apparatus:*
> *icebox, cabinet, toasters, stove;*

> the hosts seemed to live with room
> enough only for cooking and sleeping.
> My remark on this score was under-
> stood but not appreciated. I was
> offered refreshments, which I accepted.
> I ate a sandwich of pure meat; an
> enormous sandwich of human flesh;
> I noticed, while I was chewing on it,
> it also included a dirty asshole.
>
> More company came, including a
> fluffy female who looked like
> a princess. She glared at me and
> said immediately: "I don't like you,"
> turned her head away, and refused
> to be introduced. I said, "What!"
> in outrage. "Why you shit-faced fool!"
> This got everybody's attention.
> "Why you narcissistic bitch! How
> can you decide when you don't even
> know me," I continued in a violent
> and messianic voice, inspired at
> last, dominating the whole room.

There were a whole group of queens around Columbia at that time who were doing things like going down to hear Edith Piaf sing at the Plaza Hotel and interested in status and money. They had cultural interests that went back to Lotte Lenya and things like that, but at the same time it was an overly aristocratic, elitist thing.

YOUNG: Did you associate that with the faculty at Columbia also?

GINSBERG: There were a couple of guys on the faculty at Columbia that participated in that sense of things rather than in an open democratic Whitmanic gaiety, because to be open and democratic and Whitmanic meant, like, open, friendly, kissing the football players! In public, no less. Whereas the closet queen gaggle could get together and go down to the Plaza...

YOUNG: Well, was kissing the football players in any sense a reality, or just a Whitmanesque fantasy?

GINSBERG: I was kissing Jack Kerouac, who was on the Columbia varsity team in those years. It was a Whitmanesque fantasy, which, like all Whitmanesque fantasies, were practical realities. Of course, then a faculty guy probably couldn't do it, but nowadays a faculty guy could.

I was silent about it [homosexuality] at Columbia the first year I was there, between the ages of sixteen and seventeen. At seventeen something shook me loose from the authoritarianism of the culture and from the authority of Columbia. I think it was the jailing of a friend, who I loved, who knew Jack well. And then also I was interested in Rimbaud and Whitman, and I had met Burroughs by then. I was getting teaching from Burroughs that included Blake and Spengler (*The Decline of the West*); and semantics was important, separating words from the objects they represent, not getting confused by labels, like gay or queer, in those days.

So it was just a whole change, growing up out of high school and puberty and closed-in-ness. It wasn't closet; it didn't have that much style about it. It was just timidity and fear of rejection. All through high school I was secretly in love with all sorts of boys—particularly one boy from East Side High, Paterson, who I actually followed to Columbia.

YOUNG: Whose name begins with "R." You mention him in one of your poems.

GINSBERG: Yeah. Very soon I was babbling at great length. The permission for that openness came from Burroughs and Kerouac, who I was living with. They were wide-brained, international, hip, Jack London, Doctor Mabuses, all.

Kerouac was a very funny, strange, heroic figure, a seminal figure for many ideas and attitudes. He had a lot of trouble; he drank himself to death. And he ended, like many older writers, reactionary in a funny, interesting, characteristic way, a way that's teaching rather than negative. But the basic thing about him was Character, with a capital C, was an enormous mellow, trustful tolerance and sensitivity. And that's why he's such a great writer and observer. You know, he held everything dear, as a sensitive young fellow, even my fairy woes. In fact, we wound up in bed together.

YOUNG: You're saying that this really wasn't where he was at sexually?

GINSBERG: Well, he was very mixed sexually. He had a lot of trouble with attachment to his mother and his mother's dependence on him. He was a football player, and he liked girls. He liked to eat girls and was really hung up on them. That's what really excited him: black panties! black stockings! He also appreciated beautiful boys and had a really novelistic, personal appreciation of older queens—which was like a sharing of common humanity, and a sharing of emotions, even a sharing of the erotic, except that he didn't feel it was right for him to participate in the erotic.

As a novelist, he opened himself to the art of gaiety and some of its attitudes and styles in writing. In some of his poems there's a lot of stuff about himself, where there's all sorts of high teacup bullshit. In those days "high teacup" was a lifted pinky infra-language. I'm saying he had mixed feelings at different times, but I think it would have been abusive of his character to point an accusing finger and say, "You're a fairy!" There was a certain tendency among gay people there to plaster labels over everybody, including themselves, instead of seeing the nameless love that everybody is. Just as there was a tendency among macho heterosexuals to plaster labels, so there was a counterbalancing tendency among homosexuals to overreact to that and camp too heavily, so that he was sensitive about being put down as a fairy, which he wasn't. [*Calling over to Peter Orlovsky on the other side of the room where he was not listening to the interview:*] Was Jack a fairy?

ORLOVSKY: Was Jack a fairy? No... in a tiny sense of the word.

GINSBERG: Perfect, in a very tiny sense of the word. [*To Peter:*] We all made it with Jack once.

ORLOVSKY: [One time] he was so drunk he couldn't even get it up.

GINSBERG: [*Laughs*] Yeah. Well, no he came that time. We were at Clellon

Holmes', remember? I blew him and you screwed me.

ORLOVSKY: What about on Second Street? Do you remember that? Jack was gallantly drunk, lying in one of the small, side rooms, and you tried to blow him. He couldn't get it up and he was talking about his little cock; it was so tiny, so small, shriveled up, sad.

GINSBERG: He was very apologetic. But ten years ago he was asking me to blow him all the time. In '64–'65 he said: "I'm old, ugly, redfaced, I'm beer-bellied and I'm a drunk and nobody loves me anymore. I can't get girls, come on and give me a blow job." There were times he'd get drunk and be really insistent on it. By that time he'd gotten beer-bellied, florid-faced, and I no longer saw him as the romantic, handsome, young glamor-beau of postwar, dark, doomed, maddened Spengler hippiedom.

So, I got freaked out at the whole idea of bodies and sex, in fact. That was one of my first lessons in chastity. There's a line in Yeats: "Old lovers yet may have all the time denied, grave is heaped on grave that they be satisfied." I found actually in the course of time that everybody I really loved and wanted to go to bed with, I finally did. It may have taken twenty or thirty years, and we may have both fallen into ruins and baldness and all our teeth fallen out, but desire always found its way, even if it took decades. There's a lesson there. Once you become a little detached, once you lose neurotic, obsessive attachment, then, when things are floating lightly, then you find love objects that you once worshiped drifting in on the tide, back to you, more than you can deal with; in fact, horrifyingly rottened up from the sea.

An element in the gay lib struggle and metaphysics that I don't think has yet been taken up is that of disillusionment with the body. I'm not trying to be provocative in that—just the age-old realization of over-forty, over-fifty, and over-sixty, and over-seventy and over-eighty, finally, the age-old grinning skeleton, with the spiritual lesson behind it, of detachment from neurotic desire. I think there's a genuine eros between men that isn't dependent on neurotic detachment and obsession, that's free and light and holy and lambent—which is more or less what we all get during out first fantasies, loves and devotions. Some of us are lucky enough to be able to act out and receive back and forth. But it can only come in like the tide when you're free to float in it. If there's too much of a neurotic grasping to gaiety, to gayness, even to gay lib, then it makes everything too tense, and the lightness of the love is lost. So the gay lib movement will have to come to terms sooner or later with the limitations of sex.

If you consider sex from a Hindu, Buddhist, Hare Krishna, even Christian fundamentalist viewpoint—a warning about the body and a warning about attachment itself—it becomes interesting. Burroughs has actually written about it at length in a way which hip people and even radicals have found very interesting: the sex "habit"—sex as another form of junk, a commodity, the consumption of which is encouraged by the state to keep people enslaved to their bodies. As long as they're enslaved to their bodies, they can be filled with fear and shock and pain and threat, so they can be kept in place. The road of that, he said, leads to the great palace of green goo, the garden of green goo, green goo trap, with everybody schlupping together in this green stuff.

I find, as I'm growing older, no less flutterings of delightful desire in my belly and abdomen. But also I'm becoming more tolerant of other resolutions between people besides sex. When I was in Australia, I had a crush on a beautiful young dobro player who traveled around with me. He sought me out and waited all day at my hotel and put himself at my service to play music with me. He wanted to play mantras and then turned out to be a great blues player, and he taught me blues. And he went to bed with me the first night, when I really got entranced by his... servility... and availability, and generosity, genius and sense of duty. And then he didn't want to go to bed with me after that, but he loved me. I was the first man he had ever been to bed with. How am I going to deal with somebody who really loves me but doesn't want to play with my cock and doesn't necessarily want me to blow him? But he didn't mind sleeping in bed naked with me, you know, because he loved me. There was a weird thing... but is that any more weird than my desires?

So I finally got into a scene which was like the old nineteenth-century thing recommended by Edward Carpenter, and Whitman—people sleeping together. It's called "carezza," a platonic friendship in which people sleep together naked, caressing each other, but don't come, saving their seed for yogic or other reasons. So I did that with this kid.

For the next couple of weeks we were running around Australia. I found the intensity of my devotion to him in the heart area—a warm, aching feeling in the heart—growing and growing and growing, and becoming more and more desirous and narcotic-like, and more and more satisfactory to carry around with me. And I found him responding in a similar way to me, and I realized that that same warmth was growing in his breast to me, and that what was building it was the naked chastity that we were practicing together. When we got on the stage and played together—I was singing mantras, blues and playing harmonium and he was playing dobro—the erotic communication between us got ecstatic and delirious. And it couldn't be withheld. We'd keep bursting out in song and eye glances which turned the audience on completely, and turned me on, and turned him on. So I was feeling another kind of very subtle, ethereal orgasm that seemed to occupy the upper portions of the body rather than the genital area.

Though I've always been prejudiced against that kind of sublimation, thinking of it as some sort of sublimation of primary, holy sex drives, the experience was so delicious that I can't really put it down for any moral reason at all. I recommend it; everyone should have that experience, too. You can get real close with people that you love who wouldn't otherwise want to sleep with you sexually. But you could have like a total relation. So there's all sorts, all forms.... "Smash sexism!"

I know lots of men who are thinking along those lines. They may not want to sleep naked together but there's a love thrill in the breast they have for each other, and yet are completely heterosexual. And I wouldn't be surprised if that *is,* among the mass of men, a universal experience, completely accepted, completely common, completely shared.

The idea of a buddy is just the thin, label, vulgarization of it. The tradition of comradeship, of companionship, spoken of in the Bible... between David and Jonathan... all the way up to the body relationships as we know them... all these probably are intense love relationships which the gay lib group, in its political phase, has not yet accepted and integrated as delightful manifestation of human communication, satisfactory to everybody. In other words, there's a lot of political and communal development open to the gay lib movement as it includes more and more varieties of love, besides genital, and it may be that the bridge between gay liberation and men's liberation may be in the mutual recognition of the masculine tenderness that was denied both groups for so long.

YOUNG: In "Kaddish" you say something about the weight of your homosexuality: "Matterhorns of cock, Grand Canyons of asshole." Did you use those big metaphors because homosexuality was a heavy thing for you?

GINSBERG: When I was a sensitive, little kid, hiding, not able to touch anyone or speak my feelings out, little did I realize the enormous weight of love and numbers of lovers, the enormity of the scene I'd enter into, in which I finally wound up a public spokesman for homosxuality at one point. In that sense, "Matterhorns of cock, Grand Canyons of asshole." Taking off my clothes in public and getting myself listed in *Who's Who* as being married to Peter.

YOUNG: In a number of poems your homosexuality flows very naturally. Did that really happen?

GINSBERG: About 1953 I wrote a big, long, beautiful love poem to Neal Cassady called "The Green Automobile." I made the love overt. I didn't make the genital part overt but I made every other aspect: tenderness, kneeling together, holding on, traveling together, and then ultimate separation.

The next poem that had some overt thing was a little poem in '53–'54, that mentioned the "culture of my generation, cocksucking and tears."

Living in Neal Cassady's house I wrote a little poem, from a line by Whitman, about lying down between the bride and the bridegroom. This was one of Whitman's great lines. In a fantasy I just wrote a description of what I would do, my love fantasy, between Neal and his wife, say, given permission by his tolerance.

The crucial moment of breakthrough in terms of statement came while writing "Howl": "let themselves be fucked in the ass by saintly motorcyclists, and screamed with joy." Usually the macho reaction to that image of being fucked in the ass would be just like in this new James Dickey film *Deliverance* where it's supposed to be the worst thing in the world.

YOUNG: You have a line somewhere: "who wants to get fucked up the ass, really?"

GINSBERG: That's in the book *Kaddish,* in a poem "Mescaline." On mescaline, who wants to exist in the universe to begin with? Who wants to have a name? Who wants to have an ego? And also who wants to be queer? Who wants the pain of being fucked in the ass at times when it is painful, when it occasionally is. That's part of the scene, too. Sometimes you never know it in advance. Things seem to be all right, and all of a sudden it turns out to be painful. So, who wants to be fucked in the ass that way, really?

The outrageous presentation came with "Howl," where I suddenly realized how funny it would be in the middle of a long poem, if I said: "Who let themselves be fucked in the ass . . . and screamed with joy," instead of "and screamed with pain." That's what the contradiction is in that line. An American audience would expect it to say "pain," but instead you have "and screamed with joy"— which is really true, absolutely, one hundred percent.

And again I have a line like: "who blew and were blown by those human seraphim, the sailors, caresses of Atlantic and Caribbean love," referring to Hart Crane, actually. It was an acknowledgment of the basic reality of homosexual joy. That was a breakthrough in the sense of a public statement of feelings and emotions and attitudes that I would not have wanted my father or my family to see, and I even hesitated to make public. So that much was a breakthrough: literally coming out of the closet.

YOUNG: Did critical reaction to you ever focus on the fact that you were homosexual?

GINSBERG: Yes, Norman Podhoretz, in *Partisan Review*, made a big attack on all the beatnik literature, the "know-nothing bohemians." He said that though my poetry was not too bad, its chief force rested on this somewhat questionable insistent proclamation of being queer, homosexual all the time, which, if frank, was not that interesting socially. It was a put-down which acknowledged and at the same time dismissed, while it called Kerouac a "brute."

Walt Whitman is very important on male tenderness. He's never been brought forth as a totem or as a prophet by either gay lib or by the radical left for some very precise statements he made on the subject of men's lib, this is in *Democratic Vistas*, or prospects for democracy, in which he's talking about how possibly materialistic competition in America will turn it into the fabled "damned of nations"—which it now has become. It may be that "we are on the road to a destiny, a status, equivalent, in its real world, to that of the fabled damned." It says, "intense and loving comradeship, the personal and passionate attachment of man to man—which, hard to define, underlies the lessons and ideals of the profound saviours of every land and age, and which seems to promise when thoroughly develop'd, cultivated, and recognized in manners and literature, the most substantial hope and safety of the future of these states—will then be fully expressed."

Then in a footnote, he says:

"It is to the development, identification, and general prevalence of that fervid comradeship, (the adhesive love, at least rivaling the amative love hitherto possessing imaginative literature, if not going beyond it,) that I look for the counterbalance and offset of our materialistic and vulgar American democracy, and for the spiritualization thereof. Many will say it is a dream, and will not follow my inferences: but I confidently expect a time when there will be seen, running like a half-hid warp through all the myriad audible and visible worldly interests of America, threads of manly friendship, fond and loving, pure and sweet, strong and life-long, carried to degrees hitherto unknown—not only giving tone to individual character, and making it unprecedently emotional, muscular, heroic, and refined, but having the deepest relations to general politics. I say democracy infers such loving comradeship, as its most inevitable twin or counterpart, without which it will be incomplete, in vain, and incapable of perpetuating itself."

Then, in the preface to the 1876 edition of *Leaves of Grass*, he adds, in a long footnote:

"Something more may be added—for, while I am about it, I would make a full confessions. I also sent out *Leaves of Grass* to arouse and set flowing in men's and women's hearts, young and old, (my present and future readers,) endless streams of living, pulsating love and friendship, directly from them to myself, now and ever. To this terrible irrepressible yearning, (surely more or less down underneath in most human souls,)—this never-satisfied appetite for sympathy, and this boundless offering of sympathy—this universal democratic comradeship—this old, eternal, yet ever-new interchange of adhesiveness, so fitly emblematic of America—I have given in that book, undisguisedly, declaredly, the openest expression.... Poetic literature has long been the formal and conventional tender of art and beauty merely, and of a narrow, constipated, special amativeness. I say, the subtlest, sweetest, surest tie between me and Him or Her, who, in the pages of *Calamus* and other pieces realizes me—though we never see each other, or though ages and ages hence—must, in this way, be personal affection. And those —be they few, or be they many—are at any rate *my readers*, in the sense that belongs not, and can never belong, to better, prouder poems.

"Besides, important as they are in my purpose as emotional expressions for humanity, the special meaning of the *Calamus* cluster of *Leaves of Grass*, (and more or less running through that book, and cropping out in *Drum-Taps*,) mainly resides in its Political significance. In my opinion it is by a fervent, accepted development of Comradeship, the beatiful and sane affection of man for man, latent in all the young fellows, North and South, East and West—it is by this, I say, and by what goes directly and indirectly along with it, that the United States of the future, (I cannot too often repeat,) are to be most effectually welded together, intercalated, anneal'd into a Living Union."

So, that's really the direction, I think, for gay lib, for men's lib, the whole thing, you know, the release of emotions, finally a release of tenderness and that's the thing being suppressed.

YOUNG: Some people in the gay movement who call themselves "effeminists" would say that this sort of romanticization of masculine love is anti-woman, that it's another expression of male supremacy along the lines of Greek love; that the Greek society which tolerated and nurtured homosexuality was at its root a male supremacist society.

GINSBERG: I don't know. I don't think that's so in the long run. I think it's too genuine a feeling. With Whitman it didn't seem to interfere with his relations with women, because he had women friends who felt the same as he and who were, I think, married householder lesbians.

Whitman was saying that emotional giving between men, acceptance between men, has not been developed in America. One would say nowadays that it's been repressed by the spirit of competition and rivalry characteristic of capitalist home economics. A concomitant potential of a communal fraternality would be brotherly tenderness at least. That tenderness has been denied to the Southern redneck and is responsible for his disrelation both with men and women. We don't yet know what the result would be of men forming closer emotional ties, or of the making conscious of those emotional ties and the acceptancy of them as a political significance.

What's the alternative? You can bring up the specter of Greek love and its anti-feminist concomitant and point out aspects of that in behavior of the beatniks—a fear of women, at least with me. But you would also have to see it as a real, heartfelt, native development, out of the fear and restrictiveness of the situation that we were brought up with: distrust, hatred, paranoia and competition between men rather than cooperation; and the same also between men and women.

Whitman was most sensitive and conscious of that because of his blocked love for men, because he couldn't make it with men openly and publicly. He had to find a way of expressing his adhesiveness, as he calls it.

I think a liberation of emotion between men would also lead to a liberation or straightening out of relations between men and women, because men would no longer have to be men in relation to women in the sense of hard and conquistador. They might have a much more relaxed relationship in which they weren't continuously obliged to be sexualized but could be just friends, or fond. Men's non-sexual friendship with women is now considered unmanly. So the development of frankly emotional, non-genital friendships with men might mean also the development, the opening up of frankly emotional non-genital friendships with women.

What is the effeminist alternative position between men? In other words, what do they propose besides saying, "No, you shouldn't feel good with your fellow man; heterosexuals should not develop toward emotional relations with heterosexuals?" They're pointing out the danger of an exclusive club, but we've already had that exclusive club in another form with the Hemingway macho scene, or with the military muscular macho scene. I'm saying and Whitman is saying that the antidote to the Hemingway macho and military macho scene is the development of frank, emotional tenderness and an acknowledgment of tenderness as the basis of genital or non-genital emotion. It may resolve itself in more men friendships, a democratization of friendships, so that it's not exclusively friendships between men and women on a sexual basis. I think it would resolve a lot of the macho conflict and contradictions.

I think that's one of the definitions of gaiety, or homosexuality: that there is a built-in conditioning, from very early times, in which both genital and emotional flow goes toward men more than, as is more usual, toward women. I thought the point of gay lib was to admit that variety of development as being viable, making a place for that. Otherwise, what is a homosexual? Unless you want to have a homosexual liberation front which proposes that men should develop out of homosexuality to a more equal and democratic relation with both men and women. But I think you could say: let the straight flower bespeak its purpose in straightness, which is to seek the light, and let the crooked flower bespeak its purpose in crookedness, which is to seek the light. The crooked flower has to go around the rock to seek the light. But the point was to get to the light of love, and the straight flower just grew up straight, right into the light of love. So you have either biological or conditional man-love and a gay lib movement which purports to release and make public those emotions. One thing that gay lib could do would be to break down the fear barrier that queens have against women. Breaking down the fear barrier between men and men would probably tend toward that.

Another point I'd like to take up is the traditional, effeminist possibly, objection to the "sexist" relations between older men and younger men. I saw some effeminist manifestos [on this point] in Berkeley. I took that question to Gavin Arthur, who died this year in San Francisco. He was a great gentleman, with beautiful manners, an astrologer, a teacher, a guru, and a grandson of President Chester Arthur. Neal Cassady slept with him occasionally, taking refuge in San Francisco from his travels with Kesey, back and forth from the railroad; and Gavin Arthur had slept with Edward Carpenter, and Edward Carpenter had slept with Walt Whitman. So this is in a sense in the line of transmission... that's an interesting sort of thing to have as part of the mythology. Kerouac's heterosexual hero who also slept with somebody who slept with somebody who slept with Whitman, and received the Whispered Transmission, capital W, capital T of that love.

YOUNG: Kerouac's heterosexual hero? Who would that be?

GINSBERG: Neal Cassady, Dean Moriarty, who slept with Gavin Arthur, who slept with Edward Carpenter, who slept with Whitman. And I slept with Dean, so... So speaking from that line of transmission... what was whispered to me in that line of transmission by Gavin Arthur on the subject of older and young people making it: he says that's like an ancient thing, and it's very old and very charming for older and younger to make it—which you realize as you get old, too—and nothing to be ashamed of, defensive about, but something to be encouraged—a healthy relationship, not a sick neurotic dependency.

The main thing is communication. Older people have ken, experience, history, memory, information, data and also power, money and also worldly technology. Younger people have intelligence, enthusiasm, sexuality, energy, vitality, open mind, athletic activity—all the characteristics and sweet, dewy knowledges of youth; and both profit from the reciprocal exchange. It becomes more than a sexual relationship; it becomes an exchange of strengths, an exchange of gifts, and exchange of accomplishments, an exchange of nature-bounties. Older people gain vigor, refreshment, vitality, energy, hopefulness and cheerfulness from the attentions of the young; and the younger people gain gossip, experience, advice, aid, comfort, wisdom, knowledges and teachings from their relation with the old. So as in other relationships, the combination of old and young is functionally useful. It's far from sexist, in the sense that the interest of the younger person is not totally sexual; it's more in the relationship and the wisdom to be gained.

In Edward Carpenter's and Whitman's theory the older person made love to the younger person, blew the younger person, and there was the absorption of the younger person's electric, vital magnetism (according to a charming, theosophical, nineteenth-century theory). And it's something that somebody older like myself does experience as a natural fact. When you sleep with somebody younger you do gain a little vitality of breadth and bounce.

YOUNG: You've referred to Whitman and Edward Carpenter, and in some of your poems you mention García Lorca. For me it was a very recent discovery that these famous writers were gay like myself, that I had this bond with them. I'm curious as to how you made this discovery?

GINSBERG: Lorca's "Ode to Walt Whitman" speaks of "the sun singing on the navels of boys playing baseball under the bridges," which is an image of such erotic beauty that immediately you realize that he understood, that he was there; that was an emotion he felt. Then, later on I met somebody in Chile who knew him and said that he'd slept with boys. In fact, some sort of argument about a boy may be cause of the shooting of Lorca. I don't think there's any written biographical history.

This sex epiphany is all in Whitman's texts, his homoerotic rhapsody, including a description of the time he lay down with a friend—it's in part 5 of *Song of Myself*:

> I mind how once we lay such a transparent summer morning,
> How you settled your head athwart my hips and gently turn'd over upon me,
> And parted the shirt from my bosom-bone, and plunged your tongue to my barestript heart,
> And reach'd till you felt my beard, and reach'd till you held my feet.

YOUNG: You don't get it in high school.

GINSBERG: But school is irrelevant to poetry and everything else anyway. I mean school is something from the nineteenth century. Poetry has gone back to 15,000 B.C. There's Whitman's "We Two Boys Together Clinging":

> *We two boys together clinging,*
> *One the other never leaving,*
> *Up and down the roads going, North and South excursions making,*
> *Power enjoying, elbows stretching, fingers clutching,*
> *Arm'd and fearless, eating, drinking, sleeping, loving,*
> *No law less than ourselves owning, sailing, soldiering, thieving, threatening,*
> *Misers, menials, priests alarming, air breathing, water drinking, on the turf or the sea-beach dancing,*
> *Cities wrenching, ease scorning, statutes mocking, feebleness chasing,*
> *Fulfilling our foray.*

In "No Labor-Saving Machine" he writes:

> *But a few carols vibrating through the air I leave,*
> *For comrades and lovers.*

And Whitman says [in "A Glimpse"]:

> *A glimpse through an interstice caught,*
> *Of a crowd of workmen and drivers in a bar-room around the stove late of a winter night, and I unremark'd seated in a corner,*
> *Of a youth who loves me and whom I love, silently approaching and seating himself near, that he may hold me by the hand,*
> *A long while amid the noises of coming and going, of drinking and oath and smutty jest,*
> *There we two, content, happy in being together, speaking little, perhaps not a word.*

Perfect! And real, absolutely real! That is actually life. That's even heterosexual life. That's the undescribable reality of human relationship in America. It can't be called gay ... it's ... that's something in the line of what I was talking about before in terms of what needs to be ... the adhesiveness that Whitman spoke of that is latent in all of us now, and that's ready to be opened, and god knows how many, in the last ten years, how many younger boys that I've run across that I just sat and held hands with anyway and felt love feelings toward them and felt love feelings toward me, in situations like this which were maybe in a college, or somewhere, which had nothing to do with quote queer unquote, or even gay. Gay is too much of a category!

YOUNG: From what you said before, this existed to a certain extent with the bohemians or the hipsters...

GINSBERG: Oh, it existed back to Cro-Magnon man!

YOUNG: I think definitely a tension exists today between gay freaks and straight gays. There are some people in gay liberation who say, "I have more in common with a heterosexual freak than with a gay person who's into very short hair and alcohol." And then there are other gay people who say, "My loyalty is to other gay people, and the freak culture is very macho."

GINSBERG: The form I felt it in was between the heartfelt, populist, humanist, quasi-heterosexual, Whitmanic, bohemian, free-love, homosexual tradition, as you find it in Sherwood Anderson, Whitman, or maybe Genet, a little, versus the privileged, exaggeratedly effeminate, gossipy, moneyed, money-style-clothing-conscious, near-hysterical queen. Of course, there's nothing more ancient or/and in a sense honorable than the old shamanistic transvestite that we see running up and down Greenwich Avenue or, among the American Indians, a shaman who dresses himself up like a woman and even takes a husband. The screaming young queen—there's something very ancient and charming about that; great company, total individuality and expressiveness. Sometimes you fear it's the screaming, hysterical outside of somebody who's going to have a nervous breakdown and wind up in the church, or something. But then there's also the pettish, spiteful, anal retentive, disciplinarian.

But when I was younger the split was more between the grubby, beatnik, open-hearted... I couldn't call myself a fairy exactly... queer?... I have used that, but I've never found the right word... the nameless lovers, the nameless gnostic lovers... and the monopolistic queens, say, who had privilege and money. So that was the distinction. It was more between the cold-hearted and the warm-hearted.

YOUNG: In the gay bars of New York did you find both?

GINSBERG: Oh, I found both definitely. There were lots of outspoken, funny old sailor queens from the twenties; and then there were all sorts of prissy-mouthed, paranoiac, fearful, conservative-reactionary, short-hair, worried advertising martinets. And everything in between. There is a manneristic fairydom that depends on money, chic, privilege and exclusive, monopolistic high style, and I would say that it is usually accompanied by bitchiness and bad manners and faithless love, too. I like homosexuality where the lovers are friends all their lives, and there are many lovers and many friends.

YOUNG: Could you say something about your relationship with Peter Orlovsky?

GINSBERG: We met in San Francisco. He was living with a painter named Robert LaVigne in '54. I was having a very straight life, just trying it out, working in an advertising company, wearing suits, living up on Nob Hill in a nice big apartment with Sheila, who was a jazz singer and worked in advertising. Things were somewhat unsatisfactory between us. We'd been taking a little peyote, so we were into a psychedelic scene, too.

We got into an argument, so I wandered down one night into an area of San Francisco I'd never noticed then called Polk Gulch, now known as a notorious gay area with lots of gay bars. It was then more of a bohemian section, somewhat gay, artistic. Hotel Wentley was there, right on the corner of Sutter and Polk, and a Foster's cafeteria. I went and sat in the Foster's, late at night. I ran into Robert LaVigne and got into a big, interesting, artistic conversation about the New York painters I knew—Larry Rivers, de Kooning, and Kline. LaVigne was a provincial San Francisco painter, so I was bringing all sorts of fresh poetry, art news from New York.

He took me up to see his place and his paintings, about four blocks away on Gough Street in an apartment that I subsequently lived in for many seasons and still use now. I walked into the apartment and there was this enormous, beautiful, lyrical, seven-by-seven-foot-square painting of a naked boy with his legs spread, and some onions at his feet, with a little Greek embroider on the couch. He had a nice, clean-looking pecker, yellow hair, a youthful teeny little face, and a beautiful frank expression looking right out of the canvas at me. And I felt a heart throb immediately. So I asked who that was, and Robert said, "Oh, that's Peter; he's here, he's home." And then Peter walked in the room with the same look on his face, a little shyer.

Within a week Robert said that he was going out of town or breaking up with Peter, or Peter was breaking up with him. He asked me if I was interested in Peter, and he'd see what he could arrange. I said, "Ooh, don't mock me." I'd already given up. I already had had a historic love affair with Neal Cassady a decade earlier. So I was already a tired old dog, in the sense of the defeats of love, not having made it, not having found a permanent life companion. And, in 1955, I was already twenty-nine. I wasn't a twenty-year-old kid with romantic notions. That night we were in Vesuvio's bar. Robert had a big conversation with Peter, asking Peter if he was interested, sort of like a *shachun,* a matrimonial arranger.

Then I went home one night. I went to Peter's room. We were to sleep together that night on a huge mattress he had on the floor. I took off my clothes and got into bed. I hadn't slept with too many people. Never openly, completely giving and taking. With Jack or Neal, with people who were primarily heterosexual and who didn't fully accept the sexualization of our tenderness, I felt I was forcing it on them; so I was always timid about them making love back to me, and they very rarely did very much. When they did, it was like blessings from heaven. If you get into it, there's a funny kind of pleasure/pain, absolute loss/hope. When you blow someone like that and they come, it's great! And if they touch you once, it's enough to melt the entire life structure, as well as the heart, the genitals and the earth. And it'll make you cry.

So . . . Peter turned around (he was in his big Japanese robe), opened up the bathrobe—he was naked—and put it around me and pulled me into him; and we got close, belly to belly, face to face. That was so frank, so free and so open that I think it was one of the first times that I felt open with a boy. Then, emboldened, I screwed Peter. He wept afterwards, and I got frightened, not knowing what I'd done to make him cry, but completely moved by the fact that he was so involved as to weep. At the same time the domineering, sadism part of me was flattered and erotically aroused.

The reason he wept was that he realized how much he was giving me and how much I was demanding, asking and taking. I think he wept looking at himself in that position not knowing how he'd gotten there; not feeling it was wrong, but wondering at the strangeness of it. The most raw meat of reasons, for weeping.

Then Robert hearing, seeing the situation, came in to comfort Peter a little bit. I was very possessive and I pushed Robert away. That got me and Robert into a funny kind of distrust that lasted for a year or two before our karmas finally resolved. He then realized he was well off on his own; and I was burdened with the karma of love.

Peter was primarily heterosexual, and always was. I guess that was another reason he was shocked—the heaviness of my sadistic possessiveness in screwing him. For the first time in my life I really had an opportunity to screw somebody else! I think that wounded him and thrilled me a little bit. So we still had to work out all that in our relationship over many, many years. It's painful sometimes.

We slept together perhaps one more time. Then I had to go to New York for my brother's wedding at Christmas, '54. I came back and moved into that apartment where they were living, at their invitation. And then there was a triangle of

Robert, me and Peter. Peter had not made up his mind whether or not he wanted to make a more permanent relationship with me. I had my eyes on Peter for life-long love; [I was] completely enamored and intoxicated—just the right person for me, I thought. Robert was not sure he hadn't made a mistake, seeing the flow and the vitality that was rising up in both me and Peter. And Peter began withdrawing. He was caught in this rivalry between me and Robert, and, at the same time, there was his unsurety of me and his relation to me. Basically he liked girls anyway, so what was he doing lying there being screwed by me?

So I moved across from the Hotel Wentley and got a room. I was working in a market research job. I had the brilliant inspiration that all the categorizing and market research I was doing could be fed into a machine, and I wouldn't have to add all those columns anymore. So I supervised the transfer for the company, and that left me out of a job just nicely, like a seamless occlusion. Then I got unemployment compensation.

I was being psychoanalyzed at Langley Porter Clinic, an elite extension of U.C. Berkeley Medical School. He was a very good doctor, and I said: "You know, I'm very hesitant to get into a deep thing with Peter, because where can it ever lead. Maybe I'll grow old and then Peter probably won't love me—just a transient relationship. Besides, shouldn't I be heterosexual?" He said, "Why don't you do what you want. What would you like to do?" And I answered, "Well, I really would just love to get an apartment on Montgomery Street, stop working and live with Peter and write poems!" He said, "Why don't you do that?" So I said, "What happens if I get old or something?" And he replied, "Oh, you're a nice person; there's always people who will like you"—which really amazed me. So, in a sense he gave me permission to be free, not to worry about consequences.

So then I waited for Peter, and Peter stayed up at the Gough Street apartment and went to school. I got this room and started writing a lot and waited and waited for Peter. Neal Cassady came by a couple of times. I made it with Neal. I can remember one of the last really wild times I made it with him, because I had a room of my own and there was privacy, finally. He was lying there naked, and I was sitting on his cock, jumping up and down trying to make him come.

And I just waited and waited [for Peter]. There was nothing I could run after or pursue, because I couldn't claim anything by force. Things got too difficult where Peter was living, so he got a room himself in the Wentley, across the street from where I was. And there was embarrassment, coldness—not knowing where each other was, what we would do. I was waiting for him to make some sort of decision. A couple of times we drank a little to see if we could get over the low. We didn't sleep together at all, though I was longing to.

Then one day he was lying in bed, and he started crying again. He said, "Come on and take me." I was too overwhelmed and frightened to even get a hard-on. I didn't know what to do. We both had our clothes on. I was afraid he was interpreting it as me screwing him again, rather than really just having each other. But that soon got resolved, and we moved in together, into an apartment in North Beach. We found an apartment, and it had a room for him, a room for me, and a hall between us; and a kitchen together. So that gave us both a little privacy, and, at the same time, we could make it when we wanted.

He was very moody, very sweet, tender, gentle and open. But every month or two months he'd go into a very dark, Russian, Dostoevskian black mood and lock himself in his room and weep for days; and then he'd come out totally cheerful and friendly. I found after a while it was best not to interrupt him, not to hang round like a vulture; let him got through his own yoga.

The key thing was when we decided on the terms of our marriage—I think it was in Foster's cafeteria downtown about three in the morning. We were sitting and talking about each other, with each other, trying to figure out what we were going to do, who we were to each other, and what we wanted out of each other, how much I loved him, and how much did he love me. We arrived at what we both really desired.

I'd already had visionary experience: an illumined audition of Blake's voice and a sense of epiphany about the universe. He had had an experience, weeping and lonesome, walking up the hill to his college, and having a sense of an apparition of the trees bowing to him. So we both had some kind of psychedelic, transcendental, mystical image in our brains and hearts.

We made a vow to each other that he could own me, my mind and everything I knew, and my body, and I could own him and all he knew and all his body; and that we would give each other ourselves, so that we possessed each other as property, to do everything we wanted to, sexually or intellectually, and in a sense explore each other until we reached the mystical "X" together, emerging two merged souls. We had the understanding that when our (my particularly) erotic desire was ultimately satisfied by being satiated (rather than denied), there would be a lessening of desire, grasp, holding on, craving and attachment; and that ultimately we would both be delivered free in heaven together. And so the vow was that neither of us would go into heaven unless we could get the other one in—like a mutual Bodhisattva's vow.

That's actually the Bodhisattva's vow—"Sentient beings are numberless, I vow to enlighten them all. Passions are numberless, I vow to quench them all, cut them all down. The nature of the dharma, the doors of nature are endless, I vow to enter every single one of them. Buddha path very high and long and endless—vow to follow through all the way—Buddha path, infinite, limitless, vow to go all the way through." Sentient beings, numberless, unnumbered—countless, vow to count every one, enlighten every single one of them. Basically a vow to be reborn as everybody, one after another, every stone, every leaf blade, vow to be every individual part of the universe at one time or another, and accept the fate of that particle, so to speak.

Well, this is like a limited version of that, almost intuitive, the vow to stay with each other to whatever eternal consciousness: him with his trees bowing, me with Blake eternity vision. I was more intellectual, so I was offering my mind, my intellect; he was more athletic and physical and was offering his body. So we held hands, took a vow: I do, I do, you promise? yes, I do. At that instant we looked in each other's eyes and there was a kind of celestial fire that crept over us and blazed up and illuminated the entire cafeteria and made it an eternal place.

I found somebody who'd accept my devotion, and he found somebody who'd accept his devotion and who was devoted to him. It was really a fulfillment of fantasy, to a point where fantasy and reality finally merged. Desire illuminated the room, because it was a fulfillment of all my fantasies since I was nine, when I began to have erotic love fantasies. And that vow has stuck as the primary core of our relationship. That's the mutual consciousness; it's the celestial social contact, valid because it was an expression of the desire of that time, and it was workable. It's really the basic human relationship—you give yourself to each other, help each other and don't go to heaven without each other.

There's this mythology of Arjuna, from the *Bhagavad Gita,* getting to the door of heaven. He's got this little dog following him, and they say, you can come in but you can't bring your dog. And he says, well, no, if I can't go in with my dog, I won't go. And then they say, Oh, come on, you can go in, just leave him behind, it's only a dog. And he says, no, I love my dog, and I trust that love, and if I can't bring that trust in, then what kind of heaven is this? And the third time, he says, no, no, no, I'll stay out and put the dog in heaven but I won't go in without the dog. I vowed to tears with my dog, I can't leave my dog alone. And so, finally, after the third time, the dog turns out to be Krishna, the supreme lord of the universe and heaven itself. He was only trying to get heaven into heaven. And his instinct was right. And our instinct was right. It was enough to bring us through very difficult times—all through the change of status, beat generation and fame, the alteration of social identity that fame entails.

Our relationship has lasted from 1954 on. The terms have changed tremendously. Peter's gone through a lot of changes, and we've separated for a year at a time. And always come back. We've gone through a lot of phases of sleeping with people together, doing orgies together, sleeping alone together. Now Peter sleeps with a girl. I very rarely sleep with him. But the origin of our relationship is a fond affection. I wouldn't want to go to heaven and leave Peter alone on earth; and he wouldn't leave me alone if I was sick in bed, dying, gray-haired, wormy, rheumatic. He'd have pity on me. We've maintained our relationship so long that at this point we could separate and it would be all right. I think the karma has resolved and worn out in a sense.

The original premise was to have each other and possess each other until the karma was worn out, until the desire, the neurotic attachment, was satisfied by satiation. And there's been satiation, disappointment and madness, because he went through a long period of speed freakery in the mid-sixties which really strained things. We had times of hostile screaming at each other such as happens in the worst of homo- and heterosexual marriages, where people have murder in their hearts toward each other. That burned out a lot of the false emotion of youth, and the unrealistic graspings, cravings, attachments and dependencies. So he's now independent, and I'm independent of him. And yet there's an independent curiosity between us.

YOUNG: There were some vague stories going around about your visit to Cuba in 1965 and departure. I'd like to know more about what you did in Cuba and what you said that eventually got you deported.

GINSBERG: Well, the worst thing I said was that I'd heard, by rumor, that Raúl Castro was gay. And the second worst thing I said was that Che Guevara was cute. The most substantial thing was that I went around wondering why their marijuana policy, as of 1965, was so down and unscientific. I didn't accept the answer I got which was that the Batista soldiers used to get high and shoot at them, because I didn't think that was true. By hindsight, it doesn't seem really relevant to their needs, but at the same time, the denial of marijuana doesn't seem relevant to their needs, either.

There was persecution of homosexuals in the primarily gay-oriented theater group at the time. Instead of finding a place for that, they tried to break it up and sent everybody out to the sugar-cane fields to work. This was an attempt to humiliate them, to use sugar cane for humiliation rather than community. And it wasn't in the newspapers. It was a secret campaign, with all the Young Communist League party-hack, flag-waving kids, like the Nixonettes, so to speak, accusing everybody they didn't like of being faggots.

It was considered bad form to wear beards and long hair, even though that was the characteristic style of Castro and the liberators up on the main drag, La Rampa. People were being stopped by the police and busted for having long hair, accused of being existentialists and degenerates. A bunch of young kids belonging to a poetry group I knew, El Puente (The Bridge), were being bugged by the police, not allowed to publish, and were called fairies. One evening the whole group of Escritores del Encuentro Inter-Americana, sponsored by Casa de las Américas, went to the theater to hear a concert of "feeling" music. We were joined there by a whole bunch of young poet kids. When we left the theater, they were all stopped by the police, arrested and told to stop hanging around with foreigners. Some of the young poet kids were translating my work.

So there was this police bureaucracy in Cuba that was very heavy and was coming down heavy on culture, in terms of beards, sexual-revolution tendencies, sociability, and homosexuality. In other words, there was no real cultural revolution; it was still basically a Catholic mentality. As in many Communist countries, the police bureaucrat party hacks were like Mayor Daley ward-heelers: flag-waving, fat-assed square types. Self-seeking squares, not at all spiritually communist, were getting control of the police and emigration bureaucracies and setting themselves at odds against the people who screw with their eyes open, listen to the Beatles and read interesting books like Genet, and *fought* at the Bay of Pigs against the Americans. Even people who had been up in the mountains with Castro were very secretive about smoking grass. The press was monolithically controlled and boring, and the newspaper reporters for the press reminded me very much of the self-righteous newspaper reporters from the *Daily News* as far as their opinionation and argumentativeness.

I just continued talking there as I would talk here in terms of being anti-authoritarian. But my basic feeling there was sympathetic to the revolution. I had friends living there, was invited there as a guest, and I took part as a judge in a literary contest, and I just shot my mouth off! The worst thing was the talk about homosexuality and the challenge to the official position about it. Castro had taken an official position in a speech at the university in which he had attacked homosexuality. He called it degenerate or abnormal, saw it as a cabal, perhaps, a conspiracy. I think he praised the Young Communist League for turning in fairies.

I suggested to Haydee Santamaria that they invite the Beatles and got the answer: "They have no ideology; we are trying to build a revolution with an ideology." Well, that's true, but what was the ideology they were proposing? A police bureaucracy that persecutes fairies? I mean, they're wasting enormous energy on that. Some of those "fairies" were the best revolutionaries—people that fought at the Bay of Pigs, Playa Girón.

I slept with one young poet, secretively. I took one stick of grass one day, walking along a shady street with a bearded fellow who said he'd been up in the mountains with Castro and that they had smoked up there. But that was the extent of my "criminal behavior."

I thought one of the most brilliant and interesting results of gay liberation was the confrontation with the repressive, conservative police bureaucracy in Cuba. I think the confrontation between the Venceremos Brigade and gay lib showing the Cuban mental block on the subject of homosexuality was one of the most useful things that gay lib did on an international scale. At least it brought the question to front-brain consciousness. Gay lib people went there to offer themselves and, I think, less to confront the Cubans than to find out what the scene was. They were, obviously, faithful in terms of change and sympathy with the revolution. Since it was a gay lib group, the right-wing, capitalist press couldn't take advantage of the confrontation to put shame on Cuba, because otherwise they'd have to defend gay lib! So, it was gay lib taking the bull by the horns, within the context of brotherhood, challenging the Cuban macho, repressive mentality in a constructive way. I don't think the Communist Party there reacted very well. What was the result?

YOUNG: In the interim period the brigade has adopted a policy of excluding gay liberation people. There was a fifth brigade that did not have gay liberation people on it. The Cubans have since come up with a detailed, rather specific policy statement on homosexuality, declaring it to be a "social pathology." The pro-Cuban Venceremos Brigade people have related with hostility to the radical gay lib movement. Large numbers of New Left people who formerly were very sympathetic to Cuba have reduced their expression of sympathy for Cuba because of the gay question. The Cubans, basically, have forced a lot of people to choose between the Cuban revolution and gay liberation, and they're quite surprised to find people choosing the gays.

GINSBERG: When Castro originally had his revolution, he said it's a Marxist revolution but it's still a humanist revolution. If it's a humanist revolution, they cannot put down gays. Otherwise, it's doubletalk. I think it's important to support any separation out from American imperialism and conspicuous consumption, and any sort of independence from American psychological domination. But, on the other hand, the reason for doing so is to become human again and independent.

If the definition of human and independent means sustaining an old, authoritarian viewpoint toward sexuality—the monotheistic, Catholic viewpoint—then it would be better that American radicals at least realized that they're dealing with human beings in the Cuban situation rather than with divine authorities. I am willing to accept the fact that the Cuban revolution is a genuine relief from Mafia capitalist domination, the previously corrupt society of Cuba, and a release from America.

In other words, I feel the Cuban revolution is important and should be supported. They'll learn, soon enough. They're gonna see the end of the world anyway and end up with long hair and pansexualities. They're going to have to take it as state policy before they're over, just to relieve their population problem. I think the gays are dealing in the long run from a position of great strength, because their position is founded in ancient rules of mammal behavior and ecological necessity as far as the future and the recognition of common humanity. So I think gays can afford to say, "Ahhh."

I saw a lot of other things there in terms of cultural persecution. I was interested in *santería* [Afro-Cuban cults]. With a group of writers I went to a *santero*'s house in the outskirts of Havana for a Congo ceremony and also for a Yoruba ceremony. In the middle of the ceremony the police came in, wanted everybody's name and address and harassed everybody. They said you had to have a permit for any meeting of more than ten or twelve people after a certain hour or even at any time in a private house. They knew who we were perfectly well; we had representatives there from the Casa de las Américas. So again it was the police bureaucracy hassling the cultural side.

One of the boasts in Cuba was the acceptance of black consciousness. The *santería* religion was one of the great ancient tribal things that had resisted the white, honky, Christian church, and here they were interrupting this ceremony! There was apparently an attempt to discourage the practice of *santería* because it was like a rival spiritual authority to the state.

In Cuba I remember that most of the honkies from a Catholic background were indifferent to black culture and to the heart of it which was the *santería* cult. But among the appreciators were some of the old gay painters and poets.

YOUNG: A couple of friends of mine who were recently in Cuba told me that the persecution of the *santerías* continues. At the same time there is peace between the Cuban government and the Catholic Church. The Cuban Declaration of the Congress on Education and Culture specifically attacks the *santería* but speaks very positively about relations with the Catholic Church, especially in terms of the support of the Catholic Church in other Latin American countries for left-wing forces.

One of these black *santeros*, who was wanted by the police, escaped and hid in the house of a homosexual friend. They were both caught and arrested. The news report about the arrest emphasized the connection between *santería* and homosexuality. They used the stronger taboo against homosexuality to reinforce the attack on the *santería*.

Edward Carpenter says that one of the things that made him a revolutionary was going to Africa and through his gayness becoming familiar with the humanity of the African people.

In Cuba I met the three people who run the puppet theatre, the Teatro de Guiñol, a brother and sister and another fellow. The brother and the other fellow are both gay. The people in the theater are mostly gay. When I was there in 1969, I hardly even perceived that they were gay, because of my own closet situation. They told me they were producing a Yoruba play. Pepe Carril wrote it and it has been translated into English by Susan Sherman. Carucha, one of the directors of the theater, told me that they had to fight to do this Yoruba play. They did a theatrical puppetry presentation of the Yoruba cult, and afterwards the party hacks thought that it was o.k.

GINSBERG: The original humanist, Marxist approach was that Western monopoly capitalism, homogenized, turned into a commercial mass cult, a plastic, degenerate commodity. From a revolutionary point of view, the rights and cultural heritage of workers and minorities had to be preserved from the depredations of the evil banks and cultural monopolists. By revolutionary theory the Yoruba tradition among the blacks should be cultivated and subsidized, kept as folk art of the people, as their art and religion. So, it's a contradiction in basic Marxist approach to have a rivalry between police bureaucracy and Yoruba priests.

YOUNG: I think it has something to do with plain old racism; white supremacy.

GINSBERG: I suppose so. It means that blacks have a culture of their own, and whites don't want that. So what do you say to Castro? Has anyone had an intelligent conversation with Castro in the last seven years? He used to have conversations with interesting people like Sartre.

I was in my hotel room one morning toward the end of my stay in Cuba when three uniformed, olive-clothed, mute soldiers came in with an officer. He said he was head of immigration, that I had to pack my bags, and that I was being deported on the next plane out, to Prague. I asked if they had informed the Casa de las Américas, and the answer was, no; there will be time enough later. They wouldn't let me make a phone call to the Casa, which was my host, and they took me downstairs. I shouted in the lobby to Nicanor Parra that I was being deported and they should get in touch with the Casa de las Américas and warn them. I was driven out to the airport. On the way I asked why I was being deported. The officer said, "For breaking the laws of Cuba." And I said, "What laws?" He responded, "You'll have to ask yourself that." And that answer, I thought, was like the answer I got from Dean McKnight at Columbia University when I got kicked out for staying overnight in my room with Jack Kerouac. And we hadn't made love at all. We just slept there because Kerouac had no place to sleep that night.

I didn't go round screaming to *Time* magazine that I'd been unjustly kicked out of Cuba. I just gave them the benefit of the doubt, understanding that I was a like a pawn. It was a fight between the liberal groups and the military bureaucracy groups. I realized also that the more the United States put pressure on Cuba, the more power the right-wing military, police bureaucracy and party hacks would get. The real problem was to relieve the pressure in America, to end the blockade rather than to "blame" the Cuban Revolution, Castro, or Marxism—although I don't think Castro was very tactful on the question of homosexuality. There was an excessively macho thoughtlessness on his part, and insensitivity.

YOUNG: When I was there in '71 at the journalists' conference, there was a reception, at the side of a big swimming pool. Everybody was crowding around Fidel. He was loving it and getting involved in lively conversation with different people. I was feeling very out of it. I was the only male that didn't have short hair, a suit and a tie, except for some Africans in African dress. The whole idea of pushing into a crowd to talk to a famous man was something I wasn't exactly into.

I decided to get involved in conversation with some other people. I spoke with a very important comandante, a black guy, who had fought with Fidel in the hills and was on the central committee. Karen Wald, an American who was with us, asked him what he thought about machismo. And he said, "Oh, man, that's good!" I can't figure out to this day whether he was putting her on or whether he was simply expressing his very gut reaction—which is that machismo is an important thing for a Cuban man to appreciate.

GINSBERG: The question does finally boil down to machismo, both here in the United States, and there, in terms of revolutionary tactics. Gay lib, in a sense, has a good approach to straight people with smug, middle-class ideas about power coming out of the barrel of anything, actually.

YOUNG: I think there's been a certain schizophrenia in the radical section of gay liberation. People have said they're against power. In fact, most of the people I know in the radical wing of gay liberation don't even like and don't use the slogan "gay power" because of the word "power."

GINSBERG: Gregory Corso has a great poem called "Power" which I invite you to check out. It was written in 1959: "Standing on a street corner waiting for no one is Power"... "A thirst for Power is drinking sand."

YOUNG: On the one hand people were attacking the whole notion of power, trying to do away with power in personal relationships. On the other hand, there was this desire to be a part of the left, a desire best epitomized by the slogan, "Go left, go gay, go pick up the gun"—a variation of the Panther slogan.

GINSBERG: Though it may serve as a vehicle for machismo among gays, it also serves as a deflating slogan for the pompousness of black- or white-power slogans that are actually a bit ridiculous sometimes.

The slogan "Power comes out of the barrel of a gun" was irrelevant in the American situation all along. There wasn't enough imagination in terms of tactics and poetry. How do you transform and convert America? It was a sign of the poverty of imagination that finally people fell into violence, when all along the whole problem had been mental violence, blindness and rage. Gay lib really did turn all of the machismo of the left inside out.

YOUNG: Do you feel that gay liberation has influenced you personally in any way?

GINSBERG: I use the word "gay" now which I never did before. And that's important when you change somebody's language. I find myself drifting toward the gay lib group whenever there's a big parade, because it's generally so sincere and interesting. The ideology there at least is personal. Gay lib has influenced my thinking on a few other things—like junkie liberation.

If you can have gay liberation from the oppression of the macho oppressors, then you can have junkie liberation from the oppression of the macho Mafia CIA, fuzz AMA, the Truman-Nixon oppression of punitive treatment of junkie illness rather than medical treatment. There should be a Junkie Liberation Front. They're the most oppressed group in America, in the sense that they're hunted down like dogs by people with guns. They're always under the threat of jail. They're sick. They've got a legitimate illness, and they're not being treated with legitimate medical means. But they are thrown over into the hands of the most corrupt police agents in America—narcs who have relations with the Mafia and peddle—as proved by the Knapp Commission and various other documented analyses. They've suffered the greatest image distortion of any group in America. There was never a category of human being in America that was invented as low as the fiend category for heroin addicts. They didn't even say liquor fiends.

And they are the victim of slander. They're called a criminal class, violent murderers when they're not; when it's the alcoholics who are really out of control.

YOUNG: Half of the Pentagon generals are alcoholics, too.

GINSBERG: So, I mean, there should be Junkie Liberation. The idea of the gay liberation front turned me on to the terminology Junkie Liberation Front. It added a little fillip to the relationship that Peter and I have.

YOUNG: One of the quotations that floats around gay liberation ascribed to you is your reaction to the Stonewall riot: "The fags have lost that wounded look." What were the circumstances?

GINSBERG: It was an interview in the *Village Voice*. I wasn't there at the riot. I heard about it, and I went down the next night to the Stonewall to show the colors. A crowd was there, and the place was open. So I said [to myself], the best thing I can do is to go in; the worst that can happen is I'll calm the scene. They're not going to attack them when I'm there. I'll just start a big Om.

I didn't relate to the violent part [of Stonewall]. The trashing part I thought was bitchy, unnecessary, hysterical. But, on the other hand, there was this image that everybody wanted to make that they could beat up the police, which apparently they managed to do. It was so funny as an image that it was hard to disapprove of, even though it involved a little violence.

YOUNG: Did you at that moment anticipate that this might lead to something called gay liberation with organizations, publications and so forth?

GINSBERG: It seemed to have been there all along, somehow. There was already that in rudimentary form with the Mattachine Society and One. They were more sedate, but they did some interesting things in their time.

I published the poem to Neal, "The Green Automobile," in 1959 in *The Mattachine Review*. Because it was a frank love poem, approving of the gay love relationship, it brought forth a rebuke from psychiatrist Karl Menninger of Topeka, Kansas. He wrote a strange letter to the Mattachine Society, denouncing the poem and saying they were trying to cure everybody, and here was this terrible poem boasting of these perverted feelings!

I went to a few of Mattachine's meetings and gave a little poetry reading there in San Francisco. But I never got involved politically with them, just literarily. Of course, San Francisco was always more advanced than New York in terms of the acceptance of homosexuality. It's like a Parisian city. There was a historic, famous bar [the Black Cat] in San Francisco's North Beach, near what was called the Monkey Block, which was maybe the greatest gay bar in America. It was really totally open, bohemian, San Francisco, Viennese; and everybody went there, heterosexual and homosexual. It was lit up, there was a honky-tonk piano; it was enormous. All the gay screaming queens would come, the heterosexual gray-flannel-suit types, longshoremen. All the poets went there.

YOUNG: Martha Shelley has a great first line in "Gay Is Good," one of the first gay liberation articles: "Look out straights, here comes the Gay Liberation Front, springing up like warts all over the bland face of Amerika, causing shudders of indigestion in the delicately balanced bowels of the Movement." At the end of the article she says, "You will never be rid of us because we reproduce ourselves out of your bodies."

GINSBERG: There's too much of a conflict there. The point is that nobody's straight. It's like calling someone a pig. Everybody has dreams that have some homoerotic content. So the problem is to make it safe for "straights" to feel the whole spectrum of feelings instead of single-level feelings, just as it's important for gay people to feel a whole spectrum of feelings. The politics of challenge in that sense doesn't seem to make too much sense. You don't woo somebody by challenging them. You woo them by giving them a place where they're comfortable, making it safe for them to get a hard-on...

YOUNG: I think there are definitely tensions in the movement now between the people who say having lots of blow jobs is liberation, and those who say that we are trapped in a meat-meets-meat approach and have to get out of that and relate to each other as people.

GINSBERG: It's an important human experience to relate to yourself and others as a hunk of meat sometimes. That's one way of losing ego, one holy divine yoga of losing ego: getting involved in an orgy and being reduced to an anonymous piece of meat, coming, and recognizing your own orgiastic anonymity. It's not a place where you want to live all your life, but it's certainly a place where you want to see and experience as a lesson, experience of consciousness that's valid for a certain level, and experience of great, divine beast consciousness. That's what they used to have the Dionysian orgy for; it's an ancient ritual; I don't think there's anything wrong with relating to people on the level of pure meat, as long as you don't get trapped into that all the time as a single level of consciousness—as some queens do.

The gay lib answer is obviously not going to be just simply lyrical sexuality. The use of sex as a banner to *épater le bourgeois,* to shock, show resentment or to challenge, is not sufficiently interesting to maintain for more than ten minutes; it's not enough to sustain a program that will carry love through the deathbed or help out Indochina. Or even get laid, finally. You have to have something more. You have to relate to people and their problems, too.

I dig baths and orgies. I think orgies should be institutionalized: impersonal meat orgies, with no question of personality or character or relating to people as people.

Anyone who insults Dionysus had better watch out! The leopards come and get them, or else they get turned into vine leaves, in Ezra Pound [Canto 2], when they practice god-slight, the insult to Dionysus.

YOUNG: The problem with that approach is that as long as your meat is young and attractive, you're doing o.k. But if it doesn't meet the standard...

GINSBERG: When you get to be my age, that's when you really appreciate orgies, in the dark when nobody sees anybody and doesn't give a shit who they're being screwed by. The paranoia in Turkish baths, are you acceptable or not, is another problem. But orgy is one way for people to equalize—for fat people, thin people, handsome people and ugly people, hunchbacks and one-legged people and rachitics all together in the dark.

Peter and I used to get into scenes in San Francisco with girls and boys together, very nice. He liked girls, and that situation would set up a nice vibration when other men would come in. Since Peter and I were already close and making it, that opened the door to anybody. He'd make out with girls and I'd make out with boys. Sometimes I'd make out with girls too. Or we'd make out with each other. We had a two-year period in San Francisco where almost every party we went to we took off our clothes and wound up in bed with one or two people. We didn't try to start orgies; we just took off our clothes, wandered around the party, had a good time and didn't make a big scene out of it.

YOUNG: When I saw the dedication of *Howl* and found out about Carl Solomon, I was curious as to your relationship.

GINSBERG: That was never an erotic relationship. I went to a mental hospital in 1948 as the result of a bust involving grass and stolen cars—a typical, college fuck-up bust. In the old days when you were from a genteel family they sent you off to a bughouse to get out of going to jail. So it went through that middle-class resolution to my bust. I wound up in the New York State Psychiatric Institute on 168th Street.

The day I walked in with all my bags I met this big fellow [Carl Solomon] just coming up from electric shock. I was waiting to be assigned a room, nervous and strange and wondering what I was doing in this psychiatric institute with all these people supposed to be crazy. And a little worried that I'd lost my grip on reality.

Carl Solomon asked me who I was. He seemed so intelligent and literate that I wanted to see if he had any soul. So I said, "I'm Prince Myshkin" (a saintly character in *The Idiot*). And he said, "I'm Kiriloff (a hard nihilist in *The Possessed*). So we had a funny understanding. Then we had a literary time, writing imaginary letters to T. S. Eliot. He introduced me to Genet's work and to Artaud's work. He was very learned in French literature and surrealism. He turned me on to a lot of French literature that I'd missed. Then he took me down to the Village, and I began digging the whole subterranean Village of 1949–50 through his eyes. He's written several little collections of pithy *contes*—stories and aphorisms.

He's still a friend and was here about a month ago. A couple of times a year we get together and spend some time. He was heavily ideologically Marxist at one time and then anti-Marxist. He went through all sorts of chameleon-like mad changes, searching for a sane way of approaching the fact that everybody in the world is mad, anyway.

YOUNG: I remember hearing that around the time of the original excitement about LSD, Timothy Leary made some statement saying that it cured homosexuality. I recall you said you had a heterosexual experience under the influence of LSD.

GINSBERG: [I had] an emotionally heterosexual fantasy experience in relation to my mother and girls. But everybody has that on LSD. It was a breakthrough of heterosexual feeling/emotion in relation to my mother, and there were so many girls that I'd rejected. When Leary was looking around for information and rationalization on LSD, I told him that it probably would loosen up some of the blocks in homosexuality. The reverse is true, too: it would probably loosen up some of the blocks in heterosexuality, which it's notorious for doing. Leary or someone else carried the ball a little too far on that one, to say that I experienced heterosexual breakthrough for the first time in my life. I've got a venerable heterosexual or bisexual history to begin with.

In the context of the arguments about LSD I gave congressional testimony:

"One effect I experienced in Peru I would like to explain. From childhood on I had been mainly shut off from relationships with women, possibly due to the fact that my own mother was, from my early childhood, in a state of great suffering, frightening to me, and [she] finally died in a mental hospital. In a trance state I experienced in a *curandero*'s hut [in Peru] a very poignant memory of my mother's self, and how much I had lost in my distance from her and my distance from other later friendly girls. For I had denied most of my feelings for them out of old fear. And this tearful knowledge that had come up while my mind was opened through the native vine (some yage) did make some change toward a greater trust and closeness with all women thereafter. The human universe became more complete for me, and my own feelings more complete...."*

YOUNG: When you traveled to the Soviet Union, what were some of the most significant things you learned there?

GINSBERG: The commonly accepted figure around Moscow, among people who

---

*Hearings of the Special Subcommittee on the Judiciary, U.S. Senate, Senate Resolution 199, "LSD and Marijuana Use on College Campuses," June 14, 1966.

are in the Writers' Union, as well as writers who are not members of the Union but are on the outs, but have been in bughouses or in Siberia, is that between 1935 and 1953 under Stalin twenty million Russians were arrested and sent to Siberia and fifteen million didn't come back. And then outside the Writers' Union, Yessenin-Volpine said the number was fourteen or fifteen million, give or take a million. It's the commonly accepted figure around Moscow.

The explanation for the present heaviness in the Russian mentality, compared say with Prague in 1965, or even Cuba, is that "all the bureaucrats who did that are still holding their chairs and you have to wait for them to die off." The younger poets think that they'll create a cultural revolution with the young scientists, engineers, physiologists, doctors and athletes who all listen to poetry, and that they'll be more liberal.

One poet in the Writers' Union told me that under Stalin almost every family in Moscow had somebody taken away who didn't come back. For instance, Yevtushenko has people in his family who were taken to Siberia and never returned. One thing I heard was that everybody got it in the neck until there was nobody left, and then the police got it in the neck. Stalin created a whole new sub-bureaucracy of police who arrested the old police, who were compromised by killing everybody. There was a twist in the party line, so there were perhaps several waves of police who found themselves in the same situation as the people they arrested; themselves under arrest, exiled, with no coming back. The police who are in now, after Khrushchev, know that, so they don't want it to go too far anymore. The police don't want that kind of absolute, poisonous police state anymore with mass secret arrests. So that is a kind of safety brake in Russia—the police realize that they can't go too far or else they'll be swept up in the terror. I've never seen this explained in the West.

YOUNG: Do you think this is an actual reason for the liberalization?

GINSBERG: It's not so much for the liberalization, as a reason why things are not likely to go back to horrific Stalinism. The people that would have to carry out the worst police state orders realize that those orders would finally be carried out against them. Stalin was so strange, so weirdly humored, with such a sinister sense of humor, that no one wants to get into that box again. The police got smart finally, realizing that it was their karma that got trapped.

YOUNG: Did you ever go through a period where you idolized the Soviet Union before you went there?

GINSBERG: No. My mother did. My mother was a Communist in Paterson, New Jersey, and she took me to Communist Party meetings, right off River Street, when I was seven years old, back in 1933. I remember them selling garbanzos. And I heard Israel Amter speak, and Scott Nearing, in those days. In my family, among my aunts in New York and the Bronx, there was an idolization of Stalin, the party line. My father was against it, as a Socialist. On the other hand, my father went all the way to the other extreme; between 1961 and 1965 he was still backing the war in Vietnam. So between the Scylla of Stalinism and the Charybdis of anti-Stalinism, there was not much of a left in America, really, until the independent hippies came along, with the beatniks really, and introduced a whole new anarchism, which was the old American anarchism like the Wobblies, up to San Francisco and Kenneth Rexroth. That was always a viable tradition of intellectual anarchism, communalism, free love.

YOUNG: Did the 1950s hipsters all think of yourselves as anarchists?

GINSBERG: Oh, yeah. Kenneth Rexroth and Robert Duncan back in 1948–49, in San Francisco (I wasn't there); and in 1943–45 Brother Antoninus and Philip Lamantia, both poets, had an anarchist circle in San Francisco. They were reading Kropotkin, and gay lib was accepted among them. That was the traditional bohemian-Anarchist-West-Coast-Wobbly-Chicago-American Populist tradition.

YOUNG: What do you mean when you say that gay lib was accepted among them?

GINSBERG: I mean there were all sorts of gay cats around. Robert Duncan was gay and he was a sturdy member of the anarchist circle, I think. The panoply of tolerances and understandings and gnostic (mystic, psychedelic) awarenesses, as well as social hopes and humors, were already fully developed in the 1940s, and that continued right on through in San Francisco, and in some circles in New York.

YOUNG: In your development as a yoga person, have you come across the somewhat anti-homosexual writings of certain yoga masters?

GINSBERG: No, I've never seen any of those. A couple of months ago I got into a conversation with a teacher I'm working with now, Chögyam Trungpa Tulku, incarnate lama, and asked him what he thought about homosexuality. He said he thought it was interesting. I asked him if he thought it was negative or bad. He said, "No, it doesn't make any difference what forms the bodies are; the important thing is the communication." This is very sensible, clear and really important. With communication overt, homosexual lovemaking is obviously terrific and charming. Without communication it's a drag, and heterosexuals the same.

YOUNG: I've always felt there was something particularly mystical about two men doing sixty-nine, something in the configuration of the bodies.

GINSBERG: Yes. There's a mysticism when you screw somebody in the ass, or in being screwed. There's a mysticism in being screwed and accepting the new lord divine coming into your bowels—"Please Master." There's a great mysticism in a girl being screwed, or climbing on a guy. Any position is mystical.

The official answer of my Tibetan teacher was interesting: the quality of the emotion is important; communication is important. And the form is not, obviously.

There's a tradition against marriage in the Gelugpa, a yellow-hat sect of Tibetan Buddhism. It slowly evolved historically that the monks all make it with each other. But basically the bias, if any, in yoga is toward chastity, retention of sperm. Sperm is art, poetry, music, yoga. Sperm is *Kundalini*, serpent power: a shivering tingling that runs and takes over the top of your head and spreads throughout the whole body. Retention of sperm is apparently one of the basic understandings of some forms of yoga.

So it's not really homosexuality or heterosexuality that would be disapproved. It would be attachment to any kind of "pleasure," as a neurotic attachment. As Burroughs might say, an attachment to the green goo factory, an attachment to body. The body itself may be the by-product of a large-scale conspiracy by certain forces as Burroughs says, trying to keep people prisoners in a prison universe made out of parent matter, subjected to appearances and apparent physical conditions defining their limitations. As Blake, the Buddhists, and Burroughs would say, the real world is a world of complete, blissful, empty silence. In other words, the anti-body yoga position is not anti-homosexual; it's pro-empty or pro-transcendental. We are so free of our bodies that we are able to stay in them; and it's all right to be in them and use them. That's the Buddhist position. You're so free of the body you don't have to be afraid of it.

We have the question of what is sex, which William Burroughs has addressed himself to. He's one of the few gay lib "heroes," one of the few homosexual theorists who has theorized up to the point of outside-of-the-body, and detachment from sexuality. In fact, the cut-ups were originally designed to rehearse and repeat his obsession with sexual images over and over again, like a movie repeating over and over and over again, and then re-combined and cut up and mixed in; so that finally the obsessive attachment, compulsion and preoccupation empty out and drain from the image. In other words, rehearsing and repeating it over and over, and looking at it over and over, often enough. Finally, the hypnotic attachment, the image, becomes demystified. His particular sexual thing is being screwed, because Burroughs can come when he is screwed; he's one of the few men that can.

YOUNG: You mean without manipulating himself?

GINSBERG: Yeah... look, no hands!

YOUNG: I remember he has that image in *Naked Lunch,* but I couldn't believe it.

GINSBERG: Burroughs and I made it a lot over many years, back in '53, so I know his body. And there's the image of the hanged man in Burroughs, the guy that's being hanged and coming involuntarily. At the end of "The Blue Movie" [episode in *Naked Lunch*], there is a sequence of rehearsals over and over again, like cut-ups of the same scene and the same characters over and over: getting hung, and spurting, and the hangman coming up and sucking it, and Mark coming up, and Mary coming up and gobbling at his crotch just as his neck is being snapped, and he's involuntarily coming—just as Burroughs involuntarily comes when being screwed. At the end of that "Blue Movie," they all appear on the screen, bowing, tired, a trickle of saliva, or come, on someone's lower lip, a rope around Johnny's neck, Mary completely worn out and tired. The image is completely washed out through experience.

That's very early Burroughs—'58 or '59—and leads to more and more cut-ups of his most favorite and tenderly sentimental images. He can finally look at it at the end of the spool; he can look at his most tender, personal, romantic images objectively, and no longer be attached to them. And that's the purpose of the cut-ups: to cut out-of-habit reactions, to cut through rehearsed habit, to cut through conditioned reflex, to cut out into open space, into endless blue space where there is room for freedom and no obligation to repeat the same image over and over again, to come the same way over and over again.

So Burroughs is one of the very few gay liberation minds who is thinking in ultimate philosophical terms about sexuality, about the nature of "apparent sensory phenomena" (that's his phrase). He's one of the few that has actually questioned sex at the root—not merely rebelled from heterosexual conditioning or heterosexual, social/moral fixed formations—to explore love between men as he has experienced it. He's seen it inside and ouside, divine and degraded. But also to go beyond that and look at it through the eyes of a Sufi or a Zen master, or a sufud adept Tibetan monk saying, "Ah."

Burroughs has contributed a great deal of space which a new generation hasn't yet caught up with. His style was picked up by younger people. The whole cut-up-collage thing did influence even underground press writing quite a bit. The further philosophical, practical Yankee examination of sensory phenomena perception that Burroughs had gone into still awaits discovery by the gay lib left. Otherwise, you just get into some kind of a funky scene. There are a lot of young kids who carry sex banners and march around saying sex, sex, sex, great, great, great—doing it humorlessly, reacting to just the initial superficial attraction.

Let's see, what haven't we covered? I asked Swami Shivananda where I could find a guru, and he told me, "Your own heart is your guru." The main slogan, instruction, teaching, compass and fidelity of the whole love situation is the heart which must always be followed because there's no other place to go. And that will dissolve perplexities of ideology, or complexities of the political fix we're into. Following the heart a little more—there's a way of avoiding the pitfalls of hyper-intellectual, ideological dead ends, which both homosexuals and radicals have gotten into.

Rely on your feelings and trust your feelings. I think a lot of homosexual conflict comes from internalizing society's distrust of your loves, finally doubting your own loves, and therefore not being able to act on them. The other thing is I think it's important to accept rejection because the more you learn to accept rejection, the more you leave yourself vulnerable to be rejected, the more you have a chance of getting laid, of scoring, both for heart and for cock. The more you open yourself up and give yourself, continuously without rancor, and accept rejection from people who are either too timid or are afraid socially, or who just don't want you ... the more open you'll be to your feelings, the more you'll communicate, the more likely you'll just connect.

One of the greatest difficulties, especially for the younger sexualists of all kinds, is the fear of making a move, because they're afraid of being rejected. So, the only thing is frank revelation of the heart: that applies politically, subjectively, personally.... It's the lack of trust in the heart that's messed up radical mentality as well as sexual mentality in America. If we don't interest ourselves in your hearts and accept our hearts, if we don't find our reality in our hearts, then the rest is a perpetual void of intellect, Urizen, Blake's Urizen, your-reason, rationalization, common error, and, ultimately, the heart becomes brightly empty. Thinking of that in terms of making judgments politically: does Tom Forcade have a brightly empty heart, or does he have a heart loaded with silver shit? Is Mark Rudd's heart brightly empty this day as he goes to the anonymous cafeteria for his oatmeal? Is Mother Machree's heart brightly empty as she comes out of the Capri bar at 3 a.m., leaving the most beautiful boy in San Francisco with long curls flowing down his lion-like shoulders with a smile in his eye and pearly teeth showing in the moonlight?

> *Beauty is but a flowre,*
> *Which wrinckles will devoure,*
> *Brightnesse falls from the ayre,*
> *Queenes have died yong and faire,*
> *Dust hath closde* Helens *eye.*
> *I am sick, I must dye:*
> *Lord, have mercy on us.*

This is "Time of Pestilence" (1593) by Thomas Nashe. It's maybe *the* great poem in the English language, and the greatest line is "Brightnesse falls from the ayre"...

* * *

EDITOR'S POSTSCRIPT: In the above interview Allen Ginsberg mentions Gavin Arthur in connection with Edward Carpenter and Walt Whitman. The following document which attests to that line of "gay succession" originally appeared in *Gay Sunshine* 35 (1978). It is published here for the first time within the pages of a book. It is preceded by biographical notes on the two principals involved.

GAVIN ARTHUR (his real name was Chester Alan Arthur III) was the grandson of President Chester Arthur. Educated in fashionable boarding schools, he was just as happy working on ranches in his native Colorado. He took the name Gavin and worked his way around the world in the merchant marine, panned gold, and even sold newspapers for a living. He was a friend of Havelock Ellis, Kinsey, and other famous sexologists. Gertrude Stein consented to his naming her as the archetypal "Ten O'Clock Dyke." In 1930 Havelock Ellis introduced Gavin Arthur to Dr. Magnus Hirschfeld, the great German gay sexologist with whom Arthur collaborated for several years. Arthur's own philosophy is set forth in his book *The Circle of Sex* (1966).

EDWARD CARPENTER (1844–1929) was a writer and gay mystic and lived in England all his life. Although ordained an Anglican priest in 1869, he soon renounced religion and became a Fabian socialist. Among his works on social reform are *Towards Democracy* (1883-1902), a long unrhymed poem revealing the influence of his friend Walt Whitman; and *Civilization: Its Cause and Cure* (1889). He edited the first gay literary collection, *Iolaus: An Anthology of Friendship* (1902), and wrote the gay anthropological study *Intermediate Types among Primitive Folk* (1916). He is one of the most important precursors of present-day gay liberation. See his autobiography *My Days and Dreams* (1916); also the selections from his writings in *Gay Sunshine* 7 (1971), p. 3.

* * *

ALLEN GINSBERG WRITES: The late Gavin Arthur, San Francisco Astrologer & companion of Sufi Sam, died in 1972 after long loving life. I asked him to set account in writing of his memory of encounter with Edward Carpenter, who in turn, G.A. said, had love encounter with Walt Whitman when, as Arthur said as well, he directed Carpenter to Ramakrishna in India where Carpenter was to travel. Thus this is a document given me by G.A. in 1967 the year of the First Human Be-In in San Francisco.

* * *

GAVIN ARTHUR WROTE: You asked me to tell you about my visit [in 1923 —*Ed.*] with Edward Carpenter, who gave up the chance to be tutor to Queen Victoria's grandchildren and even as a DD crossed the Atlantic steerage to sit for a whole year at Whitman's feet. I was 23 and came up the garden path with the letter of introduction awkwardly in my hand. He seemed to know I was coming for he opened the door and held out his arms. "Welcome my son" he growled affectionately as if he had known me for ever. He did not read the letter but drew me into the cozy study by the fire and introduced me to his comrade George and George's comrade Ted. George was about 60 and was pouring tea. Ted was about 40 and was sticking flowers in a vase. Both were warm in their welcome. I was about 20 and Carpenter about 80.

They all talked to me as if we were old friends. That is what Mother used to call "Le don fatale de la familiarité" which only a few people like Havelock Ellis, Kinsey and F.D.R. possess. We talked about Walt and E.C. gave me the young picture which is the frontispiece of his book about WW. He said Walt would have loved me and the others agreed and my heart beat hard. He also talked about their friend Mrs. Gilchrist and how she had wanted to go to bed with Walt and how gently Walt had put her in her place and consoled her by letting her be his hostess to all the European celebrities that kept coming to see Walt.

I started back to my inn, but Carpenter insisted that I stay for supper. After supper Ted suggested a walk in the moonlight (it was June) and we talked all the time about Carpenter and he said "Why don't you spend the night? It would do Eddy so much good to sleep with a goodlooking young American like you. Even Peter the Great in his old age used to sleep between two of his healthiest guards. It used to recharge his battery, so to speak."

I said I would love nothing better—that next to Whitman I admired Carpenter more than anyman anywhere anytime. Ted said he would put a flea in the old man's ear. Which he did.

We had some matté someone had sent him from Brazil (his mail snowed in from all over the world). Carpenter asked me if I would do him a favor and sleep with him. "George and Ted need a rest," he grinned. He had a growly way of talking like an old dog that growls his affection. The other two went up to bed, and the old man and I sat by the fire. I wish I had had a camera. The firelight on that wonderfully human face with its sensitive bones and rough silver beard, the skin so coppery from the sun, the eyes so blue. He said he was looking forward to dying, to see if reincarnation was really true. I asked him if "The Secret of Time and Satan" was not the distillation of his wisdom—what he had learned from the great YANG guru in America (WW) and the great YIN guru in India. He agreed. I asked him if he had ever been to bed with a woman and he said no—that he liked and admired women but that he had never felt any need to copulate with them. "But that wasn't true of Walt, was it?" I asked.

"No, Walt was ambigenic," he said. "His contact with women was far less than his contact with men. But he did engender several children and his greatest female contact was that Creole in New Orleans. I don't think he ever loved any of them as much as he loved Peter Doyle."

"I suppose you slept with him?" I blurted out half scared to ask.

"Oh yes—once in a while—he regarded it as the best way to get together with another man. He thought that people should 'know' each other on the physical and emotional plane as well as the mental. And that the best part of comrade love was that there was no limit to the number of comrades one could have—whereas the very fact of engendering children made the man-woman relationship more singular."

"Had he no interest in bringing up his own children—in the husband-father relationship?"

"No. He said his women had been married to men of wealth and social standing who could not engender children of their own, but who wanted the children Walt engendered to regard them as father. He said he felt that his mission as Answerer did not require specific paternity and that all the young men of America were his spiritual sons and all the young women his spiritual daughters."

"How did he make love?" I forced myself to ask.

"I will show you," he smiled. "Let us go to bed."

It was a warm night and we had just a light eiderdown over us. We were both naked and we lay side by side on our backs holding hands. Then he was holding my head in his two hands and making little growly noises, staring at me in the moonlight. "This is the laying on of hands" I thought reverently. "Walt. Then him. Then me." I had recently seen some neophytes made priests in Maynooth and their faces had shown the same emotions as I now felt.

He snuggled up to me and kissed my ear. His beard tickled my neck. He smelled like the leaves and ferns and soil of autumn woods. A song my shipmates used to sing obtruded rudely into my worshipful thoughts. "If you can't get a woman, get a clean old man!" Is that what he wanted from me? I remembered Walt's indignant denial to Symonds' inquiry was he a pederast. The old man at my side was stroking my body with the most expert touch. It was as exquisite as the little bubbles that come up from the decaying vegetation in a mud bath, caressing the flesh with a feather lightness.

I just lay there in the moonlight that poured in at the window and gave myself up to the loving old man's marvelous petting. Every now and then he would bury his face in the hair of my chest, agitate a nipple with the end of his tongue, or breathe in deeply from my armpit. I had of course a throbbing erection but he ignored it for a long time. Very gradually, however, he got nearer and nearer, first with his hand and later with his tongue which was now flickering all over me like summer lightning. I stroked whatever part of him came within reach of my hand but I felt instinctively that this was a one-sided affair, he being so old and I so young, and that he enjoyed petting me as much as I delighted in being petted. There are so many possible relationships, and one misses so much if one limits oneself to one sex or color or age.

At last his hand was moving between my legs and his tongue was in my belly-button. And then when he was tickling my fundament just behind the balls and I could not hold it any longer, his mouth closed just over the head of my penis and I could feel my young vitality flowing into his old age. He did not suck me at all. It was really *karezza,* which I knew he recommended in his books. I had not learned the control necessary to *karezza* and he did not want to waste that life-giving fluid. As he said afterward, "It isn't the chemical ingredients which are so full of vitality—it's the electrical content, like you get in milk if you get it direct from the cow—so different from cold milk!" He was in no sense a succubus like so many old men, draining the young men of all the vitality they can get, like a vampire. The emphasis was on the caressing and loving. I fell asleep like a child safe in father-mother arms, the arms of God. And dreamed of autumn woods with their seminal smell.

The next morning he made love to me again, this time gazing at my body rapturously between kisses and growling ecstatically. And the same thing happened at the end. I had the distinct feeling that he felt my coming as if he were coming himself—that in that moment he *was* me. Afterwards he said: "When I was a clergyman I thought at Communion I was at one with God. But I realize now that this is a much more intimate communion—for is not Man made in the image of God? And I have reason to believe that this was the beginning of the Communion Service—the young man laid out on the altar to be circumcised—and all his male relatives eating his 'body' and drinking his blood." Much later I heard Kinsey lecture on this subject and say this was still practiced in very remote Jewish communities near the Caucasus. Carpenter had been dead for many years but in that western lecture hall I could see him bending over me so reverently and hear his loving growl.

PHOTO BY PETER HUJAR ©

JOHN GIORNO

JOHN GIORNO was born in New York in 1936. He is founder of Giorno Poetry Systems, which sponsored the Dial-A-Poem series (Museum of Modern Art, New York City, 1970; Philadelphia Museum of Art, 1973, etc.). He has published several long-playing record albums of poets reading from their own work: *The Dial-A-Poem Poets; Disconnected; Biting Off the Tongue of a Corpse; Totally Corrupt;* and *William Burroughs/John Giorno*—this last album contains Giorno's long poem "Subduing Demons in America" and shorter poems "Suicide Sutra" and "Eating Human Meat." Among the contemporary poets who have read on these albums are Allen Ginsberg, Frank O'Hara, John Cage, Charles Bukowski, Diane Di Prima, W. S. Merwin, Charles Olson, Sylvia Plath, Jack Spicer, William Carlos Williams, Robert Creeley, Michael McClure, and Anne Waldman. Giorno was involved in the movie *September on Jessore Road* with Allen Ginsberg, 1971. His own books of poems include *American Book of the Dead* (1964), *Poems* (1967), *Balling Buddha* (1970), and *Cancer in My Left Ball* (1973). His work has appeared in many anthologies, among them *Anthology of New York Poets* (1970), *Angels of the Lyre* (1975), and *Orgasms of Light* (1977).

THE PRESENT INTERVIEW with John Giorno was taped in July 1974 in San Francisco at the apartment of Winston Leyland, editor of *Gay Sunshine* (see biographical note on p. 326). It appeared originally in *Gay Sunshine* 24 (Spring 1975).

Winston Leyland interviews
JOHN GIORNO

LEYLAND: Why don't we talk about your recent trip to India as a start?

GIORNO: My first trip to India was before I got sick and my second was after. I have a teacher who lives in Darjeeling. His name is Dudjom Rinpoche. I go there to see him. This last visit was very brief, four months, three in Darjeeling and a month in Calcutta. I love Calcutta. In Darjeeling I lived in a Tibetan monastery where I did a five-week retreat. It's like no matter how much you want to change it, you will always find yourself sitting in a Greyhound bus station waiting room. And you work at it. You are given specific meditation practice, which quiets the rattle of your internal dialogue or you might say transforms it, so you get into the space inside and around you, and play with the energies reality is made of and not made of. Your mind is like the person who never shuts up, who just keeps talking and talking and talking to you, until you say, "Listen, man, please shut up. I can't take it anymore." And everything gets quiet for a while. It's like this idea, plus a lot of expansiveness and giving in to the situation. There are specific disciplines, which are as excruciatingly painful as they are alternately blissful, and totally boring.

LEYLAND: What was involved in these disciplines?

GIORNO: It's Tibetan Tantric Buddhism and the idea is to get enlightened. It's a little hard to describe it in a journalistic way, but it's like you're in San Francisco and it's easy to think about Darjeeling; in an instant you see all the pictures, but to get your body there is a whole other trip. You have to get time and money, and get your shots and buy an airplane ticket and then do it. Meditation is like that. I am in the Nyingmapa Lineage. You take refuge in your teacher, who is the Buddha and guides you along a path, a system of practices that lead into or open into each other. After having emptied or quieted your mind, the use of devices such as visualizations and mantra and prostrations produces amazing results. You aren't visualizing an external deity, but projecting some element of your own nature, manifesting it out in space and then reabsorbing it.

LEYLAND: Is this a similar kind of thing to Eastern Orthodox mysticism? The Jesus Prayer? The mantra is the name of Jesus which they repeat over and over. That's on the surface, and below is the inner meditation.

GIORNO: I don't think so. Buddhism is nontheistic and it even isn't a religion. It's a way of being aware of reality. Just emptying yourself.

LEYLAND: Emptying yourself with the idea that the spirit will enter in, or in some other sense?

GIORNO: Emptying yourself because you basically are empty. Except the TV is always on; there's a TV in your mind, you're always tuned in to one channel or another, which prevents you from just being where you are, just being open with the space around you.

LEYLAND: How long do these particular disciplines last; do they go on a few weeks?

GIORNO: They never end. They just vanish. Or the difference between doing them and not doing them doesn't exist.

LEYLAND: When did you go to India for the first time?

GIORNO: In 1971. It was either going to jail again or going completely out of your mind or thinking of some alternatives. It was back in the days when you still thought there were political solutions to the horrors of the world. Abbie Hoffman and I were working on WPAX. We were making radio programs for broadcast on Radio Hanoi. The North Vietnamese government had offered us radio time to broadcast in North and South Vietnam, particularly to our boys fighting there. It was a totally great idea. Abbie's main interest was to get busted for treason. He wanted to be the first poet since Benedict Arnold to be busted for treason on grounds of freedom of speech. Abbie was a visionary. But then there was the usual movement bullshit. Everybody liked to talk a lot and I ended up doing all the work.

LEYLAND: What was involved exactly in this project?

GIORNO: Making radio programs for broadcast on Radio Hanoi to the troops in South Vietnam. It was no different from funky hip FM radio. Good music and talk shows with good music. We had a gay show, and a women's show, and anti-war shows. The idea being that it was information we heard here which was not accessible to the guys in South Vietnam.

LEYLAND: Were there investigations by the FBI?

GIORNO: Vice-President Agnew called us "The Would-Be Hanoi Hannahs." There was a congressional committee ready to investigate us. They were about to descend upon us, which was cool. The hassle was the typical Movement hassle: a community of thirty people, nobody doing anything and everybody fighting about who makes the decisions, and how authority is shared. So it was Abbie battling with everybody and me doing all the work, because I knew how to do it. It got exhausting and depressing and I said, "Fuck It!" I got on a jet plane and flew to India. I had some friends who were living in Almora, and two weeks later I was driven in a VW bus across northern India and found myself in the Dalai Lama's living room with the Dalai Lama. It all unfolded without too much effort. One thing just led to another. I met Nyichang Rinpoche and went to live in Sarnath and after a while was taken to Darjeeling to Dudjom Rinpoche.

LEYLAND: Had you been into the Tantric way before that?

GIORNO: Not really. Just the usual 1960s "take LSD and see Buddha." Then somebody laid "Om Mani Padme Hum" on me. You did the best you could given the fact you didn't know what was happening.

LEYLAND: What do you feel is the main thing you've gotten out of Buddhism?

GIORNO: It has to do with basic sanity, dealing with yourself, using your neurotic pain as something to work with, as a very good place to start, and the people around you and the world around you. It's not getting rid of anything, but using what you got as a basic reality. From this arises a strong clarity.

LEYLAND: It intensified the sensitivity which you had already to the karmas of reality?

GIORNO: Meditation makes perception clearer. Reality is very haunting. It's always there. It's like we all live in a giant haunted house, and the point is make friends with it.

LEYLAND: Did you feel that this clarity came by gradual stages, or just as illumination, say after weeks?

GIORNO: It's very gradual. It can't be measured in time, because everyone is working with a different set of variables. It also comes in leaps and bounds. As for signs of progress, when your meditation is difficult and boring and painful, you are really making progress. You're dealing with ego, so it's when you're about to throw in the rag, give up the whole thing, that's when it's really happening to you, when you're cutting through. This is different from other kinds of spirituality occurring in the United States. Their approach is quite opposite. They make you feel good, bliss you out, and it stops there.

LEYLAND: Are you referring to Transcendental Meditation?

GIORNO: TM and the others.

LEYLAND: Do you want to talk a little about the difference between TM, which so many people are getting into now, and your experiences? Your experiences were mainly in Tibetan Buddhism.

GIORNO: I have great respect for Satchananda, Maharishi, Guru Maharaj Ji, and the rest, but they only take you so far. They bliss you out and leave you hung up there. Which is better than not doing anything at all, but why not go the whole way? In the Hindu yogas, it's all milk and honey, and cheesecake. Making everything good and easy and sweet. Purifying yourself, removing yourself from the problem. Whereas there's this giant shithouse of the world made up of good and bad.

LEYLAND: Would you say that Tantric Buddhism sees the dualism more than the Maharishi and TM?

GIORNO: I think we're aware of dualism. Hinduism is theistic, the belief is the reality of god, Atman. So there's another heaven for you and I've had enough of heaven.

LEYLAND: I don't know very much about Maharaj Ji and his group, but they tend to be very apolitical—wishy-washy about Nixon, for instance. Perhaps they have lost a certain sensitivity to evil.

GIORNO: I love Nixon. He's a great American folk hero, like Billy the Kid or Jesse James. He did more to destroy the authority of the president than any other man in history. They should write folk songs about Nixon. If you just look around, you can see all the realms of Samsara. What you read classically as heaven and hell are not just abstract phenomena. The god world is the super-rich, the billionaires, the Rockefellers and Mellons and Duponts living in ignorance with everything money can buy, all the pleasures and comforts; and the Asuras are the Pentagon and the B-52 bombers and nuclear-warhead missiles and hundreds of billions of dollars in weapons; and hamburgers and juicy steak, the sad world of the animal; and being burned by napalm or a mortar rocket is a hell world; and dying of starvation in Bangladesh is either a hell world or a hungry ghost world. A lot of heavy cruising in the gay world could be described as pale hungry ghost.

LEYLAND: You're saying that groups like TM tend not to see these distinctions, tend to blur good and evil.

GIORNO: They avoid dealing with them, they remove themselves from the problem, which doesn't make the problem any less real. But I'm not suggesting anyone get involved in politics. However good the intentions, politics tend to waste all your time, consume your energy, confuse you with a lot of hope, and all of that is totally beside the point.

LEYLAND: But it isn't good to go to the other extreme either. Take Rennie Davis for instance. I talked about this with Harold Norse [see pp. 234-235]. Davis went from one extreme of making political activity almost a religion, a constant drive, to the other extreme, a complete dropout from all political activity, a belief that all is hopeless and the answer is in the Guru. I've always thought that the ideal should be something in between: not where you're immersed in politics to the point of not having a spiritual center in yourself, but having both a spiritual center and an awareness of political realities, and sensitivity to the evils that you're talking about. I gather from what you've said that you've found some kind of golden mean.

GIORNO: Buddhist meditation. It's like everybody has a living room or a bedroom or at least a bed or a place to sleep. Each person's place is very intense, because it's an extension of themselves. They generally fill it with some kind of activity, working on something, or cleaning, or talking to someone, or talking to someone on the telephone or watching TV when there's nothing to do, or just talking to themselves, having this dialogue go on inside their head. So all you got to do is stop the talking, let the internal dialogue fall away, quiet the mind and be where you are. In that space you do nothing and you deal with whatever arises as it happens. It's very joyful.

LEYLAND: And you've found that this awareness has permeated your life from day to day?

GIORNO: It's the same space. Right now.

LEYLAND: In your last book, *Cancer in My Left Ball,* you talk about your illness. Maybe you could talk a bit about that? Did your illness come before that book was finished?

GIORNO: The poems were being written at the same time the cancer was growing. Only I didn't know both things were happening. I thought I was just writing poems. I knew something was wrong, but who likes to go to a dentist? Actually I was living on Allen Ginsberg's farm in Cherry Valley. Allen had had a hernia operation and we went over to the Cooperstown hospital to have his stitches taken out. I mentioned it as a joke, that my ball was the size of a hard lemon, and he mentioned it to the doctors, and the doctors whipped me into a room and made an instant diagnosis: "Operate!" And I said to them, "Hold on, folks! Let's not rush into anything." Then I came back and went through these tests, and they painted a dismal picture and said I should be operated on. I said, "Don't call me,

I'll call you." This was the summer of 1972, and Allen and I were about to leave for the Democratic and Republican conventions in Miami Beach. There was no choice. Miami we went. The last attempt at a political solution. I wasn't having any part of the idea that I had cancer. I didn't want to hear about it, and Allen kept bringing it up, and telling everybody to tell me to go to the hospital. They were getting to me.

Then I gave a reading in St. Mark's Church, and we had a party in the church afterwards. It was Nanao, this Japanese Zen Buddhist yogi, who got to me. He said, "You look sick." So the next day I went to Bellevue Hospital, and they said, "We're not letting you leave the hospital. You're being operated on today." I couldn't believe it, there are these perfect strangers saying they want to cut one of my testicles off. I said, "Wait a minute! I promise I'll be back in three hours, just let me out of here." I managed to dance out the door. Actually I was pretty depressed. I called Anne Waldman and went to see her, and she called her doctor, who said I should go to Memorial Hospital, which is the cancer hospital. Bellevue is the dirty snake-pit horror of all time. I took a taxi up to Memorial with Anne, crying in the taxi. It was so intense, so sensational. It was one of those situations where there's no way out. Memorial made all these tests and checked me in. It's really amazing when those things happen to you. I mean you say to yourself "Wow, look at all the bad karma I'm shaking off." It happens in meditation when you're in progress. To let go of obstacles is sometimes painful. It sometimes goes in leaps and bounds, and the leaps and bounds manifest themselves in reality. The reality is inescapable pain and suffering, sickness and death. Poisons come out of you, when they normally would remain hidden or unexpressed.

LEYLAND: You mean many of the negative qualities of one's character become clarified?

GIORNO: The situation arose out of cause and effect. The cancer is a result of something. I think we're a storehouse of agonies we will have to live out, caused by action in the past. Of course it isn't all bad. Along with the agonies are bathtubs of bliss, and oceans of boredom of everyday life. I think the point is to get rid of both things, all the bad and good karma, so there is no karma. The result of that is totally amazing.

LEYLAND: What is involved in getting rid of good karma?

GIORNO: You just lay back and smoke good dope, just having a good time and not being too aware of what's happening. Americans are experts in this area. We consume sixty percent of the world's resources, each of us has riches and leisure by general world standards; our lives are filled with wealth of consumption and we fight these incredibly cruel wars, with hundreds of billions of dollars of weapons. Then you break that down into specific images, like the average two-car suburban household, or the Vietnam war or the hungry-for-oil Twilight of the Gods. It seems that America has become a cancer on the earth. Then cancer becomes the national disease and I get my ball cut off, and the president's wife gets one tit cut off, and the vice president's wife gets both tits cut off. So the book of poems were written in those two years, during which I had cancer, and they essentially deal with American karma. It all seems connected.

LEYLAND: So all of the poems had been written, and then you decided to name the book *Cancer in My Left Ball*.

GIORNO: Yeah, I thought it was a good idea.

LEYLAND: I think it's a very arresting title.

GIORNO: It is being in hell. They cut off your ball, which is easy enough. Then they do a biopsy and find that you have four kinds of cancer: embryonal cell, corial, teratoma and seminoma. And they give you all these statistics on how long you have to live, if you had each one separately. Nine out of ten die in one year. They try to get you to have this second operation. At this point it sounds convincing enough and "What the fuck! Do anything you want to me, I don't care." So they slit open your stomach and take all your intestines out and your liver and whatever else is in the way. They cut out fifty lymph nodes going up your spine. Then they stuff all the intestines and meat back into you, clipping it together with forty steel clips, and sew you up like a turkey. It is being in the deepest of the hot hells, where the pain is so ceaselessly agonizing that it's like a continuous flash of white lightning.

LEYLAND: After the operation? While it's happening you're anesthetized.

GIORNO: First they shoot you up with morphine. Then they cut a little slit in the vein in the crook of your arm, and they stuff a plastic tube up the vein into your arm and down into your heart. They feed the anesthetizer into the plastic tube and into your heart. Afterwards they feed you intravenously through the tube, and a week or so later when they pulled the tube out, they pulled three feet of tube out of me. I couldn't believe it. It didn't hurt. You tend to become desensitized. They're shooting you up with Demerol every hour and a half, twenty-four hours a day. So it doesn't hurt so much, but you are sort of conscious of everything that's happening from beginning to end.

LEYLAND: But the pain afterwards was intense?

GIORNO: Yes, but you just learn to deal with it. And it actually isn't so painful. It's like the pain in any situation, like sitting in this room or watching television or not watching television, except it's more intense. Anyway I just wanted to get out of that hospital. So I told the doctors to stop giving me the painkillers and after two weeks I checked out and got on an airplane and flew out to Jackson Hole, Wyoming, and saw Trungpa Rinpoche, who was giving a Padma Sambhava, a crazy wisdom seminar. It was December and it was really cold and we would take these hot sauna baths and then run out naked and roll in the snow. When you're that hot, the snow is warm. I think it was the shock of it that jolted me back to life. Among other things, cancer is sort of an internal schizophrenia. Some of the circuits get crossed or go haywire, and you start consuming yourself. I have no idea whether it's gone or not, but I feel terrific. Meditation is a way of cutting through that poison.

LEYLAND: Do you tend to devote a certain period of every day to meditation or do you try to integrate it into your life?

GIORNO: Both those things. I do a formal meditation practice, and the clarity or space that it creates I try to bring through the whole day.

LEYLAND: There was a similar practice in medieval Christian meditation—Dame Juliana of Norwich, for example. The Jesuits ruined it later with their Ignatian exercises. Fortunately, true mysticism and meditation were maintained by Teresa of Avila and John of the Cross. How long do *you* meditate?

GIORNO: An hour and a half in the morning. What happened to Christian meditation is they lost all the teachings. Rome destroyed all agnosticism or nondual teachings by feeling threatened by it. Well, if there's any truth that's inescapable, it is, "I can't get no satisfaction. I can't get no satisfaction. No, no, no! 'Cause I try and I try and I try and I try."

LEYLAND: Maybe we can talk about the evolution of your poetry. Your first book of poems came out in 1967. Had you written much poetry before that?

GIORNO: I've been hauling ass for a long time. You might say I've been writing poems since puberty. Somewhere in the early sixties, it seemed totally beside the point to go on scribbling things on pieces of paper. So I stopped writing for a year or two. Also it seemed at the time that all poetry being written was incredibly boring. I mean among the world of poets I knew, the New York School of Poets, etc. I'm not going to make any judgments, but it all seemed totally out-to-lunch.

LEYLAND: Don't you think some exciting things were happening in the late fifties and early sixties?

GIORNO: Yes, but Allen Ginsberg and Kerouac and Frank O'Hara did what they did in the 1950s. I mean, by the 1960s they were still doing the same thing, a little weaker, and a whole new generation was happening. Anyway, about that time, 1962, my friends were artists, painters and sculptors. Andy Warhol and the Pop Artists. It was a working situation. Everyone was just working and living and seeing each other every night. How I started doing found poetry was I read a lot of newspapers and magazines. It seemed more interesting to read *Time* magazine than to read a book of poems. The information was more real and the images were more vivid.

LEYLAND: Are you talking about hard news, like the *New York Times?*

GIORNO: Yes. Just anything: *Time* magazine, the *New York Times,* the *Post,* the *News.* So one day I was reading this article in the *Times* about extinct wildlife in North America and I was totally enraptured with the words. I thought to myself, "This is more interesting than John Ashbery." So I picked up a pencil and made slash marks in the sentence at points where the mind paused. Then I typed it up in a vertical left-hand column. My doing that seemed to light up the image in the sentence and make a poem of it. That was how the first found poem came into being. From there it was a gradual evolution.

LEYLAND: This is similar to the cut-up method?

GIORNO: In a strict sense it's not cut-up. Not the way Brion Gysin invented it or Burroughs developed it. It is simply discovering images that are inherent in reality all around you. Images that glow and appear to have a larger space inside them. Wisdom manifesting in mundane objects or occurrences, symbolically or actually. It just is. And you take it and use it. By taking it out of its ordinary context and putting it in a new context, other people might take notice of it. After a few years of doing this, it gave rise to the long poems. Taking the individual images and weaving them together and splicing them into each other to form a new poem. Essentially in some weird way those long poems seem to me to make use of T. S. Eliot's "objective correlative," where you build successive unrelated images to form a larger whole. I like using images which are prosaic. The garbage of your everyday life, which has a very powerful, funky strength. These days I'm into the words spoken on television. All those words on the news or in commercials or just in the TV programs. These days, not only don't I read books of poems, but I don't even read newspapers and magazines. Anyway the concept is any verbal input, oral or written. Whatever images in words enter your mind, whatever externally comes into you. In recent years I've also included images which arise in my mind from the internal dialogue. So your mind sometimes catches on an image, and you have a special reaction to it. Generally it's for a good reason. You take it and separate it from wherever it comes. When you look back on it later, you are very aware of why you chose it. When you're working on a long poem, it's generally over a period of two or three months, and the poem is a pile of very specific images, both personally and in a larger sense.

LEYLAND: So this began in the early sixties.

GIORNO: Yes. It started simply at first. Then it seemed to me it wasn't good enough. It wasn't interesting to go on doing the same thing. So it occurred to me to double the lines.

LEYLAND: Your poetry is basically oral.

GIORNO: By further splitting and repeating phrases and doubling them, it slows down, stretches the space and makes the mind more aware of it. Then after doubling it, tripling it, because I found musical rhythms developed in the flowing of the words, and two and three and four repeats would build its intensity and make it sing. Chanting. Then as it appears on the written page, doubling it again and making two parallel columns, which further breaks the linear patterns of reading, and besides reading either column, you can read the whole thing from right to left. Expanding the process a little more. Or at a poetry reading, two people can read it, one person reading down the left column and one down the right, and you start playing with the sound of each other's voices saying the same words, and get into really doing it together or bounce the words off each other.... All that gave rise to a bunch of books of poems. First is *The American Book of the Dead,* a part of which was published in *Poems by John Giorno;* then came *Balling Buddha,* published by Kulchur Press; then came *CUM,* published by *Adventures in Poetry;* then came *Cancer in My Left Ball,* published by Something Else Press.

LEYLAND: So you feel that your themes come from many areas?

GIORNO: Yes. Any speech input: words you see written, spoken, heard on the radio, heard on TV, just the reality of speech. You are picking up manifestations of wisdom, which appear in the form of an image. My whole take on art is that art is not an amusement, is not entertainment. If it is painting, it is not decoration. The whole point of poetry is to cut through the person who is hearing it, destroy the conceptions they have, pull out the rug from under them and let them deal with it from there.

LEYLAND: Your poetry does do that. There's a clarity that is similar to some of the things you were talking about in Tantric Buddhism. It comes through when one reads them or especially when one hears them. I found that happening to me in "Suicide Sutra." Do you feel you're getting into this more in depth and exploring new ways of doing this? Or do you feel you're following similar patterns of writing? To what extent do you feel your writing on this level has evolved?

GIORNO: I just do what occurs to me. If an idea comes to you, there are a couple of possibilities: it's a good idea, it's a bad idea, it's a boring idea; you want to do it, you don't want to, you can't or you're doing it. It's spontaneous and it's like surrendering to the possibilities. Then because we all have personalities, we develop our style. Which is just like a person's face. Then you use your style and the skills you've been developing, and they become stronger and more potent. My karma: "I'm John. I look a certain way. I talk a certain way. I've got these recognizable human features—arms and a head." You might say style, in the best sense, is skill, and your skills develop and become stronger and more potent. Until they get weaker, and you die a ravaged old man. It's an old story. So you become easy with it, which becomes openness. From there arises whatever you should do and whatever will happen. And then you truck your ass working at it.

LEYLAND: Are you somewhat influenced when a particular poem really zaps people? Then do you ask yourself why this particular poem has been so effective?

GIORNO: I would say so. When you're doing something, you don't really know what you're doing, and it's more by mistake than not. So when you do something that really works, you get into what it's doing to people, and an amazing amount of possibilities open up, which lead to more possibilities. And it's all horribly painful.

LEYLAND: What is your life like in New York now? You said you're living in a loft in the Bowery?

GIORNO: I live in a loft in a building that used to be a YMCA. It was built in 1884. I'm in this giant room with fifteen-foot-high ceilings and huge Sullivan windows and a baronial fireplace. I think it was the game room in the YMCA, where the boys played checkers. There's still vibrations there. Then there's the gym, which used to be Marc Rothko's studio, and an abandoned swimming pool and several other lofts. William Burroughs is moving in. He's selling the loft he bought last April and moving into the space that used to be the locker room, below the gym and above the swimming pool. It's got these big porcelain urinals.

It's in the Bowery, which is the skid row of all times. So outside the building are all these drunk derelict bums, lying all over the sidewalk or lying passed out on the curb with their legs sticking into the street and cars come by and don't see them and run over their legs, which get all crushed. Or in the winter the bums just pass out drunk and freeze to death. Or they just die like flies in the flophouses. Where I live is next door to the Prince Hotel and the walls of my building are four-foot-thick brick. So just a few more feet away from my head all the time is this flophouse with totally penniless old men frozen in a booze stupor, crowded together lying in their own piss and shit. Or last winter I was coming home late one night, about two in the morning, and this bum was sitting on my doorstep frozen to death. An ambulance came, but since he was frozen stiff, they couldn't put him on a stretcher. They had to get a wheelchair. Totally hopeless.

I must say living there is very refreshing. It keeps you on very real ground. Pain and suffering and death. You might say it's a charnel ground. But somehow we live in the middle of it in this heaven world. All these famous artists and poets, stoned out, with everything they want, doing everything they want, and most of the time totally unaware of what's a few feet away from them. It freaks me out sometimes. Then a short block west of Bowery starts Little Italy, which is headquarters for the Mafia. It's great—beautiful Italian boys hanging around streetcorners and restaurants riddled with bullet holes from the Mafia murders. Then a couple of blocks south is Chinatown and the great Chinese food.

So you might say it's a great teaching to live in New York. There are all the realms of Samsara in vivid color: the heavens and hells and hungry ghosts and pollution in the air and the pollution which keeps people from being enlightened. You know when it rains in New York and you're walking down a street and a raindrop falls in your eye, it burns, because the raindrop is full of acid which it picked up in the air while it was falling. Anyway I live in a loft, which is this good large space to work in. I live alone when I'm there and I'm there about five months a year. I love New York, because there's this incredible amount of energy to work with, which means there are all these possibilities. I'm into poetry and I work with media—the electronic approach to communication and media techniques for making it happen. New York is the best place to do it, because everything is at your fingertips. All the manufacturers or engineers or fabricators or whatever you need are there. You just have to pick up the telephone and dial with your fingers. It enables you to easily keep twenty-five big projects going at one time. All that consumes a lot of energy, so you tend not to spend too much time in New York, because if you're there twelve months a year, you do it for twelve months a year. You can go insane.

LEYLAND: You can do all these things if you can stand the pace and pressure. I got acute claustrophobia in New York after being there two weeks.

GIORNO: Trungpa Rinpoche says New York is a holy place and people should make a pilgrimage to New York. What more can you ask for, all the god worlds and hell worlds and the hungry ghosts and cruising the trucks and gay bars and wanting and needing and totally being unable to be satisfied. Plus an added attraction is all the riches and power of the world. David Rockefeller and Jacqueline Onassis and a vast assembly of modern-day nobility living in modern-day places controlling and consuming the wealth of the world. Then there's the human world, all these millions of people who live and work and go through all the emotions we've been talking about.

I can never forget I was living in this loft on Fifth Avenue and Twenty-third Street. It was a New York commune. With Wyn Chamberlain and about fourteen people. It was 1969 and we were tripping on Sunshine acid. About three o'clock Wyn said to me, "Around seven o'clock, you should go look out of the front windows." He said it again around six o'clock. At about seven o'clock I remembered. So Wyn's wife Sally and I went to the front windows. The loft was on the second floor with big windows looking out on the street. There was a subway station on the corner. It was winter and it was gloomy and the street was empty. Then all of a sudden little people started coming out of the subway entrance. Short, squat and ugly ugly people scattering like ants going to work. As I say, we were still sailing on orange Sunshine. Then again more people came out of the subway. Fat, ugly people stuffed in big, bulky clothes, and it was cold. We started laughing and laughing and laughing, and it was that total complete laughing blissful joy of LSD. Then more and more came out of the subway filling the streets and it got lighter and lighter. All of a sudden it began to seem totally horrible. These poor pathetic people, totally imprisoned, going through some ghastly routine. Slowly Sally and I started to cry. Ignorance. It seemed more horrible and more horrible and totally hopeless, and we started to cry more and more. Insects crawling out of the ground and scurrying away. Then we collapsed to the floor, screaming and crying and writhing in great convulsions of grief. Great fat heavy tears. It was like your best friend died. Then Wyn came and put his arms around us and said, "It's gonna be all right. I told you to look out of the window at seven o'clock." Actually everyone's just got to look out the window. In New York it just happens to be very intense, but it's the same all over the country. It tends to slow down into the innocuous American style.

LEYLAND: I think San Francisco's a little gentler.

GIORNO: Yes, San Francisco's great, but it's slow and gentle. It's light and love. It has a whole other thing going. Everyone is blond and beautiful and laid back, and it feels to good to live here and in Berkeley. All of that tends to make your mind into mush. Other parts of the country don't even have that going for them. All the possibilities have been scrubbed away with Ajax. Or it's taken an Anacin to alleviate the pain. Then there's all the young people living in the country and surviving well enough. But living in the country, without any formal practice, tends to become rather sleepy. I mean you talk about the weather and you talk about food, because there isn't too much information, but you keep on talking to yourself. America is this juicy compost heap. It consumes so much that it shits out a gargantuan amount of garbage, which is a very rich situation. You might say, organically speaking, that American has more protein in its shit than anywhere else on earth. So it's out of some hell world of the suburban kitchen that all of us arose. Except America tends to want to wipe the possibilities away with some fantastic spray cleaner, which is totally poisonous and kills even the seeds. Or it coats the beauty with some plastic chemical impenetrable film that eliminates anything from happening.

LEYLAND: As in a city like Chicago?

GIORNO: Anywheres in between New York and San Francisco—Nebraska.

LEYLAND: You could be accused of chauvinism.

GIORNO: I didn't make New York. I'm just looking at it.

LEYLAND: But artists do function throughout the country, not just in San Francisco or New York. There's great creativity.

GIORNO: I think America is so intensely repressive, as well as intensely open, so it tends to want to erase or anesthetize the artist, unless he's really able to endure the pain and make it on his own alone. New York is the same, but somehow there's the support of a community. There are a lot of other people working intensely in similar ways, that it forms a sangha. Or more simply a bunch of people working on poetry projects. It's not only New York. There are all these fantastic places with amazing people living in them like Boulder and Santa Fe. It generally takes the shape of an indiscriminate bunch of people living in what could be called a neighborhood, who form a community, who support each other as a system.

LEYLAND: So you feel there's been a supportive community for you in New York.

GIORNO: You see I'm from New York, so I've been there a long time. Fortunately growing up in the late fifties and sixties, you had this automatic dumb access to this artist community. I mean coming from a straight rich middle-class family with all the ego orientations, the only escape was through being an artist, and being with your friends who were artists or poets, who existed in a larger structure of the art world of the Village. Then as time went on the people who you had these magical attractions to were Bob Rauschenberg and Jasper Johns and Andy Warhol, except nobody was famous then; they were just these guys living on twenty-five dollars a month, or hassling with people hating their work, and seeing their friends who were totally into each other's work, plus weird heavy emotional involvements. Now they're these incredible superstar names, but then they were just a heartache.

LEYLAND: How do you feel that fame has affected some of these people—Rauschenberg, Warhol and so on?

GIORNO: It's totally fucked them up. I love them all. They've all been my lovers and I still have a great attachment. But listen man, when you're earning $100,000 a year for fifteen years, it fucks you up. Your ego gets to be the size of a rotting melon. It feels good, oh so good to be rich and powerful and totally adored, because they've never stopped fucking you over anyway. So you have to keep fighting mixed with the momentary calm of power. Then this gigantic ego that has been force-fed by society limits your possibilities. Jasper is the totally great artist, and he's cool in a certain way. But his paintings sell for $200,000 and when he does an edition of a series of lithographs he rips off $500,000. That kind of conceptualization of the success of work in fame limits the way he deals with space in art, because he deals with it the way he feels secure, and in his case it affects the way he deals with the reality of the space he lives. Jasper is not totally open. None of them are into any form of meditation, which would enable them to cut through the situation. Bob just ruthlessly gives away his money. It's horrible.

LEYLAND: It's a major trauma for him to do that? Or not a cathartic thing?

GIORNO: I don't think so. They're all doing the best they think they can do. But it has to do with territory. When you got a lot of territory it feels good and you want to keep it. As soon as it gets threatened, you react in this way, in ways you may think are enlightened, but they're not. You just support your ego more. Listen, those guys are like decadent princes presiding over a vanishing art world. Like where they live. Bob Rauschenberg lives in a giant building which is a former church and orphanage. He lives in the whole building as his residence. And Jasper lives in what used to be a bank. His living room is this huge white marble hall which used to be the inside of a bank and his bedroom is the bank president's office and his incredibly valuable collection of paintings is locked in the vault in the basement. So there are these huge palaces, because Bob and Jasper don't spend so much time in New York anymore. Bob lives in Florida on an island in the Gulf of Mexico, and Jasper lives on St. Martin in the West Indies and in Stony Point up in New York State. They're totally into the bottle. Booze heads, you might say. They're still locked into the scene as it was in the 1950s, only they never dug or went through the drug scene of the 1960s. Jasper and I broke up because he refused to take LSD, among other reasons. I mean I would do some acid and he would get angry with me for doing it. You know what it's like to be on acid and have someone be cross with you. It's horrible. So they're still into being drunk out of their minds, torturing everyone around and torturing themselves.

LEYLAND: Are you saying there's a high incidence of alcoholism among these affluent artists?

GIORNO: It's indigenous. The 1950s of Pollack and de Kooning, and guys like Bob and Jasper, who arose out of the 1950s and made it in the 1960s. I love booze too.

LEYLAND: What about Allen Ginsberg? How do you feel his fame has affected him?

GIORNO: I think it would be fair to say that he's a pushy Jew—speedy and aggressive—whose expertise at public relations makes him rank equal to the boys on Madison Avenue, what Allen fondly calls "Hotspur." His ability to manipulate his own image in the media explains his incredible success. I mean his guru trip in the 1960s. How can you be a guru if you're not enlightened? He's a founding father of the bullshit liberals. He is ravenously desirous, gets angry at the drop of a pin and won't listen to any criticism of himself. His brain is so quick that he will rationalize, twist or justify anything you might say. The only time you cut into his ego is when you say it in the media. He can't justify or rationalize it, because it becomes historical, being in twenty thousand minds, like this *Gay Sunshine* interview. He will scream and scream with hate at me. So Allen is a mess, but at least he's getting the picture that he's a mess, and is beginning to try to do something about it. Which is as much as you can expect of anyone. I think his early poetry is totally great, otherwise it's very uneven.

LEYLAND: By his early poetry, do you mean *Howl*? Before that I think his poetry's very uneven indeed.

GIORNO: Allen Ginsberg hasn't written a good poem in years, and hasn't written a great poem in twenty years. When he wrote *Howl* he was the voice of the moment, mirroring what everyone felt, the moment in a larger sense. Now he's more or less a bad poet and everyone listens to him because he's famous. I think it's as simple as that and it doesn't matter anyway, either way. What happens when you get famous is that people constantly want things from you. You want to give it to them, and you develop these skills and styles, and it becomes easy and you become a very good performer. There are occasionally amazing things he does, like "CIA Calypso" or a poem like "Morning," which is a safe poem for a great poet to write. It feels totally great when five thousand people pour all this energy at you. It's like fucking in a hot shower. Then you want to do it again, you sort of fall in love with it, and you're hooked. What you're doing becomes entertainment, for you and the audience. You're feeding them and they're feeding you. Poetry is not entertainment.

LEYLAND: Perhaps at times that does happen to Allen. He's an enormously good entertainer.

GIORNO: Well, he used to be. I think I've OD'ed on him. His music is simply awful and his blues melodies are worse. At this point no good musician can stand to be in the same room with Allen and his music. They leave instantly, saying, "Man, that's totally great." You might say his whole music trip is self-indulgence in the name of spontaneity. Or, as one young guy in Chicago said on hearing Allen sing, "Is that the same guy who wrote *Howl?*" However, personally Allen is improving. That is, he's into meditation very seriously now, and it's quieted him down. He's down to just working with himself and his own garbage, rather than bellowing out mantras over a microphone to a captured audience, which is totally beside the point.

LEYLAND: You feel that it was good but that it wasn't in the right direction?

GIORNO: It was just beside the point. Allen used mantra as entertainment. I'm sure he was not aware of it.

LEYLAND: His mantras for the destruction of the Pentagon and that kind of thing?

GIORNO: He used mantra as prayer and that's very ego-oriented: "I want this good thing to happen." The idea that you can save the situation. That's just more bullshit, that there is something to save. It serves no useful purpose to sing a mantra to a crowd; you're just entertaining them, making them high, leaving them high and dry. Mantra is very powerful. But it should not be used that way. Mantra is a device of speech that can be used with visualization and has a very powerful effect. Quieting the internal dialogue rattling in your mind and releasing extraordinary internal energies, which can be a dangerous thing. So you should do it with the instruction of a teacher. Tantric practices are very complicated and in progression, and not doing it properly can really weird you out. Or block any real dealing with your space.

LEYLAND: As you say, Allen's getting into the Tantric approach, but he's also doing the chanting of mantras in public too. For instance, in the concert he gave in San Francisco recently.

GIORNO: I know. Allen is hopeless.

LEYLAND: I felt it was a cathartic experience for the audience. You're right that one doesn't get a deep clarity, but there can be a certain catharsis for at least part of the audience entering into it, and that goes beyond mere entertainment.

GIORNO: What it does is make you feel good for three days, like the touchies and feelies approach or encounter groups. There's nothing wrong with encounter groups. You do what you're supposed to do; you scream or you and somebody feel each other up, and you get accepted by the group, and they say you're doing it right, and it feels good, except it's not enough. You may even feel good for three days. But you haven't gotten anywhere, you haven't gotten to the boring ground that made you freak out in the first place: that it is totally pure to be fucked up. The whole American trip is anesthesia, "Relieves Pain Fast." America's the master of anesthesia. The drug culture is like the drugstore. What it does is separate you from feeling and experiencing the pain of the space you're in, and then letting that pain fall away. Heroin is bogus samadhi.

LEYLAND: Did you feel that as a result of your involvement in Tantric Buddhism some of this pain that you're talking about has fallen away?

GIORNO: It's the difference between looking out a window and looking at a wall. Or you've just continued looking at the wall after the paint's dried. Or that the wall is really opaque or transparent. If there is still pain, then you know where it came from, from your fucked-up neurotic mind. If you realize what causes it, then you can let it fall away. Or you can breathe into it and transform it.

LEYLAND: You're talking about neurotic pain?

GIORNO: Yes. All pain is that, essentially. It just manifests itself in a billion different ways: the Ajax woman on TV scrubbing away at her sink, or cancer in your tit, or you're waiting for the subway at Fourteenth Street and you're freaking out on a January night. You name it, you got it. Neurotic pain is that you can't see the sky from the clouds of pollution in your mind. The sky over New York City.

LEYLAND: How do you feel that your growing fame has affected you?

GIORNO: I want to become famous, so I can make a lot of money. How's that? It's my 1970s theme song. Do you remember the 1930s? It's on television all the time, movies of the 1930s. Let me tell you about the 1930s. Everyone was rich and beautiful and wore gorgeous clothes and jewels and furs and had giant cars and huge houses and fell in love with each other. It sounds like the 1970s, doesn't it? The great depression. Otherwise you take it as it comes. I'm anonymous all of the time, except when I get up on a stage or walk into the Museum of Modern Art. Besides being anonymous, I'm getting old fast. I mean old and fat and ugly. I don't know how I am dealing with fame. There's not much choice in the matter. You tend to try to be aware of what you're doing, and this tends to cool you out. You're this poet, and you have all these friends and you love them and leave them, and besides being very boring, it's very vivid. The great thing about poets is they're never paid for their work. Nothing, ever. Or just tokenism. We're all always broke, or you're given enough money to pay the telephone bill or the rent. We're not like the painters and sculptors, like Rauschenberg and Jasper who make $200,000 a year. William Burroughs is broke. He never got paid very much for his work and the millions of dollars *Naked Lunch* made went into the pockets of the people along the way. As Bill said to me last week, "If I was a dentist, and I had reached the prominence in my profession that I've reached, I sure would be well off, Baby." And I tell him, "You're lucky. If you were like Bob or Jasper or Andy or Norman Mailer and they paid you $100,000 a year for twenty years, and then they took it away, you would be totally fucked up. But they never gave you anything, so they haven't anything to take away. When you're lying on the floor, all they can do is kick you, and that's where you started from, and it's good to know you're on solid ground." You see poets don't produce a salable object or a commodity. You can't market it the way you do a McDonald's hamburger or a Jackson Pollock painting. Poetry is a razor blade that cuts through ego, cutting through the ego of American karma. People find it less pleasant than Diana Ross and the Supremes.

LEYLAND: You mentioned that you have two new records out?

GIORNO: Yes. *Disconnected* was just released, which is a two-record album. And we have five more in the works, which will be released simultaneously in September 1975: a William Burroughs album, a Frank O'Hara album, an Anne Waldman album called *White Woman,* a John Giorno album called *Subduing Demons in America,* and a new Dial-A-Poem album called *Biting Off the Tongue of a Corpse.* Giorno Poetry Systems has become an institution. It's called Giorno Poetry Systems Institute, Inc. We've used, as a format, Rockefeller as a Mafia

Don organization. That is, we're a nonprofit, tax-exempt organization with me as president, William Burroughs as vice president, Les Levine as treasurer, and an illustrious board of directors consisting of Marion Javits, wife of the New York senator, Kynaston McShine, curator of painting and sculpture at the Museum of Modern Art, Allen Ginsberg, and Anne Waldman. The foundation is a device using prominent American poets as a group, organized in a way to raise money to continue what we've been doing for the last ten years.

Giorno Poetry Systems has essentially been working with the idea that you have a poet and you have an audience, and at some point between the two, they make contact. They connect in some way and that point of communication is open to a limitless number of possibilities. Traditionally, a poet writes a poem and then mails it to a magazine or publisher or maybe reads it to some people sitting on a chair, and that's the end of it. No more further thought has been given to the process. I've found that the point where a poet and audience meet, where a poem employing some form of media makes a connection, where the two join is a fantastic experience. The energy of the two coming together is what makes the possibilities. That's what I've been investigating and finding new ways of using and developing, which has given rise to an endless number of projects such as Dial-A-Poem, LP poetry records, radio, TV, color video cassettes, Consumer Product Poetry, which are poems replacing the garbage words on the cornflakes box, on the milk container and on the candy-bar wrapper. So instead of reading some dumbness when you're cooking frozen broccoli, you can read John Cage on the frozen-broccoli package. America is so good at developing those techniques. America produces so much. So it's just using and transforming what America is good at doing, producing materialism. Only trying not to produce more garbage.

LEYLAND: Dial-A-Poem was a situation where a person could dial a certain number in New York City and get a poem, a different one every time?

GIORNO: Yes. Dial-A-Poem was on at a bunch of different places. For example at the Museum of Modern Art we had twelve telephone lines, each connected to an automatic answering machine, each holding the recording of a poet reading a work. A person calling would get randomly one of twelve poems, and could call back and randomly get a different poem. All the poems were changed every day.

LEYLAND: There was a big controversy with one of the councilmen in New York because of what were considered obscenities.

GIORNO: There were lots of freak-outs and endless hassles. Which I must say were joyous, if not excruciatingly boring. It's like you got these poets and got this audience and at the point where they communicate, there are the protagonists. The guys who try to throw in a monkey wrench and fuck up the works. But it's these protagonists who bring a great deal of energy to the situation, which makes the situation more dynamic, and that is a crucial ingredient.

LEYLAND: Didn't that affect it to the point of closing it down?

GIORNO: Yes, it never fails. We're all losers, and we wouldn't have it any other way. But before we'd get closed down, we'd have a good solid five or six months. We'd get millions and millions of phone calls and the energy would start to intensify and there would be freak-out after freak-out, which would become part of the intensity of the situation. For example at the Museum of Modern Art. In

1970 the consciousness of the country was very political, so we put on lots of political poems. The idea was to intensify the experience of political awareness. Along with this was the work of Frank O'Hara, John Ashbery, John Cage and broadly most of the interesting poetry that was occurring or happening at the time, plus Bobby Seale, Kathleen Cleaver, Bernardine Dohrn right after the Weather explosion on Tenth Street, Diane Di Prima on how to make a Molotov cocktail and how to go about building a bomb. These were on the day bombs wrecked the IBM building.

The *New York Post* picked up on it and on page two was a two-column story with headlines on how you could call the Museum of Modern Art and learn how to build a bomb. Then the *New York Times* picked up on it because the *Post* had made news of it. Then came the *Daily News* and *Time* magazine. *Time* did a column on the Nation page, which is right at the beginning of the magazine, on how you could call the Rockefeller brothers' museum and find out how to be a revolutionary. They ran the story next to a photograph of a cop shot dead while talking on the telephone in Philadelphia, with the phone in his hand. It read like it was illustrating Dial-A-Poem. A totally unrelated story.

The Board of Directors of the Museum of Modern Art totally freaked out. You might say they had a few moments of panic. David Rockefeller just wanted it stopped, wanted Dial-A-Poem closed instantly, and there's no two ways about it. John Hightower, who was director of the museum at that time, had this twinge of moral consciousness; his WASP righteousness arose and he said firmly: "John is a poet and cannot be censored." He stuck by it and later it was one of the contributing factors to why he was fired from the museum. Then the FBI arrived at the museum. They're so dumb they arrived at the front desk and flashed their badges, asked some questions about Dial-A-Poem and were sent to the ninth floor, where the offices are. Well, you can imagine what the reaction was to the FBI wandering through the offices of the curators. There was this blast of panic. They were totally shook up. The inner sanctum of the Museum of Modern Art violated.

It's really interesting using media that way. Media feeds upon itself, and in doing so creates this giant energy blob. All the publicity we got just made everyone want to call Dial-A-Poem. The telephones rang like crazy. The equipment worked at maximum capacity, receiving 60,000 calls a week and giving out three times that many busy signals. If we would have had more lines, we would have received 200,000 calls a week or more. It turns people on to listening to poetry, which is the point. It should get through to some of them. An opening experience. When you get into that sort of thing, it freaks people out.

LEYLAND: Using American technology against itself?

GIORNO: It's more like transforming American technology. Filling the space with poetry instead of garbage. The commercial is getting people into their own minds to deal with their garbage, rather than just constipating it with more frozen TV dinners. It's interesting why people call Dial-A-Poem. It seems that they call out of loneliness. They dial the telephone out of some anxiety about being bored. They are alone in their space and they want to fill it up, or they're bored where they are and Dial-A-Poem can change it for them. The majority of the calls came between nine in the morning and five in the afternoon, which means in New York people imprisoned in their glass office buildings, sitting behind desks nervously dialing. It would taper off around six o'clock, then it would pick up strongly after dinner around eight or eight-thirty. It would taper off again around one-thirty in the morning. Between 1:00 and 3:00 A.M. there'd be a burst of calls, until about five; between 5:00 and 8:00 A.M. would be the quietest time. When I programmed what poems went on, sometimes I did it for the people who called between 5:00 and 8:00 A.M.

LEYLAND: People going to work?

GIORNO: No, people who'd been up all night. What one is doing is giving people information, information by poets who occupy the same space as them. Information from sixty poets. One selects poems that are particularly strong, or have a strong impact, or clarity.

LEYLAND: Did each poet choose a poem?

GIORNO: No, they would come to my loft and we'd make a tape of them reading a whole bunch of poems, or they would send me a tape, or I would tape them reading to an audience, which is the best, because when a poet reads to a group of people, there is this flow of energy between them and a dynamic situation results. Anyway we had thousands of poems and I would pick from them. There were twelve telephone lines and each day a different poem is put on each line. So I choreographed each day as a whole, each poem played against or with the other poems on the other lines. Somebody calling back would be hit by something totally different yet somehow relating, or another view of what they had just heard.

LEYLAND: The museum did this at two separate times?

GIORNO: Dial-A-Poem was at the Museum of Modern Art. Then at the Architectural League of New York and the Philadelphia Museum of Art and the Museum of Contemporary Art in Chicago and it's been started in a lot of small places around the country. We're going to start it again in New York this fall. Sponsored by ourselves this time. As you mentioned we're a nonprofit, tax-exempt foundation now, and we're raising money so we don't have to be sponsored by an institution, but we will sponsor ourselves as an institution. We're planning to raise a huge chunk of money, so we'll be budgeted for a year and pay everybody who works on it and pay the poets, rather than everyone just doing it free. You might say it's an attempt to make the structure of poetry organic. It's the poets who are the center of the organization, rather than businessmen. Actually it's happening all over the country, with small presses, poets publishing other poets. There is St. Mark's Church in New York, which organizes poetry reading and publishes several magazines, and has started a full-scale publishing company to do books of poets.

LEYLAND: Hasn't there been a tendency to use poems mainly by famous poets?

GIORNO: Most poets you would call famous are just my friends, and they represent generally what poetry is in America. They are fully developed skillful poets plying their trade. Anyway I just talk about them because they're recognizable images, but always at least half the poets are just young people writing poetry that's really interesting. I do the selection, rather than some innocuous bland democratic process. It's the poems I get off on or respond to in some way. It becomes a personal thing, but better that one person has strong feelings than nobody. I mean as opposed to the out-to-lunch academic poets. It's that, seeing

I'm interested in these poems, maybe somebody else would be too, and that may be one of the reasons it's worked.

LEYLAND: I like to do the same thing in *Gay Sunshine*. I make the poetry selections. We've had controversy in the past because some people believe that in alternative newspapers everyone should decide what poems go in the paper. But it's an unworkable system, because there were people who didn't care anything about poetry voting on a certain poem. So you might have half good poems and the rest mediocre. One is always accused of elitism. Someone has to take responsibility, even at the cost of being vilified.

GIORNO: You got to be ruthless. What you like and what you don't like. We've produced two double albums of the Dial-A-Poem poets. So far it's a four-record set. Now you start off knowing that poetry records don't sell. So you get Les Levine to design gorgeous albums and you produce it the way they do a rock-musical album. It's all in the packaging. That's one thing America knows best. Like a Wrigley's chewing gum commercial on TV or "Fly the friendly skies of United." Then traditionally poetry records have been one poet reading his poems for thirty minutes, which is this boring experience. There is scientific proof that most people can't listen to anything for more than ten minutes without their minds wandering hopelessly, and longer than that some hearing mechanism turns off. So on the Dial-A-Poem poets LPs the poems are one to six minutes long, thirty-eight poets on *Disconnected*. The poems are powerful, lead into one another or are juxtaposed to one another so you're constantly held. The idea is that of a rock album, where a side is made up of all these cuts. You can listen to one side as one unit of listening, or they can be played as single cuts, like on the radio. That's one of my pet projects—two- or three-minute poems being played on the radio, along with the three-minute commercials and the pop songs, as a sort of public service. Anyway, since records are sound whether you sing or talk, there is a close connection with poetry.

LEYLAND: So you can just dip into it.

GIORNO: The next three albums are going to be of three different poets. So it's something new to work with. Burroughs' is going to be the greatest moments of a reading tour we did together. Bill's whole approach to reading is timing and sometimes he's more perfect than others. So his record will be the best readings of individual works. The best of Boston, Berkeley, New York. I'm working on it now. We just finished a reading tour and William developed a new routine for it. Two routines, for where we had to give two readings in one city. It's all show biz. The routines consist of work from all the novels, from *Naked Lunch* right up to the one he's in the middle of writing.

LEYLAND: When did you first meet Bill Burroughs?

GIORNO: In 1964, when he came back to New York for his first visit. Then we spent a lot of time together in London and Tangier. I love William. We have dinner together about three times a week and it's going to be a total joy when he moves into my loft at the end of the month. It's really an intense trip living with William. He's one of my gurus. He's a great teacher. The way it's been for the last ten years is we get drunk and stoned together, a quart of Scotch and lots of dope, and we discuss the basic nature of reality. I was pretty lame when I first met him, and he's taught me an amazing amount of things.

LEYLAND: What is Burroughs like? Is he as taciturn in conversation with his friends as he seems to be?

GIORNO: Bill is very shy and gentle. He sees very few people and is very attached to those he sees. He's very quiet and always tries to appear anonymous in any situation. He's into silence now. Stop talking to yourself, stop the internal dialogue and just be with another person without talking incessantly. Then inside he's incredibly funny; he's the funniest man around. He talks just like the dialogue from *Naked Lunch*. He's this aristocrat American folk hero. Besides being the grandson of the man who invented the adding machine. The man who invented the American version of what the Mayan Codices were about. His mother was Laura Lee of the Robert E. Lees of Virginia. One amusing story is his uncle, his mother's brother, was named Ivy Lee, and he was John D. Rockefeller I's first press agent. He took care of all his public relations and thought up the idea that John D. Rockefeller give away dimes to the poor people. Ivy also invented the idea of a press release, and he was so ruthless and so horrible that he was known among the Madison Avenue trade of the time as "Poison Ivy."

LEYLAND: Did Bill Burroughs inherit the Burroughs fortune?

GIORNO: No. When his grandfather died, around 1910, the lawyers sold off all the Burroughs stock, because they thought it was a poor investment. So they never had a giant fortune. William still says, "I've been robbed of all the Burroughs money." They were just rich midwestern upper middle class, living in a large house with a bunch of servants. His brother is an engineer at Emerson Electric in St. Louis, Mortimer Burroughs. When his mother died two years ago, every last dime was gone. About five years ago they sold the Palm Beach house, which was the last property, for $200,000. She went into a nursing home and by the time she died it was all gone.

LEYLAND: Have you been influenced by his writing?

GIORNO: I would think so. When two people see a lot of each other, even though they're working on different kinds of things, there is a magical exchange between them, and ideas grow and develop with mutual influences. Each encourages the other in ways he sees look good.

LEYLAND: Do you know much about Thomas Merton's ideas on linking Christian and Eastern mysticism? Merton's work has had a great influence on me.

GIORNO: I brought Merton's *Asian Journal* to Darjeeling and showed it to all the lamas who Merton talks about in the book and showed them their photographs and they loved it. Chatral Rinpoche remembered Merton very well, and said that he was the most open of all the Westerners who have come, and the most realized.

LEYLAND: He seemed close to developing that link.

GIORNO: Whenever you're getting close, the obstacles really do their thing, and sometimes it wipes you out.

LEYLAND: What kind of attitudes and clarity do you feel you've gotten into your sexuality as a result of your experiences with Tantric Buddhism?

GIORNO: I've become like a rose. A big red rose. You know it has to do with openness, surrendering to the space around you. Being naked and being in that space with another person. Developing openness to cut through the fantasies or conceptualization of the situation. The reason most people are fucked up in relating to each other is that they start the relationship with some preconceived idea about what it is, or who they are, or who the other person is, or what they expect out of it and how much it costs. I mean all the horror of surrendering yourself, abandoning yourself to being.

LEYLAND: Instead of building constructs.

GIORNO: Without air-conditioning. Without conditioning, just where it starts. When you want something, it's always conditioned by something, by some cesspool of karma that's in you, that makes you want something specific, to your own specifications. It seems to me sexuality has less to do with desire than with communication.

LEYLAND: To what extent has this been put into effect in your gay relationships? Do you feel you have explored your gayness?

GIORNO: I'm gay. But since I grew up in a heterosexual world, I tended to duplicate their patterns, wanting the same things they want. I'm this macho asshole. So one cuts through that bullshit, plus a whole lot of other restrictions like attachment and longing. It's like dancing, the freedom of gently and continuously dancing. As opposed to hysterical dancing or getting drunk and stoned and having all your senses blown out, and you're exhausted and wiped out, and you pass out before you get around to making love to anyone. Actually, there's nothing wrong with that, either. It's the continuity, one moment leading to another moment, that's really interesting. As Trungpa Rinpoche says, "It's like a motion picture; where one frame ends another begins." When each moment dies another is born, and if you don't get the picture, when you really die you really get the picture. So you're in this space, and when two people are in this space, it is a powerful thing. Feeling your feelings and feeling your emotions, because the only way you can dance with them is to be aware of them. They are no more real than Johnny Carson. It's a little like a blind man dancing on a subway platform. So you feel the fuckers as they arise, and they become these transparent images, which teach you all you need to know. And you don't get hung up on them, you just kiss them and let them fade away. I hope I'm not painting a too pretty picture. Life is pretty dismal. It's always the same old story. Pleasure and pain, you get this, you lose that. So you just experience them, pain equally with pleasure, and you don't hold on, and they begin to transmute themselves. So after the movie, we're talking about two people fucking. It's all in the concentration, folks. Just keep that few seconds before coming going for hours, and when you shoot, suck the cum back up into your cock and into your bladder, and then feel it rushing into your heart. Then don't start thinking for a while.

LEYLAND: Do you feel this kind of current is tending to happen more in your own life within the past couple of years as a result of Tantric Buddhism? Have there been other influences besides that?

GIORNO: I would say it's Buddha dharma and clearing enough space in your life to do practice. That is, as a start, you make time every day for meditation practice, like an hour every morning, no matter what happens. I mean you start because you don't know anything about anything, no matter how much you've learned, and you're in a state of panic, and you have all these feelings and all these anxieties, and you don't know what to do, except tighten up like a nut or flail your arms about helplessly. Then you find there are alternatives, and you move cautiously in their direction. When you get to know yourself better, you get to know other people better. When you make friends with yourself, you make friends with other people. You just have to give an inch. When you give an inch to other people, you'd be surprised how far it goes. It goes a million miles. Making love is meditation. It's surrendering to the space around you, making love to that space, and when there's somebody in that space, you focus your attention on them. You concentrate on them, you're there with them, and you're not thinking too much, so that the thoughts don't interfere with the flow between you. It's just openness, without too many preconceptions. Having preconceived notions about what you want happens particularly among gay people. I mean you go out for cruising for a particular image, which makes for limited possibilities. Or there is a highly stylized attitude towards sex, which tends to limit feelings and stop the flow between two people. Sometimes it's just acting out fantasies again and again. I love fist fucking and poppers, but sometimes you get the feeling that there are no feelings, just a pornographic movie going in the other guy's head. It's being hung up with a point, with what you want to happen, that blocks the whole thing.

LEYLAND: What kind of point are you talking about?

GIORNO: Being hung up with wanting to make it with a certain type, getting turned on by certain types, and uncontrollable promiscuity, making it with an uncountable number of people continuously. The large number of hours spent cruising each day by gay people. That seems uptight. You find yourself saying "Please come so I can get out of here." I love balling a lot of people. You just got to move slowly. Or surrender to the feeling that you want to extend your relationship with a friend. However you get off being totally bare.

LEYLAND: Are you talking about the difference between traditional gay promiscuity and the political implications of the gay movement? I do feel there has been a spiritual dimension missing in many Gay Liberation manifestos. There's been a certain franticness, maybe to the detriment of the general flow that you're talking about. I think there's a great need for more gay people to enter into gay relationships with this dimension in mind. The usual visual approach may be the reason for encountering one another in this stylized sense. How do you think gay people can become more aware? Are you advocating a mass involvement of people in Tantric Buddhism?

GIORNO: Mass involvement by Americans in Tantric Buddhism would be like 210 million Americans going out to the airport near where they live and trying to get on a jet plane going anywhere. But instead of that, all they got to do is be themselves and allow another person bald ass-naked openness. I mean being with another person is not wanting them, needing them, thinking about them all the time, wanting to be with them all the time, being in love and having it break your heart. You might say that's the world of desire. When you desire something, the idea of gain and loss, acceptance and rejection, tends to turn the whole thing to poison. "Let me out of here, I can't stand it anymore."

It seems to me gayness is just two people who are Buddhas or bunches of energy on one Buddha, and it's just allowing emotions to flow on both sides of being. It's not rejecting any feeling that comes out of you, and accepting all the neurotic behavior as well as the good times which come from the other person. It's giving an inch, to yourself and to another person, going toward it, holding it, and then letting it go. You can do it again. If you're making love properly, there's no two guys, just like there's no man or woman; there is nothing there and it is blissful and you don't know it's blissful because there is no ego. It's amazingly simple. Pleasure and more pleasure and it feels so good and then it ends. But because we're not enlightened, the emotions tend to turn into barriers. What generally happens between people is they want to do it, but something tells them it's going to be weird, or it is weird, and there's a little fear, and you get out of that spot. Whereas there's nothing to be afraid of, and you just surrender and it's light and love, and it falls away. Feeling something is allowing it to happen. Allowing it to happen and not holding on to it, because when you hold onto something, you become afraid of losing it. At that moment you've blown it. When you've done this a number of times, you say, "Wait a minute, folks. I don't want to do it anymore." Your actions become more and more conditioned, giving less and less. Sometimes it makes an inability to relate to anyone, but then it's always very subtle.

Americans are totally hung up on their bodies. It's a case of extreme materialism. For gay people it's blind overconsumption of bodies. For straight people it's never thinking of your body. You are just this thing, you're born and you're fed and your shit is taken away, and you reach a point where you can get rid of your own shit, eat your own steak and potatoes, and drink your own beer. That's about where Americans' awareness of their bodies stops. I don't want to seem to be putting down America. I think it's amazing here. You go to any other part of the world, Africa, the Sahara, South America, India, any part of Asia, and you think back on the United States and the people seem like a bunch of Bodhisattvas. I mean all the Movement politics—Gay Liberation, Women's Liberation, etc.—doesn't exist in any other part of the world. There are a billion women who could not conceive of Women's Liberation. In the context of their lives, they wouldn't know what you're talking about. Gay Liberation doesn't exist except in Europe and America, and Australia.

America is the richest place on earth, and it consumes so much, and it produces a vast amount of garbage, which makes it richer yet, and it starts rotting and worms crawl in and out, but it's this incredible energy, which makes all we've been talking about possible. I have this theory that America was so gargantually addicted to materialism, so hopelessly uptight, that LSD had to be invented to deal with the situation. Acid was the only thing that could slightly open it, like blowing somebody's mind with a sledgehammer, but there was no alternative. And that just left you cruising the supermarket for a way out. . . . Relations between men in other parts of the world is worse, even in Morocco or among so-called bisexual Arabs. They are totally structured by heterosexual society and conditioned by the same poisons.

LEYLAND: Male chauvinism in a different form. I agree with what you say about gayness and the flow of energy. I think Joe LeSueur was right in a recent letter he sent me. He said that *Gay Sunshine* should be more concerned with exploring interpersonal relationships and that kind of thing. I have tried to aim the paper in that direction for some time, to cut down on rhetorical articles and concentrate more on poetry and personal kinds of articles and more in-depth political articles —material which has the right kind of energy flow. What you're talking about in regard to gay energy flow is very simple on one level and yet on another level very hard for Westerners, Americans in particular, who have been conditioned to act in a certain way. Even in the gay culture, there are certain conditioned ways of acting.

GIORNO: Exactly. It's like you're living in this gloomy roach-ridden apartment, and while you were out somebody broke in and robbed the TV and stereo, and you haven't paid the telephone bill and the telephone's been disconnected, and you are totally alone and you are lonely. There isn't even the possibility of anyone coming to visit you, and it's too cold to go out, and the whole thing is like a heartache. Well, what you can do is sit up straight and breathe into it and just keep breathing into it, filling the empty space with love, flood the space around you with love that circulates in and out of you, a spherical field of love. That creates a ground from which to work. A place to begin from. Rather than just staying freaked out and just wanting somebody to jerk you off. It's allowing it to happen in your space.

LEYLAND: I find that kind of thing happening to me on *Gay Sunshine*. I let things flow and articles, poems, graphics come in as I need them, without having to search frantically.

GIORNO: It's a very simple technique: "Don't try too hard." It can be applied to anything. Everybody thinks what's happening to them is the most important thing in the world. Everyone is the center of their own world. When you got everybody doing it, it's a pretty funny scene. I think the point is to work through whatever it is and quiet it. Sometimes it seems that gay people have this extreme sexual orientation, endless wanting just leading to more endless wanting, which can be described as baths or bars or cruising the trucks.

LEYLAND: What do you think about revolutionary promiscuity?

GIORNO: It's a step in the right direction. Toward openness. Marriage is a heterosexual construction, but there is such a thing as two people wanting to extend their friendship, to enlarge their commitment to each other. You might say to be friends in many lives until they reach enlightenment. I don't know how prevalent this practice is. Gay people seem to be so involved with pleasure, and the dissatisfaction that comes from wanting, wanting pleasure and pain.

They tend to be uptight in only allowing the pleasure to happen, with no further involvement, because of not wanting the difficulties that brings, but you can't have pleasure without pain.

LEYLAND: You feel that with many gay people there's an avoidance of pain?

GIORNO: Well, when you've been burned a thousand times, you say, "Listen, man, I know what the story is." You tend to cool out on neurotic pain. "Leave me out of it, folks." The difference between sustained gay and heterosexual relationships is that gay people are pointedly involved with sexuality. Whereas the heterosexual structure is a whole complex of species survival, wives and children, alimony payments, big business.

LEYLAND: Gayness is more than sexual.

GIORNO: Of course. I'm saying one of the obstacles that sometimes happens with gayness is the hysterical search for pleasure. The pleasure becomes a way of trying to escape from the person's everyday life.

LEYLAND: In a recent article, "Indiscriminate Promiscuity," [by Charles Shively; *Fag Rag* 9/*Gay Sunshine* 22], the author felt that this flow can come from indiscriminate promiscuity.

GIORNO: Absolutely. It all boils down to everything is just like pornography. If it gets you off, what the fuck! It's anything you want to make it, any time and any place. It's also an excellent revolutionary device, because it cuts through the conceptualizations of straight society with a clean cut. The point of the pornographic poems I've written is that they break the rules of the heterosexual world. When that very early poem of mine called "Pornographic Poem" got printed in Random House's *Anthology of New York Poets* it became homework in English classes across the country, totally straight American English Class 101. It's like getting down to the nitty-gritty. Pornographic images have a very valid use in that kind of audience, whereas in a gay audience everyone is already convinced. Becoming naked and exposed is true promiscuity, because you're cutting through everything you've been conditioned to believe.

LEYLAND: I think people can make this breakthrough initially, but the problem comes after that.

GIORNO: You can get hung up there. As Ed Sanders says, "If you can't bite your way through the bars with your teeth, you always got your fingernails to scratch through the walls."

LEYLAND: Also, I think there needs to be more open discussion of the relationship between affection and sex. Much writing on promiscuity tends to bypass this.

GIORNO: That's what I've been talking about. Affection and sex go together. It's having a basic generosity with other people, a giving out, a breathing into them. When an imbalance occurs, then a nasty situation takes place. Hysterical promiscuity is just as off the wall as totally locking into the fantasy of loving somebody.

LEYLAND: Do you feel you've been doing this more in your life?

GIORNO: Absolutely! I love when guys say, "I've never felt like this about anyone."

LEYLAND: Are you into an ongoing relationship with one person or friends whom you are close to?

GIORNO: I'm not into one person at the moment. A couple of lovers and a bunch of close friends.

LEYLAND: Don't you feel that this is more difficult to do in a city like New York?

GIORNO: New York is the personification of difficulties, it's a very vivid picture of the world. It sure ain't Coffeyville, Kansas.

LEYLAND: Do you feel you've tried to get into and express this clarity, this flow, in your erotic poems?

GIORNO: I just finished a long poem called *Subduing Demons in America*. It's fifty-seven pages long.

LEYLAND: Do you want to talk about the poem as a totality and explain what you do?

GIORNO: Are you asking me to make another poem on the spot? Or translate the poem into rhetoric? I can say the constituents of the poem are images, which I described how I got before, of all the states of existence, which we've been talking about, whether actual or psychological: the heaven worlds, the hell worlds, the hungry-ghost worlds, just the range of our experiences translated into words.

LEYLAND: Did you know Frank O'Hara?

GIORNO: Yes.

LEYLAND: What kind of person was he? I guess he had many facets to his character.

GIORNO: Frank O'Hara was the bitch of all time. Somehow from the beginning we never got on. I loved Frank and I loved his work, but he was always just incredibly mean to me. So I took it that we were two opposing elements which were just not compatible. Then Andy Warhol and I were seeing a lot of each other all the time and Frank hated Andy, hated Andy's work, hated everything about him and was mean to him too. It was only six months before Frank died that he came around to saying Andy's work wasn't so bad after all. But it was that reason the Museum of Modern Art didn't acquire any Andy Warhols in the early years. Frank actually hated all the pop artists. So there's dynamics in that kind of situation. Frank O'Hara, John Ashbery and Kenneth Koch formed the power center of something they created called the New York School of Poetry. They hated my poetry and still do. But then Burroughs and Brion Gysin and I were hanging out together, and Frank hated us too, for no discernible reason. Brion used to say, "I can't figure it out. They came to Paris and we organized a reading for them and we were as good as we could be to them, and they were always hating us." Frank also had a certain antipathy for Burroughs. So Frank was a totally great poet, and I loved him, but he sure was a bitch. A ruthless bitch. I was real young then, so it hurt a lot.

LEYLAND: You mean in encounters with people?

GIORNO: Frank was into the bottle. He would see your weak points and then go at you with an ice pick. He was great when he did it, really mean and really funny. But he told the person exactly where they were at. Execpt he made lots of mistakes. I mean to really dislike the work of Andy Warhol. And in the early days, Frank used to laugh at Andy, make fun of him to his face and torture him. Frank's territory was the abstract painters, de Kooning, Pollock. Looking back at it, Andy turns out to be an abstract painter. He chooses an image and uses it continuously, the image is unimportant. So essentially he was interested in the same principles as the abstract painters. It was the vigorous pop thing cutting through the pretentions abstract painting, and ending up just an extension of it.

LEYLAND: What was your reaction to Gerard Malanga's criticism of Warhol's ruthlessly exploiting people?

GIORNO: It's one hundred percent correct. Andy has this great gift for using other people's ideas. Around the Factory were all these kids stoned out on speed. Henry Geldzahler used to call them "the squirrels." When you're on speed you get lots of ideas, and Andy used to pick the best ideas and do them. For the paintings, for the sculptures, for the movies. Andy is the only real movie star, nobody in his movies. Andy is the only one who's made untold millions of dollars. All the kids, if they haven't committed suicide, then they're totally penniless with their brains like mush from too many drugs. That was characteristic of the sixties Superstars; they were unbelievably ruthless. Bob Rauschenberg was worse than Andy, and Timothy Leary was as bad as that. Leary just consumed people whole. Chomp! He'd take them in one bite, chew them up, digest what he wanted and spit the rest out. That's the way all the Superstars were. They'd rip off anyone in sight who was supporting their careers or emotions, or both when you scored. But those guys are totally great. Each in their own way has opened up American consciousness, cut through conceptualization. That's rare enough. They also happen to be only human, with just as many poisons as you or me. A great work of art is the result of a mistake. You have this artist and he works away at his work, and it's completely unglamorous, and he makes this piece, which afterwards turns out to be absolutely great, is this great breakthrough affecting all of the world. He doesn't know why he did. It was a mistake. He stumbled on it. Stumbled on his natural mind. Then it's easy to go on from there. So they have this ego like everybody else, and it gets pumped up by society, and they say, "Man, you're great!" It feels good and you become rich and famous. It feels so good, you want to hold onto it. That's where the trouble begins.

LEYLAND: But if in one's personal relationships one is ruthlessly exploiting, even though one's art may be a breakthrough and catalytic, I wonder if that's not overbalanced by the exploitation.

GIORNO: The karma of those guys is horrible. Then it starts falling apart. Every decision Timothy Leary made in the last six years has been a mistake. An ordinary mistake in this case. I mean his mindlessly supporting the Weathermen and supporting mindlessly Eldridge Cleaver, supporting them like a PR scam, and the Swiss trip and the idea of going to Afghanistan. He must have been out of his mind. And heaven knows what he's doing now turning state's evidence. It's just totally fucked up, but if it wasn't, you and I wouldn't be here and it wouldn't be here.

LEYLAND: But genius, art, writing, are not necessarily dependent on ruthless exploitation.

GIORNO: Well, my dear, it's all perversion and accumulation. You can't really say that they shouldn't have done it, or what would have happened if they didn't do it. And it isn't so much anymore; those guys have been put out in the pasture. Did you know that Allen Ginsberg, Bob Rauschenberg and Andy Warhol are all the same age and they're all going to be fifty this year. As Rita Hayworth said recently (you know she's been in total secluded retirement for twenty years), well, recently she came out of retirement to give a press conference in support of some charity. Rita Hayworth had gotten a little fat, to say the least. Well, it was this auditorium full of press people and Rita on the stage, and one reporter asked the question, "Miss Hayworth, how does it feel to get up in the morning and look in the mirror and see this ugly person, and know that you were once beautiful?" Rita Hayworth answered, "I don't get up in the morning." I love Rita. How does the old show biz saying go? "You're only as good as your last act."

LEYLAND: But isn't it also true that many of these artists helped prop up the American system.

GIORNO: Not only that, but now that we're in an economic depression, if you take away the National Endowment for the Arts and the New York State Council on the Arts, the poetry scene would vanish from the United States. Everything is more or less funded with government money. Poetry readings, magazine publishing, small press, you name it. Poets never get paid by society. They are never paid the way other artists are. They never gave you anything, so you got nothing to lose. Or as I tell Burroughs, you're just lying on the ground, so what if they start kicking you. Poets are in a fortunate position, relatively speaking.

LEYLAND: Do you see Andy Warhol these days?

GIORNO: Not too much these days. Andy has withdrawn into a world of Nureyev, Jacqueline Onassis and Yves St. Laurent. He's totally out of the art world. And so am I. We haven't been close in years. In the sixties we hung out together. As I said before, nobody was really famous, and we just bumbled along together. It was loose and intense at the same time, and it's when all the great work was done. Like in 1962, when Andy made *Sleep*. We used to go see a lot of underground movies. Jack Smith and Ron Rice and Taylor Mead and masses of movies that were garbage. Andy had never made a movie, and he would say, "They're so terrible. Why doesn't somebody make a beautiful movie, there're so many beautiful things." About a week later he bought his first Bolex 16 mm camera. He didn't know how to use it and would ask Jonas Mekas questions like, "How do you focus it?" A week after that we were in Old Lyme, Connecticut, visiting Wyn Chamberlain who had a farm there. We were up really late one night to five in the morning. It was one of those ninety-degree sweltering June nights. I got really drunk on black rum. Andy didn't drink, because he did a lot of speed: Dexamil, Oberdrin and Purple Hearts. I just passed out when my head hit the pillow. I woke up an hour later, as the sun was coming up, to take a piss. I looked and there was Andy in the bed next to me, his head propped up by his arm, wide-eyed awake from speed, looking at me. I said, "What are you doing?" He said, "Watching you sleep." So I went back to sleep. A couple of hours later I woke up again and there was Andy in the same position. I remember I had a great pain in my head and I said, "What are you doing?" He said, "Watching you." I went back to sleep and when I woke up the next time, Andy was doing the same thing. I looked at my watch, it was 11:30 in the morning, boiling hot with a hangover. I said, "What're you doing, Andy?" He just laughed and said, "What do you want to know for?" The next time I woke Andy was gone. It was one in the afternoon and he had watched me sleep for eight hours. So that's how Andy Warhol got the idea for his first movie, *Sleep*. Coming back on the train he said to me, "Do you want to be a movie star? I want to make a movie of you sleeping." We started shooting a couple of weeks later.

LEYLAND: I wasn't aware of that because I've never seen that film.

GIORNO: I slept a lot of the time. Fourteen hours a day every day. It was the only place that felt good. Everything was so horrible. Every time Andy telephoned, morning, afternoon or night, I would be asleep. He would say, "What are you doing?" and I would say, "Sleeping." Or he would say, "Don't tell me, I know. Sleeping."

LEYLAND: Were you living with Warhol at that time?

GIORNO: We each had our own place. When I would go to sleep at night, Andy would set up his camera on a tripod and start shooting. It took about a month to shoot, because Andy's Bolex had to be loading every three minutes. We stopped when we had taken these thousands of rolls of film.

LEYLAND: Did you feel, from what you said, that you got burned out too? From what you intimated, you went through a lot of pain.

GIORNO: Everybody got ripped off. At least you can say I've survived. I didn't commit suicide like Fredie Herko or Edie Sedgewick, or get lobotomized by shock treatment in some hospital or have my mind fried crisp with methedrine. Years later Andy said to me, "I want to make another movie of you. It's called *Suicide*." And I said, "Okay, I'll call you when I'm going to kill myself and you can bring the cameras over."

LEYLAND: What has been your reaction and attitude towards political activity in the gay movement?

GIORNO: Everything I do is a political action for the gay movement. I've lost interest in being directly involved with political organizing. I also don't have the time, but I'll do anything anybody asks me. Give a benefit reading, anything you want.

LEYLAND: Are you writing in prose at all, or have you written in prose?

GIORNO: The only prose I do is "Vitamin G," my gossip column. I've started doing it again.

LEYLAND: What is this?

GIORNO: In 1969/70 I wrote this gossip column called "Vitamin G" for a newspaper called *Culture Hero*, which was published by Les Levine. The idea was that the poetry and art world incessantly talks about itself. Everyone is always gossiping about what everyone else is doing, like who's making it with whom, who has done what to whom, and all the weirdnesses. Ordinarily it just seems like boring gossip, but it actually is the dynamic relationships between artists, between artists and poets, the hardcore of art history. The really sordid details which came to me at the time. It was what people said to each other, like in the back room at Max's. The things people scream at each other in laughter or telephone each other and say, "Listen to this!"

LEYLAND: That you dug up?

GIORNO: No, it's what people would call and tell me or the stories one hears at a party. The gossip column was sensational. Like the size of their cocks hard: Bob Rauschenberg, Jasper Johns, Andy Warhol and Brion Gysin. Then what they like to do. It freaked everyone out. People either loved it or hated it. They said I was ruthless and malicious. I didn't feel I was being malicious by just mirroring their maliciousnesses.

LEYLAND: After a while they became cautious about what they said to you?

GIORNO: That should have only happened.... Actually people started hating me. Sometimes I'd feel this huge negativity coming at me, like a child. I only did the column for a year and then I stopped it. But I've started writing it again, because that's really art history. You have all these art critics, like Clement Greenberg and Barbara Rose and David Bourdon and Peter Schjeldhal, and they write this fiction. Their art criticism creates the art or artist, which then becomes a commodity, which has this monetary value, and is then traded in the New York art galleries just like it was the New York Stock Exchange. I mean the Abstract Expressionists and Pop Artists and Minimal and Conceptual. It's all so righteous. They only show you one side of the coin. Whereas I think who's fucking who is where it's at, or the size of his cock hard, or what he likes to do. And all the neurotic pain between people, which has some effect on their work. The horror story of Jackson Pollock, Ruth Kligman and Lee Pollack. Wow, did Lee Pollack freak out!

LEYLAND: That's why I asked you about Frank O'Hara, because I think there's been a certain romanticization about him. Gossip doesn't always have to be vicious.

GIORNO: Just the facts. They can be very horrifying. I started doing "Vitamin G" again. I just finished a piece on Jane Bowles' death. Her obituary. Paul and Jane had this glamorous public image of themselves. It was Tangier and *Vogue* magazine and everyone was sublimely civilized. Well, I lived in Tangier with Brion Gysin and the story firsthand is a nightmare. Jane was poisoned, went out of her mind and died in an insane asylum in Malaga. The last five years of Jane Bowles' life, she didn't know her name was Jane Bowles.

LEYLAND: Did she die of poison?

GIORNO: It's a long story. She was poisoned over a long period by Shirifa, her lover, who was this formidable Arab woman, as tough as they come. It all began thirty years ago in Tangier, when Jane was walking through the grain market. She sees Shirifa majestically selling her wheat. The grain market was run by women, each woman having her own stall, weighing out the flour. Shirifa, young and beautiful, was the undisputed boss, Queen of the Grain Market. Jane fell in love at first sight. Jane courted Shirifa and they became lovers and Shirifa moved into her house. That was the best of it. The rest was a nightmare. Shirifa always threatened to kill Jane if she left her.

LEYLAND: Because there had been quarrels?

GIORNO: Shirifa controlled Jane. She would say, "If you leave me, I'll make it so you can't eat, can't sleep, can't write, and don't even know your name." Shirifa was heavy on magic. Around 1950, Jane fell in love with another woman, and started drifting away. Shirifa with poisons or herbs or spells drove Jane out of her mind. Jane was taken to a hospital in England, where she received six shock treatments, after which she never wrote another word again. This was after she wrote her last work, a play called *In the Summer House*.

LEYLAND: There's also a romanticization around Paul Bowles, for instance the recent interview with him in *Rolling Stone*.

GIORNO: Listen, man, in 1966 I was living with Brion Gysin in an apartment in Tangier, and Jane lived in the apartment next door with Shirifa and a harem of Arab women they'd collected over the years. Paul Bowles lived in the apartment above Jane's and had his Arab boyfriends. During this time Jane was having an affair with Princess Martha Ruspoli. Martha was this middle-aged American woman, who was the Longworth heiress from Maryland, and had married a Roman prince, and was living in a villa on the mountain outside of Tangier. Jane would go and visit Martha for two weeks, and then come back and be with Shirifa for two weeks, and then back to Martha. That wasn't the way to do it and keep healthy. Shirifa was now this wizened old woman behind a black veil and really mean. She started poisoning Jane with arsenic. Two serious ladies. Jane got pretty wiped out. She got real thin and her skin got chalk white and she always looked dazed. Paul would come and visit us, and say as he puffed on a cigarette in a long white cigarette holder, "I'm so worried about Jane, she's so pale." Then one day he came rushing in after lunch, really shaken up, saying, "The parrot's dead. The parrot ate some of Jane's food and died. He fell off his perch and died." The parrot may be known to some readers as the bird on Paul's shoulder in the photo on the back cover of *100 Camels in the Courtyard*. Martha went on an extended trip and Jane recovered. About three years later, Jane totally went out of her mind, moved out of the apartment down into the Medina, and lived at the Parade Bar, a crowded gay bar where a piano player sang love songs. Jane drank day and night and bought everyone drinks and six months later had run up an $8,000 bar bill, which Paul paid with the American Express traveler's checks he kept in the suitcase under his bed. Jane was so far gone she had to be committed to an insane asylum near Malaga, where she spent the rest of her life, not knowing her name was Jane Bowles. And about a year after Jane died Shirifa went mad, and now is in an insane asylum near Tangier, where in her lucid moments she's on this super-romantic guilt trip, mumbling, "I killed Jane. I said I would make it so she couldn't eat, she couldn't sleep, she couldn't write, and she wouldn't know her name. I love Jane and I killed her and I've lost my mind as payment."

LEYLAND: Harold Norse said to me that Paul Bowles would never agree to be interviewed in *Gay Sunshine* because of the self-image he has. In fact he refused to be included in my forthcoming gay poetry anthology with the apology that he doesn't believe in *littérature engagée*. I wrote him back: I've long admired your work, and you *are* in fact a supporter of *"littérature engagée"*—viz. your long championship of Mohammed Mrabet's writing and other Moghrebi literature, surely a minority literature if anything is.

GIORNO: Exactly. That's literary history, not some straight commercial self-serving image.

LEYLAND: It's certainly an important background to know about people's lives and not to romanticize people.

GIORNO: Get the facts out into the open.

LEYLAND: You knew Paul Bowles quite well in Morocco?

GIORNO: Yes. He's one of Brion's life-long best friends and we all lived in the same building. Paul was very aware of the situation. He once said to Brion, "Nobody's ever going to find out about this." And Brion said, "Don't be silly, Paul. We all write each other letters."

LEYLAND: Some people want to create this aura and don't want reality to come through.

GIORNO: They try to avoid coming to terms with reality. They package this image of themselves, complete with credentials. In the Bowleses' case it's international intellectual chic.

LEYLAND: The recent film made with Paul Bowles is very interesting. But the film passed over in silence much that is crucial to an understanding of him. It was all very beautiful and he was the "artist in Tangier." A very nice film, but it was doing the same thing that these histories do that you're talking about. They whitewash the situation. Even the *Paris Review* interviews are not very personal at all. It's good to hear about the person's writing, but beyond that they are often bland.

GIORNO: Jane lived the life of her greatest novel, *Two Serious Ladies*. She was able to transform the poisons into this great work. That's all anyone asks of a writer. If you're not doing it, you're just wasting time, making entertainments. They were all great entertainers.

LEYLAND: When the poisons have not been dealt with, the creativity dries up.

GIORNO: The poisons are the creativity, transformed.

PHOTO BY BETTY FREEMAN

LOU HARRISON

LOU HARRISON was born in Portland, Oregon, on May 14, 1917. "He was brought up on the West Coast, facing east," writes Wilfred Mellers. Yet, most of Lou Harrison's life and education has occurred in California, while his central interest lies in the sonorities of Asia. He was, in 1934-35, a pupil of Henry Cowell in San Francisco, and later of Schoenberg in Los Angeles. During these years he organized recitals of percussion music with John Cage while "moonlighting" as a florist, a record clerk, a poet, a dancer and dance critic, a music copyist (his handwriting is famous for its beauty), playwright, and builder of instruments using found objects: the tack piano, automobile brake drums, graduated coffee cans and flower pots, clock coils, gongs submerged in washtubs, plumber's pipes.

In 1943 he emigrated to New York, where Virgil Thomson became an intellectual (though not a musical) influence and a champion of his works. Here too he commented professionally in such lamented periodicals as *View, Modern Music,* and the *Herald Tribune.* He also briefly acted as editor for the trailblazing *New Music Edition,* wrote a pamphlet "About Carl Ruggles," and conducted the first performance of any Charles Ives symphony, the 3rd complete. In 1947 a breakdown provoked an extended retirement into the New York Psychiatric Institute, although the same year brought a sizable grant from the American Academy of Arts and Letters. Soon after, he quit New York for good, teaching first in Portland, then at Black Mountain College, finally returning to California and into his present home in Aptos.

He received a Guggenheim Fellowship in 1952, and again in 1954. During the latter year he also won the Twentieth Century Masterpiece Award, and attended the International Conference in Rome where Leontyne Price premiered his first opera, a monodrama titled *Rapunzel.* The following year he received a Fromm Foundation Award, and a commission from the Louisville Orchestra to write the *Four Strict Songs* (eight baritones and stylized orchestra) on his own text, in Esperanto, about certain of his constant concerns—love, plant growth, peace, and mutual enjoyment on our travels to death.

From 1957 to 1960, in preference to a lucrative job at Buffalo University, he worked full time in an animal hospital, composing at night with the aid of Benzedrine. He then "withdrew" again for a year. The early 1960s took him to the Far East. A Rockefeller grant provided study first in Tokyo and Taiwan, then in Korea with Dr. Lee Hye Ku and Liang Tsai Ping who, in teaching him the principles of Korean court music and Chinese classical music, made of him America's first true orientological composer since the late Colin McPhee.

In 1963 he became a Senior Scholar at the East-West Center at the University of Hawaii. He also intensified his schedule of building new instruments (now incorporating such exotica as choirs of jade flutes) conforming to his lifelong obsession with pitch relations and a need for what he calls "just," rather than "tempered," intonation. From 1965 until the present he has been variously occupied as ballet accompanist, researcher in Oaxaca, beneficiary of the Thorne Foundation, composer of his first film score, teacher at San Jose State College, and, with a nucleus of friends, as touring concertizer and lecturer on his own and oriental music. He is devotedly involved with pacifism and with Esperanto as a means to world peace, with hiking and poetry, and with civil rights for homosexuals. Indeed, these involvements are conjoined in his art, the most recent example being an opera for puppets called *Young Caesar* based on an early (male) love affair of the emperor.

Lou Harrison's music is not easily pigeonholed. Although most of his hundred some works are first rate, they are of a wild and willful variety of genres. Especially during the 1940s they were "occasional," speaking a langauge, as required by the commissioner (usually a choreographer), ranging from the strict Schoenbergian twelve-note formula, through the Coplandesque diatonic and the Ivesian total sound fields, to studies for groups of non-pitched percussion. In general, however, Harrison is a melodist. Rhythm is pronounced in his work too, though rather more four-square than eccentric. Counterpoint is not essential to his typical scores today, harmony even less. His *Koncherto* (sic, an Esperanto spelling) for Violin and Percussion Orchestra is virtually all in line, while other of his pieces from every period are solely melisma with ostinato or drone background. The effect is exceedingly Romantic, but, curiously, neither Chinese nor Western—removed in time and space.

Harrison has never had a mass following, for he has lived recluded, flirting with neither the New York market nor the college circuits which in America remain the chief outlets for contemporary music. He nonetheless is protected by a circle of friends (notably Peter Yates, the twentieth-century specialist, and Oliver Daniel, the publisher) who are focal in keeping his production before a discriminating public.

—Ned Rorem
(adapted from Grove's *Dictionary of Music*)

THE FOLLOWING INTERVIEW with composer Lou Harrison was taped by Winston Leyland, editor of *Gay Sunshine,* at the composer's Aptos, California, home in summer 1973. Musician Bill Colvig also participated in the interview, which originally appeared in *Gay Sunshine* 23 (November–December 1974).

Winston Leyland interviews
LOU HARRISON

LEYLAND: Why don't we start by talking about your earlier life, your background in general?

HARRISON: I was born in Portland, Oregon, in 1917. I came to California at an early age, and so I really regard myself as a Californian, more specifically as a San Franciscan, though I've had my troubles of late with that city. Nonetheless, it's there I grew up and came out. When I was growing up there, it had lots of concertizing. John Cage was in and out; he had been introduced to me by Henry Cowell. We began giving concerts and we did percussion concerts. That was the golden age of percussion. Things that now are recorded and have become part of the repertoire are things we were doing then.

At that time, San Francisco was really fairly relaxed already about being gay. I never had any trouble with it at all. None of my friends did either. The first time I encountered that feeling of tightness and constraint, or uptightness, was in New York. When I went to New York for the first time I did see that there was a certain difficulty, but it never really occurred to me in San Francisco, particularly when young. Of course, when you're young, you're immortal; the world is marvelous, and it's springtime. Just before I left San Francisco, I lived for three years with a man who is now dead. He was older than I. I generally like people older than myself. That's been a pattern all my life, though I've had little affairs with younger people.

We were very active at that time in giving concerts on our own. We established the basis of a free-lance musical activity which was experimental and exciting just by doing it ourselves. John Cage and I, for example, would go out and rent a hall like the California Club where we gave a now famous concert. Later, I did something at the Fairmont Hotel where they had a little theater downstairs. We had a few friends who were able, really very skillful musicians. Then we would either compose or ask our friends to compose pieces for the concert. John Cage used to do this at the Cornish School in Seattle before we were together in San Francisco. Henry Cowell had stimulated both of us to all of this. At that time John Cage was married to Xenia Cage, and he and Xenia were very dear friends with Sherman and myself. Sherman and I had rented a big studio where we all rehearsed; it was a dance studio.

During this time, I was working at Mills College with dancers, and I taught musical form to dancers and composed for dancers a great deal. The main thing I remember of that period is living with Sherman for about three years. Then we separated. At that time my emotional life was very intense as you know it is for some young people. It was a real upset in my life. Then I took up for a couple of years with a young man who became a dancer. We lived together while I was working as a florist. This was in the very early forties. Then we moved together to Los Angeles where I also worked at UCLA and where I studied with Schoenberg at the same time, and accompanied and composed in the dance department. Also, I worked with Lester Horton, who was a marvelous man, just lovely, and had a studio there.

He was a very great choreographer. It is now being realized slowly that he corresponded to and had all of the same genius and excitement that in New York was given to Martha Graham, Doris Humphrey, Charles Weidman and all this school. Lester had his own group; and his principal dancers are still dancing.

Then we went to New York around 1942. Shortly after that, I found myself alone; my other friend vanished. That was the war period and New York was wide open. Friends helped me. For example, John Cage introduced me to Virgil Thomson. Virgil or John Cage introduced me to Minna Lederman, editor of *Modern Music Quarterly,* and she gave me reviewing for the summer. So I covered band concerts and new pieces that were being played around during the summer. But right away Henry Cowell also gave me some work from Charles Ives, and I worked for Ives. I was in the big city and alone except for these personal friends. My private life began to take the form of the random cruising that New York made madly available at that time. During the war, New York was host to all the armies and navies of the world and everybody else. It was quite a free and open sort of life, which, incidentally, no longer exists. I took up while I was there with a minister. That was a sort of extraordinary period in my life. He had a black congregation in the Bronx. At that time I was a little bit militant on the black situation, and helped him a bit like that. Every so often he'd get a blockage and come over Saturday night, and we'd do the sermon for Sunday, which was fun. He was a very nice man, rather melancholy, from the South, and needed cheering up every so often. He now is very happily married and has a congregation in Brooklyn, I think.

LEYLAND: At the time you lived in New York were you also friendly with literary people?

HARRISON: No, I wasn't, because they were very much older and established people. I knew Robert Duncan. He was very young at that time. He taught us poetry one night which was grand fun. He gave us some words and we made poems up. I used to, in fact, see him quite frequently. I also knew John Henry Meyer, who had a gallery and did puppetry. Paul Bowles wrote him a little puppet opera. As a matter of fact, Jane Bowles wrote him something which is still in the repertoire, too.

LEYLAND: You knew both Paul and Jane Bowles?

HARRISON: Yes. As a matter of fact, it was Paul who, in a sense, gave me his job on the *Herald Tribune* when he went to Morocco for the first time and stayed. He came down to my house and offered me the post. So I went up and started to work. I knew Paul quite well, as a matter of fact. A very mysterious person, and utterly charming. Still, what a marvelously skillful writer. Last time I saw him he brought one of his Arab friends in New York to a party at Leopold Stokowski's. I think Peggy Glanville-Hicks had set some of his letters for voice and orchestra. Oh by the way, Peggy was always part of our scene in New York. She's a charming woman. We're all very dear friends. Paul was composing at that time you know. He was a composer for the most part. Once he took up writing, he simply abandoned composing, which was too bad because he was a very good composer.

LEYLAND: I have a recording of his *Scènes d'Anabase* and *Music for a Farce*.

HARRISON: Well you know then that he's a good composer. He had also an absolutely fascinating way of working. He showed me how he did it once. He would write down a measure or some ideas just a few bars long or something like that on a scrap of paper. Then he'd dump it in a wastebasket. When the wastebasket got three-quarters full of just these little fragmentary ideas, he'd take them out and start putting them together in different ways, like a mosaic. Some of them would work, some wouldn't. He's wait until he'd find something else. Occasionally he'd copy out more of one because that would come back a couple of times. He'd piece together his whole pieces this way. It was a marvelous mosaic way of working, sort of a way of sneaking up on the subconscious too because you could emit these little sparks and then finally the whole work would appear as you contemplated the entire board or field, as it were. I thought that was fascinating. I've never really tried it; I should sometime to see what that would work like for me. It worked for Paul, I thought very well. I think he did the *Sonata for Two Pianos* that way, a beatiful work. Fizdale and Gold have been playing it for years.

LEYLAND: The relationships you had in New York were not satisfactory?

HARRISON: Because of so much else they tended to be not. I took up with a young artist, and that was catalytic because he helped me with calligraphy. I learned a lot from him. We still are good friends. But that one was the only catalytic and interesting relationship. As a matter of fact, it was somewhere around then that I decided that the next person that I had to do with would either be a musician or a functioning artist of some sort. New York was most valuable in acquisition of knowledge. I really gained an awful lot in the experience of reviewing, having to think about music, the presence of an incredible number of museums which I haunted. I had lots of artist friends, painter friends especially. The painter world I've always liked too because they have a certain easy camaraderie that is a great pleasure. It was very different from the literary or musical worlds because they are dealing with subverbal things too. They relate to music, and they love music most of them. So New York was a very widening experience in many ways. But it also brought me into conflict in some sense because on the West Coast my experience had been that the nearest relation we had as Americans was Asia. You know, San Francisco is close to Asia, whereas in New York, you are just a stone's throw from Europe. It's a completely different civilization. So that took some difficulty, made some difficulty for me. When I got back I immediately refelt the connections with Asia. Then, of course, I plunged into them at once when there was the opportunity of going to Asia actually. Since then, of course, I've been better balanced, back on home ground and also Mexico.

We had a group that was more or less stable in New York, but it was heterogeneous. It was mixed as to sexual orientation. We all believed, though, in advanced technical procedures. The whole circle included the younger ones like myself, John Cage, Ben Weber, Frank Wigglesworth and Alan Hovhaness. Then the older age level with whom we were very close included Henry Cowell, central information as you know for a whole generation or more of musicians, and Virgil Thomson. Edgar Varèse was in the periphery and Carl Ruggles and, of course, I did some work for Charles Ives; there were also Wallingford Riegger and Otto Luening. Harry Partch had not come into the picture. He was still working, I believe, out here. He came to New York when I was there. I do remember writing a review, a dreadfully uninformed one, of one of his concerts there.

It was what I call the new music group that most of us were interested in. We were developing advanced procedures, trying to hear the music of the previous generation that had not been done. Neoclassicism was very strong when I arrived there, and the Americanistic thing. I and several others drew attention to the work of previous generations that were not being heard. For example, there were no performances, at that time, of Ruggles and Ives, or very few indeed, and of Varèse and his group. It was that which I wanted to hear. So we stimulated interest in that and did give concerts and succeeded in swerving the course of music a little bit in that way I think. So at that time, it did not basically devolve on sexual orientation, though some of us tended to group together because it was comfortable. Some of us collected and spent time together simply because we could share common feelings and understandings. That also passed clear over the aesthetic; we had no common aesthetic at all. I don't think anybody does, do they? At that time, of course, nobody had in mind doing a gay movie involving all of the arts, or for that matter, a stage work or anything of that sort. There was no reason for any collective action as specifically being gay. Consequently there were a hundred different aesthetics, ways of doing things, different interests in the arts too because there was no way publicly of doing anything about being gay at that point.

New York for me, Winston, was not a productive period as to composition. In the first place it's too noisy. I don't see how anybody lives in New York. I can't anymore. Also there is so much going on, and as a young person you feel like you have to do it all. Besides, there was the question of earning a living, which involved a good deal of copying, and then also music reporting. Music reporting I found, at once, good for me because it makes you think about music; but also, it has that awful business of while you're sitting listening to a piece, you are at the same time trying to think of something to say about it. And that's not good. It means you're not really listening to the music. Eventually I had a breakdown. I'm sure New York's noise and the general complexity of everything all contributed to it. Since then I have not liked to review or write about music except more abstractly. Then I took to country living, and as you can see, I still live in the country. I like the quiet. I came back here around 1953, following a two-year interlude at Black Mountain College after the breakdown, and I've been here ever since.

LEYLAND: Maybe you could talk a little about your involvement in the Black Mountain School in the early fifties.

HARRISON: That was a strange and difficult period in my life because I had a big breakdown before I went there. I think John Cage suggested me as a possible teacher. I went down and I had a very bad reaction to it at first. Later I began to like it; it was a conversion. At that time, Charles Olson was our faculty head and Mrs. Rice from the earlier institute that Black Mountain broke off from in Florida. Max Dane, whom I used to think of as the Great Dane, was there. He was a mathematician, a perfectly charming man who played the cello and liked to play a Bach sonata every so often. I had only two or three pupils. One of them was Merrill Gillespie, now in Berkeley. During the summer we had Bob Rauschenberg and Cy Twombly, both of whom I enjoyed very much, and Paul Goodman, such a nice man. John Cage and Merce did one of the first of their "things," you know, with various things happening, timings by the watch and so on. It was like one constant festival, people were arriving all the time. Robert Duncan was there. Bill Masselos came down and played a piano concert. I arranged that. At the same time Franz Kline was there painting. I put one of Kline's paintings over the grand piano. Bill Masselos played one of the Ives sonatas, with the Franz Kline abstraction hanging in the air right above the piano; that was a marvelous thing. I also worked with Catherine Litz, the dancer, who is now in San Francisco working with Sheila Xoregos.

Black Mountain was based on a farm, you know, and it was a co-op. The pupil-teacher relationship was fantastic. We had one or two pupils apiece, you know. It was also quite free. I took a class with Johana Yalovetz. Her husband, who was a musician, had died and she stayed on. She taught bookbinding, and I learned to bind books there with her. Our student body ranged from people who have gone on to become quite well known to people who seemed to drop out and have stayed dropped out, as far as we know. We had a good time, and it was an extraordinary experience for me, quite intense at the time. Part of that getting along was in some sense coming to terms with my own homosexuality in terms of a community, too. And it wasn't until much later that my homosexuality was in some sense valuable. And it does stand to reason that if you are going to have young people growing up being homosexual (and nature herself produces this generation after generation), any good school should have at least one model. This seems to have been part of the attitude of some of the other faculty members and students there too. There had been another homosexual faculty member just before I came there. Nothing was made of it, and I think Black Mountain was one of the few institutions in the United States where that was true.

I moved back to the West Coast about '53. Then I went to Rome in 1954 for a conference that Nicholas Nabokov and Virgil Thomson had invited me to. I won an international prize there. Stravinsky gave me the certificate. I had a nice conversation with him and with Malipiero. I cruised the Tiber at late hours with other distinguished people, and had a good time. Also I had an Italian lover while I was there, who was charming. We made love in Michelangelo's old studio, which was the waterworks at that time. Then I came back here, and my parents gave me this place so that I could work.

I moved here to Aptos nineteen years ago, in 1954. The last six or seven of those years Bill [Colvig] has been in my life. As I approached fifty, I tended toward alcoholism. I was producing all right, but when I came out here I was in a fury against all of New York and all of the difficulties it had meant to me. I have had periods, even here, when I could not even talk about music with anyone except possibly Bob Hughes, who has some magic gift with me about this matter. But it has been very productive out here. During my life I've earned my living different ways. When I was living in San Francisco I earned my living at the Palace Hotel as a florist for a while before I went to Mills College. And then here I worked for four or five years as an animal nurse in an animal hospital. Then I got the Phoebe Ketchum Foreign Award for composers. The award ran for three years. It's the biggest award that can be given a composer in this country. I went to Mexico then for a year and came back. At the same time, I was asked to teach at San Jose State, and I've been there ever since, six years, seven years just about.

I met Bill in the first year there, and he moved down here right away. We've been living happily ever after. I've involved Bill, or rather Bill got me reinvolved. When I first met him I was in another period of hating music. Then Bill got me reinvolved because he comes from a long musical family. He seemed to like to give concerts, so I roped him in on the concerts I was asked to do, and gradually I got to do more of them. Now we're madly busy all the time giving concerts. I've written my best music the last few years, too. Also, he has become an instrument builder. In short, he is so much a part of my life, both professionally and personally, and it's an inextricable compound now. We're really one person in some sense.

LEYLAND: Do you think this is the first time in your life that you've had this kind of relationship both in your personal life and in regard to your work?

HARRISON: Yes. There was only one other and that was with a young New York artist. It was a personal relationship, and he was part of the art world too and had an independent role. He's now quite famous and well known in a special field of art. That was the closest. I never had to do personally with a musician as part of my life. It works very well now because Bill seems to be just part of everything. He's also extremely bright and able to do the special things that I want done. He also is interested in doing them, so it works out beautifully. Obviously, we're living happily ever after. When we met we already knew many people in common and had a background that was curiously intertwined for years and years; it's surprising we didn't meet before. As a matter of fact we first formally met when Ned Rorem and I were reading *Façade* at the Old Spaghetti Factory in San Francisco. Ned Rorem came out to do some pieces of Bob Hughes' for the Oakland Youth Chamber Orchestra. It was Bob Hughes' suggestion that Ned and I read the verse in a performance of *Façade*. So we did it and Bob Hughes conducted, and a friend introduced me to Bill. I took one look at him and listened to his voice, and I knew.

I'd had three- or four-year relationships in my past. But this is the first real permanent relationship that I've ever felt strongly about, that it really was an integrated life. I think that being fifty had something to do with it. By the way, Ned and I have been talking about this subject. Forty hit him pretty hard because he realized he was no longer a youth. Oh, he dreaded that moment. But fifty is when it hit me. When you're forty, after all, you might easily have another half to your life. By the time you're fifty, you are fairly certain you're not going to have another half. Boy it hits you. So there is no more nonsense; you're going to have things the way you want for the rest of it. I think that really helps give a mind-set that makes a permanent relationship possible. What do you think about that, Bill?

COLVIG: I think it did in our case. A lot of it is just getting more realistic about everything in general. Younger people are so idealistic, hetero- or homosexual. A lot have a hard time making a permanent relationship. They always expect too much, overidealize the whole thing.

HARRISON: And also they are immortal, so they can afford to hold ideals, more imaginary images. I think that young people now are much more realistic and much more sensible than when Bill and I were young. They know so much more than we did. You've no idea how tiny and protected and tight the whole thing was by comparison. Well, there were so many fewer people too. Nowadays the kids encounter great masses of people with all sorts of different ideas. They encounter through the media a thousand things that we had no access to either. They are much more informed, much cooler characters than ever in history probably. I'm full of admiration. When you deal with a young person nowadays, by the time they're in their twenties they're already really mature and sensible. But still that sometimes doesn't really alter what goes on in your body. You can't alter those anabolic and catabolic processes; they just happen. We're timed inside the genes. That does make a difference too. So there is at any rate a certain point to that business of mortality hitting you when you're about fifty, the knowledge that you are going to have things you own way. That's the way I reacted. I suppose some people give up, or some people get neurotic. I'm stubborn; I'm a Taurus, very much the bull; so that's the way it hit me.

LEYLAND: I think it's very beautiful to see the kind of integrated relationship that you have.

COLVIG: We're both very accustomed to it and every once in a while we reflect on what it would be like not to have it, and we don't even want to think about it.

HARRISON: It's unthinkable for me, really unthinkable. That's why we worry about becoming a "duprass." In Kurt Vonnegut's *Cat's Cradle* a "duprass" is a couple so close together that they really pity the rest of the world and do not have any further social feelings. We're not really a duprass, I'm sure about that. In the first place we give too many concerts.

LEYLAND: Do you feel that if you had had this kind of integrated relationship in your twenties, it would have affected your work as a composer?

HARRISON: Oh, I think it would. But then, of course, it's almost impossible to think back. For example, it might well have released me as a composer. But would I have had the knowledge that would have made such an integration possible for both of us, and would he have had it. I'm just happy that it happened when it did, and that we are living happily ever after.

COLVIG: Zappily ever after.

HARRISON: Zappily ever after. Bill has a very good sense of humor. That's also a help. I tend to get very solemn. I've got a drive. I'm not really happy unless I'm finishing things. I'm happy for a while, then I have to start finishing something else. I have to be sobered up by funnies every so often, and he's a great help along that line. One of the nicest things Bill said to me after we met was, "I've always wanted to live in a cabin in the woods with a dirty old man and now my dream is realized." When I took up with Bill, those things I used to do when I was young with my first lover, like climbing mountains and going out backpacking, all came back. It was a great joy because I do need to be out in nature. We are, as a matter of fact, very well integrated in this community. We're always invited together; there's never any problem. Of course, we're also a functioning professional team; that's understood as well. So it works very well. It's a marvelously integrated life for us.

COLVIG: Should we put in here about my having been invited to the Institute as your spouse?

HARRISON: This last year I was elected to membership in the National Institute of Arts and Letters along with Allen Ginsberg, Joe Campbell (an old friend of mine), James Brooks, the painter, Jasper Johns, and Kurt Vonnegut Jr. Induction ceremonies were held in the hall there, and there was a luncheon beforehand. I told them that Mr. Colvig would be coming too and that he needed tickets. Then it was stated on one of the letters that they were expecting Mr. Colvig for luncheon too. So we both appeared and sat at the same table.

COLVIG: That's all that were at the reception, the inductees and their spouses and older members of the Institute. So I was actually invited along just as a spouse as a matter of course.

HARRISON: Well, Bill, I think it's more than that. You're a colleague too. We're so integrated a functioning team that it would be hard to separate us at this point for any reason. There is that lovely story about Tennessee Williams. When he was making a movie, there was a young man around at a party. One of the directors came up and said, "What do you do?" And he said, "I sleep with Mr. Williams," which is a position in itself. Bill's function is, of course, not like that; neither is mine for him. It's much more elaborate than that. We met through music, and we continue to operate through music, of course. It's our business.

After we met I found out that Bill came from a long family of musicians. Oh, it's a marvelous family, just darlings. They've invited me right in. It's really marvelous to live, as it were, in an extended family. His mother writes both of us with affection. We visit them. All the brothers and sisters are affectionate and warm to us. I've felt very included in a family that is much larger than I had any knowledge of before, and all musical, too.

COLVIG: He was the only one invited to a family birthday party for my father's eightieth birthday who wasn't a blood relative or actually related by marriage. He sat at the head of the table along with Papa and me. There were about thirty-five or forty people.

HARRISON: I was astounded at one point to realize that yes, there his eldest son was at his right hand, and I was beside the eldest son. On the other side was the eldest daughter and her husband, and so on right down the line. It took a while for that to dawn on me. But I was thus included; so it was an extraordinary experience for me. We have continuing good relations with the family. My mother balked a little at first, but she finally accepted Bill.

LEYLAND: Both of you have found that your creativity has been stimulated by the deep interpersonal relationship?

HARRISON: Oh, I'd say yes. Don't you agree with that?

COLVIG: Oh, yes.

HARRISON: I am perfectly certain that I wouldn't have composed the things I've composed in the last four or five years without the stimulus from Bill. He's part of the very mechanism by which it's done. I don't mean the spiritual or intellectual or emotional mechanism. I simply mean he builds instruments, he plays. It's all part of doing it. Also, the creativity from our relationship keeps me going. I don't know if you could even call it a stimulus; it's a sort of release he gives me that makes it possible to do these works. I find that for the first time I'm actually doing the larger works of my maturity because I have in some sense a normal life for the first time too. I'm no longer on the road to being an alcoholic. I get more and more stable and can do more things.

COLVIG: The only trouble is, the more things you find you can do, the more you try to do. We're forever having this awful struggle trying to do so many things. I think my life changed for the better getting involved with all this personally, helping Lou to get his composing done.

HARRISON: Well there's more to it than that. When Bill first came down, he didn't perform in public. Now, he's a professional musician performing in public quite constantly, and he has his own acclaim as such. He gets reviews and comments and he is known as a professional musician on a national scale. Now he has gone on to become an instrument builder. A long time ago I used to ask people to build things for me, and I'd make designs and take them down to a carpenter. Now I just give Bill the problem generally, and he comes up with extremely inventive solutions. About a year ago he produced the entire gamelan for the *Heart Sutra* and for *Young Caesar*, which is no small achievement. This last year he's been concentrating on the monochords and the transfer instrument. He comes up with new ideas, very inventive, for construction and perfection. So he does all sorts of creative things. The Mode Room is the project now.

Many years ago I thought of the idea that there was nowhere on the planet where you could go to study all the various musical modes that mankind has made in the course of history. It suddenly dawned on me that it would be a marvelous thing to have a Mode Room. I first proposed it in an article at the Tokyo Conference in 1962. Then the idea lapsed, because, after all, it would require a room somewhere, probably a host university, and then a fund to keep it going. What I had in mind was a set of drawers. For example, you could pull a drawer and there would be Ptolemy's intense diatonic. Then you would have bars, or tuning forks, for an octave. Somewhere in the room there should be a harp or a large instrument which you could tune up over many octaves to really study its characteristics and be able to compose on it. Then there should be a big book which should tell you when the mode was first written down, or where it was first discovered, or what its history in diffusion among people was. Well this could amount to quite a large library of material; and it fascinated people. I called it the Mode Room, of course, because that's what it would be. I thought: some day I'm going to do something about it.

About a year ago, for one of my classes, Bill and I whipped up a plain monochord, just a stick. Within a week he had gone and produced a really good professional monochord with a steel tube and exact to within a millimeter in a whole meter's length, which is indiscernible to the ear, and almost indiscernible to laboratory instruments. Then he perfected a method of playing the modes on the monochord. Then we decided to go on and make a transfer instrument to transfer the modes. All of a sudden it dawned on us that the Mode Room should be a kit that anybody could have instead of a place where people had to go. It could probably be produced fairly inexpensively. So that's what we are up to. There will be a book that Dr. John Chalmers is writing, *The Divisions of the Tetrachord*, which I regard as probably the most important book on music in many centuries. Then the production of a monochord, a transfer harp, and a book of history about intonation. Then also the publication of these strips because on the monochord you have to have paper strips which measure off the modes, and so we'll be able to publish those too. The whole thing is going to be the Mode Room. We hope to get it in functioning operation in about a year. I think it's one of the most important things musically that I will ever do. It fills a real need; and it is also endlessly stimulating. Each one of these modes is a world, you know, Winston. It's absolutely fascinating to hear modes and, for example, to cross history like that, to realize that the mode you are listening to, because it was notated in true mathematic ratios, is exactly the way Ptolemy was hearing it in Alexandria in the second century B.C. It's like having a phonographic time machine, and it's a very exciting musical experience.

LEYLAND: Is much information about the modes taken from books of research?

HARRISON: Oh yes, and some of it's quite hard to find. I did discover that there are two great periods in musical intonation. There is the Greek period from Pythagoras through Ptolemy. Then there's a gap of several centuries. When the Arabs took up Greek learning, there is another great flourishing. Avicenna, for example, turns out to have had a very exciting life. So now I'm writing on that as well. It's very exciting, this world of intonation across the planet and through civilizations. It's going to take a long time. We'll gradually just collect modes from all over. There are a lot of ethnic records from various civilizations, and we can transcribe those modes and date them. It's like the early days when they first began to take astronomical observations.

LEYLAND: What about the earlier relationships that you've had? You mentioned that you lived with a few people for periods of two or three years. Were those catalytic in any sense?

HARRISON: They may have been in terms of my inner growth and understanding, but I'm not sure of that, Winston, because really for a great deal of my life I was an awful prig. I suppose I still look back on things that simply shock me that I said and did, the way I behaved. But I suppose we all shock ourselves occasionally. Cocteau had a wonderful phrase for that, he said, "I have an angel in me whom I am constantly shocking." I was much too preoccupied with my work, with my art, with my music, and a sort of interior selfishness.

COLVIG: I don't think I would have been able to stand him. I'm not sure he would have been able to stand me either.

HARRISON: Again, we arrived at just the right time. The gods have been plotting this for a really long time.

COLVIG: I was fairly neurotic when I was younger. I was sort of uptight. We never would have got along at all. Another thing, he was a heavy smoker, and I couldn't stand people who smoked a lot. I wouldn't have had anything to do with him on that score. Luckily he quit a couple of years before he met me.

HARRISON: So everything conspired to make that work. It turns out that Bill and I had mutual friends, even one of his brothers and I knew one another many years ago. We played recorder together at San Francisco State. We had a lot of mutual friends as composers. Bill collected composers; he likes them. I take it that comes from being in a musical family; sooner or later you get to the source.

COLVIG: I only had two before him.

HARRISON: Yes, I felt as though I had joined a "barem" at first. I wrote to one of the other members to that effect. They've all dropped out of his life.

COLVIG: Unluckily, the one who meant most, a great deal to me, was dying when I was making the gamelan. I was so busy with the gamelan I did not have time to write him and I knew he was getting worse all the time. But I sort of ignored him and the news of his death came as a great shock. It was just one of those coincidences that happened.

HARRISON: Well, I think that's forgivable. Now he's got an angel that's being shocked.

LEYLAND: I saw on the shelf your big book on angels, *Dictionary of the Angels*. I'm an angelophile, too.

HARRISON: That's wonderful. Do you know that's the only source book in English on angels. When you consider that it is a dogma for three separate religions, it's about time somebody wrote a book on the subject. It turns out, too, in my recent studies on Avicenna, that he was a great angelologist. Apparently it was Avicenna's work that prompted the wonderful chapters on angels in St. Thomas Aquinas. I want to do something eventually in honor of the angel Israfel, who is the angel of music and who sort of softened up Mohammed for Gabriel's takeover.

LEYLAND: Carl Ruggles has a piece called *Angels*.

HARRISON: That was a work I conducted in New York once. People kept shouting *Bis! Bis!* from the auditorium and I didn't know what it was. Edgar Varèse came and said, "Go on, do it again; it means repeat."

COLVIG: You thought they were calling you a beast?

HARRISON: Yes. I didn't know what they were saying. So I went out and conducted it again. *Angels* is a beautiful piece. I think angels are a nice idea.

LEYLAND: And very prominent in Cocteau's work, too.

HARRISON: Yes, he had his own angel, Heurtebise. I love Cocteau. I was going to send him a record of my music but he died. He had such a marvelous mind, and he's such a wonderful artist. At the same time he produced a lot of trash too. It's like finding opals amid autumn leaves. At his best he was marvelous, particularly, I think, in the theater. His movies, of course, are wonderful. I thought every city should have a playhouse that was exclusively devoted to showing *Beauty and the Beast* just over and over and over again. It's sort of all you need to know, it's so beautiful, absolutely enchanting. Everybody falls in love with the beast, of course. Cocteau realized that. I have an edition of the fairy tale *Beauty and the Beast,* which he wrote a little afterward. He said that he realized that people in fact fall in love with the beast. There's a bit of a shock when the beast turns into a handsome prince. In the movie when Beauty looks upon the prince, who is the beautiful Jean Marais, he says, "You will get used to it," because he's been transformed from the beast she loved into this handsome man. So Cocteau realized that impulse too. It's extraordinary, one of the most beautiful movies ever made. It had lovely music by Auric.

LEYLAND: Do you want to talk about how you started composing? Were you into music from your childhood?

HARRISON: Yes, really. From the very early times I had the usual piano lessons, along with dancing lessons. I remember learning the schottische when I could barely toddle and the polka and things like that in a dancing class. I played in recitals and played the piano all through childhood. When I was about ten I started to compose. I have, of course, a few fragments from that period. They were all piano pieces. Then I assayed grand things very shortly afterwards, sonatas and things like that which were perfectly awful, but they were some indication of ambition along the line. I started studying composition when I was an adolescent. I never went through any courses in school; it was all private. I won a little scholarship and studied with Howard Cooper in San Francisco for two or three years. He was a pupil of Domenico Brescia. I studied variation and fugue and these classical compositional studies. It's like learning to do sonnets and odes. Then I studied with Henry Cowell. I wrote a letter, I think, and then met him out at Olive Cowell's house, in the old days. That was the first modern house in San Francisco. It was done by Irving Marrow, who did the Golden Gate Bridge.

When I went to Los Angeles, I studied with Schoenberg. Then when I went to New York, I got acquainted with everybody, Virgil Thomson, Henry Cowell (who was there then), Wallingford Riegger, Otto Luening. I knew Aaron Copland by that time too. And I was part of the New York scene for about ten years. It was there that I conducted the Ives Third Symphony complete, and Ruggles. I gave some concerts. I helped edit the *New Music Edition*. It would be hard to enumerate the things I was into, but then all of us were busy all the time doing everything.

So I began composing early. I just haven't stopped, and I don't suppose I ever will. Sometimes I regret being a musician because it's so complicated. I'm not awfully skillful at patience, let's put it that way. Music really requires a lot of patience. That's why I have to have backup arts like painting and writing because there's so much just plain chore about the art of music. Nowadays the kids often don't bother to write anything down; they just improvise it and put it on a tape. But I am of the classical persuasion; I like precision; I like to decide as many things as I can, coordinate them. It makes a difference for me. So I just have to pay the price, which means an awful lot of patient work. Just before I met Bill, I was teaching Esperanto, a language I dearly love, in San Francisco. I spent a little time here in my lonely days in the country working with animals and forestry for a while. I spent most of my time with calligraphy and Esperanto. I did some pieces, of course, but those were the things that after work every night I was doing here.

LEYLAND: Could you talk about your opera *Young Caesar* and how your relationship with Bill was catalytic in its composition?

HARRISON: Bill got me used to the idea of being a musician again in the first place, and not hating everything about it. I was asked by the Encounters Group, in Pasadena, a modern composer presentation group, to do a concert. They pay a certain amount of money and were willing to commission a work from me for first presentation on their series, which often happens. I didn't know what to do for them, but I had wanted for a long long time to write a second opera. My first one, *Rapunzel,* is on a text by William Morris. I wanted to write a puppet opera; I love puppetry. I kept thinking in terms of a Southwestern Indian thing. All I could see was a white, sort of adobe stage with kachinas, and beautiful color in the puppets. But the music idea was a little restricting. I could only hear drums and maybe a flute or something. This wasn't quite what I was up to, because in the meantime I had had this long Oriental period, the beginning of the writing of a book on Korean music, and the exploration of Chinese music. All of this was very strong in me, a surge of this interest and knowledge. So, Bill suggested, why don't you do a gay subject, which had somehow never occurred to me.

Within fifteen minutes I had remembered the episode in Caesar's life, his affair with the king of Bithynia. Immediately I decided that's what I would do. I began getting lots of ideas for it right away, both for the production, and for the music.

The gist of the story is that Caesar, who comes from a republican atmosphere in Rome, finds himself in an Oriental court with an Oriental king. He actually has an affair with the king; and I'm sure he was absolutely dazzled there because this king was apparently a very intelligent and brilliant man who had already ceded his kingdom to Rome. As a matter of fact, Caesar like Bithynia so well that he went back to do legal defense of friends he had made at the court, and there are other evidences that he really liked it. It was the only time in his life, outside of with Cleopatra (when they went up the Nile) when he took some time off. To me what this meant was the young Roman, in a brilliant Oriental court. It meant, also, the combination of Western music with Asian music. It was, as you can see, a focal point, and it was exactly what was in my spirit at the same time. I wanted to do something which had this combination of world music. I had trouble finding librettists and finding a puppeteer to do it. It was terrible; I went through three puppeteers and two authors. Finally, Robert Gordon made me a very good libretto, his first. I set every word of it conscientiously. Eventually, I want to take time out and concentrate it. But basically it's a good opera. It's in fourteen scenes. We just finished recording excerpts from it, instrumental excerpts because there are a lot of tunes that everybody likes.

My idea was, Winston, that it should be a chamber opera in every sense. There is a precedent in modern writing, and that's Manuel de Falla's lovely opera for puppets, *El Retablo de Maese Pedro.* That has only twenty-one instruments, three voices, something like that. I wanted to go a little further and have only five players but lots of instruments because I don't write for a clarinetist, a flutist, a violinist. What I write for is a musician who can play four or five instruments, at least. I expect them to play four or five. So if I had five players, I would expect at least twenty-five or thirty instruments to be available to me in various combinations. Usually, you can get it; so that's the way I compose. I do more and more of that. Then I wanted five puppeteers, five players, and five singers, because it's a big cast, but I thought five singers could change their voices enough to do it. They would all be backstage, and all you would see would be puppets. That's the way it turned out except that it required another few puppeteers, so there turned out to be seven or eight puppeteers. All that got out of hand was the puppetry. Finally I did find a professional puppeteer, Bill Jones, art director of KQED, and he did finally produce the whole set.

Young Caesar had a number of performances. We tried two or three preview performances which were almost complete. Then we did the first full premiere at Pasadena. That was quite successful. It roused the oddest press I've ever had. Some people enjoyed it, and some people were absolutely flabbergasted and insulted.

LEYLAND: Why do you think they felt insulted?

HARRISON: They couldn't believe that I would do such a thing seriously, present this episode from Caesar's life as a puppet opera. One reviewer couldn't imagine that there could be such a thing as a serious puppet opera.

COLVIG: I think also that a lot of people thought Caesar couldn't possibly be that silly. The image they had of Caesar was as the great leader, and they couldn't believe he could have gone through such a period. It rubbed them the wrong way.

HARRISON: Some of them didn't know the old saying about Caesar: Every man's woman and every woman's man. There is a story in the books that when the Senate was mad at him in later years, they used to hail him as he came in, "Hail, Queen of Bithynia!"

LEYLAND: In what way did you treat the relationship between Caesar and Nicomedes, king of Bithynia?

HARRISON: Caesar was sent to Bithynia in Asia Minor to collect boats for a campaign against Mytilene. He went to the client king, Nicomedes, to demand boats and had a love affair with the king. He got the boats, too. At the end of the opera there's a great sailing of boats for which I wrote a barcarole which, of course, means boat. I'd like to more, too, on such themes. They're grand fun. I would like to do some of Alexander the Great's life, which is a marvelous subject.

LEYLAND: Have you read Mary Renault's novel *The Persian Boy,* a very sensitive treatment of Alexander's later life?

HARRISON: Oh, isn't it marvelous? Bill read it to me. And I'd like to do a number of other operas or works. I really did fall in love with puppetry. It can do so much, you know; it can be so fluid and so full. For example, if you want to show a big banquet, you can. If you want to have a fleet of boats leaving, a fleet can leave. It's one of the virtues of puppetry that you can be lavish, and I like my theater lavish.

Gilgamesh is a big favorite of mine, too. I was going to do Gilgamesh for the York Festival when I realized I couldn't leave my mother because of her illness. But I will do it anyway sometime. The *Epic of Gilgamesh* is the affair between Gilgamesh and Enkidu. It's heartrending, the original poetic epic, and also it cannot really be construed in any other way than a romance, a very powerful and deep love between Gilgamesh, the hero, and a sort of wild man who must have represented all sorts of things. When Enkidu dies, Gilgamesh really goes wild, mourning. Then, of course, the mortality idea hits him and he spends the rest of the epic looking for some sort of immortality. In the end everything fails and all he can take is pride in his work, which is building the great wall at Uruk. Incidentally, I have a piece of the wall at Uruk right here. It's a loan from the Oriental Institute in Chicago and comes from the eighteenth century B.C. But It is astonishing that our first literary epic should have this subject, the relation between two men, as a very important thing. I am happy to see that Benjamin Britten has done a more overtly homosexual theme [his opera *Death in Venice —Ed.*]. I'm very happy about that.

LEYLAND: Don't you think the climate is right now and has been for the past few years? Would such works have been performable and acceptable twenty years ago?

HARRISON: No. I think that all the freedom we feel to do subjects of this kind now is due to the intervening strength of the gay movement. For myself, half of it was the McCarthy period. Senator Joe McCarthy was the one who resolved me never to hide in any closet about anything ever again in my life. When you get to the point that you don't know what's in your mailbox, the only counter-power you have is to live an absolutely open life, and I think that's really important. Some of the same feeling I had is back of the gay movement: the opening up and fighting for civil rights. You never get a thing by not fighting for it. Minorities do have to continuously keep the majority aware they exist. It seems to me that homosexuality is a cautionary minority for the rest of the world. It is the only minority which is produced spontaneously by nature herself generation after generation. And you'd think that would be a caution to the straight world that they don't have everything exactly their way all the time.

LEYLAND: I think the artist has a very catalytic role in this area.

HARRISON: Yes, I think so too, and I think that the public who accepts a work of art should sometimes think of its origins. I think that's only fair; they cannot expect that the origin is going to be the same for every work of art. In a way we really do have a privileged position as artists in this society. It's extraordinary. I've been to other societies, and I can tell you we do. But I do want to re-emphasize that we are a minority that is produced by nature. Other minorities dissolve. For example, if you have color minorities, they can just get dissolved into the bloodstream of the whole group. Religious minorities may disappear or get absorbed again. I can't think of another major minority that is produced directly by nature over and over again.

LEYLAND: And it's interesting too, that through recorded history so many major artists and writers have been gay. Their gayness has been a stimulus in their work, an important part of creativity.

HARRISON: Yes, whether known or not, I'm sure that's true. We know a little bit from Tchaikovsky's diary, though how directly it relates to his work we don't know. It must have because, after all, the Sixth Symphony is dedicated to the nephew with whom he was having an affair at the end. A recent psychological study of Beethoven shows that he was probably a repressed homosexual. It's funny how these traditional rumors have been going around for years. The gay world has always known about Tchaikovsky, of course, and there have been rumors about Schubert, for example, and his friend. They combined names at one point you know, and came out with a name that was sort of halfway between both of their names.

COLVIG: When are we going to do that?

HARRISON: Well, I don't know, we've tried all sorts of things. We used to cut out the C&H sugar cartons, Colvig-Harrison, very sweet. But the sense of community I think that we have had. How many years has it been really?

LEYLAND: Mattachine started in 1950 as an activist group, the first of the homophile organizations.

HARRISON: I joined Mattachine many years ago. What happens, of course, is that every generation reinvents the whole thing. But every time there's a little more progress I think.

LEYLAND: The tempo has been accelerated within the last three or four years.

HARRISON: Yes, I agree with that. We can even have feature-length movies about us too. Television now accepts the subject. That's a fair indication, I think, that the general community is beginning to accept the facts of life. It seems to me that *Gay*

Sunshine has turned in some sense into our major cultural journal, which is an interesting transition.

LEYLAND: It's not a change so much as an evolution. The political and cultural have been integrated. For instance, in the Ginsberg interview [reprintd in this volume] much of what Ginsberg said was both political and literary at the same time. Not political in the polemical sense. But I think we're coming to a new understanding of what we mean by political, too. A work of art, a piece of music can raise consciousness. A work like *Young Caesar* is a beautiful work of music, and at the same time it also raises consciousness in the sense of treating a gay subject in an open, honest way, without being defensive about it. But if you had written *Young Caesar* fifty years ago, it probably would not have been performable.

HARRISON: Oh yes, I think so, and not that far back even, just very recently. I think that change is clearly the result of emboldened honesty. I wonder about the absolute political connections, of course, of the revolutionary movement. I have the feeling that revolutions are much too busy to worry about our problems generally. The Castro pronouncement about gays, for example, has proved very disagreeable to numbers of us, and of course we read of distressing things in Maoist China, too, which is an exaggerated example of a certain kind of revolution. It's apparently very hard to make a successful humanistic revolution that includes everybody. It doesn't seem to have happened in our time, at any rate in this century. Segments of a full revolution occur here, there, and yon, but it doesn't all coalesce. As a matter of fact in the United States we are really freer now, and we're having a more thoroughgoing revolution in many ways than other parts of the world that are professing revolution.

LEYLAND: Don't you think there is a kind of dichotomy here? In one sense there is a great deal of artistic freedom in the United States. Yet at the same time—in the sixties for example—there was a massive bombing of Vietnam, torture, and the My Lai massacre. It's a schizophrenia. Artists are free in our society—up to a point; as long as their art doesn't shake up capitalist structures too much.

HARRISON: Of course, all of us were fighting on both fronts then; we were fighting both for minority rights and against the war. I devoted a fair amount of time to writing *Peace Pieces,* which were literally political activist music. Some of them were good music, some weren't probably, but I had to do something. Vietnam was a dreadful disaster. Yes, you're right, a very mixed bag, wasn't it; and it's still a mixed bag as we see, at the present time, the government having such an imbalance. If the present situation holds with an obviously weak president, then maybe Congress will take back powers that it relinquished slowly, and we might get a better balance again.

LEYLAND: I think one of the roles of the artist is to be prophetic and to speak out against injustices. You have done this with your *Peace Pieces,* just as Picasso did it with his painting "Guernica." And I hope that *Gay Sunshine* can do likewise.

HARRISON: One of the great protests was Robert Duncan's *Passages 22,* that one enormous single sentence against the Vietnamese War and Johnson at that time, which I set as one of my *Peace Pieces.* We got our only "boo" at the Cabrillo Festival from that. Some little lady said "boo." After that, there was silence in the hall and some lady said "boo" and one of the double-bass players looked around and said "shame!" So mild a riot.

COLVIG: And of course, Associated Press quoted, "Amid cries of 'boo' and 'shame'." It was marvelous music.

HARRISON: I've done four *Peace Pieces*. The *Heart Sutra* is the fourth.

LEYLAND: Could you talk a little more about the *Heart Sutra* and about Esperanto, the language in which it is written and in which you're an accomplished linguist. I heard it at the Cabrillo Music Festival and was immensely moved by it.

HARRISON: Esperanto is an international langauge. It really works. I found myself in Italy not being able to speak the language. I'm very sensitive about being articulate. So when I came back here I thought surely somebody has done something about this. And I remembered then when I was a very early adolescent, the daughter of a professor at Stanford had introduced me to the language of Esperanto through a book. So I immediately went up to San Francisco to the international bookstore. From that time on I made use of Esperanto.

I am currently a member of the Esperanto International Musicians League. I was for a while a member of the Buddhist Esperantist group with headquarters in Belgium. The musicians' group headquarters is in Turin, Italy. Within the last year I've written a large work in Esperanto. It's the *Heart Sutra* (*La Koro Sutro* in Esperanto), which was performed here at the Cabrillo Festival (summer 1973), with Carlos Chavez conducting. Bill's instruments were used. The whole gamelan that he made was used along with a chorus. So the work is for chorus and gamelan. It's the text of the Heart Sutra translated from Sanskrit into Esperanto by a friend of mine in San Francisco, Bruce Kenedy, a superb linguist. I commissioned the translation several years before I actually composed the piece. It's about half an hour long. Every year the Cabrillo Music Festival does one large work by me. Last year we did a Chinese concert, and the year before that we did almost the complete *Young Caesar,* which is an opera that comes from the relation with Bill, just as the *Heart Sutra* does.

The Heart Sutra is one of the great documents of humanity in the area of what the West knows as Hagia Sophia, Holy Wisdom. The Mahayana Buddhist version of that started fairly soon after the Buddha died. By the second century A.D. a huge literature had developed. For example, I think the major book of that is the *Perfect Wisdom* in a hundred thousand lines; each of those lines is thirty-two syllables. You can imagine the size of the book. Then it's had condensations clear down to a single letter, the letter *a* in Sanskrit. But the most successful, and the most noble, and the enduring one is the Heart Sutra. It's called that because it's the heart of the matter. It's seven paragraphs with an introduction, and the mantrum at the end. It concentrates all of the paradoxical beauty of this whole area of philosophy into a very brief, sharp space. I had wanted to set it ever since I was in Asia in the early sixties, and it just brewed for ages. It's psychological insight on the question of Nirvana, which is the Buddhist problem.

Buddhism, as you probably already know, is a self-evaporating religion. The minute you're talking about it it's no longer Buddhism; it's a practice. The Heart Sutra, which is about the practice and its evaporation, is just full of paradoxes. It comes out to a mantrum. Also there is a question about one phrase in the translation I find absolutely fascinating. The Sanskrit phrase at one point can be construed in two ways. With the fullness of the practice of perfect wisdom the Bodhisattva, who is the person doing all this, finally attains Nirvana or finally is sustained by Nirvana. When you're completely with it, of course you're in Nirvana. The doctrine can be construed as meaning that that's the fixing point, the nonbacksliding point, and that you are then sustained; no matter what comes up you can't be shook up. It's the same thing in Epicurus' philosophy. The word "atarax" in Greek means the same thing fundamentally as Nirvana, the state in which you can no longer get shook up, or shaken up. Nothing will budge you; you're in the unwobbling pivot in the confusion sense too. So it's the same thing. In fact, Epicureanism is very close to some parts of Mahayana Buddhism. Epicurus lived just after Alexander's conquests, and he very carefully questioned all those who knew of things from India. So it is a kind of refined Buddhism in the Epicurean doctrine; it relates to it at any rate. That's the question in the Heart Sutra, the question as to whether all this practice leads to Nirvana, or whether Nirvana happens on the way and then sustains you when you get shook up. It's a question of being with it all the time and not getting swerved. So I vote for the sustaining point of view; it seems to me the more sensible. I retranslated that one word in the Esperanto text to conform with that notion, but it can be read either way as a matter of fact. It's a marvelous text. There is, I think, almost no moment on the planet when the Heart Sutra is not being intoned somewhere. It's the favorite text, you know, for all walks of Buddhism. Every Mahayana sect uses it. I think it's been translated even into Pali. It's probably used in the Theravadan area too now. So fundamentally, it's really the quintessential text of this kind of philosohy.

I had wanted to set it for a long time, and all of a sudden it started to roll because there was a congress of Esperantists in Portland last year. A lot of them came down afterwards to San Francisco for what they call a post-Kongresso trip. We entertained them as Bay Region Esperantists. Bill and I organized and presented a concert at San Francisco State on August 19th, 1972. That's when we presented the first performance of the *Heart Sutra.* So it was written specifically for an Esperantist conference. They loved it. In fact, the San Francisco papers did announce it at my request, that it was going to be happening, but they didn't bother to review it. But we didn't mind that because, of course, reviews started coming in. Two from Holland, at any rate, and we got one from London too. Well this is the advantage of having an international audience that is literate and has access to the press.

LEYLAND: So the crucial element is one's being sustained by Nirvana in this life and beyond, as opposed to obtaining Nirvana.

HARRISON: You're right about sustaining Nirvana in this life. As I understand it, proto-Buddhism involves being totally with it all the time, not having any objections, not being shook up, perfect equanimity about everything at all times. Fundamentally, it's a formula for being happy, if you want to be happy. Now it's surprising the number of people who don't want to be happy; so it doesn't help them. But if you do want to be happy, there is a formula, and if you'll just follow it and get with it all the time, then that's Nirvana. If you get to the sticking point about that, you are in Nirvana all the time, which is the idea. It's the Epicurean "atarax," complete equanimity and not being shook up. As in Epicurus, you have to control your environment a little bit to do this, because otherwise you are at the mercy of the elements, so to speak. Buddhism makes no point about the question of life after death at all. As the Buddha pointed out, if you want life after death, and you don't get it, then you'll be disappointed. If you don't want life, or if you don't care, and there is, you'll be surprised. In any event there is no way it can help you at all while you're here to be happy. So the question is completely irrelevant, and he wouldn't discuss it. He said it simply doesn't matter. Reincarnation, I suspect, in the original prototypic Buddhism simply meant from minute to minute. What we have done in the past does determine our reincarnation minute to minute, you know. The real point is not to want anything to be other than it is, in any way that it is; that is, not any more or less than it will be, nor your attainments either.

LEYLAND: So it's more a sense of equilibrium and not an insatiable ambition kind of thing; a gradual developing evolution of one's being, one's talents.

HARRISON: Yes, you're right, that's it. For example, if you want to be happy, you can't just all of a sudden say, "Oh, yes, now I want not to want anything to be more," because automatically you're off the beam. It's very poised and almost inexpressible. As a matter of fact, when it's happening, Buddhism evaporates. The desire, the way, the path, everything's gone because there, whatever is, is. I think that's the basic idea of the Heart Sutra too. Through a list of marvelous paradoxes, you know, form is the same as not-form. The fourfold business is very frequent.

Here's one of the fourfold things he says: "Here, Shariputra, form is emptiness and the very emptiness is form. Emptiness does not differ from form, nor does form differ from emptiness. Whatever is form, that is emptiness; whatever is emptiness, that is form." The same is true of feelings, perceptions, impulses, consciousness. You just are intended to apply the four opposites all the way down the line. It's a kind of wiping out of intellection by the use of extreme intellection. It's self-evaporation. "Here, Shariputra, all dharmas are marked with emptiness. They are neither produced nor stopped, neither defiled nor immaculate, neither deficient nor complete...." James Broughton gives it more clearly in his Zen Poetry:

> *This is It*
> *and I am It*
> *and You are It*
> *and so is That*
> *and He is It*
> *and She is It*
> *and It is It*
> *and That is That*
>
> *O It is This*
> *And It is Thus*
> *and It is Them*
> *and It is Us*
> *and It is Now*
> *and here It is*
> *and here We are*
> *so This is It.*

LEYLAND: There is a clarity, à la Gertrude Stein, here.

HARRISON: Yes, well, it does come down to that. To quote another of his poems, "Round Table":

> *It's all in your head,*
> *the first man said.*
>
> *It's all in your heart,*
> *said another.*
>
> *It's all in your stars,*
> *said the man with scars.*
>
> *It's all in your guts,*
> *said his brother.*
>
> *It's all in your soul,*
> *said the man who was slow.*
>
> *It's all in your balls,*
> *said the fast one.*
>
> *It's all in your things,*
> *said the fellow with rings.*
>
> *It's in no thing at all,*
> *said the last one.*

That's what the Wisdom literature is all about. Incidentally, the Christian literature developed about the same time as the developed form of Mahayana Buddhism. Do you know that marvelous intersection, intellectually, in Syria?

LEYLAND: Do you mean Pseudo-Dionysius the Areopagite of the fifth century A.D.?

HARRISON: Yes. His work is related to the Perfect Wisdom literature of the Mahayana Buddhists. It was in Syria that that exquisite confusion between Christian and Buddhist saints came about: the Balavariani, Saints Barlaam and Josaphat; a real divine comedy. The Christians in Syria had an extremely rich intellectual life. They apparently knew of the life of the Buddha, and the Mahayana business of the Bodhisattva; they simply adopted lives of such conspicuous sanctity into Christianity.

LEYLAND: This was connected with the Nestorian schism of the fifth century and its subsequent history, as I recall.

HARRISON: Right. It was the Nestorian Christians who spread into Asia as far as China, and this information probably came into the Christian Church through them also. It is only recently that the church decanonized, unsanctified Barlaam and Josaphat. Otherwise, you could walk into a Catholic church and light a candle for the Buddha and the Bodhisattva. But to return to the gay subject—though there is no fundamental problem about gayness in Buddhism, the way of the elders, all of the uptight groups still make prohibitions or did at least scripturally. Nobody pays any attention, the same thing as the advanced Catholic situation.

LEYLAND: That quotation in the Ginsberg interview was interesting. Ginsberg asked his Tibetan Buddhist guru what he thought about homosexuality. The response was that the important thing is communication. And surely that is one of the basic approaches of gay liberation.

HARRISON: Right. That was very stimulating reading. I really just loved that. Allen is stimulating. He's a marvelous guy.

LEYLAND: Was the *Heart Sutra* your first work utilizing Buddhist texts?

HARRISON: No, I set the *Invocation for the Health of All Beings* from the Metta Sutta, which is a beautiful text. It's part of a large Sutta in Pali and is a very well known Buddhist text: "May all beings be happy and at their ease, may they be joyous and live in safety, all beings whether great or small, born or unborn, visible or invisible.... May all beings be happy and at their ease, may all beings be joyous and live in safety...." Another part of it is that you are instructed to think of every living thing, every being in the world as though you were a mother and had an only child, to extend good will and love to the whole of the animate conscious universe. It's part of the good will feeling of Mahayana Buddhism. It's a beautiful sutta.

That was my first *Peace Piece*. It's dedicated to the memory of Dr. Martin Luther King. That's for unison chorus with a small orchestra including percussion, two harps, some strings, a trombone, very small. All these *Peace Pieces,* by the way, were done at the Cabrillo Festival in Aptos with Gerhard Samuel conducting. They took a whole half program because I collected them. My very first *Peace Piece*, or my first protest piece, because I didn't label it a *Peace Piece* back in those days, was done in 1935/36; it was a protest against the Spanish War. It had a quotation from Milton. It was for a percussion and string quartet. Then I did to my own text a little song which was another *Peace Piece*. It was about the atom bomb. It has a lot of things, but it wasn't a Buddhist text, it was my own. So I think fairly surely, Winston, that the Metta Sutta, the *Invocation for the Health of All Beings,* was the first Buddhist text I set.

Another one I want to set is the ten ox-herding pictures of Zen. They're just beautiful. There's a whole series of different sets of them, so I could choose from a lot of texts. Fundamentally there are ten pictures. They represent the psychological journey of finding one's rather violent libido in the shape of an ox. First you get glimpse of the landscape, they you find the ox, then you grab the ox, then you tame the ox. The ox finally gives up and listens to you play the flute. Then finally you release the ox, and it's all blanked out, endless white moon. Some groups add a further one where the fat, jovial old man goes back to society as a sort of buffoon. He's the enlightened one, of course, who has tamed the ox. The ox-herding pictures have all sorts of charming things in them. It took me nearly ten years to brew up the *Heart Sutra*. Eventually the ox-herding pictures will brew up too. I want to set them probably for soloist and chorus and a small ensemble of some sort. Then I want to project those woodcuts on a screen or even make a puppet show of the ten scenes. I'm not quite sure, but some ritual presentation of the material because it exists graphically in so many versions. It would be beautiful to project all those along with the music. Many commentators have commented on the pictures and the meaning of them; so it gives a lot of different texts.

LEYLAND: You mentioned last night about some medieval Arab musicians being transvestites. Maybe you could talk a little about that and homosexuality in the East.

HARRISON: In the earliest histories of Arab music the first important musicians were apparently transvestites, apparently also homosexuals. That's not always true you know. Much ill will attached, as a matter of fact, to them. Drinking wine and listening to music and like that are not orthodox in Islamic practices. That didn't stop them because there were periods, of course, when Islam resounded with song and instruments and much consumption of wine. The tradition of the minstrel in Europe in the Middle Ages apparently derived from the habits of the musicians of Islam, that is to say, the costumes, the wearing of certain hairdos and/or long hair, henna hands, use of makeup, and so on. In fact the word "mascara" is an Arabic word. Homosexuality has, of course, been a frank part of the Islamic tradition for a very long time. One reads of Turkish sultans, for example, even in the last century or before in history, and the advice given them in growing was not to scorn either sex. So certainly a bisexual habit was a part of their tradition and background.

In the Far East homosexual practices have been largely associated with the literati and are much more closely connected with writing than they are with other arts. This is largely because the musical foundations, the big foundations of the court and the church are largely hereditary. In Japan even the clergy marries. The court orchestras continue to practice generation after generation, from father to son, so that the habit of musicians being homosexual does not hold in Far East Asia—China, Japan, and Korea. There used to be a tradition in Korea and Japan of Buddhist monks who would go about with young men to raise money for their monastery. There is a good deal of homosexuality in the history of Japan among the samurai and so on. There was in fact one monarch who offered rewards for any of the samurai who would marry and have children.

The Wharang tradition in Korea seems to have had homosexual overtones. It was during the Silla dynasty, roughly contemporaneous with Tang in China, and was a courtly institution involving young men. It's very romantic, at any rate. It was involved also with the shamanistic practices. As we know, shamanism includes homosexuality very often as a part of its structure. So that the Wharang institution, very poetic, seems to have been part shamanism, part court, part poetry and music, the singing of songs, and part Buddhism. It was an institution all of its own.

LEYLAND: I had wanted to talk a little about the relationship between your gayness and the creative process. This perhaps is more pronounced in writers, as you said before, than in composers.

HARRISON: Yes, I think so, and for the very simple reason that to say "I am gay" is done with words. That as a public matter is entirely verbal. I think that a musician, composer at any rate, deals with generalized terms. That is to say, for example, depicting making love in music works no matter what sexual combination you have because it's a matter really of the fundamental expression of sensuality and it simply doesn't matter what form it is. You rightly point out, Winston, that there are fewer musicians who have declared themselves homosexual for the simple reason that there is no real public need for it, or there is no problem in that sense because there is no verbal problem except as you pointed out too. If a composer is writing a great number of songs and they all have gay texts, then someone might inquire at some time. Of course, I have written an opera on a gay subject and one song which I myself construe as being a gay love song, as it were.

Has Ned Rorem set any gay texts? I don't specifically remember any gay texts from him. Texts by gay authors, yes, but I don't remember any involving actual gay material.

LEYLAND: He did set work of Frank O'Hara, Paul Goodman and Walt Whitman.

HARRISON: He's a very skillful composer and I'm always looking forward to things. I think he feels, because of the *Time* article, perhaps that he's less important as an instrumental composer. I think that's nonsense; he's a very good instrumental composer. *Time*, you see, said that he's the best song writer that we have. So now he feels that he has to be the best song writer, has to turn them out by the millions. Overlooked, for example, are the beautiful pieces he did for Louisville, his orchestra pieces. He's an all-around composer. I think he has had an unfair press in that sense. He's an all-around composer, and a very sensible one I think too. Is Ned the only declared gay composer?

LEYLAND: Well, Virgil Thomson hasn't openly declared himself, although his gayness is an open secret. I suppose Ned Rorem is declared more or less because of his writing in the *New York* and *Paris Diaries*.

HARRISON: Yes, they're very specific on the subject. That just goes to show you how far we've come. I remember being quite surprised that a fellow musician, a fellow composer, had written such a diary, and delighted, as a matter of fact. I wrote a review of both of them right from the start. I hope that more gay material will be used more naturally in the arts; and I think it will be.

LEYLAND: Don't you think that in the past many artists felt compelled to make a dichotomy between their personal lives as gay people and their art, whether it be writing or music; and that there's been a breakthrough within the last decade or so?

HARRISON: Yes, I think so. Also rousing, out of gratitude and natural group feeling, a kind of loyalty to a group which was not there before. I used to envy minority composers who had behind them a whole minority group. For example, the Armenian bishops used to fight to sponsor concerts by Alan Hovhaness. I used to think, how marvelous to have a minority that supports you, that you could write for, and that you had a real response to. I shouldn't be a bit surprised that that brewing underneath also helped lead to my opera, *Young Caesar,* because of that feeling of support from minority group. I like that.

LEYLAND: How has your relationship with Bill affected your own creativity?

HARRISON: There is one thing that I have observed over the years. I do not go along with the pseudo-Freudian notion that sexual frustration, or sublimation as they call it, is a help to creative processes. I think, in fact, exactly the reverse. Unless you have plenty of love, plenty of sex, plenty of affection, it just gets in your way if you're trying to do creative work. When that's expressed in fully living, then I think you can live the life of a creative person. But I think that you're just gummed-up otherwise. If you are all frustrated, what can you do? The proof of the pudding is that I have been very happy with Bill, increasingly happy; and I am increasingly composing and doing big works, the natural thing you know. So, in my own case, that's the plain proof of it. I think a lot of people are rethinking that notion these days too, don't you? This is another reason, too, for outright living, all the way down the line I think.

PHOTO BY PAT YORK, SANTA MONICA, 1972

CHRISTOPHER ISHERWOOD

CHRISTOPHER ISHERWOOD was born in Cheshire, England, in 1904. He left Cambridge without graduating, tried to study medicine, and in 1928 published *All the Conspirators,* an unsuccessful first novel. From 1928 onwards he lived mostly out of England: four years in Berlin, five in various European countries. His Berlin experiences furnished him with the materials for what are probably his best novels: *The Last of Mr. Norris* (1935) and *Goodbye to Berlin* (1939)— reissued as *The Berlin Stories* (1946). These books form the basis for John Van Druten's play *I Am a Camera* (1951), and for the Broadway musical and later film *Cabaret.* The two Berlin novels report on the period of social and political turmoil during the Nazi rise to power and illustrate Isherwood's concern with the problem of the intellectual in a tyrannical society.

With W. H. Auden, a friend since their early schooldays, Isherwood wrote three plays and a travel book, *Journey to a War,* which describes China in 1938 during the Japanese invasion. In 1939 he emigrated to the United States. He worked with the American Friends Service Committee during part of the war. In 1946 he became a U.S. citizen. A few years later he was elected to the U.S. National Institute of Arts and Letters. During the forties his interests also turned to Hinduism.

Since living in America Christopher Isherwood has written five novels: *Prater Violet* (1945), *The World in the Evening* (1954), *Down There on a Visit* (1962), *A Single Man* (1964), and *A Meeting by the River* (1967). A play with Don Bachardy, based on *A Meeting by the River,* was first performed in 1972. He has also written a travel book about South America, *The Condor and the Cows,* and *Ramakrishna and His Disciples,* a biography of the great Indian mystic. In 1966 a collection of his stories, articles, and verse was published under the title *Exhumations.* His study of his parents, *Kathleen and Frank,* appeared in 1971. And in 1976 his autobiographical account of his life in the thirties was published under the title *Christopher and His Kind.*

Christopher Isherwood lives with artist Don Bachardy in Santa Monica, California, his home since the 1940s.

TWO SEPARATE INTERVIEWS are printed here: Interview I was taped in summer 1973 by Winston Leyland, editor of *Gay Sunshine,* and originally appeared in *Gay Sunshine* 19 (September–October 1973). Interview II was taped in San Francisco in December 1976 while Isherwood was touring with his book *Christopher and His Kind.* It was conducted under the auspices of Fruit Punch, gay men's radio, which broadcast an edited version over KPFA (Berkeley) in February 1977. Roger Austen, who conducted the second interview, is a San Francisco free-lance writer, author of *Playing the Game: The Homosexual Novel in America* (1977).

I
Winston Leyland interviews
CHRISTOPHER ISHERWOOD

LEYLAND: In the introduction to your *Berlin Stories,* you say that you destroyed your past and that the real Christopher Isherwood disappeared. What did you mean by that statement?

ISHERWOOD: Well, that's a literary phrase. My religion, Vedanta, encourages me to believe that there isn't one single *real* Christopher Isherwood, in a personal sense. There are many, all equally real or unreal. When I started writing about Berlin, I found that the story would be more coherent and indeed *truer* if I fictionalized it to some degree. And so I started rewriting my life and therefore manufacturing a different Christopher. But the story never departs from my own essential experience. It's still Berlin as I saw it. I never gave my fictitious Christopher any characteristics or virtues or vices which I didn't have myself. I agree with Hemingway—one should only write what one knows.

Of course, the Berlin experience seemed different to me then. While I was there, it didn't seem as glamorous to me as it now does. As a matter of fact, there were long periods which were dull and quiet, when things went on much as usual. Nowadays, people often say to me: "Jesus, if only I had lived in those days! If only I'd been with you there!" I smile to myself, because I think how bored they'd have been a lot of the time. And yet, the funny thing is, I can look back at Berlin through their eyes—looking through the telescope of my stories, as it were—and see Berlin as they see it.

LEYLAND: Don't you think that people are romanticizing the San Francisco beat period in the fifties in the same way?

ISHERWOOD: Of course they are. But there *are* periods in one's life which one finds romantic at the time as well as afterwards. For instance, my trip to China with Auden in 1938 seemed just as romantic at the time as it does now. But Berlin—because I stayed there several years—became simply a way of life. In the winter it was a very dark and drab city; heavy buildings. I gave English lessons, day after day. A boyfriend would come by in the evenings and we'd go to the movies. It was enjoyable but certainly not a scintillating or brilliant period. It was appetizing, because I was young and full of life and tremendously happy to be away from all the restraints which England represented—above all, to feel completely free sexually. Also, it was a great freedom to be able to speak a foreign language. I could say things in German which it would have still embarrassed me to say in English: things about love and sex, particularly. And that made me feel like a new person. Nevertheless, at the end of three and a half years, I had gotten pretty used to all that. It was no longer a thrill.

LEYLAND: Were your characters in *The Berlin Stories* taken from real life?

ISHERWOOD: Yes, certainly. No important character in the Berlin books is without a model from real life.

LEYLAND: What about Baron Kuno von Pregnitz? He's almost a caricature of the Prussian homosexual.

ISHERWOOD: The imaginary island where he lived with all the boys—I took that from another character, actually. This sort of baron—I mean, someone who put on the airs of being an aristocrat, even though his title was often invented by himself—was a stock figure in the Berlin homosexual bar world.

I suppose I was always aware, in the back of my mind, of an intention to write about Berlin, even while I was there. That was why I kept a diary. It was very terse and fragmentary, but it helped me to remember a lot of things later.

When I started to write the novel about Mr. Norris in 1934, about a year after I'd left Berlin for good, I was very much under the spell of another experience I'd just had. In 1933, I got a job—the first of that kind—writing for the movies, in England. (That's all described in my story *Prater Violet*.) Because of this job, I became intensely cinema-minded. I had always been a great movie fan, anyhow. Now I was in love with plotting, action, and trying to tell a story in visual terms. Even while writing this novel, I kept thinking how its scenes would look on the screen. That was good. But the effect of my plot-mindedness was that I put my portrait of Mr. Norris into a primitive, pre–Eric Ambler story, with some absurd melodrama about espionage. I adore spy stories, both in books and on the screen; but in this case the two styles of story-telling didn't blend very well.

LEYLAND: But the character of Mr. Norris certainly does come alive.

ISHERWOOD: Yes, he has managed to exist independently, outside the book itself, as it were, in the minds of many readers. The original of Mr. Norris also existed independently—alas, he's dead now—and often did things which I could never have invented in my wildest dreams. But he was very conscious of the fictitious Mr. Norris and even wrote a book called *Mr. Norris and I*. His real name was Gerald Hamilton.

I'm often asked if I regret that I didn't say outright in *The Berlin Stories* that I was homosexual. Yes, I wish I had. But I should have had to say it very *casually*, if I *had* said it; otherwise, I would have made the Christopher character too odd, too remarkable, and that would have upset the balance between him and the other characters. Christopher is the narrator, so he mustn't stand out too prominently. To have made him homosexual, in those days, would have been to feature him as someone eccentric. I would have made a star out of a supporting actor. That's a valid literary reason. But I must also frankly say that I would have been embarrassed, then, to create a homosexual character and give him my own name.

LEYLAND: Do you think you could have gotten an explicitly homosexual book about yourself published in the thirties?

ISHERWOOD: Oh yes, I could have got such a book published if I hadn't gone into too many details about homosexual lovemaking. But I must come back to what I've just been saying: in those days, people expected you to announce the theme of homosexuality with a flourish of trumpets. By the time I'd finished introducing and explaining and apologizing for Christopher the homosexual, there would have been no room in the book for my other characters. It would have overbalanced the boat.

LEYLAND: It's difficult now to get interviews with some well-known writers and poets who are gay in their private life but have never let the gay dimension into their writing. Some are uptight about being interviewed in a journal like *Gay Sunshine*.

ISHERWOOD: If a writer doesn't want to admit to his homosexuality publicly, that's his affair. But to refuse specifically to do so in the gay magazines, that's sheer snobbery. That means he's ashamed of his brothers and sisters.

LEYLAND: In *The Berlin Stories* you yourself came more to the surface in the Peter and Otto story. Did you have an affair with the boy Otto when you were in Germany?

ISHERWOOD: Yes. In that story, I took a real person, a friend, and described him in the character of Peter, an English homosexual. As a matter of fact, it wasn't Peter who was living with Otto Nowak on Ruegen Island; it was I myself. Otto and I were lovers for quite a long period and lived together some of the time. Actually, there were only two boys who were really close to me during the whole time I was in Berlin. First Otto, then another boy who left Germany and traveled with me. To some degree, the other one is described as Waldemar, in *Down There on a Visit*.

Toward the end of my stay in Germany, I became much more conscious of the political situation. The Berlin books were written with a good deal of political hindsight. I couldn't resist posing as someone who had been deeply concerned with the fate of Germany right from the day of my arrival. That simply wasn't true. To begin with, I was both indifferent and ignorant. And even as late as 1932, I find that I wrote to my mother and spelt Hitler's name wrong!

In the working-class world of Berlin, every young attractive man was under economic pressure to become a hustler; nobody was getting enough to eat. These hustlers were apt to become gang-minded; they joined political parties which fought in gangs against other rival political gangs. These boys were pretty vague about the political part of it. They just wanted some action to relieve the frustration of their lives. They switched sides continually. Many of them who had called themselves Comunists became Nazis when it was obvious who was going to win.

LEYLAND: Were Spender and Auden in Berlin at that time?

ISHERWOOD: Not nearly as much. Auden came before I did, to brush up on his German because he intended to become a schoolmaster. But he soon left. We were old friends; we'd met at school when he was seven and I was ten. We met again in our teens and I discovered to my amazement that he wrote poetry. Then we became really intimate. Later, Stephen Spender came to Berlin from Hamburg, where he had been living. (You can read all about that in his autobiography, *World within World*, which is pretty frank about both our lives.)

LEYLAND: There is an unfavorable mention in *The Berlin Stories* of the German Youth Councils of that period. What were your feelings behind that comment?

ISHERWOOD: I don't like that passage and I don't know why I put it in. It strikes an insincere, rather puritanical note. I may have written like that because I felt that these people were in a fair way to becoming fascists. But that in itself has an unfair implication and a very dangerous one. I should have discussed the whole question fully or left it alone. Does homosexuality predispose you to join group movements of young men and hence, in certain historical circumstances, to become part of a totalitarian group? Maybe so. But that isn't the whole story. An awful lot of homosexuals who were conned into doing this in Germany later discovered to their cost how totalitarian regimes deal with homosexuals. At the time of the Roehm scandals in 1934, there was an out-and-out attack on homosexuals as such, although the real reason for the liquidation of Roehm was entirely political. And in Soviet Russia, about the same time, homosexuals were being denounced as fascists. Both Communists and Nazis regarded them as potential traitors.

LEYLAND: And, of course, gay people ended up in Nazi concentration camps. We had a short article on this in *Gay Sunshine* 18. A lot of people associate homosexuality in Germany in the early thirties with Roehm's SA gang. A caricature of homosexuals has been built up, as exemplified in the movie *The Damned*.

ISHERWOOD: Yes, there's a strong suggestion in *The Damned* that homosexuality is a factor in the damnation. People ask me nowadays, "Wasn't it kind of decadent there?" meaning, actually, homosexual. It's infuriating; it's such a vicious oversimplification to say that pre-Hitler Germany was decadent and so a Sodom and Gomorrah punishment fell upon it through the Nazis who in their turn of course were decadent too. You end up by saying, "It's those Germans; they're all decadent anyway, whatever party they belong to!" [*Laughter.*] As a matter of fact, I think Germans, when they're homosexual, make very good homosexuals. They're not in the least decadent, as far as my experience goes. They're simple and natural about it, and they have a strong natural capacity for tenderness and unashamed sentiment. I have often thought that I detected some of this same quality in Americans.

Sometimes I'm asked about my relationship with the girl who was the original of Sally Bowles in my stories—and of the Sally Bowles in the play and the film *I Am a Camera* and in the musical play and film *Cabaret*. My relationship with the real Sally Bowles was the simplest imaginable. She knew that I was fond of her like a sister and that I was a contented homosexual. We had no problems. Never were there any coy suggestions that I might be partly in love with her or secretly longing to go to bed with her. That's what I found a bit dirty about the film *Cabaret*. First the boy's supposed to be gay, and then he isn't, because he can make it with Sally, and then he is, after all, because he plays around with the Baron; and then he wants to marry her but she reminds him that he may lapse at some future date and run after boys again. His homosexuality is presented as a kind of indecent but ridiculous weakness to be snickered at, like bed-wetting.

LEYLAND: When did you first come to a realization of your own gayness?

ISHERWOOD: Quite early—by the time I was ten or so, in the sense of being physically attracted to boys at school. I managed to have orgasms with them while we were wrestling and I guess some of them had orgasms too, but we never admitted to it. I fell in love a lot during my teens, but never did anything about it. I was very late in getting into an actual physical affair. That happened while I was in college. There was no question at all in my mind about my homosexuality. It was like a choice which my mind-body had definitely made. I was even willing to agree that I might have become heterosexual if I had decided to. I tried it a couple or times. It was quite workable. But I preferred boys and I already knew that I could fall in love with them. I have been perfectly happy the way I am. If my mother was responsible for it, I am grateful.

As I have said, coming to Germany was a psychological release for me. It was in Berlin that I first came in contact with an organized homosexual group. It was centered at the Institute for Sexual Science which was run by Dr. Magnus Hirschfeld. He was a great pioneer and himself a homosexual. He had managed to re-educate the Berlin police and liberalize their attitudes to sex. He and his associates were deadly serious about their work in a typically German way which often seemed funny to a foreigner. I laughed at them often, then. Now I see them as heroic and noble. (Their institute was later wrecked by the Nazis.) Many people came to see Hirschfeld from all over Europe.

I remember how Hirschfeld put on a special scientific demonstration for André Gide. Among other exhibits, they brought in a boy with two perfectly formed female breasts. Gide sat there judiciously holding his chin. He had a very pragmatical attitude toward the whole thing and didn't want to listen to a lot of theories. Gide liked very young boys. At the bar he visited (it was one of my regular hangouts) they couldn't find anyone young enough for him, so they produced a boy who was actually about twenty-three but looked fifteen. There were no complaints. Gide was rather grand and gracious, with a cape. He liked to be called "maître." I didn't appreciate his greatness then as I do now. I thought him a snob—but then I thought anybody was a snob who didn't live in the slums.

LEYLAND: Isn't that an upper-class English romanticism—an idealization of the lower classes and a desire to associate with them?

ISHERWOOD: Typically upper class, yes. My own snobbery was simply inverted. Upper-class homosexuality in England tended to fixate on working-class boys. I didn't really recover from that state of mind until I began to live in America. When I found myself living in the working-class section of Berlin I felt I had transposed images and was playing the role of my own lover, so to speak. I had enough money to live in a more respectable part of town if I had wanted to, and I did, later. I moved into a slum tenement because of this boy Otto. I lived with him and his family.

LEYLAND: What was the attitude of your contemporaries in England to homosexuality?

ISHERWOOD: Most of my friends were either homosexual themselves or very relaxed in their attitude toward it. They had been to upper-class schools and were therefore quite accustomed to it. But then, I instinctively avoided people who I thought might disapprove of me. I never allowed anyone I knew intimately to be under any misunderstanding about my own homosexuality.

I came to the United States to live in 1939. I was very drawn to the Quakers because of their pacifism. And, more recently, they have put out an admirably positive statement about homosexuality. It was maybe a little condescending in places but it did say flatly that homosexual love can be, under certain circumstances, just as worthy of respect as heterosexual love.

LEYLAND: Were they idealizing monogamous gay love in a typically liberal approach?

ISHERWOOD: That's probably so. I agree that it's very dangerous to equate a homosexual relationship with heterosexual marriage. You drag in the whole bourgeois system of obligations and the concept of ownership.

I would very much like to write a novel about gay life itself, but it's terribly hard to do so. I have never written much about homosexual relationships—just some references to them in *The World in the Evening* and *A Single Man*—although I myself have lived much of my life in a series of quite long relationships. In my diaries I've tried to examine my fantasies about sex and how they relate to the kind of relationships I've had. One of them is incestuous, the desire for a brother who is also a lover. A younger brother.

LEYLAND: Have most of your relationships followed this pattern?

ISHERWOOD: Yes. All the relationships I've had have been with people younger than myself. I say "brother" rather than "son" because I don't like to think of the person I love as being a reproduction of myself. The idea of a brother suggests a greater polarity between us.

In my novel *A Meeting by the River,* and even more explicitly in the play which Don Bachardy and I have made out of it, there is a good deal of metaphor surrounding the two brothers who are the principal characters. One of them becomes a monk in a monastery in India and therefore has "brother" monks. The other, a married man, takes up with a California boy because he yearns for an ideal brother who is also a lover—a sort of Walt Whitman camerado. The two actual brothers have a love-hate relationship which binds them in spite of themselves until it is resolved at the end of the story.

LEYLAND: Do you think that the deep relationships you've had during your life have been satisfactory and fulfilling?

ISHERWOOD: Fulfilling, yes. I'm a bit shy of the word "satisfactory." It suggests that something has been delivered as ordered, according to specifications. It suggests the phrase "fit and forget," as applied to something absolutely reliable and predictable; you install it and it functions from then on, no need to worry. With love there *ought* to be a need to worry, every moment. Love isn't an insurance policy. Love is tension. What I value in a relationship is constant tension, in the sense of never being under the illusion that one understands the other person. When you fall in love, you feel you've discovered the bird of paradise, the magic person from the Other Land. You suddenly see a human being in all his magic extraordinariness. And you know that you can never understand him, never take him for granted. He's eternally unpredictable—and so are you to him, if he loves you. And that's the tension. That's what you hope will never end.

In my novel *A Meeting by the River* the married brother's romantic feelings go out to men; he regards his marriage as a kind of fortress. He sallies forth from the fortress to have adventures. Then he rushes back into it and his male lover is left standing outside in the cold. This kind of bisexual interests me a great deal. I have met many of them during my life. I describe another of them in *The World in the Evening,* but the one in *Meeting* is far more convincing, I think.

LEYLAND: Do you feel that such people are really bisexual or basically homosexual?

ISHERWOOD: It seems to me that the real clue to your sex orientation lies in your romantic feelings rather than in your sexual feelings. If you are really gay, you are able to fall in love with a man, not just enjoy having sex with him. That's the test I would apply to such people.

LEYLAND: In the gay world a dichotomy is often set up between the sexual and the romantic resulting in the one-night-stand syndrome. It's very hard (but very important) to integrate friendship and sex.

ISHERWOOD: Yes, that's true. Some people I've talked to have been very amazed when I told them I have sometimes been to bed with friends. Auden says somewhere in his writings: "Awareness of likeness—kindness; awareness of difference—love." Friends have this awareness of likeness. The combination of sex and friendship can be beautiful, but it's apt to be short-lived because excitement doesn't last when you feel the awareness of likeness. The love remains, but it's a love without tension, a different kind of love. How could you fall in love with someone about whom you could say, "He's exactly like me"? That would be sheer narcissism. Once, when I was in my early forties, I met a boy who was at least fifteen years younger than I was. Everybody noticed how alike we were physically. "He could be your younger brother," they said. And I found him wildly attractive! He didn't take the slightest interest in me.

LEYLAND: When did you first feel the need for this creative tension?

ISHERWOOD: When I was young. I didn't philosophize about it, but the need was undoubtedly there. When there was no tension, I wasn't really in love. But sometimes I tried to kid myself that I was, because the person I'd met was so "suitable" in every other way. I mean, he was somebody who would have done exactly what I wanted and never interfered with my work and waited for me when I went out and stayed home with me when I wanted to stay home. That was one side of my character, and it demanded a kind of chauvinistic marriage relationship. The other side of me knew it had to wait for the magic person, who would awaken real love and consequently tension and the destruction of convenience.

LEYLAND: You were tempted to isolate youself from relationships by devoting yourself to writing?

ISHERWOOD: Yes. When I was young in Berlin and apparently engaged in sowing my wild oats, I was terribly sensible about working. I got up early in the morning and wrote. At night I did go round to bars, but I always returned home early, with or without company, and managed to have a good night's sleep, sex or no sex.

LEYLAND: Have you been able to maintain this discipline?

ISHERWOOD: Yes. I do keep at it. The important thing is that you do something every day, no matter how little. If you form the habit of work when you're young, it makes things easier later.

LEYLAND: Was the character of George in your novel *A Single Man* autobiographical?

ISHERWOOD: Yes, to a large extent. But there are important differences. Unlike poor George, I've never had a lover who has died on me. Then again, George is a stoic and an agnostic, without any religious faith to help him through his life. He defies fate. He fights with bared teeth up to the last moment. I'm not a bit like that.

Again, George is a professional college professor. When I lecture at a college, I do so as a guest speaker. Therefore I can allow myself a great deal of freedom in what I say. I am expected to behave like a celebrity, not a professor, to amuse rather than instruct. The things I make George say in the classroom are the things that I would say. Coming from him, they are a bit out of character. But

I feel *A Single Man* is the best thing I have ever written. This was the only time when I succeeded, very nearly, in saying exactly what I wanted to say.

LEYLAND: In his book *Homosexual Oppression and Liberation,* Dennis Altman quotes you talking about the "annihilation by blandness" which liberals adopt towards gays. To what extent have you been exposed to this in your own life?

ISHERWOOD: Well, I've never been annihilated by it. But I've been very conscious that I was exposed to it. At one campus where I was lecturing, I asked a friend, "How many of my colleagues know I'm gay?" He answered, "All of them." I wasn't surprised. But, just the same, it was kind of spooky, because not one of them had ever given the faintest sign that he or she knew. If I had spoken about it myself, most of them would have felt it was in bad taste.

I suppose my own role as a gay is to try and get people out of their closets. When you're elderly and well known, closety types are apt to approve of you. Your books encourage their fantasies of freedom.

LEYLAND: What was the attitude of your parents to your gayness?

ISHERWOOD: I've written about my parents extensively in my recent book *Kathleen and Frank.* I always felt that my mother had a built-in defense against the whole idea of homosexuality. She was unable to believe that a relationship without a woman in it could be serious, under any circumstances. She thought it was a sort of pose, a mental game that I played. I told her that I was gay, very soon after I grew up. She appeared to accept the situation. She was always polite to the young men I brought to the house, and in one or two cases she genuinely liked them. But I believe her imagination refused to accept the fact that I was actually having sex with them. Sometimes my mother's attitude made me furious. I think it even helped to confirm me in my homosexuality. I had to *prove* to her that there really is such a thing as a homosexual! But, since she lived to be ninety-one, I had time to outgrow my antagonism; we ended by accepting our misunderstandings.

I think it would have been much harder for me to tell my father that I was gay. But that crisis never arose, because he was killed in World War I, when I was ten years old. I realize now that I was sexually attracted to my father, in my childhood. I used to go into his dressing room in the morning while he was doing physical exercises almost naked, in his undershorts. I can still remember liking the hardness of his muscles and the smell of his body.

I had a gay uncle with whom I had an amusing relationship after I grew up. He used to invite me to dinner at his flat and we would talk about boys. At the end of the evening, I would get a kiss from him which was rather too warm and searching for any nephew, even one's favorite.

When I started to write *Kathleen and Frank,* it was obvious to me that I couldn't tell their story without making my own gayness absolutely clear. So I kept stating this fact throughout the book. And this led naturally to similar statements on television, in public talks and in press interviews. So now I have officially "come out." Those who have always known that I was gay can now no longer pretend that they don't know. Those who have been prejudiced against me as a homosexual will now be confirmed in their prejudice. My fellow gays will mostly say "So what?" I don't risk being fired from a job, or sent to prison, or run out of town. Society can afford to overlook the deviant behavior of an elderly, otherwise respectable literary man who has sufficient savings in the bank. It may be that what I have done will inject a little courage into the souls of a few timid brothers. If so, good. If not, also good, because I at least feel a certain satisfaction.

About eighty percent of my friends have always been gay, and I feel curiously ill at ease when I have been away from gay people for long; it's a feeling almost like a lack of oxygen.

Many of my brothers have suffered terrible guilt because of their nature. Many more have been made to suffer because of it, by others. My life has been extremely lucky. To quote from *Kathleen and Frank:* "Despite the humiliations of living under a heterosexual dictatorship and the fury he has often felt against it, Christopher has never regretted being as he is. He is now quite certain that heterosexuality wouldn't have suited him; it would have fatally cramped his style."

II

Roger Austen interviews
CHRISTOPHER ISHERWOOD

AUSTEN: in your latest book, *Christopher and His Kind,* you have given an autobiographical look back into the years 1929–1939, which provides a real-life commentary to the fiction that you wrote at that time, with particular emphasis on the gay realities which were occasionally muted in such novels as *Goodbye to Berlin, The Last of Mr. Norris,* and, later on, *Down There on a Visit.* Did you ever sense in the thirties that there would come a day in your lifetime when such a frank book as this could be published?

ISHERWOOD: I suppose so, yes. I suppose I took it for granted that things would get better rather than worse. But that wasn't really the reason that I didn't write more frankly, although it was one reason at the time. There was also the reason that I was just trying to narrate this whole thing in the most unobtrusive manner possible. If the narrator were something as unusual as a homosexual, this would have made him too interesting, and then we would have got drawn aside into his affairs, his way of looking at things, his prejudices, his view of the world, and taken the interest away from Mr. Norris and Sally Bowles and all these characters. It's a different kind of writing.

AUSTEN: I suppose that because of your living at the Hirschfeld institute and seeing things that were being done thirty and forty years ago that your perspective on gay liberation is much broader than it is for those who believe everything began with Stonewall. Things were really happening in Berlin in the twenties and thirties?

ISHERWOOD: Oh, my goodness, yes. Hirschfeld was certainly one of the great heroes of gay liberation, one of the earliest people. He several times actually risked his life by going to Munich, where there were already an awful lot of Nazis around, and did get beat up on one occasion. He was almost killed—they left him for dead. And he went right back! He was fantastic in that way, because he was very much the sort of funny German professor, with glasses and everything, and one didn't see him as a fiery, daring person. But, in fact, he was.

AUSTEN: Was there anyone comparable to Hirschfeld in England at the time?

ISHERWOOD: The great figure, of course, was Edward Carpenter, who was one of the greatest figures anywhere in the liberation movement and was not only writing about it and speaking about it but living a life of domestic bliss with his lover. And that was quite something—people were horrified. There's that wonderful story about when he was visited by some sort of religious person who started this spiel about hell and "Don't you care about your soul?" and "Don't you want to go to heaven?" Carpenter's lover said, "Listen. We're in heaven right here."

AUSTEN: But in those day there were a lot of people who were much more pessimistic, too. In 1906 Lytton Strachey wrote a letter to Keynes saying that he felt it was impossible to make the dowagers understand that feelings were good and that very often the best of feelings were sodomitical. He felt that only a hundred years hence could this ever be done.

ISHERWOOD: Yes, well, that's very understandable. It must have seemed incredible before the War, but World War I was, psychologically and philosophically speaking, much more of a disturber than World War II. There was a different world at the end of World War I.

AUSTEN: In choosing the title "and his kind," was that the phrase that was used fifty years ago? Weren't homosexuals supposed to go away and live with their own "kind"?

ISHERWOOD: As a matter of fact, it was Don Bachardy, my friend, who found the title. As you know, we write together. In the book I'd been using the word "tribe" to describe gay people, but "kind" was deliberately chosen as being more ambiguous, and it also suggested "my kind of person." Because after all I do have quite a lot of intimate heterosexual friends of both sexes, and they had to be included. It's not just about my gay friends.

AUSTEN: Have you read Martin Green's *Children of the Sun*, the overview of what it meant to be a "dandy" in England in the twenties and thirties?

ISHERWOOD: Yes, I looked into it.

AUSTEN: He's not very sympathetic towards people like Brian Howard, for instance.

ISHERWOOD: Well, of course, Brian was a bird of another feather altogether. And yet he had a great deal of courage—admittedly a rather destructive kind—but courage is always remarkable.

AUSTEN: Did you think of Brian as a dandy, and did he think of himself as a dandy, and was there any correlation between being a dandy and being gay in the thirties?

ISHERWOOD: Well, he was the sort of person who got into tuxedos and tails, all of which were absolutely taboo to me. The reason I'm dressed up like this is because of our quaint idea down south that when one gets to San Francisco one must put a tie on. [*Laughter.*]

AUSTEN: All you need to do is to go to Eighteenth and Castro to see how little we wear.

ISHERWOOD: Well, I think it would be very amusing to go to Eighteenth and Castro and have a tie on—it would be like appearing in evening tails.

AUSTEN: To get back to Martin Green: although I realize he started out in his book not to be particularly kind to you all, he ends up with a sort of grudging admiration. He pegged you as a *naif*—there were rogues and dandies and *naifs*—and he says "*naifs* were men who offered their minds and hearts as being all limpid sensitiveness—always about to join the Communist Party, to become comrades, fighters, members, but most of them didn't." Would you quarrel with Green's pigeonholing you this way?

ISHERWOOD: I think pigeonholing is a foredoomed operation. It's much beloved by certain types of minds, but really, people won't go into pigeonholes. You have to start chopping bits of them off in order to get them in. Of course, the basic thing about Russia was that when the revolution took place in '17, the Communists had come out with a big platform which included the idea that private life was not the concern of the state. That it was bourgeois to have all these laws regulating behavior between consenting adults. Hirschfeld took this very seriously and welcomed them as allies—and, therefore, added to his crimes (of being gay and a Jew) the crime—according to the point of view of the Nazis—of being a Communist fellow-traveler. Of course, if Hirschfeld had lived and witnessed the turnaround when the Soviets began arresting gays and deporting them to Siberia and so forth, he would obviously have denounced them. There was a feeling, as you've quoted just now, about "brotherhood" and so forth, and that was sort of nice, and had something to do with comrades and thus had something to do with Communists. But if we were woolly-minded, we had good cause. Somewhere we probably smelled rats that we didn't like to refer to. All was not well, because there was always the suspicion that the Party felt we were decadent and bourgeois.

AUSTEN: Did you think of your generation (i.e., you and Auden and Spender) as more enlightened because of your politics than the preceding Bloomsbury group of Strachey, Woolf?

ISHERWOOD: You know, just speaking for myself, I really wasn't all that political. I was very much concerned with getting on with the job, which for me was just writing books, having decided that I was a writer. Everything else was rather secondary. Among my friends were some perfectly serious Communists, who were Communists in the way that Quakers are Quakers, and you can't criticize that. They were so totally different from us—we weren't serious in that sense. Auden, too—his eye was on something quite different. Although he was prepared to risk his life to go to Spain and all that, his fundamental thing was to write poetry.

AUSTEN: In literary history, though, it seems to me that Auden particularly has been pegged as a poet whose political views have colored his works. The left claimed him as their own—in those days, at least.

ISHERWOOD: In those days. Later he moved much more across the center and in some positions toward the right. He was very individualistic.

AUSTEN: Let me ask you a little about some Americans whom you may have met during the thirties but did not mention in this book. Did you ever bump into Parker Tyler, Charles Henri Ford, Robert McAlmon, Frederick Prokosch, Hart Crane?

ISHERWOOD: Prokosch, but I couldn't swear when I met him, exactly.

AUSTEN: Were you reading any of his books?

ISHERWOOD: Well, I certainly read the first one. I met Paul Bowles very briefly —that's why Sally Bowles is called Sally Bowles—but in fact I had no idea that he was an extremely talented composer or writer. He was nineteen at the time, and there was no reason I should have known. He said I had a very "superior" manner, and I don't doubt it because I was in my late twenties, which, of course, *was* superior.

AUSTEN: One of the Americans, McAlmon, wrote some stories during the twenties about Berlin gay bars in which his main characters were usually just slumming, going to watch the "decadent" people. There seems to have always been this sort of remove for Americans—they could not admit in print to being gay themselves. Did you sense there was a difference between the British point of view and this American nervousness?

ISHERWOOD: No, not necessarily. There were an awful lot of slummers who came by, and I was meanwhile, being very salty and dressed like a hustler myself most of the time. I wore one of those sweaters with a great big turn-over neck and bell-bottom pants. But in retrospect none of those bars seems to have been very rough and tough—nowadays it seems much more violent—but I think they committed murder and stole, of course, and other things people do when they don't have very much money.

AUSTEN: Most of the German boys in the Cozy Corner bar were just hustling because they were poor? And then they would go on to get married?

ISHERWOOD: Oh, yes. One of them said, "I'm homosexual for economic reasons."

AUSTEN: And everyone else there was homosexual for other reasons?

ISHERWOOD: Oh, of course, One wouldn't go there, otherwise. No, heavens, what for?

AUSTEN: When you were describing these bars in your earlier novels, you referred to them obliquely as "amusing," but the gay reader could sense that when you wrote "amusing" that you meant "gay," right?

ISHERWOOD: Yes. People like my uncle, who belonged to an earlier generation, talked about "frightfully amusing" places.

AUSTEN: So that there were these code words that gay readers could pick up on—

ISHERWOOD: Oh, yes.

AUSTEN: And what you're saying in *Christopher and His Kind* is merely confirmation, or sort of a key to the code.

ISHERWOOD: Yes.

AUSTEN: One reviewer in the thirties called your narrator Christopher "this sexless nitwit"—

ISHERWOOD: Wasn't that beautiful? Yes, I've always treasured that.

AUSTEN: Do you discount the validity of this criticism?

ISHERWOOD: No, I don't discount it. I think it was one of the disadvantages of my method.

AUSTEN: Or all gay men's methods in those days when they had to be obscure and oblique.

ISHERWOOD: Yes, I was in a dilemma, and the dilemma was not solved by just avoiding the subject of the narrator's sexuality, which is in fact what I did. It's a valid criticism. "Nitwit," I don't know. I don't see him as a nitwit.

AUSTEN: No, I don't either. Going from the specific to the general, though, do you think that gay writers of the thirties and the forties who had to "pass" through one ruse or another wrote things that, as a result, suffered aesthetically? They could not be as forthright about their minority status as, for instance, Jews who were writing "Jewish novels" or blacks who were writing "black novels."

ISHERWOOD: Yes, I do feel a sort of lameness in some books that are otherwise quite remarkable. There's an excellent novel by William Plomer that I was re-reading the other day. It's called *The Invaders* [1934] and it has to do with someone from the upper class and someone from the lower class. But the whole thing is blunted by the fact that Plomer can't really quite come out and say it. It's really a moving love story without any lovemaking of any kind, but something in the reader nowadays calls for something more—at least one explicit scene.

AUSTEN: Let's go into the concept of the upper class and lower and into what the parallel was here in America. My idea of the average gay man in the thirties here—and I was born in 1935 so I don't really remember this—is that he must have aspired to a certain Clifton Webb elegance, and they all considered themselves a mystical brotherhood just a little lower than the angels. Was this part of the gay mystique in England as well, this sense of elitism?

ISHERWOOD: Well, certainly we fortified ourselves with that to some extent, as all minorities do. Everybody is the Chosen People. You have to have something to give you gumption, a quiet superiority—at which the British are very good, anyway. There's nothing like our "superiority" anywhere to be found, and the less there is to be superior about, the more valuable it is, of course.

AUSTEN: But I think American gay men were pretty good at that—they wore all the right scarves and subscribed to the *New Yorker* and had very smart apartments. However, to get to the parallel with the lower class. I'd say the American counterpart to going to Berlin to look for a lower-class German boy would have been to go out and look for what used to be called "rough trade." Can you explain why the members of the upper classes felt a certain virility did not seem to be obtainable among wealthy young men, and why gay men everywhere used to place such a great premium on seducing someone who was supposed to be straight?

ISHERWOOD: It probably has something to do with the awareness of difference and likeness in other people, and how this awareness leads to loving or merely liking someone. When you suddenly feel you can bridge the frightful gap between the Montagues and the Capulets, that's the awareness of difference, which love leaps over. When you realize that you and the person you just got into conversation with are both crazy about stamp collecting, that's awareness of likeness, but that usually leads to friendship rather than love.

AUSTEN: Were you in Germany at this time, had they started to round up the gay men and send them to concentration camps?

ISHERWOOD: You see, I left Germany only a few months after Hitler got into power, so they really hadn't got under way.

AUSTEN: Did you know of anyone who was impounded, or who died wearing the pink triangle?

ISHERWOOD: No, no I didn't.

AUSTEN: Apparently there were hundreds of thousands.

ISHERWOOD: Oh, yes, undoubtedly. There's no question about that.

AUSTEN: We haven't heard very much about them, though, have we?

ISHERWOOD: No, they never had a spokesman, really.

AUSTEN: And the rationale was that the Nazis didn't want any men who were not virile for the Third Reich, that all gay men were effete?

ISHERWOOD: Yes, that was the excuse, I suppose.

AUSTEN: And yet there's quite a mystique today here in San Francisco revolving around neo-Nazi menace and so forth. Are you troubled that some gay men are flirting with all of this Nazi memorabilia and storm-trooper trappings?

ISHERWOOD: I must confess to a terrible ignorance of S & M, and I really don't know what goes on in their heads quite, but as I have tried to find traces of it in my own libido, it seems to me that one might quite as easily just pretend to be a Jew being tortured or something and get a kick out of that without necessarily subscribing to the Nazi philosophy. Is it a political question under those circumstances? You could just as soon say, "Today I'm going to be a homosexual being beaten up in the Lubianka Prison by the Soviets." Now does that mean you've changed your political orientation? I think it's better to get all that junk out in the open. In a word, I'm not so terribly frightened by it.

AUSTEN: Let me ask you about George Orwell. Did you see eye to eye with him during the thirties and later?

ISHERWOOD: I saw eye to eye with him much more later. We were tremendously shocked at first by his monumental book *Homage to Catalonia*, in which he said that the Russian Communists were destroying the cause of the Spanish revolution.

AUSTEN: By the time he wrote *Animal Farm*, you tended to agree with him more?

ISHERWOOD: Oh, yes.

AUSTEN: There's a contemporary of yours—maybe a little older—Joe Ackerley, and in his letters you get the idea that his gay life was not quite as happy and breezy and successful as yours. He just had his dog. He did not seem to love life quite as much as you have. Was there some difference in his not accepting his gayness?

ISHERWOOD: Oh, he was one of the greatest pessimists who has ever lived! But it was constitutional, I think. He was constitutionally melancholy. He was an extraordinary man, blessed with amazing good looks, great literary talent, a very intelligent person, a hero in World War I at the front. And this man, who might have had everything, had that sort of fatal flaw of melancholy.

AUSTEN: Was there a good deal of that in gay men you remember thirty, forty years ago as compared with the younger gay men today?

ISHERWOOD: No, I can't feel that. It's just as varied. Temperaments vary just the same in both categories.

AUSTEN: You have never been of the melancholy temperament yourself, I would gather, for any great length of time?

ISHERWOOD: I played with it when I was young, then when I began to see what life was like, I realized that it's dangerous and intolerable.

AUSTEN: To be consistently melancholy?

ISHERWOOD: Yes, I mean, you're just destroying yourself.

AUSTEN: Your reaction to coming to New York and America at the end of *Christopher and His Kind* is the sense that New York City is saying to you, "Do things our way or take the next boat back." Do you feel that America in the late thirties was not particularly congenial to one of the British temperament?

ISHERWOOD: Well, it enormously attracted me as a challenge, but I did feel it was very rough and tough.

AUSTEN: Has Santa Monica been less rough than New York City?

ISHERWOOD: Oh, I feel perfectly at home in Santa Monica. I've lived longer in this country now than I did in England.

AUSTEN: At the end of your book, you suggest that with Don Bachardy there may be a sequel to this. Are you now writing *Christopher and His Kind, Part Two*, that will pick up in 1939?

ISHERWOOD: Oh, much more so than that, you see. What I have—and it's all finished and typed—is massive diaries covering the years from '39 through 1944. I was going to publish them. I said to myself, "The moment has come that I'm going to edit them and publish them." And I thought, well, before I do that I'll have to have just a chapter which explains how I came to the States in the first place. That book's the first chapter. In other words, it got longer and longer. I went further and further back in time and finally I decided that in the sense that one's life is a chess game, the moment that I made the move to go to Berlin all the other moves were inevitable.

AUSTEN: Is this diary going to be published shortly?

ISHERWOOD: I don't know, because there are grave difficulties. First, the embarrassment of material—far too much. And secondly, the question of people who are still alive who might be hurt. Certain indiscretions of one kind or another. But all that is secondary. I could produce it with some amputation in about six months, and there's a lot of interesting material—all about Huxley, the Hindus, the Quakers, Garbo, Ingrid Bergman, the stars.

AUSTEN: So one way or another we may well be able to look forward to reading a continuation of this book?

ISHERWOOD: Oh, yes, sure, one way or another.

PHOTO BY NEIL HOLLIER, SAN FRANCISCO, 1973

HAROLD NORSE

HAROLD NORSE was born in New York City in 1916 and received his M.A. from New York University. He left the United States in 1953 and spent fifteen years of self-imposed exile in Italy, Paris, Spain, Morocco, Germany, Switzerland, Greece, and England. He returned to the United States at the end of 1968. He lived for five years (1972–1977) in San Francisco, where he edited the literary magazine *Bastard Angel*. He currently lives in the country in Monte Rio, California, and is working on his memoirs, "Adventures of a Bastard Angel."

Norse's writing has been acclaimed over the years by a large number of contemporaries—Anaïs Nin, James Baldwin, Paul and Jane Bowles, Allen Ginsberg, Dylan Thomas, William Burroughs, and others. William Carlos Williams wrote in 1959: "You have breached a new lead, shown a new power over the language which makes theories of composition so much blah." In reviewing Norse's collection *Carnivorous Saint* (1977), W. I. Scobie wrote: "I know of no other collection of homoerotic poetry by one author spanning an entire lifetime of writing—some four decades.... In his best poems he does succeed in catching that magical latent element that touches something older than the present organization of man's nature.... Harold Norse is our American Catullus."

Norse's poems have been translated into six languages and have appeared in numerous magazines internationally. In 1966 the American literary magazine *Olé* devoted an entire issue to his poems with tributes by Burroughs, Baldwin, and W. C. Williams. Norse's books include *The Undersea Mountain* (1953); *The Roman Sonnets of G. G. Belli*, translations and adaptations (1960); *The Dancing Beasts* (1962); *Karma Circuit* (1966); *Hotel Nirvana: Selected Poems* (1974); *I See America Daily* (1974); and *Carnivorous Saint: Gay Poems 1941–1976* (1977). *Penguin Modern Poets 13* (1969) also featured his work.

THE PRESENT INTERVIEW was taped at Norse's San Francisco apartment on Guy Place in April 1973 by Winston Leyland, editor of *Gay Sunshine*. It originally appeared in *Gay Sunshine* 18 (June–July 1973).

Winston Leyland interviews
HAROLD NORSE

LEYLAND: We first met, Harold, at the time you sent some of your poems in to *Gay Sunshine* in 1972. What impelled you to send your work to us?

NORSE: I had just come to San Francisco from Venice, California. I picked up a copy and thought it was a remarkably good gay newspaper. I was casing the situation here, felt lonely, and looked through some of the local publications. I thought your paper superior in quality to any of the underground tabloids so I sent you some poems.

LEYLAND: Did you start writing poetry in a committed way when you were very young?

NORSE: I began writing when I began reading, at the age of seven. I didn't begin to talk until I was four; my mother called me tongue-tied—and then I never shut up. My mother was an illiterate factory girl. She made fun of my lisp and probably ridiculed me even earlier than that. When I was nine, I sent a poem to the *Brooklyn Daily Eagle*, which published it. Later I discovered that Walt Whitman had been the editor of the *Eagle*—not when I sent the poem; I'm not *that* old [*Laughter*], I hasten to clarify, lest we start off on the wrong foot immediately [*More laughter*]. The *Eagle* published another poem, about a thunderstorm, when I was eleven. I wrote it during a tempest that lashed the trees and windows while my mother and the landlady took to the clothes closets. They don't make thunderstorms like they used to, have you noticed? They were terrifying when I was a boy in Brooklyn.

When I first read Whitman at the age of fifteen, it was the most mind-blowing literary event I had ever experienced, and I was confirmed in my decision to write poetry. *Song of Myself*, in particular, had a lasting effect on me, like a religious experience. I still think it's the greatest poem ever written. It moves me in a way that the *Iliad* and the *Odyssey* and all the great long poems do not move me. "Cross out, please, those immensely overpaid accounts," Whitman says to the Muse about the old classics, thereby putting a whole new writing show on the road.

The *Cantos* of Pound I admire intensely. I can read six of the foreign languages he uses and correct the mistakes. It will be a source book for poets for the next hundred or two hundred years. It may be what he set out to accomplish, the American epic Odyssey. But it doesn't grab me on the gut level, the level of the whole being, like Walt's mind-boggling poem. Pound is both our Homer and Dante in some respects. But it's literary; it comes from books and learning. Walt's poem comes from himself, a man, a myth, a living self. He is both the epic and the hero, in one person. Walt Whitman brings his whole person and his era into his work without skirting the homoerotic element. In fact, and he says so in the Calamus poems, this is the meaning of his work, what it is all about.

I've only recently been re-reading Whitman. "Calamus" and "Children of Adam" are homosexual poems. They can't be read in any other way; they wouldn't make sense. When I first read him I felt that he was the archetypal poet and that if I did nothing else I would have to somehow write poetry and bring out as much as I could about the truth of my life as an autobiographical record. But I ran into obstacles from the beginning because I had no current precedent, and my early stuff was so hairy it must have been either very unusual or just a chaotic mess. The forties was hardly hospitable to that sort of poetry; it was a period of critics and professors who regarded Whitman as a flop. Now, thirty years later, we know that Whitman was the father of American poetry, homoerotic poetry at that.

Hart Crane, another homoerotic poet, was my second illuminating poetic experience. I didn't know he was homosexual, but then I hardly knew that I was. I identified with Crane—his first name was also Harold. He was also a Cancerian only child who had to "shoulder the curse of sundered parentage." His parents also never got along together, and he loved young men. So Whitman and Crane in my teens became the guides, points of departure for me. They were my lasting influences, although I departed from both of them in other stylistic directions.

LEYLAND: Were you born and brought up in Brooklyn?

NORSE: Actually, I was born in the Bronx. Since I was illegitimate, my mother had to give birth to me out of Brooklyn so that my grandmother wouldn't know about it. Brooklyn was where I grew up, and went to school.

There was a plaque to Walt Whitman, where he first printed *Leaves of Grass,* on the red brick wall of a cheap diner. The plaque was on Cranberry Street over some garbage cans that stray cats scavenged in.

Also, a few blocks away, Hart Crane had lived and written *The Bridge.* His apartment was then occupied by one of my English professors, so I knew it firsthand. It was on Columbia Heights, and the rear windows overlooked the Brooklyn Bridge. Crane used to go up to the roof when drunk. He would cry and often attempt suicide, but his old friend and lover, Samuel Loveman, whom I met later in Greenwich Village (he was then an old man) would rescue him. He told me that story and others about Crane which later came out in the biographies. He also said I bore a startling resemblance to the young Crane—he called him Harold.

It's amazing when I think about it—so close to the venerable departed greats who meant everything to me as a boy. Their spirits were in the air, hovering over me. Right next door to Crane's old apartment I lost my cherry to a college professor and learned about homosexual love, with Whitman and Crane nodding sadly and mellowly over us. The foghorns from the "river that is East" sounded from the tugboats.

At the age of seven, after I'd been stashed away in Irish Catholic nurseries while my mother worked in the factories, I acquired a stepfather. He really hated me (but not more than I hated him) and never stopped belittling and humiliating me. He called me "Sissy" and "Mary" because I wouldn't go out and play ball with the other boys but preferred reading and writing at home. He was jealous of the hysterical guilt-stricken attentions of my mother who was probably trying to make up for those years she had abandoned me. I was already a rebel, suspicious of women and needing attention and love from the eternally missing male parent. To me homosexuality was not so much a rebellion as a need for approval and affection from the male, which I never got from my stepfather.

When I was about fourteen, I slowly became aware that I was staring at other boys, especially when we were naked in the swimming pools and locker rooms. I wanted to feel them up. Then I had a sudden flash: what I really wanted was to kiss and fuck. I had no such feeling for girls at all. I had some kind of a nervous breakdown at the age of sixteen. Frustration and secrecy about all this were more than I could handle. I thought I was a complete freak, the only one in the world of my kind. The last thing I would have told my friends was the way I felt about them. I grew up butch, in a very butch environment. I tried to slash my wrists when I was sixteen, a severe case of sensory deprivation. I didn't even know one was allowed to touch *anyone*. Girls used to throw themselves at me, and I got pretty good at dodging them. But nothing came of it till I was nineteen, when I had my first straight experience, and that didn't last too long. Something was missing and only I knew what it was.

When I was fifteen, I also read some very lurid accounts of homosexuality as a perversion, a disease, in Krafft-Ebing and in Wilhelm Stekel's *Bi-Sexual Love*. The title, of course, had attracted me. They were very German. I remember reading about a young boy in Vienna who picked up filthy old piss-stinking bearded bums and enjoyed having them shit on his chest, the only way he could get his rocks off. I felt degenerate, depraved, and thought I was diseased. In reality, I was a love-starved, fresh-faced, innocent, blooming virgin, starry-eyed with romantic idealism, who masturbated six or seven times a day and grew more introverted and unhappy as no outlet for my love materialized. All I wanted was just *one* boy my own age. I had all kinds of crushes in every school I went to—my family moved frequently. I remember many of them now; even their names bring back some of those first pangs of puppy-love, hero-worship: William Gilmore, Nick Gaponovitch, Irving Brodsky, Joe di Bona. They're as alive for me now as they were then.

At nineteen I took the subway to Manhattan and padded the streets around Times Square. I was getting ogled and whistled at everywhere. Guys would lick their lips at me, and I didn't even know what that meant! I thought they were making fun of me.

One day I was vaguely wandering around Bryant Park behind the Public Library with the statue of William Cullen Bryant all green with pigeon shit. It was dusk and someone that I took for a very pretty girl approached. But the "girl" had a bass voice under the lipstick, eyeshadow, plucked eyebrows, and asked me to go home with him. We rode uptown in the subway. In his room it was dark and he didn't switch the light on. He grabbed me and kissed me—my first kiss. There was a flash of electricity like lightning from my lips and the boy jumped back as if he had been electrically shocked. I was startled too, but I was used to my own tensions and sexual magnetism. It was static electricity, like touching a doorknob when you're standing on a rug with crepe soles. He said, "My god, that's what I've always wanted—electric youth!" [*Laughter.*] Being electric, having animal magnetism, is not only figurative. It's real! I lit up the dark room with my desire.

He told me later that there were lots of boys my own age who wanted the same thing, that if I hung around Times Square I'd meet them, but I mustn't look belligerent or scared—something that was almost impossible for me. I used to stand against the corner cigar store on Broadway and Times Square for hours. But I probably looked like a straight, uptight kid, so I never made out. I had been conditioned in Brooklyn as a macho boy and could never lose that almost fierce, provincial, tough-guy appearance under such conditions. Otherwise, I was gentle and clowned with the other kids I knew to hide my feelings.

I grew up with Italian, Jewish and Russian kids who were very macho, and I'd rather have died than be called a fag. This defensive behavior remained for many years, as a façade, until I returned to America and Gay Liberation was under way. In that sense, gay lib was really responsible for my second coming out. I'd never been in the closet once I knew what gay life was. I was heavily into it in New York, but I kept it secret from my straight friends, since I was afraid of their contempt and disapproval. Being rejected under any conditions was unbearable to me. I had no ego-identity at all. Soon afterwards, I got to know W. H. Auden and my provincial youth slowly began to vanish.

LEYLAND: Were you in college when you met Auden?

NORSE: I had just gotten out of college, where I won the gold medal for poetry (as a lower freshman) and was editor of the college magazine. I met Auden, Spender and Isherwood soon after my graduation. This was during the war. They had come to the United States because of the war. Auden scandalized the English literary world by refusing to return. He was regarded with disfavor for many years afterwards because the English considered him a deserter while they were undergoing the Blitz. Auden's reasons for staying here were largely pacifist, I think, and at the time he was also a leftist. Apart from his poetic skill, his early reputation was based on his leftism. In the heavily Marxist era of the thirties and forties almost every intellectual was a Marxist. We used to attend Marxist Writers' Conferences together—I was the youngest one there.

LEYLAND: Isn't it sad in Auden's case and in that of other writers, too, like John Dos Passos, that they start out as leftists, quite radical, and in old age are transformed into political reactionaries.

NORSE: It happened to Wordsworth long ago. And to Kerouac more recently. One changes not only physically but mentally, too. Needs change, feelings change. And revolutions that promise the Earthly Paradise soon end up with Earthly Hell. You can't expect too much from social revolution, although I think the next one will either be the worst failure or the greatest success.

At the time I met Auden my best friend was another young poet, Chester Kallman, then still at Brooklyn College. Spender, Auden, Louis MacNeice and Isherwood gave a reading in New York. Chester said, "Let's go sit in the front row and wink at them." After the reading we went over to meet them and Isherwood gave us their address. Chester went to see them without me. He became Auden's lover. Isherwood was interested in me but I couldn't respond to anyone much older than myself. I regret that now because as you get older you realize that you've missed out on people merely because of ageism, or sexism.

This is a difficult question to deal with simply because it isn't really so much sex chauvinism as it is a question of taste. Just as society cannot successfully legislate sex or tell the individual what to do with his body, so we cannot legislate taste. On the other hand, much as I would love to see youth making it with older men, I can't condemn them for not doing it if it repels them. Intellectual and artistic youth can learn and experience a lot from older artists, writers, who can save years of mistakes and false starts for the younger man. There is an interchange of complementary gifts and abilities between the older and younger man, so long as they do not set it up as a purely arbitrary sex relationship which can be exploitative and cynical. I was always afraid of this kind of sexual exploitation as a youth, but was perhaps overreacting in the case of Auden and Isherwood.

I would not like to subject a young man to any form of coercion in sexual relations. I don't see how it could really benefit either party in the end. If there is real feeling between them, it can work out. Unfortunately there aren't that many really gifted youths around who can take advantage of such a relationship. If money and cold ambition are involved, I don't think such affairs stand a chance. I think there is a good chance of success if there is mutual admiration: on the one hand for artistic achievement and, on the other, for beauty.

LEYLAND: Did you discuss poetry much with Auden and Spender at that time, or was it just a brief encounter?

NORSE: Spender, as I said, returned to England. With Auden, a friendship continued for years. This friendship deteriorated into bad feelings—mostly because of touchiness on all sides. I don't recall discussing poetry with Auden so much as listening to his opinions. He was very forceful, witty, sometimes bitchy, often kind. I was very quiet and shy. I was his secretary for a while. I needed a job badly and he was really helpful. He said I could type his poems and correspondence. I became his secretary.

Once we were all at a Village restaurant. Auden talked a lot and everyone told jokes or stories, but I said nothing for hours. Auden turned to me and said, "Do you suppose that Harold is secretly remembering everything we're saying and taking mental notes for his memoirs and that's why he doesn't open his mouth?" I was, in fact, painfully shy. This was my first friendship with a famous literary person and I was overwhelmed, feeling my own inexperience, youth and provincial background. Auden's Oxford accent at the time was not always easy to follow. He sort of gulped his final syllables and spoke very fast. I was uncomfortable, too, because I felt I didn't know how to express myself, and he dazzled me. So I couldn't discuss poetry or anything else. He was hard on Hart Crane, whose work he found turgid or turbid, and Crane, you know, was my hero.

Dylan Thomas had just hit the scene, although he had not yet come to America. Auden had similar reservations about his obscurity or obfuscations, whereas I found him the most stimulating poet since Crane. Later, when Dylan's reputation seemed to overshadow Auden's, I recall some bitterness on Auden's part about him which I couldn't go along with. And although I made it with Auden once, I couldn't accept a follow-up on that either.

I got to know Dylan Thomas when he came to America, and found myself much easier and more open in his presence. He was warm and boozy, spontaneous and anarchistic and desperate. A mutual friend of ours, the Scots poet Ruthven Todd, who had known Dylan intimately since they were about eighteen, phoned me and said, "Dylan's coming to this country, and he has nowhere to stay. Can you put him up? He won't burn the house down." Would I put him up! I had a Third Avenue apartment on East Thirty-eighth Street, in the Irish Bar area, which he would love. When he arrived, I got another call from Ruthven. "Dylan's staying at the Beekman Towers and I can't go to see him right now. Give him a ring and tell him you're a friend of mine and I'm sure he'll see you." It was a glacial January winter, as I recall.

I phoned Dylan and when the hotel operator connected us, there was a silence. I said, "May I speak to Mr. Thomas." I heard a voice coughing and hacking and choking. "Mr. Thomas?" More hacking. Then the voice, deep and resonant, "Oh, I wish I were dead! Hullo, who's this?" "I'm a friend of Ruthven Todd's and . . ." "Any friend of Ruthven's is a friend of mine," said Dylan. "Come right over." I was broke as usual but hopped into a cab. When I got to the penthouse bar, I saw him at a table, sitting with John Malcolm Brinnin. This was the first time he had come to the States and I was probably the second American poet to lay eyes on him.

I went over to the table and Brinnin, whom I knew, did not look happy to see me. I think he said, "What are *you* doing here?" I was dressed in blue jeans and old clothes, which literary people just did not do in those days in social situations. But Dylan rescued me and said, "Sit down! I wanna talk to you." He seemed bored with the situation until I came, and he actually leaned over to me and said in a stage whisper that could be heard distinctly by Brinnin, "How can we get rid of this bastard?" Brinnin got up and said he would be back in half an hour. We rapped for more than an hour. He told me that he came to America to make money because he had a wife and three children to support. He said he couldn't write any more, that everything he wrote was self-imitation, not growth or development; but that in the glow of his fame nobody really knew that, least of all the Americans, who worshiped him. So he'd better cash in while it was still good. He was entirely natural and unassuming and I appreciated that. He made me feel he was interested in me.

When Brinnin came back, Dylan was three sheets to the wind, pinching the waitress's ass but not loud or offensive. When we got into the elevator, a tall distinguished elderly man in formal evening dress stood uneasily in front of Dylan with a homburg held reverently over his heart as if he were at a funeral. Dylan began to make doggy sounds; he snarled and barked and finally leaned towards the man's back and began to bite it. The man twitched and squirmed and never turned his head, maintaining his poise and dignity, like Marjorie Rambeau, the big woman in the Marx Brothers movies. When we got to Brinnin's car over the ice and snow, Dylan slumped in the back seat, with me next to him. "We've got to go and meet Allen Tate and the *Partisan Review* people," Brinnin said, "and you're not invited, Harold." "If Harold doesn't go, I don't go," Dylan muttered thickly. Then he passed out and I got out of the car, said "Fuck you," and left.

It was like the forties academic vanguard, in the person of Brinnin, versus the rebels and misfits, in the person of Dylan, the successful misfit, and myself, the uninvited outsider. I saw Dylan quite a few times after that. Once, in the White Horse tavern, when I got up to piss, he watched me fondly and boomed in his deep voice, "There goes another little Lord Byron." (Presumably including himself as we were both about the same height.) He was beautiful and tragic and too good for the thin-blooded, goose-stepping literary snobs who surrounded him and finally contributed to his death.

LEYLAND: I understand that you also knew Paul Goodman well at this time.

NORSE: I'm writing a long poem in sections about the life and death of Paul Goodman. You know, I introduced Goodman to Auden at a party I gave at my pad in Greenwich Village. Paul seemed awed by Auden. In fact, he had asked me several times for an introduction. He just lay on the floor looking up at Auden and listening. This was very uncharacteristic of Paul, who was used to just the reverse, everybody at his feet listening to the Great Mind. But at that party I was amazed at his behavior. Later that summer on the beach at Fire Island Auden and Paul, who had gotten to know each other, were arguing hotly about some issue, and Auden screamed, "Well, that's what *I* think, and anybody who doesn't agree with me can go *fuck* himself!" Paul related that story and was rather disillusioned with Auden for a while. But they had a mutual admiration society between them anyway.

LEYLAND: What were you like at that time, in the forties?

NORSE: I got drunk a lot, lived in furnished rooms and cold-water flats, had sex with thousands of people, needed a shave, let my hair grow, couldn't keep a job, cruised gay bars and johns, padded the pavements, published a lot of poetry in magazines, went to parties, watched friends destroy themselves, destroyed myself, listened to music, met everybody in music and poetry, almost collaborated on an opera with Lou Harrison, was in at the start of the Living Theatre, saw a lot of Ned Rorem (with whom I collaborated on a song cycle), Edouard Roditi, John Cage, the Becks, Alan Hovhaness, Lou Harrison, Paul Goodman and so on.

In 1944 I met Tennessee Williams and lived with him while he was finishing the script of *The Glass Menagerie* in Provincetown. Jimmy Baldwin, who I met in 1943, showed me the manuscript of his first novel, *Crying Holy,* before it was published as *Go Tell It on the Mountain,* a work which made him famous. Jimmy and I were particularly close; we had a real love for each other. I introduced Jimmy to editors and publishers and may have got him his first magazine publication. I met Gore Vidal but we never got it together, just chance meetings in bars and parties. I also met Paul Bowles in 1944 but didn't get to know him until Tangier in 1962.

LEYLAND: I gather that 1944 was a watershed year for you then. Did these writers influence you in your writing?

NORSE: No, not at all, with the possible exception of Kenneth Patchen and, earlier, Auden, for a short time. When I met Allen Ginsberg, also in 1944, I was already a published poet. He was unknown. My first appearance as a poet was in *Poetry* (Chicago) in 1943 with a long poem called "Key West." It was a Crane-like poem.

Ginsberg and I first met on a subway train. There was nobody else in the car; it must have been the wee hours. I saw this kid sitting opposite me in a red bandanna and glasses talking to himself. The train was roaring so I couldn't hear what he was saying. At the stops I made out that he was reciting French poetry. I knew the lines; it was Rimbaud, probably *Drunken Boat.* At one of the stops I said, "Rimbaud!" And he said, "You're a poet!"

Ginsberg and I went to my room on Horatio Street in the Village and read our poems to each other but did not make it. Allen liked smooth, blond, crewcut types and I was a short, hairy, dark Jewish boy. I did not know he was a virgin on his first trip to the Village. I found him sexy and appealing but had no idea of his poetic capacities; the poems he showed me were slight, four-liners, and he seemed even shyer than I was. We didn't see much of each other after that until we met again in Paris, in 1962, when he presented me with a copy of *Kaddish,* which had just come out.

I missed the whole Beat scene beginnings at Columbia. Allen met Kerouac and Burroughs shortly after our meeting. I left America in 1953 and didn't return till 1968. Fifteen years during which the Beat scene turned everything upside down. William Carlos Williams influenced my approach more than anybody by telling me, in the early fifties, to use the spoken American language, not the English literary tradition. Allen carried the ball further than anybody. He influenced the whole climate begun by Williams.

I had been to Black Mountain on an invitation from Lou Harrison to read my poetry around 1951, after Williams had singled me out as having something new to present. There I met Charles Olson, who referred to me in his class as a "distinguished poet." I also met Franz Kline, who was just beginning his action painting.

LEYLAND: I was just looking through Brion Gysin's book, *Let the Mice In,* with a text by Burroughs and Ian Sommerville on the cut-up method. I understand you were also living at the Beat Hotel with Burroughs and Gysin at the time the whole cut-up method was being worked out.

NORSE: Yes. Ian Sommerville was a young English mathematician on summer vacation when we met at the Mistral Bookshop where he was working. One day when I went to see Burroughs at the Beat Hotel, room 15, the door swung open and a guy, stripped to the waist, whom I took to be Burroughs for an instant, though I knew them both, said, "Hello, man. Bill's not in." Then I realized it was Ian, and my mind was blown. I was magicked. Ian was also tall and thin, but the strange mirage could only be accounted for as a projection of Burroughs' image onto Ian, which was a kind of magical mindfuck that Burroughs used to practice, called "the replica," superimposing yourself on another. This replica thing appears in *Naked Lunch* and elsewhere in his writings. "Where's Bill?" I asked Ian, still mystified and uneasy. "Hey, man, Bill's kicking," said Ian. "I'm nursing him back to health."

That was the beginning of a permanent relationship between them. Ian was extremely brilliant in physics, mathematics and technology, and figured heavily in bringing to the scene many concepts and ideas that went into cut-ups and in other ways influenced Bill's work, although Ian was not a writer. Ian's ideas in engineering figured in the creation of the Dream Machine that he and Gysin developed. Without being a writer or painter, Ian was a collaborator of both Burroughs and Gysin.

We all lived in the Beat Hotel on Rue Gît-le-Cœur, where you could do anything, come and go as you liked, have visitors at all hours, something very rare for Paris, where there's a lot of surveillance.

I moved into the hotel about the end of 1960, as Burroughs kept telling me how great it was. "Best hotel in Paris for the money. For two bucks a day you've got a room, gas stove, heat, and no snooping concierge. You can't beat it." I always admired Bill. He had a frightening presence, especially when he was a junkie.

At our first meeting in the summer of 1959 I was scared stiff. Corso had told me to look him up. I knocked at room 15 and there was no answer. When I was about to retreat down that smelly dark hallway—it stank of feet—the door opened and an emaciated, cadaverous man stared right through me; gimlet eyes, I wrote later, absolutely terrifying, cold, piercing, impersonal eyes. I said I was a friend of Allen's and Gregory's and they told me to look him up. He muttered, "Come in, man. Come in." It was a very tiny room, with a window over a gray court—a gray room—*breakthru in grey room*—and a gray ghost in the room. The walls were covered with his black marker drawings, a series of endless, paranoid labyrinths. I sat down and he sat down without looking at me, crossed his bony legs and dug at his fingernails with the end of a match, without saying a word. I don't know how long we sat in silence, but it seemed like eternity. Finally, he asked me where I had been, and I said I lived mostly in Italy. "Italy?" he said in a faraway sepulchral voice, "I don't like Italy. I hate the sun." I said, "Oh." Then I told him I came to Paris in May, 1959.

The conversation didn't get going, as he dug at his nails, hunched over, never looking at me. It was really weird. I think I stayed a couple of hours, and by then I was pretty strung out. I said, "It's been very nice, man, I'll come back again." At that point, when I stood up to go, he fixed his gaze on me once more, as he did when I had come to the door. He was still sitting, and he stared in a slow panning motion from the top of my head right down to my feet, a long slow look taking in everything, x-raying me, like a machine, and then he said, "Yeah, man, come back sometime" in his spectral voice.

LEYLAND: In his photos he looks severe and forbidding, which I suppose is at variance with what he is really like.

NORSE: Yes and no. He does have a very forbidding manner and look. I've always thought he looked like a Mississippi riverboat old-time gambler, and he *is* from that part of the world. Even in his worst junkie days he always wore a shirt, tie and suit, though shabby. He looked like a gentleman on the skids. And when you have a dope habit that requires fifty or a hundred dollars a day, you can be on the skids.

All this is in his first novel, *Junkie,* which documents the period when he had to roll drunks and take crazy jobs like being an exterminator, private eye and such. He looks like the brains of a gang. It took a long time for me to get over an uncomfortable feeling in his presence. Though very articulate, he's tight-lipped and taciturn. I always had the impression that he was evaluating and assessing everything you said.

On the other hand he's very fun-loving, a fabulous raconteur. As we got to know each other, in the early days, this came out in both of us. I used to amuse him with crazy stories I heard around Paris. We joked a good deal. After he kicked his habit, he smoked grass with us. He could go on for hours, in his room or Brion's or mine or Ian's, like in *Naked Lunch,* telling tales of his earlier experiences, re-living each part, with a thousand different faces and voices, until you thought you were hallucinating. I'm sure he had total recall. He made every scene come alive. I'd often hear his voice rumbling from the room next to mine where Ian lived. One night in Ian's room, with only candlelight, Bill read from the manuscript of *The Soft Machine,* which he was working on, and we were all zonked by that incredible prose and the way he read it. Brion knelt and kissed his hand and called him Master.

We used to sit on the terrasse of the Café St. Michel, just around the corner from where we lived. Once, as we were watching the endless parade of young Frenchmen and foreigners go by, mostly with guitars strung from their backs, and long hair, an hour passed without a word, a common occurrence with Burroughs. Then he snorted, and drawled drily, "Not a decent fuck in the whole generation." [*Laughter.*]

Around this time Burroughs predicted the breakdown of censorship. He also went to try the first experiments with acid at Harvard when Leary tried them as a psychology professor. He came back muttering that Leary wanted to control the world. I think Burroughs felt Leary was a con man. I don't think he trusted Leary's kind of subversiveness. It did influence a whole generation. Burroughs said it would be subversive. He meant subverting the straight, linear, logical, square, prosaic, unimaginative and suppressive way of behaving and thinking, as against what McLuhan, around the same time, was calling the all-at-onceness of experience, seeing that experience is not what logic and reason would like it to be, by superimposing on it a pre-programmed, conditioned, semantic pattern that really sets up a barrier between the directness of what you see and feel and the object of your seeing and feeling. Also the extrasensory faculties have to be accounted for in the total experience, but all such urges, intuitions, flashes, are simply left out of the spectrum by the straight, linear, conditioned thinking process, although it still exists, unaccounted for and unrecognized by the observer himself, scientific or ordinary.

Even poets, especially the academic, have been writing from the stance of a purely rational approach, discounting the complex nature of experiencing. This approach is destructive of poetry in any case, since poetry (as well as some kinds of prose like that of Burroughs or Anaïs Nin) comes out of the direct, unimpeded observation of things as they are without the intervention of learned, conditioned traditional ways of seeing. The beat and the hippie generations come out of the mind-expanding drug culture. Earlier generations of writers came out of the mind-shrinking and mind-muddling alcohol culture.

Drugs, from ancient times until now, have been related to the arts. Coleridge and de Quincey are obvious examples. But there are many others, like Nietzsche, Rabelais, Baudelaire, Rimbaud, de Nerval, Henri Michaux, Aldous Huxley. *Naked Lunch* was written while Bill Burroughs was a user. He has no memory of having written it. Kerouac wrote under the influence. He wrote all of his books under one drug or another, including alcohol. The ancient Greeks were surely taking the sacred mushroom. We know that the *Amanita muscaria* was the drug of choice. It was used by the youth of Rome during Cicero's time.

LEYLAND: It was during your stay at the Beat Hotel that you yourself got involved in cut-up writing, wasn't it?

NORSE: Yes. I began doing cut-ups and showed them to Bill Burroughs who was very impressed. I continued using it as a technique for years, until today. Apart from Gregory Corso, who abandoned the method even before the first cut-up text, *Minutes to Go,* appeared in 1960, I am the only American poet with a body of poetry in cut-up dating from the original Beat Hotel beginnings. I am collecting a volume of these cut-ups called *Harold Norse/Of Course.*

Cut-up is primarily a deconditioning of language patterns and habits. The message behind all of Burroughs' writings is "kick the habit." The chief purpose of cut-up is to cut through the normal syntax that controls behavior and shuts out alternate semantic experiences. The logic of subject, verb, predicate as causal relationships, taken from the type of Western thinking that has dominated mankind since the rise of the sciences and industry, is rejected in favor of the Eastern concept of nature and behavior based on aleatory relationships, chance, coincidence. This cuts the mind free from inherited habit patterns, based on our education, received from parents and society.

Radio, TV, the newspapers, the movies, educate us every day of our lives. One statistic shows that every American is subjected to something like 360 commercials a day on the average. This is subliminal coercion, manipulation. Cut-up undercuts this kind of education with a new kind: self-autonomy achieved by destroying the commercial messages and substituting chance messages from Elsewhere. These are messages from the Beyond, from space, from the collective unconscious. The random approach, based on chance, leaves the field wide open for something New. Chance, in the West, is thought of as gambling or play, because Western thinking is structured on causality, based on cause and effect. Not all cultures believe this, as Carl Jung has shown.

In his introduction to the Wilhelm edition of the *I Ching,* Jung states that Western scientific thinking derives its conclusions from laboratory experiments but that Nature does not act the same outside the laboratory. Every process is constantly interfered with, interrupted, by other processes. So Western science is based on limited or false data, from which it draws hard and fast rules, even moral laws, erroneous but sanctioned by authority. Western thinking is clearly limited and places us right at the bottom of Plato's cave.

The ancient Chinese based their observations of nature on the principle of synchronicity, or coincidence. Things come together by Chance which is, however, subject to inscrutable divine laws. What we consider a random throw of the dice or yarrow stalks that fall in a certain pattern once, and once only, is not considered random but inevitable and unique, with meaning. The *I Ching* is still a great book of divination and oracular power. Anyone who had worked with it, as I have, cannot fail to be continually amazed by the rightness of its prophecies and the relevance of its answers to the current situation of the individual.

When Tristan Tzara cut up a newspaper in 1916 in Switzerland, threw the scraps into a hat and pulled each one out at random to create the first random dada poem, he subverted the rational approach that had led to the First World War. He made the first aesthetic revolutionary attempt as an act of defiance to be hurled into the teeth of the comfortable bourgeois who still accepted the world as a safe and sane place.

The rational approach is not the only one to reality. Since Freud, we know that the irrational dominates our behavior. I have observed that the most irrational people often consider themselves rationalists and put down astrology, ESP, zen, yoga, mystical experiences and so on. But if you press them you find that they may hold orthodox beliefs in God and generally behave irrationally in argument.

Burroughs saw the power and usefulness of the cut-up method to go beyond Dada, where poetry, as Lautréamont and Rimbaud said, could be made by all.

Take any page, cut it down the middle and then across. Do the same with any other pages, from Shakespeare, your friend, yourself, poetry, and do the same. Then at random put the pieces together and read across, and you'll have a message, a poem, something. A voice that is not your voice comes through. The words are not your words: they're everybody's words. They are words that belong to, come from, everybody, and, as Joyce wrote, here comes everybody. Is it art, is it a game, a pastime, or what? Will it shake up the habit patterns of the reader, turn him/her on, like dope, or meditation? It will do all these things. It will defuse the charges in language that have locked words into memory and memory into the body as muscle and nerve reflexes. It will release the ancient hold of stored-up negative memory charges by cutting words loose from their traditional referents. And you will get high, if you let go, let it happen.

There is a form of psychotherapy in practice today that uses only poetry to calm and heal patients. Just as in ancient times hexameters were said to have a therapeutic effect by the regularity of the rhythms. So why not cut-ups as therapy? It intensifies your perceptions, just as grass does. There are changes in brain-cell pattern on acid or mescaline or grass, and I am sure the same happens when doing or reading cut-ups.

My first cut-up at the Beat Hotel in 1961 alarmed me. I thought I'd gone crazy. There was no precedent for what I had written, or what was being written through me. At times I felt possessed, occupied by another being, someone else's voice speaking through me. There's some evidence for concluding that everything you see or read or hear makes some kind of permanent physical change in your brain cells and nervous system. Cut-up is akin to extrasensory perception states.

When I was first doing cut-ups in the Beat Hotel, I found out a month later that an English poet in the room next to me had been writing similar things. Whole phrases and words were identical, although we did not know each other at the time of writing. I had the same experience time and again with Burroughs, who lived upstairs. We felt we had reached levels of ESP where we shared a common voice. The walls themselves were acting strangely, like magnetic conductors.

Burroughs has devised various uses of cut-ups as counter-media agencies, like taking a tape recorder into a crowd of people and playing back what they are saying but cutting in different voices into each other, until what's played back is a mad mixture of everybody's voice into one voice and then speeded up into a Mickey Mouse/Donald Duck effect. This is one of the purposes of cut-up: to create panic among those who are so set in their ways that re-programming threatens their sanity. Essentially, its purpose is to create an alternative life to the one you're leading as a controlled, manipulated unit.

LEYLAND: The most successful poems I've written over the past two or three years are the few in which I used a cut-up method. As you say, it's as if another message were coming to me, a message from the unknown.

NORSE: If you tap the collective unconscious, a remarkable voice comes through, the voice of everyman. When we reach the time that all men are poets, we won't have to fear division and separation. We will then, of course, enter that era which I think all poets, at bottom, no matter how cynical and depressed, believe will happen: "The day of Universal language linking together all thought will come!" (Rimbaud). We will be free to express our love rather than our hate. That was the vision of Whitman and Rimbaud, two gay poets. Homoerotic love plays the greatest role in that, when it is no longer suppressed and ridiculed but brought out in everyone.

LEYLAND: Perhaps you'd like to rap about the gay dimensions of your own life.

NORSE: I've always been attracted to young men. What I wanted was a life companion but never found one. I had various lovers before I left America but a lot of violence and jealousy came with them. I understand now that it was an internalization of self-hatred. It wasn't so much guilt—I never felt guilty about accepting, loving another human being—but I think we could not accept ourselves because we felt left out. Society defined us and said, if you love another of your own sex, you're criminal and degenerate. We were too young, in our teens, to argue and so we accepted it emotionally. Later we destroyed our relationships through a long habit of insecurity. Not loving ourselves, how could we love each other?

There was a great fear of becoming that stereotype, the fairy. I myself was never the victim of the Fairy Princess syndrome. But in an environment that makes you automatically a criminal, it's useless to pretend that you can get good feelings when driven underground into secrecy and pretense. (I'm talking of a period long before the gay liberation movement, of course). When you're growing up in such an environment, you haven't the intellectual weapons to combat the false labels attached to you. Feelings of inadequacy cripple your relations with others and communication problems make things worse. So you drink, you fuck compulsively, you get yourself into dangerous situations with the law and with psychotic queer-haters and queer-killers. Every other friend of mine in New York was either being psychoanalyzed or pychoanalyzing. They were gay on both sides of the couch, so to speak.

An example is Paul Goodman. Paul had first wanted to make it with me. Then, after I had acquired a lover, he wanted him, too, besides having a wife and innumerable boy friends. We both declined the honor, Dick Stryker and I, and Paul never let us forget it. I had met Paul in 1944 through Jimmy Baldwin, and Paul made a pass at me when we were alone, but I didn't respond. Rejection to Paul was unforgivable. Yet for the next decade, till I left America, we saw a lot of each other. He said that he enjoyed my company. Whenever Dick and I got to smashing glasses of booze against the wall or against each other or wrapped the lamps around our necks or chain-smoked endless packs of Chesterfields in endless discussions of our problems, we would phone Paul Goodman. He would say, "Why don't you both calm down and take it easy?" Not much help from a lay analyst. His boyfriends complained that he found their helpless condition on the couch so appealing that he could not resist blowing them right in the middle of a session. We went to Fritz Perls' therapy sessions conducted by his wife, Lore. This would usually result in playing the game of analyst—attributing to the other habits and behavior that we didn't like in ourselves. Also fantasies, repressed feelings.

So nothing was solved. Dick, who had spent three years in prison for pacifism and conscientious objection, would get drunk and bar me from going out the door, trying to make me hit him. He was usually successful. He was an ex-Catholic who had a self-punishing guilt trip that he laid on me. Dick would invite friends to come and watch the fun. Friends took sides. Judith Malina sympathized with Dick because she only heard his side of it. I kept my feelings to myself. Julian Beck was neutral, while Jimmy Baldwin, through whom I had met Dick, sided with me.

I couldn't handle the situation any longer. I had a cold-water flat on Third Avenue with a Picasso gouache on the wall, *The Dancers,* 1921, Cubist period, which nobody ripped off because they thought it was a reproduction. I sold it for $400, which wasn't very practical, and used the money to get to Europe. Before I left there was an endless party at my flat financed by the gay millionaire who had given me the Picasso. Scotch flowed like water and hundreds of people drifted in and out for days, among them Allen Ginsberg (who mentioned it years later in Paris), Paul Goodman, Julian Beck and Judith Malina and what seemed like the entire literary and art world of New York. John Button arrived from the West Coast and helped get me to the boat. I couldn't remember much. I was smashed, confused and suicidal the whole time. It took me years to realize that you can *like* yourself. I couldn't understand that self-hatred was destroying me. This is what ultimately triggered off the attacks on me. I always found, of course, a partner who was equally self-rejecting and who would accuse me of his or her own self-hatred, a kind of intricate mirror leading down labyrinthine ways of twisted bullshit.

So I left America (1953-1968) and lived in Italy, Morocco, Greece, where the sex "problem" as we know it does not exist. In a sense I might say somewhat jokingly that it's very much like what the baths are here, a way of quick and easy sexual release. But it's much more than that. In those countries you find without difficulty men who are only too happy to share their lives with you without being cut off from the rest of society. With or without sex, men are intimate with each other, less so with their wives or other women.

Of course, it's a male-oriented world in the Mediterranean. But it's truly bisexual, or more—melons will also do. In Arab countries or southern Italy, it's very common to see two men, not necessarily lovers, walking down the street with their little fingers lovingly entwined. You see this also in Spain, under Arab domination for eight hundred years, where the Inquisition made the Spanish what I call the Puritans of the Mediterranean, just as Oliver Cromwell put an end to "Merrie England," helping to create a people who "take their pleasures sadly," as Oscar Wilde observed. The Church bans sexual pleasure except to monks, priests and popes, as history reveals (I did not translate Belli for nothing.) Those bastards made the Spanish and English guilty about their bodies.

Machismo grew out of the need for men to assert their balls because they secretly worried about their manhood. That's the reason Hemingway types love bullfights. Risk your balls and you're a man. Well, it's a bigger risk, and more courageously manly, to say, "I'm a cocksucker." If the athletes and warmakers and tough guys were to admit their true desires about other men, I think we'd see a homosexual America. A homosexual planet.

In recent years America has contaminated the Mediterranean. For example, the pissoirs of Paris and Rome were pulled up by the roots while I was living there. They had existed unmolested for two thousand years, happy meeting grounds for cruising men in need of a satisfying quickie to soothe the soul. Their doom was sealed with the arrival of barbarian hordes from the West, those antiseptic American ladies reeking of chemical deodorants, alcohol and cosmetics that eat the skin away and cause cancer. But they complained of "the smell," not to mention that men were urinating in the streets! Shocking!

It reminds me of a story. It concerns the controversy over the scandal of Oscar Wilde's trial at the end of the last century. The Victorians were shocked not so much by homosexuality as the exposure of it. Mrs. Patrick Campbell, the famous actress, said she had nothing against homosexuals, "so long as they don't do it in the streets and frighten the horses!"

God knows why anybody in his right mind lives a whole lifetime in cold, duty-driven, pleasure-hating, God-punishing, unimaginative workaday mad countries where it rains and snows and life is regarded at best as penance and pain and they make damn sure that everyone else will enjoy it as little as they do! This is called Law 'n' Order, and the chief lunatic engineer throwing the switch that executes all beauty, joy, love, thought, and sex is the criminal President of the U.S.A. And his brainless, brainwashed, illiterate electorate vote against their own best interests on every issue because they are ruled by Fear.

LEYLAND: Could you talk about your stay in Morocco and your affair with Mohammed. For instance, how it differed from an affair with a boy in a Western country.

NORSE: When I first got off the boat in Tangier and set foot on Moslem soil, the entire Christian world dropped from my shoulders like a filthy cloak that I'd been wearing all my life, a ragged, tattered, stinking, stained, itching, ugly, old rag that I couldn't get rid of because it had become part of me, like my skin. Guilt went with it and the contamination of pleasure by commandments against instinctive joy. Young men offered themselves or their sisters or a kilo of grass for five dollars. They were not afraid of the police breathing down their necks.

My relationship with Mohammed explains a lot about the attitudes in different cultures towards sexuality, not just homosexuality. They don't draw the lines that tight.

I met Mohammed at the Café Central in the Socco Chico, the small plaza in Tangier's Medina, also called the Casbah. I had been around for about a week or so and would sip green tea and watch the hustlers and "guides" ply their dishonest trade, as the moneychangers sat motionless, like lizards, not even blinking their eyes, waiting for who knows what.

One day Mohammed was sitting at the next table with his older brother, Alal, who was about twenty-four, and the kid kept staring at me and smiling his slant smile. They started a conversation in Spanish, and soon Alal offered to go to my hotel with his brother. I said I'd like Mohammed (who was seventeen) alone. After that first time we remained inseparable during my year in Morocco.

When I first met Mohammed he was the most attractive and successful male hustler in Tangier. He had walked from the Rif mountains hundreds of miles barefoot to the Big City where his brother introduced him to hustling the foreign gays. He'd been at it for about three years or so when we met and seemed rather hard and professional until I got to know him. Then I saw that he was really very innocent, affectionate and loyal, a young Berber shepherd who had not changed. I taught him to read Spanish and brought out a latent talent for drawing in pastels and crayons. The results were remarkable enough to be sold to the International Set of writers, artists and dope fiends. Paul Bowles bought some, as I recall. It was Paul who suggested originally that Mohammed would enjoy this kind of creative outlet. The relationship was unlike any I had known in Europe or America because of the implicit assumption between us that what we were doing was perfectly normal.

The first time Mohammed and I went to a movie in the Medina he took out his kif pipe. I nudged him and said in Spanish—which was the language between us—"There are two policemen in back!" He blinked a moment and said, with a straight face, "Keep your eye on them!" I assumed he meant that while he was smoking I had to watch the cops to see they didn't come over and bust us both. So I kept my eye on them rather than on the film, worrying all the time. Then I saw both of them reach into their pockets and bring out sections of a kif pipe, which they assembled, stuffed with dope and turned on! Then they dismantled the pipes—Moroccan kif pipes come in sections to be fitted together when used—and put them back in their pockets. I said in astonishment to Mohammed, "They're smoking!" He laughed and said, "Of course! Everybody does!" So I turned on and the film seemed terrific, though I can't recall *any* film I ever saw in Morocco, I was so stoned the whole time.

But the trouble, as usual, was money. My funds were limited and I could not, cheap as it was, stay indefinitely.

When I told Mohammed that I had to leave for Paris, I was not prepared for the way he took it. He went out on the terrasse and bawled like a child, deep convulsive animal sounds. I was completely shaken, and soon there were two of us crying in the moonlight against the coping on the roof overlooking all Tangier and the bay below. From then on, although we continued to live together for another couple of months, his attitude toward me was more formal, more polite, a bit distant and somewhat more mysterious than usual. During the whole year we were together, living and traveling and almost never out of each other's sight, I felt there was something intangible about him that I could not reach. His eyes, at times, seemed ancient and dreaming far back into vast primitive deeps of time, desert, stars, pan pipes. Hashish and grass had a lot to do with it but also the fact that he was a Moslem shepherd. There was a great gulf between us, psychologically, that I could not bridge. He was never abusive or nasty and had a dignity and poise you would hardly expect from a peasant, which put to shame many aristocrats I knew. Although he rarely entered a mosque, as a Moslem he accepted with natural simplicity the fatalism of his culture. *Mektoub*—It Is Written. Whatever happens is destined. They don't believe you make anything happen, which is directly opposite to Western thinking.

Once when there was only enough spaghetti for an evening meal, Mohammed, who was cooking, drained the spaghetti through a colander over a bucket on the floor. But he had forgotten to empty the slops in that bucket. When I saw the black, slimy, muddy spaghetti, I said for Chrissake, what the hell is this, what are we gonna eat tonight? Mohammed said, I didn't do it. I said, Huh? Who did it? There's just you and me here and you made the spaghetti. No, he said, I didn't do it. I thought he had gone nuts. So I said, OK, who did it? Allah, he answered. He meant it, he believed it. This was another world. It is hard for us to see that there are whole civilizations where the individual feels guiltlessly immersed in his sensuality.

I read in the *San Francisco Chronicle* that a survey showed that *every* American lies and steals. But Americans don't believe they do; they prefer to think self-righteously that only Italians and Arabs do.

Before we separated, we moved into a room at the Hotel Villa Mouniria on the ground floor facing the garden. When I told Paul Bowles about this, he said, "That's the room Bill Burroughs had. I used to go round to see him. It was a complete mess, hundreds of Eukodol bottles scattered all over the place and pages and pages of writing on the floor, blowing out into the garden. I asked him what all those pages were and he said, laconically, 'That's my work.' It was the manuscript of *Naked Lunch*. He wrote it in the room you're living in."

The Mouniria was a big, pleasant, old-fashioned villa run by an aging Frenchwoman who once was a whorehouse madam in Shanghai. She was very fierce and one day she shouted, "Monsieur, monsieur! There is an American friend of yours who has been looking for you all day!" That evening Gregory Corso showed up—he was the American friend—and took the only other room on the ground floor next to mine. We had some good times there, got stoned and played fantastic verbal games. Once we were looking up at the stars at night and Gregory said, "Let's read the stars. Pick out two letters from the shape of the stars. I'll begin. I see G.C., my initials. What do you see?" "I see V.D.," I said. Gregory later played other verbal games that were less charming.

Through Gregory, I met Alan Ansen, who had a room on the top floor. He said aggressively that he had heard a lot about me from an old "friend" of mine, Chester Kallman. I was annoyed by Ansen's unmistakable innuendo. I can't say that Ansen and I became friends, although we ran into each other a lot, years later, in Athens. He always had the same belligerent air.

LEYLAND: Did you see Mohammed again after you left Morocco?

NORSE: Before we broke up in Tangier, he said, "I can't go back to the life you took me from." I had taken a young boy out of prostitution and illiteracy and taught him to express himself, to communicate, to love. He was bound up with me because of the communication between us, in a language that neither of us had mastered (Spanish) but had transcended through body language. I said, "What are you gonna do?" And he said, "Go back to the Rif." I didn't believe him, but that's what he did. A year later, Mohammed was in Paris, heaving coal for fourteen to sixteen hours a day in the *banlieu*, where Arab workers were exploited. He said, "I don't want money from you, I just want to be with you." But there was no way I could handle it. I couldn't just freely move around at will. I had to go where I could teach or take a room or apartment offered by friends. So I left for Italy and never saw Mohammed again. I heard he returned to the Rif and got married.

Anyway, there's something I've never told anyone about some of these affairs with boys. In the Mediterranean especially they often put a restriction on the amount and kind of sex they have with you: three orgasms a week, no kissing and you can't fuck them. Now I'm just not cut out for regulations of any kind on my libido. Mohammed made that kind of restriction and it became boring. This is how they probably justify their masculinity to themselves—by not allowing themselves to enjoy it *too often*. I'm more than ready now for a sensible adult kind of turned-on thing without destructive games (dear reader, please note).

LEYLAND: You mean that you would be ready for a truly intimate affair rather than one based on false values?

NORSE: Right. In all my past affairs there existed a fear of intimacy because of what we'd find under the mask. It was an unequal partnership with Mohammed, in the sense that we couldn't really know each other. Barriers of language, education, culture came between us. At times I felt incredibly close, but I never knew whom I was close to. I never knew what he was feeling and thinking. When stoned, you can get very freaked out in such a scene. At times I thought I was bewitched, magicked, by some kind of Arabian sorcery. We saw a lot of Paul Bowles, whose tales about westerners meeting with strange fates in the desert were not exactly reassuring.

A couple of years later I went to Greece, had an affair with an Irish Catholic ex-nun from Boston. A Greek boy I had made it with got jealous (he wanted her, too) and hexed me. Then I had a very intense affair with a Dutch boy for about two years.

LEYLAND: You met him in Greece?

NORSE: Yeah, on the boat from Piraeus to Hydra. He had looks, brains, beauty, talent. There was something of a déjà vu about our meeting. We spent fourteen hours rapping about poetry, the *I Ching*, coincidence, Zen, Hermann Hesse, Vedantic philosophy, modern painting, everything.

But from the start I saw the fatal split in him, gut-need versus head-trip rejecting each other. So whether it's an illiterate or a high IQ doesn't mean shit. If there's no acceptance of gut-level, instinctive self, you're a fraud. He was part Jewish, schizzy and paranoid. Our raps were crazily supercharged with imagination and energy. It was just what I needed. What I didn't need were the stumbling blocks to intimate contact. Before sex he had to be seduced; after sex he was cold and hostile. OK, so I had run into this before, all too often. But, you know, I take risks; that's how I've always lived.

I had an old house without electricity or running water, where I didn't have to pay rent. Leonard Cohen had told me about it; it was being rented by a friend of his who had left for America but had paid up for several months in advance. Gerard, the Dutch boy, tried to nail a door shut between our rooms as a permanent barrier between us. I told him he had the choice of leaving. He stayed two years. He slept on the floor with about a dozen cats who shat all over the place. In the morning I would see him on the dirty mattress with cat turds and fish heads over his face and body. He didn't bother to clean or wash himself either. He never washed a dish or clothes or anything around the house. He hated everybody, including himself. He had studied karate and got mad all the time, threatening people with karate kicks. When I'd ask for a cigarette—I bought the smokes—he'd say sarcastically, "What's this, the army?" He was surly, selfish, and parasitical. He was a compulsive liar and thief—but I was hooked; like a junkie I couldn't break the habit.

I was gambling on keeping communication open between us, to make changes. But I found that a high IQ is no match for psychosis. In the end I lost everything. I'd been stupid enough to believe his abstract con, because I *wanted* to believe it. When he came on about Truth and Love, he seemed to soften and lose some of his aggressiveness. For two years I kidded myself into believing that things would get better, especially when the early barriers broke down and he seemed to grow more human, less monstrous. I thought I'd succeeded in getting through his dishonesty. We took an oath in Athens that we'd always stick together, help each other, and that I would never leave him "in the desert," as he referred to life without me. I kept that oath but he didn't. He never even kept a promise, much less an oath.

He spoke of Spiritual Self-realization and brotherhood, while ripping me off, stealing books, energy, possessions, health, time, life. So what was wrong with me? Why didn't I pull out, stop being the "nice guy" who could always be relied upon, preyed upon. He would have screamed bloody murder had I ended it and saved myself, but I had a compulsion to play the martyr. I'm not playing this game anymore; I've paid my dues, overpaid them. The victim needs the executioner, and that was the name of the game. It seems preposterous, monstrous now. How could I have gotten into such a masochistic bind? His existential position was, "I am blameless," the stance of the criminal psychopath. His conscience just didn't exist. He could not admit he had stolen or lied. A lot of movement people are like this. Behind the LOVE button there beats a heart full of HATE.

LEYLAND: Did his talent reinforce your overpowering need to risk so much on the affair?

NORSE: Until we met he had only dabbled in poetry. He relied entirely on me for guidance and stimulation. We both wrote voluminously, mutually stimulated to a fever pitch. The quality and amount of work I was producing is what kept me hooked. There was constant feedback. I had been lonely, needing a companion on this level. But I kept clinging and didn't know how to let go. Then, too, I created his career, introduced him to everybody I knew in Greece: Leonard Cohen, Gregory Corso, Sinclair Beiles, dozens of others. I got his work published in magazines that solicited mine, put him in touch with first-class editors like Carl Weissner.

I have the ability to bring out the best in young poets, to play more than a teacher role; it's like hypnotic suggestion. They pick it up, even the less talented, and do remarkable things while it's happening. But not when it ends. Instead of exploring new areas of poetry-space as he had begun to do while we were together, he landed back in Holland with a wife and kids and never got off the ground. But he made profitable use of every introduction and lead he had gotten from me to publish, through a press he started, some booklets and a record of other English-language poets. He paid me back for everything by not publishing me, although he'd started the whole thing with the purpose, as he said, of bringing out my work in Dutch. He was what he professed to despise, a Dutch bourgeois with a commercial goal disguised behind a façade of Art and Metaphysics.

But I did write some of my best work during that period: most of the poems that comprise *Karma Circuit* and my long poem *Hotel Nirvana,* an emotional record of that affair. The swami I wrote about is Satchidananda, who had not yet gone to America and knew nobody in Greece except a few of us in the small Athens literary colony.

As for Gerard, he could never accept the homosexual side of himself which was overwhelming him. It was not his "submission" to *me* that he hated, but the submission to this need that turned into rancor and hate. So I became the scapegoat. He couldn't stand the truth of his feelings—or *any* truth, for that matter—and so he walked out on his true feelings and, therefore, on poetry. The Muse and the Duende take their vengeance upon whoever betrays them. That's one kind of karmic punishment.

At the end of all this, I was physically and emotionally a wreck. I also had chronic hepatitis. I returned to the States in 1968 and tried to put all the pieces together again. Now I'm getting back to health and sanity.

LEYLAND: In the magazine *Holy Doors,* you have an article called "Coming Back," written after your return to the States. In that article you say that American writers tend to destroy each other. What did you mean by that exactly?

NORSE: It's the same syndrome, ruthless ambition. When I returned I saw among writers here an internalization of the competitive capitalist system. Writers and poets were handling themselves no differently from deodorant manufacturers or oil men. Although they may not commercialize their work, they commercialize their relations with one another by cutthroat competition.

LEYLAND: Do you think this is true of the writers of the beat movement also?

NORSE: The beat writers—Burroughs, Kerouac, Ginsberg, Corso, Ferlinghetti and others—regarded themselves as a group, who started a new way of feeling and behaving. They helped start a new life-style that became the hippie generation. Allen's work certainly was one of the chief forces that opened up gay consciousness, took it out of the closet and made Americans see what was before their noses, in every family. Burroughs added to this when *Naked Lunch* became a success. They were identified as members of the same movement, although each was vastly different from the others in style, attitudes, approach.

The beat movement, like any other, had competitive individuals. This is natural enough when you are representing a style opposed to the current fashion, but not when you are trying to cut your weaker competitors out of existence, like some big powerful oil company. This mentality seems to be operating among many poets and writers. In certain positions, editorial and publishing, this is done by suppressing or blocking the career of someone you don't like. I can understand, for example, a poet who represents a school, like the surrealist school, as a way of life, not as merely a literary vested interest but an entire philosophy which, like a religion, dominates the psyche of the adherent; I can understand the Olson-Creeley projective verse colloquial manner, or the confessional, academically dominated, tight-form, tight-assed, English, traditional school of Robert Lowell, based on meter and rhyme as it has been understood by professors for hundreds of years. But I am not talking about genres where the artists feel militant about their style over another style. I am talking rather about individual writers who have become gangsters, hardened themselves against other writers in petty warfare. They behave like rival Mafia hoodlums and defend this as realistic in an age where everyone acts like an animal.

LEYLAND: I know some of your views on this stem from the bad experience you had with Charles Bukowski. Perhaps you'd like to expand on this.

NORSE: Before I met Bukowski, he had praised me in his writings. In his volume of *Stories* he said, in a characteristic sweeping statement, that I was the best living American writer. He was then not well known. I had, in fact, put him in the *Penguin Modern Poets 13* anthology, with myself and Philip Lamantia, and that got him his first international recognition. The Penguin Books editor had asked me who I wanted besides myself in the volume. He had never heard of Bukowski.

When I came to California Bukowski and I met. We had, I think, a good relationship. He was being careful not to antagonize me. But he's an alcoholic and plays alcoholic games. His life and his work are based on a compulsion to humiliate people, to eliminate friends and enemies alike; to make a fucking mess of everything and then blame them all for his aggressions and hostilities. He feels like a shit afterwards and begs forgiveness. But he'll do it every time. If you're the patsy or the good Joe—the role in which I had cast myself—he'll try harder next time to doublecross and destroy you, till you tell him, finally, that you've had enough. That, of course, confirms his own feelings of self-hatred and gives him the chance to put you down for not being big enough to let him destroy you! Very similar to my experience with the Dutch boy. Catholics, drunks, gays, blacks behave like this when they've accepted the definition of themselves from others, from parents and society.

Bukowski didn't mess around with me until we'd known each other for two years. I was Prince Hal, the Greatest. But as his reputation increased, he became impossible. He used to say, "I love thee in my fashion." He has got to play the Pig, I believe, in order to push way down and out of sight the intimacy he will never get in touch with—an intimacy for men. He hates women much more than the stereotype homosexual is said to.

I see dishonest games of this kind among writers all the time. We can't really be better than those around us, since we are all really one on a certain level and responsible in the end for everybody. We can only change as individuals. We can change by meditation, by mind-expanding drugs, by therapy, by our own decision to change, by actually changing our behavior.

LEYLAND: You said to me some time ago that the rise of gay consciousness over the past few years has affected your work. Perhaps we could rap some more on this.

NORSE: I remember Burroughs telling me in 1960 in Paris that he expected censorship to break down within five years. This is exactly what has happened. Miller's *Tropic of Cancer*, Lawrence's *Lady Chatterley's Lover* and Burroughs' *Naked Lunch* were all test cases that won. Burroughs is a great prophet.

The poems I wrote twenty years ago about boys are now being published for the first time. I have been pulling them out of the obscurity to which they had been relegated in folders and notebooks and submitting them to editors like yourself. I've never been a closet case, but now I don't bother to conceal my own preferences as I used to under certain conditions, in a job situation, for instance. Not that I've ever kept a job for long. I've always been aware that there's no such thing as "straight" in any case when sex is involved.

I've always been a more or less open person concerning my own erotic behavior. But after Christopher Street I thought, "Well, now I don't have to sneak around anymore." In my work there has been no change; I've always written about gay subjects. But I had never really noticed it until I began sending out poems to gay anthologies and magazines. Then I realized I'd written a great many poems with gay themes. There's been a change only in the sense of being more in the open.

LEYLAND: There is the case of Gertrude Stein and Alice B. Toklas. Gertrude and Alice were lovers for many years; it was a well-known fact among their circle of friends. An appreciation of her gayness is crucial to an understanding of her writing, especially for a work like *GMP*. And yet the literary world has almost conspired to keep this aspect of Gertrude's life hidden. I read a biography of Gertrude Stein a few years ago which didn't even mention her homosexuality!

NORSE: Yes, I just read a biography of Kerouac by Ann Charters. Not once does she mention that he had sex with other men. Yet, in his *Gay Sunshine* interview Ginsberg mentions having had sex with Kerouac over the years. And this disclosure about Kerouac's natural sex needs has already pissed off a lot of his followers who can't stand the truth.

How many people know that Henry James was homosexual? And until recently scholars had never made it overt about Walt Whitman. When I was at college, I had a crazy professor who said something about Whitman having a high-pitched voice, "like so many of his kind." And this comment was by an American literature specialist! You have to go through unbelievable contortions to make a heterosexual writer out of Whitman. The Good Gay Poet, as I've always called him.

LEYLAND: Another example is John Addington Symonds, the Victorian writer, whose personal diary talks extensively about his gay sexual experiences with Venetian gondoliers and others. After Symonds' death his executor, Horatio Brown—who was also gay—put the diary under lock and key not to be opened until 1976.

NORSE: I don't think we've ever had anything similar to the gay lib movement going on now in America—and taking root in Italy, France, Germany and other countries, too. It's the first time that gays have come out in the open, which confirms my belief that this is the showdown century. All repressed elements which have been persecuted, hounded, made to lead miserable, defensive, hidden lives of self-hatred have never spoken out militantly until now: the blacks, Chicanos, Jews, gays and most recently the Native Americans.

This society is so rotten and destructive that only a total change could make it livable. At the age of fourteen I was reading the Russian writers of the preceding century, and was influenced by nihilist-anarchist views. I am still an anarchist. I have never belonged to any political group or party. From the middle of the last century, with Marx primarily, something was set into motion that I feel got sold out in our time. It's a bigger view of social change than the repressive petty-bourgeois socialist states of today represent, an early ideal that has been destroyed and almost forgotten.

When I was fourteen I had my first experience of cosmic consciousness. I experienced astral projection. I left my body and went into the stars. They became a circle of light and I was that circle of light. I was out of Time and saw my previous lives and future lives and my death in this life. In that split second I also saw the ultimate universal brotherhood of all, through Love, and that we are all one being not separate beings. No matter how gloomy it all looked in subsequent years I never lost that vision. I've been depressed and cynical, have acted and written a good deal out of negative states, feeling immobilized by the oppression of the individual. But I still think the wheel is turning from hate to love. But the psychedelic and sexual revolution hasn't gone far enough.

If one isn't totally erotic, expressing all sides of the sexual nature in every human organism, no revolution can be complete. You're cutting yourself off from that real love experience that has something oceanic and all-embracing, mystical and vast, a soul experience of union with all life, and, through this, union with God. God is that Being in every one of us, in our bodies at the base of the spine, the serpent-power, kundalini force, the sexual drive towards the ultimate orgasm, the ultimate union, eventually to be raised up through the chakras to the third eye–pineal gland–explosion-of-light at the top of the skull in out-of-sight-spaced-out superconsciousness. Fear of this experience is fear of your own tenderness, softness, gentleness, femininity and contact with your own inner space.

Instead we have the reaction: tight-assed macho violent dollar Pentagon warlike rigid suspicious hatred in American men that you don't see very often in Europe except in northern countries. The American's sexual role is preprogrammed. He is forced to declare it at the expense of his true feelings. Most of the violence in this country comes from insecure, shaky sex roles—fighting and killing are more acceptable social activities than loving and touching other men. The American man would rather have a bayonet up his ass than a cock.

LEYLAND: I understand you'll be figuring in the next volume of Anaïs Nin's *Diary*. When did you meet her?

NORSE: We met in the early fifties. She admired my first book of poetry, *The Undersea Mountain,* published in 1953, and we've been a mutual admiration society ever since. I enter in the fifth *Diary*. In the seventh *Diary* she will publish a long prose-poem of mine, "Journal of Insomnia" in the form of a diary. It's never been published before. I sent it to her about a year ago for her opinion, since it had been violently attacked here in San Francisco by a group of poets. Her positive reaction was a vindication and reassurance. She wrote: "The Diary is beautiful, direct and unique. If you are not ready to publish, would you like me to include yours within mine, a diary within a diary . . . ? Do you feel ready to face what I faced (and sometimes regret)? You share, and people love you. Others seek to destroy you. But the kind of love you attain by sharing (as you did when you wrote from England) is worth the price."

LEYLAND: Why do you think the poem-diary caused so much controversy among the poets you read it to here in San Francisco?

NORSE: I think it was because of the tone. It's a work which can be very easily misunderstood. It's in the French tradition. I had been reading Henri Michaux, whom I met years later in Rome and Paris. The tone and rhythm of the poem is apocalyptic and epic, far from what was prevalent in American poetry of the forties and early fifties and not at all acceptable to academic types. The San Francisco group were mostly professors of poetry in the academic tradition. It's ironic that I was accused of "apocalyptic bullshit"—they said they were tired of this after fifteen years of it. As I mentioned to you, the poem was written before the beats had come on the scene. It has nothing in common with beat language, although the tone is a precursor, you might say, of this approach.

The academy has a provincial hatred and suspicion of French influence, although now it's fashionable in New York. My work is a grab-bag of influences from everywhere I've lived and everyone I've read and admired. I don't really fit into any "school."

The poets who were impressed by the poem in question were all Europeans. The local poets condemned it as being verbose, full of cliches, sentimental, a rape of language and poetry, a work based on hate instead of love and therefore "immoral"—which is missing the mark altogether.

LEYLAND: Yes, of course. A criticism which rejects a poem as being based on hate instead of love is not a valid way to criticize *any* poem.

NORSE: Right on! The man who condemned it on those grounds was himself so venomous that he was practically foaming at the mouth. Actually, it's a poem of love anyway. Nanos Valaoritis, the Greek poet and professor, said (at that same meeting) that since the trial of *Fleurs du Mal,* over a hundred years ago, moral considerations of the kind being presented had no validity in art; and that in any case, the critic had missed the point, the irony being in the love behind the hate, as in Lautréamont's *Maldoror.*

I wrote a poem about the incident but it's too long to quote here. It seems I am always putting my foot in it. As Henry Miller once wrote about himself, I don't even have to open my mouth in a phony bunch of people; they know at once, instinctively, that I'm not like them.

> *Like a meeting of taxidermists*
> *they were stuffing the winged horse with straw.*
> *They had beaten Pegasus to death*
> *for shitting on the livingroom floor.*

LEYLAND: Perhaps you'd rap about your style of writing and also how your love affairs have affected your work.

NORSE: My style changes as I change, and I hope I keep changing rather than remaining with one particular mode of writing or feeling. When my *Selected Poems* appears, it will be pretty evident that I keep moving in poetry as well as in life. Generally I cultivate clarity and spontaneity, muscular language free of baroque baloney, natural speech rhythms, surreal vision and, above all, sensuality with nervous tension.

I work best when I have a lover; otherwise I feel isolated and lonely and cut off from stimulation. Although I haven't been spectacularly successful in the past in maintaining a long-lived affair, looking back I can see what there was in me that worked against a good relationship. I chose people like myself, with similar hangups. We couldn't solve them because we didn't know how. Perhaps you do not have to get older to realize it's not merely sex and passion but that a very conscious effort must be made on both sides to get through to love and to avoid contempt and hatred, which are carried over from childhood reactions and spoil the adult situations. I no longer suffer from the self-hatred that was so devastating to me and others most of my life.

LEYLAND: Do you think it is self-hatred that militated against your having a good relationship with a lover in the past?

NORSE: Definitely. Lack of self-confidence is fatal. The partner you choose is invariably someone who complements your neurotic needs, so that you recognize at first sight, for example, someone who will play the role of victim to your executioner, or someone who will be the helper to your helpless, the martyr to your persecutor. The roles are interchangeable. All dependency relationships that exclude self-help and self-autonomy are headed for the trash can. I now recognize these compulsive roles after a few signs betray them in another or in myself, and I don't plunge into an affair just because it's been sexually stimulating. Sex is simply not enough as a basis for living together. This may not be news, but to people who spend most of their waking hours in the desire and pursuit of the penis, it's always a good reminder.

Gay people often dehumanize sex, separate it from the person they're making it with. It's always been first sex and then muddle through the personality problems. Now I would do it in reverse order. Communication has got to be kept in the open. By communication I don't mean talking about antiques, cars, clothes, movies or telling jokes—those are just pastimes. I think *gay* and straight people spend too much of their time in those pastimes and never confront the vital issues of living, namely, personality problems, existential problems. There's no way love can work without communication. You've got to be really vigilant about your psychological behavior, without feeling blame or guilt, but observing how you destroy your own best interests.

LEYLAND: The gay liberation movement has never addressed itself to some of these questions. We are only now really beginning to talk about gay interpersonal relationships, and it's extremely important that we do so. We've had a lot of rhetoric in the movement; a lot of people have gotten involved in demonstrations and zaps, but they've never really dealt with their feelings toward other gay people. As a result relationships have often been fatally destructive. The viciousness, too, with which gay movement people have sometimes put down other gay movement people is a form of self-hatred not yet dealt with. It's easy to spout radical rhetoric but more difficult to deal with the basic issues of love and communication. In *Gay Sunshine* we are trying to get away from mere rhetoric in order to communicate on deeper personal levels. This is the direction in which I, as editor, have been trying to steer the paper over the past couple of years. And with some success, if I can judge from the beautiful letters that have been sent to us from gay brothers and sisters all over the country.

NORSE: That's a very good observation. There's a lot of sex chauvinism among gay people; the butch contempt for faggy behavior is as bad as the straight contempt for it. On both sides understanding is minimal. The transvestite, the drag queen, the compulsive nellie are in many cases simply living out a fantasy buried deep in most people from childhood. The butch goes to the other extreme by suppressing these fantasies and becoming more masculine in behavior and appearance than ordinarily required for relaxed behavior. I think it's extremely important for gay movement (and non-movement) people to investigate the psychological aspects of their behavior with each other, and with the non-gay world as well.

There's also something wrong with the gay activist who doesn't look into his/her own psychological behavior and goes around offensively causing splits in the gay movement, just as in the straight radical left, because of disagreement or the desire for power. Power is oppressive whether you're black, Indian, Jewish, straight or gay, man or woman.

LEYLAND: Yes, I agree. I think most of the brothers and sisters involved in the gay lib movement are not power-driven, although there have been tendencies of this kind at times among some individuals.

Another important question that's only just beginning to be dealt with is that of age and ageism. We've printed a number of articles during the past few issues on ageism. The gay movement has been very much a youth movement, and older gay people have been relegated to the background in a second-class role, or usually just ignored. And in the current gay scene "older gay people" means almost anyone over thirty. Of course, the ageism syndrome permeates our entire society.

NORSE: I wish it were otherwise, speaking as an older gay person who was once guilty of the same ageism in youthful folly. The ageism syndrome goes through the whole American structure, more than any country I've ever lived in. America is youth-conscious and youth-struck and has a horror of wrinkles, gray hair and flabby figures. Yet of all nations the youth of this country let themselves go physically to an alarming extent, eating and drinking sheer crap and destroying their bodies with drugs.

The majority of young people in European and African countries, where I've lived, are far better looking than American youth and are not repelled by physical contact with older men and women. In the Mediterranean countries, youths are not put off by the looks of older people, because their culture still has a place for the usefulness and experience of the older ones. Young men are just as excited about making it with old women as with young, and many of them have admitted that they prefer older women. In countries like France it is customary for a boy just emerging into puberty to be taken in hand by an older woman and initiated into the love experience over a period of years.

This is also common in many countries with homoerotic relationships: a very young boy and an older man. It must go back to ancient Greek times. The young men don't shrink from the touch of an old person. When I get really old, I hope to leave this country again and go back to the Mediterranean or the Far East where old people are admired, venerated, loved. You just can't tell the youth of this country to like, love, admire and have sex with older people. It would make them vomit.

LEYLAND: I think it's a matter of raising gay consciousness gradually, something which will take many years. It is true that an older gay person can get youthful invigoration from a much younger person, as Allen Ginsberg has pointed out. At the same time, it is far from ideal to search only for the very young and to be totally unwilling to make personal contact with people one's own age, or older.

NORSE: Yeah, as you get older you realize that you can make contact with people of any age, because you're not looking only for ornamental types who look marvelous, like a new car, but for people who have a great deal to offer, to say. In general, it's more desirable to be open to people and to experience rather than to cut yourself off by a limited outlook. Beauty is always desirable at least to me, but the beast has qualities of loyalty and affection that beauty, in its narcissism and vanity, often lacks.

Beauty is very hard for a young person because in a way it bestows on the possessor a kind of godlike superhuman quality to be worshiped and admired rather than to be comfortable with. It's a gift like genius. The possessor can get away with almost anything. But the beauty must also get old and die. I've never been comfortable in the presence of great beauty. If I have sex with a great beauty, it is always followed by a kind of sadness, and I'm sure that this is because it could not continue forever.

Only when you go out to meet freely all kinds of people, without preconceived notions of aesthetic or sexual goals, can you enrich your life. You impoverish life by living in one modality only, such as looking exclusively for beauty and youth. I'm speaking from experience because that's what I did for many years. When I was young and beautiful, I was sought after. It was very easy to get what I wanted, but I was never satisfied. Nor did I find a lasting relationship on that basis.

LEYLAND: Would you care to comment on the spiritual revival that is very much in evidence as one reaction to the intense crisis in Western society on all levels, economic and social, with the constant threat of war and annihilation through technological achievements?

NORSE: We recently had the interesting phenomenon of Rennie Davis, the new left activist, one of the Chicago Seven, who has become a disciple of Maharaj Ji. Davis sees this fifteen-year-old Indian guru as the only salvation. At first his attitude was, "What! be converted by some fat little rich kid with jewels all over his body?" Not only that, but Maharaj Ji's older brother is supposed to be Jesus Christ—the Second Coming, no less! And as a second-class messiah, too, because it's the kid who's the big shot, the hottest messiah on the scene since Buddha and Christ. And this is what Rennie Davis believes. Don't forget that political activism is not necessarily exclusive of spiritual premises, witness Malcolm X and *his* guru, Elijah Muhammad.

America is at the very nadir of material decay and the corruption of spiritual values by the most materialistic society that has existed since ancient Rome. This country is now in the throes of a giant schizophrenia: you go either into the materialistic life or into spiritual illumination. Rennie Davis gave up the political solution in favor of the spiritual, but he had probably been suppressing his spiritual side and it had to come out one way or another.

I've been through both sides myself. I had left America in a completely cynical condition, nihilistic. When I left in 1953 I got involved with occult and metaphysical concerns. In Europe I met a whole bunch of clairvoyants, yogis, swamis, cabbalists, Christian mystics, witches, warlocks, white and black magicians, Arabian sorcerers, theosophists, anthroposophists, and so on. There was almost no period during those fifteen years that I wasn't in touch with some of those occultists and magicians. I've had some weird experiences. Once at a circle in Rome conducted by an Indian yogi, I had the experience of the kundalini force suddenly rising and my heart chakra opening up, which manifested as a feeling of a great wind in my back, on both sides of my spine, like the sprouting of wings. And once, through practicing Buddhist exercises in Spain, I went out of my body.

I wrote about the Aquarian Age back in 1960 in Paris, in several poems. Now everybody knows about it. Good, the mysteries are revealed. This is the time for it, as prophesied in the distant past. The people are now to assumpt, to become God. What is happening en masse is what we, as individuals, pursued fifteen or twenty years ago.

LEYLAND: While there are beautiful and deep elements in many spiritual approaches, there are also a lot of emotional excesses in the name of spirituality. There is an imbalance in saying that the final answer is in this or that particular guru. If a guru helps you to transform your inner life and your external relationships as well so that a dichotomy is not set up between the political and the spiritual, then all well and good. But I think there are a lot of phony "spiritual leaders" around, taking advantage of the genuine spiritual needs of young Americans who have broken away from a materialistic culture.

NORSE: There'll be rich pickings among them! There are all kinds of fortune tellers, tea-leaf and palm-reading gypsies, astrologers, ESP and clairvoyant mediums, psychics of all types. Many are phony, just as there are phony gurus. But some are not. I've had some unbelievable experiences in Europe with clairvoyants who knew all about me *at first sight*.

Now it's perfectly possible in Rennis Davis' case that he has flipped or is a double agent or loves power so much that he finds it at the left hand of God, in the person of young fatso, who's riding around in a Rolls Royce and is sheltered by parents making a fortune on him while the Indian people starve. My attitude is this: whether or not you have a profound spiritual experience makes no difference whatsoever to the masses of mankind who are suffering from oppression because power and wealth are concentrated in the hands of a few. If you are enlightened or not, your role should remain more or less the same with regard to social action: under no circumstances can you allow yourself to withdraw from the commitment to change the world. Transformation of self *is* transformation of society only to the extent that you raise the consciousness of all by ceaseless activities in that direction.

It is true that there has been a mad dash for esoterica. On the other hand, most people are starved in a materialistic desert where the multiplication of goods and possessions is supposed to bring the highest happiness. Quite the reverse has happened: it's brought alcoholism, cigarette smoking, loneliness, lack of identity, TV, and movie watching (because you can't relate to live people and must relate vicariously) and a superficial mechanistic determinism that produces the Ugly American riding in his big fat slimy automobile or plane while the world starves. From this there's no way to go but to start looking for the source of all values, within yourself.

LEYLAND: I think that too many people make a dichotomy between the spiritual and the political. Why can't we have both? That is the most balanced approach. Deep change will only occur when there is a union between the political and spiritual approaches.

NORSE: Yes. From my understanding, Gandhi was someone who combined the two and so was Sri Aurobindo, who in the first part of his life was a successful lawyer jailed for his role in the Indian independence movement. In jail Aurobindo had time to read and study. He began practicing yoga and became the greatest living yogi in India. In India today what he left behind as his heritage is the most important of all that country's ashrams, or spiritual centers. I've read some of his works and there's no doubt about the quality of his mind and power of vision and, under it all, unmistakably, the force of Love. Maybe the movement of the young guru Maharaj Ji is going to rival Aurobindo's in numbers, but I doubt you can compare this kid and his family, which is more like a theatrical act of some kind, a big circus show on the road, with something as genuine as Aurobindo's teachings.

I mention Aurobindo and Gandhi because I don't think there has to be a split between social action and inner light unless you make one. Rennie Davis has made a dichotomy. He may have a special problem. Time will tell. I suspect that anybody who has such a split within him is suppressing one element at the expense of another in himself. Just as a straight may be suppressing his or her own gay tendencies or vice versa. The harm comes from the suppression, not from the expression of it. Hatred comes from suppression.

LEYLAND: Not many people have integrated both the spiritual and the political. One person who has is Daniel Berrigan—poet, writer, Christian mystic, political activist, who has been in jail for his activism. He wrote mystical poems while in jail for burning draft records to protest the Vietnam war.

Another such person was Thomas Merton. His first few years as a Trappist monk were spent just in spiritual development. But he emerged from that first period and wrote activist material infused with the spiritual. He had integrated the two. I think he was on the verge of making even deeper breakthroughs before his untimely death in 1968 while visiting Buddhist monasteries in the Far East.

NORSE: If you suppress or repress a part of you that you consider unworthy or shameful, then you are going to be that kind of person who is a hater and who wants to kill others. Whether you're a mystic or a materialist doesn't matter; the same problems operate in the same way. If we do violence to any part of ourselves, we do violence to other people. We all need to express the different forces in us: materialistic, mystic, sexual. If we keep down any one of these, it will come back as contempt, hatred, the desire to kill. We have got to express, as individuals, our homoerotic urges without shame or guilt, and our heterosexual urges likewise. Suppression of one harms the other, does violence to your own personality and to other people. We also suppress the mystical at the expense of the materialistic, or vice versa, and produce monsters. "The dream of reason produces monsters," said Goya.

From the psychological point of view, all people are alike. We cry, we laugh, we need attention and affection. Our whole life is a quest for affection, for love. It's recently been discovered by neurologists that without constant handling and touching, the newborn infant begins to withdraw into itself and dies. Or if the infant grows up, he becomes the autistic child who cannot relate to anybody. All of us are like that; if we don't get constant feedback by physical and social contact, touch, attention, we begin literally to shrivel up. This lack of attention is the source of a great many illnesses. We cannot as organisms continue living in a state of sensory deprivation.

As homosexuals we are looking for someone who will give us tender, loving care, and receive it from us. But it's illegal for us to look for love. I find this barbarous, monstrous, worse than the excesses of witch-hunting in the Middle Ages and in early American society, from which our persecution derives.

LEYLAND: I think that women in this oppressive, capitalist, macho society are subject to the same kind of oppression as gay people.

NORSE: Exactly. Women and gay people have no real rights. The sexist male-chauvinist laws have relegated women to the position of goods and chattels, and this is also true of children. Without women's lib there can be no gay lib and vice versa. And until the blacks realize that their lot lies with the women and the gays, they're not going to get very far either. I think that the fault of minority militancy is in this fragmentation. That's one of the fallacies of being just politically oriented; you need a broader base of operations, a spiritual base.

LEYLAND: Blacks and Chicanos have organized, and gay people must do the same if we are to wrest control of our own lives from the Establishment bureaucracies. This is what we are beginning to do. We have to keep in mind the spiritual, too, I agree. There has to be an integration between the political and the spiritual. This is what I'm trying to do in my own life.

NORSE: Yes. Otherwise, you're operating from too narrow a base of consciousness. If you are open to mind-expanding experiences, you have a better chance of understanding the issues at stake. I define politics as the art of making the simple complex. With a greater grasp of the issues, we can fight for our autonomy more successfully. Gandhi and Aurobindo defeated the British Empire because they had a spiritual base; but they fought in the economic/political arena. You cannot beat that kind of combination. Until such men or women arise in this country, I think we will always be pawns in the game of master and slave.

PETER ORLOVSKY (LEFT) AND ALLEN GINSBERG / PHOTO BY STEVE LOWELL, SAN FRANCISCO, 1975

PETER ORLOVSKY

PETER ORLOVSKY was born in 1933. He currently makes his home on a farm in Cherry Valley, upstate New York. He has been a longtime lover and companion of poet Allen Ginsberg and has accompanied him on worldwide travels, reading and singing. Peter Orlovsky has had three chapbooks of poems published: *Dear Allen: Ship will land Jan. 23, 58* (Beau Fleuve Series No. 5, 1971), *Lepers Cry* (1972), and *Clean Asshole Poems and Smiling Vegetable Songs* (City Lights, 1978). His work appeared in *The New American Poetry* (1960).

THE PRESENT INTERVIEW was taped in San Francisco in April 1974, while Orlovsky was on his way to Grass Valley to help Allen Ginsberg build a house in the country, near Gary Snyder's home. Conversing with Peter Orlovsky were Winston Leyland, editor of *Gay Sunshine,* and Charley Shively, a coordinator of *Fag Rag,* Boston's gay liberation paper. The interview originally appeared in *Gay Sunshine* 25 (Summer 1975).

Winston Leyland and Charley Shively interview
PETER ORLOVSKY

LEYLAND: How long have you lived in the country?

ORLOVSKY: Cherry Valley? Almost seven years. That's a long time. I was drinking some wine up there but I've stopped that. And I was taking some amphetamine too but I've stopped that. So now I've got a nice 45 hp tractor, and a 20 hp tractor, and a nine-foot seeder that plans three rows three feet apart, so I can plant an acre of beets, or two acres of beets, or two hundred acres of beets. I've been up there the last seven years, more or less concentrating on the garden aspect. Now I'd like to concentrate on the overall aspect.

LEYLAND: Are you going to be keeping the farm at Cherry Valley? You're not going to be moving out to California permanently are you?

ORLOVSKY: No. Building a house is a great experience, and the land up there in Grass Valley, California, is so beautiful, all ponderosa pine, and you sleep out all night long. Gary Snyder's up there, he does all his cooking outside. I don't understand why a bunch of gays don't buy some land up there and build a house.

LEYLAND: There are a lot of gay people on the land in California. You've lived in the city most of your life?

ORLOVSKY: I've spent a lot of time in the city. We lived on the Lower East Side in the Puerto Rican slums and most of those people stayed there all their lives. It must be really horrible to be stuck in the big city that much. There must be some way of getting them out to the country.

LEYLAND: Are you doing much writing now?

ORLOVSKY: I do more work than writing, so I just keep at it. There's no time to sit down and write. Sometimes when I do have time it's a great joy, but it's rare.

LEYLAND: You lived in India several years ago; how long were you there?

ORLOVSKY: A year and ten months. It was a great time. Unfortunately I took a lot of morphine.

LEYLAND: Was that in the early sixties?

ORLOVSKY: '61, '62. I did some drawings of beggars in the streets, listened to Indian music, folk music.

LEYLAND: Was Allen there?

ORLOVSKY: Yeah. I got a sarod from Ali Akbar's son, Ashesh, took a couple of lessons with him. Then I brought myself back to New York City, got a job—we lived like gypsies, on the Lower East Side.

SHIVELY: Did you do any meditation in India?

ORLOVSKY: No, I went to Allen in Wyoming for ten days, but that was a great shock, meditation, to sit down and do it for ten days, for ten hours, it was a fantastic experience.

LEYLAND: You mentioned amphetamines. What finally made you stop?

ORLOVSKY: Speed was an essential thing for me—shooting, mainlining. I finally stopped to help my growth, to take a place in the country.

LEYLAND: What have you been growing at the farm in Cherry Valley?

ORLOVSKY: Beets, and beet greens, because there's a lot of protein and iron in beet greens. Sweet corn, hybrid tomatoes, Chinese cabbage, red, white, yellow beans, broccoli, cauliflower, Japanese radishes, cabbage. But you've got to harvest them at the right time. You don't let them grow too big. Asparagus. I didn't take care of the strawberry patch, so weeds took over. A combination of garlic and onion, edible pea pods, peas, all the ten kinds of squash, there's winter squash you can store in a cold cellar and it will last throughout the winter; carrots, short stubby "cock" carrots that don't get worms; raspberry bushes. I'm going to plant some more plum trees. It's nice. You ought to come up there some time. [*Sings garden song:*]

> *I'm going out to the garden now*
> *Oh tell me whatcha want me to bring ya back*
> *Oh bring back 36 ripe tomatoes*
> *Bring it back sweet and fresh like that*
> *I'm going out to the garden now*
> *Oh tell me whatcha want me to bring back*
> *Oh bring back some fresh broccoli with the summer rain just drippin off of it*
> *half a bushel of tender corn, oh so sweet, sweet like that*
> *Ten pounds of brussels sprouts, oh so fresh like that*

So I bring food back to the house or sometimes I would eat out in the garden.

LEYLAND: Did you begin to get into tools when you moved to Cherry Valley?

ORLOVSKY: Yes, and with Gary Snyder in the Sierra Nevada mountains. He has some nice tools. It's these ancient tools that you don't buy anymore, an old Steelmaster compact camp axe. Allen's got some very good buys on useful old tools, a twenty-year-old handmade paint scraper. [*Shows tools.*]

LEYLAND: Did both Allen and you do some building at Cherry Valley?

ORLOVSKY: Not much building—mostly interior work, wood paneling, building beds, simple repair of barn doors, chicken coop, roof, but nothing like building a whole house or a little three-room house from scratch. [*Shows English chisel that Allen got.*] There's a young carpenter that Allen likes—a beautiful young carpenter—there's a number of young carpenters, so nice and sweet. I don't think they're gay, but they're tender and Allen looks at them with such loving eyes.

LEYLAND: Is this your first time back in San Francisco?

ORLOVSKY: Yes, in eight years. It's good to be back. I used to wander these streets and drink a lot. I learned to drink in S.F. I've stopped now—I drink fruit juice instead of wine.

LEYLAND: You first came to S.F. in the early fifties?

ORLOVSKY: Yes, in '54. I lived with painter Bob LaVigne first. Do you know him?

LEYLAND: Yes, I met Bob briefly last September at Cal-Arts in L.A. He's still teaching.

SHIVELY: Could we ask when you first had your first sex with Bob LaVigne?

ORLOVSKY: Sure. I was very scared. I was trembling all over. He was showing me these big thick art books. I knew something was going on. I don't remember too much after that. I was young. I've always liked girls, but I couldn't make it with them yet, I didn't know how to do it. I was a dope, a hermit, a creep, an idiot, a moron. I was going to spend the rest of my life by myself unless I had a brainstorm. But Bob LaVigne came along and there was a whole new friendship, exciting sexual knowledge facts. He was a painter, and he showed me this big art book. It was in '54, I was in the army, a medic at the hospital at the Presidio—and I came stumbling upon him at Foster's sitting down having coffee.

LEYLAND: So you lived with Bob for a year?

ORLOVSKY: Yes.

LEYLAND: I guess maybe Bob LaVigne wanted to tell his side of what had happened. He didn't agree with everything that Allen has said in the *Gay Sunshine* interview.

ORLOVSKY: Well, we were all creeps at some time. He was hurt. I was a creep when I was taking amphetamine. I can be a creep even when I'm not taking amphetamine. I'm nasty or jealous, we all make our mistakes, but sometimes, we're lucky. We catch on to it and try to stop, but sometimes we don't and we really make a fool out of ourselves. LaVigne was carrying on a little bit, he was jealous, he was going to be lonely too. I think I was going to break up with him anyway, it was hard for me, I don't know what it was, I was having some problems with him, it was nice being together, it was very loving. I learned a lot, but there was something too limiting about him. Allen had more of a social life and was more worldly, whereas LaVigne was just too narrow. With Allen it was more exciting, you met more kinds of people; he was interested in more earth-shattering problems—could recite passages of Hart Crane or long passages of Shelley, whereas LaVigne was more philosophical.

LEYLAND: Don't you think that because you have been in love relationships with men that you might be considered bisexual?

ORLOVSKY: Probably so, yeah. But I don't have too much of a desire for men, unless it's a real nice fourteen-year-old kid or something. I tend to like feminine types. I've got a girlfriend who doesn't want me to go around with anyone but girls. So my sex life is rather small . . . there's Allen and my girlfriend. In fact I'm trying to stop orgasm, trying to go through a year and have sex, but don't come.

LEYLAND: The part that uptightens straight people most, I think, is not that gay people have sex with people their own age, but their making love with teenagers, or children. I think the taboo against child sexuality is connected with the child molestation myth. That myth is so ingrained in straight people's minds. You've felt more attracted to teenage boys?

ORLOVSKY: I'm not running after them. Only because they're young, and beautiful. I don't have the hots for them.

LEYLAND: What do you feel about child and teenage sex?

ORLOVSKY: I don't know what to say about that. If you're not going to have a good relationship, no matter who it is or at what age, then there is no point in having it. It's not going to be a good thing. It's going to be harder to seduce a fourteen, seventeen, eighteen, nineteen-year-old, but that happens you know. All kinds of love scenes happen. I was jerking off when I was twelve and a half. If the situation had been that there was a gay in my house, and my mother didn't know it, and he was blowing me before I was jerking off or something like that, or I was screwing him, well, then it would have happened. I mean, all these illegal things with a teenager, well that's going to happen because of the odd situations or the situations in the family or the community, so whatever is going to happen is going to happen.

SHIVELY: Would you make love with twelve-year-olds?

ORLOVSKY: I'd blow them—because they're so young it would be nice to blow them, but I'm certainly not going to do it and get their parents after my neck. I'm certainly not goin' to go to jail.

LEYLAND: What kind of rapport did you have with Jack Kerouac and Neal Cassady?

ORLOVSKY: It was good with Jack. Sometimes it was better than others. The winos got with Jack a lot. And again, I guess I was just a very narrow-minded fellow. Jack had so much experience, Jack had a lot of energy. He was very outgoing, such a kaleidoscope type interested in everyone and everything at the same time. A butterfly, jumping around to this person and that person, talking to everyone. It was nice seeing him. Jumping around like a butterfly, with his lips and talking, and being around and watching him do it all the time. But as he got drinking more it got sadder and sadder. Then when we got into politics in our demonstrations against the Vietnam war, he was against that, our taking part in those demonstrations.

Jack had so much faith, and love, and obedience for his mother, that he would take on her political outlook. He stayed around the house, the house that he had gotten her. He had a lot of friends coming to visit him. I don't know, I guess it was his mother. He must have just got drunk so much and every night that he had to stay home and be taken care of. Drinking just takes over. How much Jack drank in that time, the time before he died, and how much that affected him; it must have made his political thinking very difficult, and made him very tied to his mother. She was the one who took care of him after he came through. She was the one that would do the shopping and have the food in the icebox.

LEYLAND: How do you feel your relationship with Allen has evolved in the past twenty years? Do you feel it's been continuing to deepen?

ORLOVSKY: Sure, it's continuing to deepen. We still make it. I blow him. He'll screw me. I don't screw him because I make it with my girlfriend. And I'm trying not to have orgasms. So I don't probably satisfy Allen fully. It's been so long, and we've made it so much; we'll probably be making it before we die or something. There's the money thing too. I seem to be incapable of making money, or I seem to have these insanities of work habits. I'm a poet, and I like sitting down and writing. I still love Allen and I think we'll be together a long time. There are times we need each other. Like now, he needs me to help him build his house. I'm very grateful to Allen, he saved my life so many times. I almost killed myself with amphetamine. He's been very patient, thoughtful, and helpful. He has young boys and young men that he makes it with, so he's very happy. He's got poison oak right now so he can't make it with nobody. Now Allen has shown an interest in tools and in working, getting strength back in his body. He just said recently that if he works on building this house, he'll probably live another ten years.

LEYLAND: How did you feel when Allen first became famous? That had to have an effect on you too at the time.

ORLOVSKY: I was jealous and feeling inferior, but it was good, it was a good experience because he always brought new and exciting and talented things into awareness, awareness of a lot of things going on.

LEYLAND: You traveled together extensively I guess during the fifties and sixties in various countries?

ORLOVSKY: Yeah, we traveled a lot. Allen has been on trips for a year at a time, I think. He's been down in South America, then he was in Czechoslovakia by himself; he's been to Russia too.

SHIVELY: Do you get jealous of other lovers of Allen's?

ORLOVSKY: No, I think it's good for him, I'm glad. It's good for Allen, 'cause I can't give him everything he needs, and he's able to find some nice young kid, some nineteen-year-old sweet, clean ass. In fact I'm glad, because he's happy, he's a much better friend of mine when he's making it with someone else. It's not good to be together all the time; it's good for lovers to get out in different relationships. It gets too incestuous. Some people can do it, whatever feels right.

SHIVELY: Both Winston and I have trouble fitting in with our families about being gay. How do you fit in with your family?

ORLOVSKY: I don't come out and tell them that I sucked Allen's cock or he screwed me, but I think they know. I talk to them about these things, but I sign my letters "love, Peter" and they know that I love them. I guess they know that lovers do whatever lovers do. My mother says: "Well it's his life—he's a young man." My sister says, "He's crazy, he can do what he wants," or "He's a creep," or whatever she says. I love my mother and I love my father. We have many, many family problems; we argue, but we try to keep our arguments down to a very minimum because we have had such family problems in the past that we have come to a sort of calm basis of talking to each other very carefully and very thoughtfully and lovingly. My parents are getting old and they can't take arguments, and they realize I'm more calm. I love them more and more as time goes on, but I also see how limited my mother is, and my father. She is on welfare, and when a person is deaf and on welfare they develop a certain kind of way of reacting to the city that they're in, it's a very sad, narrow, pathetic relationship that they have to the whole world. They see it through their local welfare office, and the people around them in the community. Welfare turns people like my mother into raving idiots and isolated, helpless individuals. But they love me and I try to help solve their problems from time to time. I gave them jars of preserved fruits and vegetables, and tomato juice that I made myself on the farm.

LEYLAND: They were accepting of your love relationship with Bob LaVigne and Allen?

ORLOVSKY: Yes. Mother always liked Bob LaVigne, his handwriting was so nice, that he was an artist. I guess she didn't feel bad that I fell in love with him, because she probably figured that if I didn't I'd turn out worse—which is probably true. I might have tried suicide. Before I went in the army, I worked in the state mental hospital, and after a year and a half working there I was ending up crying on the wards myself, and thinking my god this is the way the whole world is. I have cured myself, I don't know. I'm not dumb or idiotic. Maybe LaVigne saved my life. So in that sense my homosexual relationship with LaVigne was tops for me, was perfect, lucky. And when I met Allen it was so much better. He was smart and worldly and had traveled. LaVigne hadn't traveled too much. Allen had just come back from six months in Mexico.

SHIVELY: How many are there in your family?

ORLOVSKY: Four brothers and one sister.

SHIVELY: What are they all doing now?

ORLOVSKY: My father's getting old and he's taking care of his health, separated from my mother, and my mother is on welfare, living with her son and daughter. She's not really taking care of him, she's on welfare, he's about to go catatonic. I love him now, love him sweetly, I'd like to help him out now but I don't have any money. I've got to make some money, he's a very sweet young man, he's thirty-three. If I took care of him, I wouldn't have this hostility, since I know more or less what I want to do—grow vegetables, work on a farm, and recognize that other people are different, that they've got their own thing that they can do, they work slow or fast. But I've lost my chance to take care of him. Or maybe it's not good for me to take care of him. He's going to end up in a very weird state, he's not getting better with my mother, he just sits in one spot. His circulation is fantastically bad. He's very skinny. His hands have a cold grimy feeling. But I'm trying to get my mother to put him in a hospital, but she thinks that all hospitals are bad. She gets medical help from welfare. It's a weird scene. I'm probably not explaining it right.

SHIVELY: Have you ever made it much in the bushes, men's rooms, or the bars?

ORLOVSKY: The sex rooms? On the spot sex? At a party once with Wyn Chamberlain I let my ass be screwed for half an hour. It was a wild party in NYC in the Bowery, same building as John Giorno's. I must have gotten a little drunk. We took off our clothes in a big pile in the center of the room; it wasn't too much of an expansive orgy, but it was nice. Have you ever—

SHIVELY: Oh yeah, wherever I can make it.

ORLOVSKY: How many times do you come a month?

SHIVELY: About ninety I guess.

ORLOVSKY: Wow! You might be short-changing yourself—you could have a longer orgasm if you cut down to thirty times a month. If you want a longer orgasm you've got to do a lot of meditating...

SHIVELY: Is *that* why people are meditating...

ORLOVSKY: That's why they're meditating—they're going to get a one-minute flood orgasm. Have you ever had an orgasm that lasted a whole minute, goes throughout your body in ripples, and vibrates? You need to do a lot of work to build up your circulation, your muscles! You should spend some time each day with your muscles—they are what's going to carry you through life. They are also what helps you feel a sexual vibration. When you drop a rock or pebble in a pond and you see the waves go out, the succeeding waves, the first one, and then the second and the third, and the fiftieth wave is a little smaller than the first five or ten. The same with orgasm, when it hits the end of the pond and starts coming back in, so there's that kind of a circular, vibrating flooding orgasm throughout the body. You can get it to when you sit and meditate.

LEYLAND: To what extent was your reaction against smoking and drinking a reaction against the beat, romantic emphasis on this—like with Jack Kerouac, and others, an almost macho emphasis on drinking? A self-destructive kind of thing?

ORLOVSKY: It killed Jack. It killed Neal Cassady. In fact, Neal came to visit me in NYC before he died, he came to visit Allen. Allen was in Europe. He stayed with me on Tenth Street. I was into amphetamine insanity and he was also, and I was in a way very horrible to him, because I wasn't feeding him, or cooking a meal, because I was obsessed with amphetamine. I was very cold and horrible, monstrous. It turned me into a monster. Greg [Corso] is not doing too well, maybe Greg will pull out of it—he's into liquor. I was drinking wine too, and I was going downhill, and if I didn't have the farm to retreat to and to recuperate and to become interested in... There is so much wine here in the city, and so much cigarettes, and so much meat. How many gays are there in the U.S. now?

LEYLAND: I think everybody needs to touch the gayness inside themselves.

ORLOVSKY: I don't think it's good to impose a homosexual experience on every male. That's going to scare them like you were going to take over. You should let things come natural.

LEYLAND: Straight people need to tap the gay potential inside themselves and most people are not doing that. Such an exploration would lessen homophobia.

ORLOVSKY: Gay, in a sense, means just being happy, it means being light-hearted; it means being kind and considerate in a very friendlied, light-ish, thoughtful way. There's no hard-on, no pulsating hot dick in the word "gay." It's more of like happy heart, uplifting feeling. In the image itself, there's no big shock, you know, of a hot dick about to squirt from here to the window. What there is in the word is a concern for the body, that it live 225 years and still be strong. A concern that you live off air for fifteen days and still be lighthearted and gay and happy. I think that is the good force that the term has.
    You're saying that everyone should have a homosexual experience?

LEYLAND: Fifty percent of men do at one time or another.

ORLOVSKY: Do you want someone who is not gay to make it with you?

LEYLAND: I'm basically attracted to gay people. I'm not masochistic in wanting that kind of a relationship with a straight person. I would hope that as consciousness is raised more straight people would tap that gay potential inside themselves.

ORLOVSKY: What is the gay potential inside themselves?

LEYLAND: It's many things, and the sexual is just part of it.

SHIVELY: I think the capacity to love and the ability to love people of the same sex, I think to love everybody in a physical, sensual, complete way. But I don't think any of it should be forced. In Boston, we had gangs of people roaming around the streets beating up on people they thought were gay.

ORLOVSKY: How do you get around that? How do you solve that problem?

SHIVELY: Bring them all "out."

ORLOVSKY: If it's a solid wall of hate, you have to stay away from them. If they're out to beat you up or kill you, they'll do it. Self-defense, self-preservation.

LEYLAND: Ann Charters in her recent biography skipped over the bisexual side of Jack Kerouac.

ORLOVSKY: Probably so. I blew Jack one time, on Second Street, when he was very drunk. He was so drunk he couldn't get a hard-on. So sadly drunk. Just fooling around, just trying to make friends with him, keep things funny and smooth. It was hard trying to stop him from drinking, but I had to do it; it was just impossible. It's hard to stop your friends' bad habits, and your friends to help you to stop. He must have loved Neal very much.

LEYLAND: Jack never made love with Neal?

ORLOVSKY: Jack could never see Neal in the sex scenes as a girl. There were orgies; he writes about it. There was a rapport, but Neal always had so many things to do. It was hard. Sometimes I wanted to go to him and talk with him, but he had so many things to do.

SHIVELY: Do you have any direction or ideas, are you writing anything?

ORLOVSKY: Writing conversations I had. Like when I left NYC on the plane to come to Sacramento, I had a funny conversation in a taxi on the way to the east side of town in NYC. So I wrote down my conversations with the taxi driver on the Vietnam war, money, asked him what he thought about Nixon, is he going to be impeached or not. He turned out to be an ex-marine. I gave him a dollar tip, and told him about the cost of the Vietnam war in a very careful way. Things like that I sort of write down, things I remember and the conversation strikes me as sort of interesting. Then other times, when I get excited about something, about eating raw vegetables, I write that down, or my shit turning green.

Oh I forgot to tell you. I plan to make five million dollars and grow eighty-five trillion trillion apples. And I'll write. I want to grow an apple orchard. A forest ranger came to our farm to talk to us about fifteen acres of woods there, this government program to thin out the woods, and says you've got some good maple trees there, we want these little trees to go so that these big maple trees will grow even bigger and better and they'll be good for timber or maple sugar. But he said our forest didn't meet the standards, so we don't qualify for this program. But he'll come and "X" the trees, so we can use them for firewood and also to help the other trees to grow. I went walking with him for about two and a half hours. He pointed out to me a wild apple tree, where there were three young trees twisting around an older tree. He said cut away those other trees so that the older tree can grow good. I haven't written that down yet. You see, the military won't let me have any farming tools to start a big multi-fruit orchard, so that's why I'm angry at the military. They've got a hundred billion dollars, and someone like me wants to come along and grow some apples, I don't get tools or land. So a lot of my poems now are about trying to get money away from the military, trying to grow vegetables and fruits and start farming going.

Withholding taxes is a very good way—don't give them any money at all. Allen has done that. His letter to Internal Revenue is in *Win* magazine. It's very good. You should read it. He says that since one-third of the national American budget goes to the military, that's the equivalent of one-third of my income; that you shouldn't pay to the military because of all these horrors they do with everyone's tax money. So he'll send one-third of his money to some organization, maybe to the WRL. It was a very good, full, long, coherent letter.

I write this in a car in North Dakota: "In a car, passing B-52 bombers in Grand Forks, North Dakota, each one of the B-52s was loaded with hydrogen bombs. 13 bombers facing another 13, their rear tail fins looked like huge whales, and the slick grey underbelly side waiting out there in the 18 below temperature, though they wouldn't let us see or go visit, go down into a silo missile. The Lt. Col. recognized Allen's name. Not to bring any adverse publicity to the presence of the silos, their rich easy no-work lieutenants and privates and Army guards some who smoke pot, guards of the silo. We were told over and over by students and teachers, laymen and Hutterite farmers that they don't fire their duds because they're waterlogged. Flooding with water the missiles in silos won't fire. There is a bomb that blows the concrete cover off of the top of the missile silo, then the silo comes shooting up so the missile is not obstructed when and if it flies it shoots up and out and up away 40 billion dollars we're talking about in North Dakota. The strongest nation in the world is North Dakota. And SAC bases, we saw a B-52 taking off. Allen reads in *Phil. Enquirer* that Philip Berrigan and his wife Sister Elizabeth McAllister do an exorcism in front of the National Security Agency in Washington. Berrigan dips and drops and covers the NSA cross with blood, trying to make people in America aware that NSA financed the overthrow of Salvador Allende in Chile."

I write about my corner vegetable man on the Lower East Side; over the years it's sometimes so difficult to talk with him, he's so pro-Nixon. Two million people had to die because the world is overpopulated. We've gotta have wars, we've got to bomb. So he talks like that. I don't know whether he's kidding or joking, but he says it to me, so he must be serious. A lot of people, a lot of right-wing people are the nicest people in the world, must feel that way. He's the old-fashioned American at work most of the time, he's an elderly man, he's got a son. His father sells vegetables. But he's willing to talk. So I write about him.

LEYLAND: Do you have anything in your diary about your reflections on coming back to San Francisco?

ORLOVSKY: Yes. "June 1st, 6:05am. I'm on the bus. Just coming out of east side terminal through 50 cent toll used to be 25 cents before that a dime I'll bet. Rainy mist and just about to pass last exit before Brooklyn. No not yet road repair work signs, 50 limit. Big graveyard. I've seen rear end fishtail says passenger seated, next to elderly grandpa driver. Rubber tires by roadside below, lay in road. Call Denise from east side terminal to tell her hello again. She's crying from 4:43am to 5:24am. And don't want me to go to Cal. and fool around with other girls. Yes and yes I'll be good so I tell her the conversation I had with a taxi driver.

"8:05 in plane just off the ground, and pulling away over the River and see the mist below now cover everything so can't describe anything out window except the white fluff of clouds of light grey and touch of greyer and almost... white puff cotton. White, bright with the sun trying to show but the white vapor clouds are too thick and even where total white puff cotton mist is outside plane window."

JOHN RECHY

NOVELIST JOHN RECHY was born in El Paso, Texas. He currently makes his home in Hollywood, California. He is the author of five novels and one documentary. His first novel, *City of Night* (1963) is a journey by a nameless hustler narrator through the gay underground in the America of the early sixties. It has attained the stature of a modern classic. His second novel, *Numbers* (1967), explores the world of promiscuous sex in the movie houses and parks of Los Angeles. There followed three other novels: *This Day's Death* (1969), *The Vampires* (1971), and *The Fourth Angel* (1973). In 1977 Grove Press published his book *The Sexual Outlaw: A Documentary*. This first work of nonfiction by Rechy is a passionate outcry against the oppression of gay people, a "nonfiction account, with commentaries, of three days and nights in the sexual underground" of Los Angeles' parks, alleys, tunnels, garages, streets and beaches—the "battlefield," as Rechy calls it, of the sexual outlaw who brings a sense of choreography, ritual and mystery to the sex hunt. "Voice Over: Interview 2" (pp. 66–71 of *The Sexual Outlaw*) is a reconstituted version of the interview which Winston Leyland, editor of *Gay Sunshine*, conducted with Rechy in April and July of 1973 at the novelist's Hollywood apartment. This interview originally appeared in *Gay Sunshine* 23 (November/December 1974) and is reprinted in the present anthology in its original form.

The following note was written by John Rechy in July 1977:

THE TEMPTATION to revise (rewrite!) an interview, a published interview, is enormous. After all, during the spontaneity of the question-answering, didn't a couple of things slip out that you might want to recall? And couldn't you have made a stronger, perhaps a wittier, point here and there? And some of the syntax! Certainly you don't really speak that carelessly at times—only at times, because, of course, you can't help but be impressed by your clarity and style, even while speaking! Yes, the temptation nags.

But soon you begin to realize that much that is valid, even where clumsy, even where not exact, is lost in revising what was spoken at a particular moment, the important conveying of your immediate thought-processes, for those who are interested.

For that main reason—and two others—I have left this interview just as it appeared in *Gay Sunshine* several years ago (and, incidentally, I consider it one of the very best interviews with me). Perhaps some of my attitudes expressed in it may have slightly altered, perhaps—as is true in some cases here—they've become surer (for example, the matter of S & M as a reactionary, straight-imposed ritual to sexual guilt).

My second main reason for leaving the interview intact is that at the time it occurred, I was grappling in my mind with concepts that would become major aspects of *The Sexual Outlaw*. To change this interview would be to change thoughts that I was then formulating. I think it is more interesting, now, to "see" those thoughts shaping, perhaps being altered by the time they appear in *The Sexual Outlaw*.

And another reason for leaving this interview intact: had I chosen to revise it—no matter how consciously I might have wanted to avoid this—the "revisions" would have inevitably attempted at least in part to answer some of the negative criticism from an element of the gay press to *The Sexual Outlaw*. When the interview was being conducted, I was confident that this book would be greeted by the gay press as a powerful statement of gay rage against heterosexual fascism. Alas, in several instances—though certainly and by far not all—the focus would turn in strident animosity to the aspects of narcissism, hustling, bodybuilding that appear in that book; its revolutionary context would be pointedly ignored in those instances.

So I have chosen to leave the interview intact, to make its own commentary on ideas as they evolve, are altered, perhaps are changed or strengthened; and on expectations, fulfilled or contradicted.

Winston Leyland interviews
JOHN RECHY

LEYLAND: Perhaps we could start by talking about the background of your first novel, *City of Night*. Did *City of Night* spring out of your own experience traveling around the United States?

RECHY: I think it's important to state that I never set out to do research on that world so that I could write about it. I never expected that I would. *City of Night* began as a letter that I wrote to a friend of mine after experiences during the Mardi Gras in New Orleans. I came back to El Paso and wrote him a letter telling him what had happened. Instead of sending it to him I sent the letter off as a story to both *Evergreen Review* and *New Directions* and both of them accepted it. There was a great deal of interest in it. I was asked if I was doing a novel and I said yes. That's how *City of Night* began.

LEYLAND: Throughout some of your books, especially *City of Night* and *Numbers*, there is a streak of pathos, despair, compulsion. Do you feel that these were prominent in your own life at the time?

RECHY: The elements of despair were not only part of my own life but they continue to be part of my life. Indeed, I feel an element of despair is very real in gay life, and that isn't to criticize gay life. Considering the pressures that we have to live with—the imposed schizophrenia—many gay people have to lead dual lives. It's like wearing a mask, putting it on and taking it off. Because of that, there is built-in despair in gay life. My first three books have been criticized because they give such a bleak, despondent picture of gay life. When I have given talks this criticism is presented to me. But I feel that I must tell what I experience. I think that no other gay writer has the experience, the ability to communicate the world of the streets, its feelings, that I know intimately. I feel that I want to convey that honestly as it is. In my speeches, in my nonfiction, I can deal with things as they should be, things that must be changed. But first you begin with a realistic appraisal of that world. It's not an indictment of the gay world to say that it's a very despairing, lonely world in many aspects. I think anybody will agree with this. It is so with any other pressured minority. For example, it's fine to be black, but the situations that surround being black certainly do not make it a totally joyous experience. I want to be honest in my books as indeed I have been. But I am criticized for it.

LEYLAND: I understand your new book deals with court cases against gay people and that you're taking a new approach.

RECHY: That book, *The Sexual Outlaw*, is nonfiction. Only one chapter of the book deals with the actual transcript of a trial and follows through with verbatim testimony about the entrapment, the lying of the police. It follows through a case from the original arrest to the verdict. But the whole book deals with the whole spectrum of the so-called promiscuous homosexual who to me is the hero of the gay world. Many people would think this is outrageous, but I am appalled by "conservative" homosexuals who are not unlike the blacks of a few years ago wanting to be whiter than the whites. There are many homosexuals who want to be straighter than straight and just show the best part of our lives and keep everything cool so everything will work out right. I am constantly appalled by them. To me much of what is called promiscuous sex is the equivalent of what happened with the blacks when they suddenly sat-in publicly. One is breaking an unjust law in private, in the closet as it were: the other is confronting the enemy on the street and saying, "Look—we are breaking your unjust laws." That is what promiscuous homosexuals did; that is what freedom fighters and blacks did in the streets. I know many people will find the comparison outrageous, but it's only because of sexual hangups. My book *The Sexual Outlaw* will explore the spectrum and try to define a very discernible homosexual sensibility, areas in which I think homosexuals are definitely superior because they have a dual awareness and sensitivity. So many of us have grown up hiding that we have developed a dual persona. I think that in many areas the homosexual can feel more acutely because of that. I'll also deal with the liberated role of women in the context of homosexuality. There's a chapter in my book called "Beyond the Fag Hag." I try to put the sexual minority in the context of other minorities. One of the saddest things in the gay world is how we are supposed to be grateful for little crumbs. When the TV movie *That Certain Summer* was shown, homosexuals were so grateful: "Oh God, did you see it; it was so good, so kind, so compassionate." Bullshit, man; it was crumbs. It was safe. They chose the safest types; they didn't take a marvelous queen, a radical queen, a promiscuous homosexual. They chose the closest they could come to middle-class America.

LEYLAND: They also managed to avoid showing the gay protagonists touching or embracing. Even when the guy was having a breakdown, there was no physical affection shown. Whereas you would not find that kind of thing in a heterosexual situation on television.

RECHY: The most pitiful thing I've heard recently was a case that was refused a hearing by the Supreme Court. In some Southern town two men were busted for sodomy in a car and they were sentenced to eight years in prison; they made an appeal which said in part that their sex act had hurt no one, and (this is what is most pitiful) they added the phrase "with the possible exception of ourselves."

LEYLAND: In a recent interview you talk about some of the themes in your novels, one of which is "no substitute for salvation"—a theme which you feel appears in all your novels. Could you talk more about this, how this appears for example in *City of Night?*

RECHY: I mean the phrase in a very religious sense, that we are raised to expect that love, kindness prevails and that there will be indeed salvation; if you live well you will be rewarded—all that bullshit. Then we discover an existential void; that there is no such thing. And part of the contemporary neurosis, the existential nightmare, is based on the fact that we try to substitute for that: some people by trying to make a lot of money; other people by acting compulsively in other areas—in sex, for instance. There is simply no substitute for that promise which was made and unfulfilled. Once you withdraw that promise, there is nothing to take its place.

LEYLAND: Do you mean "salvation" in a particular Christian sense or in a general spiritual sense?

RECHY: Both. Having been raised a Catholic I am bound to use that kind of wording that comes from a Christian Catholic attitude. But this goes for other things. Psychoanalysis, drugs are all attempts to substitute for that unfulfilled promise.

LEYLAND: That theme, of course, is clearest in your book *The Fourth Angel*, although it runs through all your novels.

RECHY: Yes, it is a note of despair and runs through all my novels. It's very much in *City of Night* and extremely strong in *Numbers*. I think that Johnny Rio in *Numbers* is a real existential creature trying to thwart the certain knowledge of doom by collecting and counting sex acts. *Numbers* is a very misunderstood book. *City of Night* took four years and my other books a considerably longer time, but *Numbers* was written compulsively in three months. I began writing it as I split from Los Angeles. Part of its power is that the same franticness that had gone into the original sex trip was carried on into the writing. I wanted to convey compulsive franticness. I wrote it in a frenzy; I wrote every single day for three months. Some friends actually strongly recommended that I not have it published. But I went ahead. The reaction to it was outrage—but it's not a pornographic book. It's a book about a nightmare, about someone trying to avoid death. It's a beautifully structured book. (I'm not modest, incidentally, about myself or my work.) Unfortunately it is flawed; it is the one book of mine that I would like to rewrite some day, I hope. The opening chapter is terrific but before Johnny Rio enters the park there is a slowness that I do not want, a confusion. I would like the thing to move relentlessly as a sexual horror story, an existential nightmare, and I think it slows down. Nevertheless, even as it is now, it's a very powerful book.

LEYLAND: Were you going through an existential nightmare in your own life at this time?

RECHY: It's a very literal book. After several years of relative "seclusion" in El Paso after the publication of *City of Night*, I came back to Los Angeles and discovered Griffith Park. I found myself out of control and courting sexual encounters. You may be surprised to learn that years later I came back to break Johnny Rio's record and yet Johnny Rio was based on myself. So now I was beginning to compete with my own character!

LEYLAND: In your novel *The Fourth Angel*, one of the characters, Shell, says, "To survive you've got to learn not to feel, even if you have to teach yourself." To what extent do you feel you have had to do this in your own life to survive?

RECHY: I'm a very feeling person. But I disguise that on the streets. I play a role.

LEYLAND: You've talked a little about the aura of hardness...

RECHY: I cultivate it on the streets. People who pick me up think I'm really tough and I'm actually very sensitive.

LEYLAND: Isn't an aura of toughness part of the gay defense?

RECHY: With me it enters an area of erecting barriers around myself.

LEYLAND: Were the characters in *The Fourth Angel* based on real persons? I gather from what you said about Shell that this is at least partly the case.

RECHY: Yes, a curious thing happened in *The Fourth Angel*. I took adults and made them teenagers. I converted myself largely into Jerry. But I have aspects of Shell who was modeled in part also on a beautiful friend of mine.

LEYLAND: After reading *The Fourth Angel* I felt that it was in large part successful but not totally so. There were times when words you put into a sixteen-year-old person's mouth sounded as if they came from an adult, and it didn't ring completely true.

RECHY: Your criticism is very well taken. There are times when the children are not children. But that never concerned me. It was the thrust of the story of loss and despair that people are driven to that I was concerned with. I think that I captured very much of the children's world, because to a great extent I'm still there, and Shell is still there. But I think you're very right, there are times when the children are adults, as indeed they really were.

LEYLAND: Did you feel that Gerard Malanga was unfair in his comments on Shell in his *Gay Sunshine* interview [GS 20]?

RECHY: I thought Gerard was not only unfair but tacky. I think it was a very low-life thing to do, certainly not worthy of what I call being a star in one's life, which I believe very strongly in. I think he misinterpreted what was happening. I certainly know that the remarks that he attributed to Shell were referring to a person that I am very close to. I think he did a very nasty thing. When he remarks that Shell's "gay friends" are indignant about some statement he attributed to her, that's bullshit. *I* am Shell's gay friend.

LEYLAND: You just mentioned the phrase "being a star in one's own life." What do you mean by that?

RECHY: I have a whole theory of one's life as autobiography, or as movie, or one's being a star in one's life. One's life is lived in such a way that there's almost a choreography to existence, everything matches one's own way of dressing, being. I believe in self-consciousness, for example, when it comes out harmoniously. I believe the body is an instrument in one's becoming a star. I'm very much into bodybuilding and weight lifting. I like appearance and I like to construct it. I dress very self-consciously. I want to look a certain way and so I work for it. But it has to work; one's attitudes have to fit.

LEYLAND: Do you feel this sort of attitude towards one's body is something you can continue to develop as you grow older into middle and old age?

RECHY: Yes. I am convinced that I will never age. I want to become better all the time. I've always had a good body but I prefer to have a constructed body of developed muscles. I think narcissism can be a very healthy attitude. Again part of being a star is being pleased with oneself. The coyness of people when they're paid a compliment offends me. They say, "No, it's not really true." And of course that's fucked, that's hypocritical. I have friends who think I've overdone that matter of my body, who think I spend too much time on it. Then I point out that I spend many hours writing a book or an artist spends many hours painting a picture. And then you want it to be the best; you want as many people to accept and love it as possible. I don't find that different from spending hours on my body and then showing it off and wanting and accepting that kind of admiration.

LEYLAND: Do you feel a kinship with, say, Yukio Mishima, the Japanese novelist who was into a bodybuilding cult (apart from his rightist political views)?

RECHY: I've never read anything that he's written. I've read about him, and become intrigued. But his political views alienate me to such an extent that I can't feel anything I would call kinship.

LEYLAND: His bodybuilding was tied in part to the ideal of the samurai.

RECHY: I do not like the military. Mine is not a political trip like Mishima's. I hate militarism.

LEYLAND: Perhaps we can talk a little more about this hint of violence and toughness in your work and whether or not it's true of your own life too.

RECHY: This is a very touchy area but one which I force myself to be open about. I'm really trying very hard to divest myself of poses and attitudes which I believe to be detrimental to me as an artist and a person. I do cultivate a certain tough appearance which attracts people sexually to me. I am often sought out by masochists. I often equate feelings of sex with feelings of power over someone. I often go out deliberately to encounter this sort of sexual experience. I think the most negative aspect in the gay world is the growth of S & M. I am completely opposed to it.

LEYLAND: We have presented both sides of the S & M question in *Gay Sunshine* [GS 15 and 16]. I think that in many cases what you say is true: there can be a negativism in S & M relationships. But some people think pain can be an added dimension in a relationship. I am not speaking from in-depth personal experience of S & M but this was one of the main arguments in Ian Young's S & M article [GS 16].

RECHY: One can justify eating dirt and say, "It intensifies my closeness to the earth." However, dirt will be full of germs and will do destructive things to your body. So naturally people who are into this reactionary area of the gay world, which is the S & M world, the Uncle Toms, the self-haters of the gay world, will justify anything. There would be greater honesty if someone would say, "I want to be hurt, I want to be humiliated." But the hypocrisy comes in when they call it love. To say that pain can bring somebody closer to love, I find totally repugnant. I'm honest with myself: when I indulge as the "S" in S & M relationships, I know what is going on. I know that I want to assert my sexual power over someone else, to humiliate that person. This is not something in my past; this is something I contend with now. I am excited by it. But I want to call it what it is. I am not going to say, I love the guy who is groveling and doing everything that I want. It is not love. It has to do with humiliating the other person.

LEYLAND: But don't you think it's possible in an ongoing relationship that pain, humiliation can be an added dimension? I have no reason to disbelieve the people who have experienced it as such.

RECHY: I do disbelieve it entirely. Pain and humiliation have nothing to do with love and respect.

LEYLAND: Your novel *City of Night* was the first novel to deal with gay hustling. What do you feel about subsequent attempts?

RECHY: I think that *Midnight Cowboy* was a very dishonest book and an even more dishonest movie. Yet people flocked to see this movie and said, "That's exactly what it's like." The "low life" emerges as filtered for *Vogue* magazine. It's also very sadistic to the hustler. Nevertheless, Jon Voight gave an inspired performance; he really got into it.

LEYLAND: Perhaps you could talk about the dynamic of this hustling in your own life.

RECHY: I have a ferocious need to hustle. There's no rush in my life like it. I know that it's not a liberated world; it's as unliberated as the S & M world. I would be a hypocrite if I put down the S & M world without upfront pointing out that hustling deals with a similar relationship.

LEYLAND: Do you feel there is a conflict between your feelings about gay liberation and your attraction to the hustling, S & M world? Do you feel the two can be reconciled to some extent?

RECHY: I objected earlier to the statement that pain brings people closer. I would be doing the same thing if I said there is a form of love that happens between the person who is paying and the person who gets paid.

LEYLAND: But there could be at least in some cases. Does the fact that money is paid mean that there will only be a nonloving encounter? In some cases can there not be a combination of pure sex and love?

RECHY: I would like to be able to say yes, but . . .

LEYLAND: Are you speaking only of yourself?

RECHY: Yes, about myself, but I'm speaking also about the other hustlers that I know on the street. I think that because of my determined awareness of what happens in these relationships, I convey more warmth than most hustlers. For me, after the sex is over and after I've been paid there's a moment in which I want to be super-kind to the person. I want to establish some kind of human contact with them, to know something about them; sometimes it works, sometimes it doesn't. I've hung around with other hustlers on the street, and I don't think this is the ordinary. You see, there is a tendency to romanticize the world of hustling as there's a tendency to romanticize the world of S & M. You can draw parallels.

LEYLAND: What sort of sexual experiences have you had outside of hustling?

RECHY: I am what is called promiscuous and I love having contacts with one person after another. Now I have at one time or another had hints of possibilities with one person. But I freak out. I become frightened and finally I fuck it up. I have great difficulty coping with one person. My reaction is that I'll go on a binge of promiscuity and hustling, as if to assert nothing has changed.

LEYLAND: What do you feel will happen in your life? Do you feel you will continue to have most of your sexual experience through hustling? Or do you feel a driving need for something else?

RECHY: I feel a need for growth. For myself I have to define what growth is. I feel almost traumatized in a child level of gratification. It's very difficult for me to be giving. In my nonsexual life I am giving but in a sexual sense, or in an emotional sense, with males, I find it terribly difficult to be giving. I want to be in control, in power. But I want, I need the thought of growth and I know the patterns I make for myself are circular.

LEYLAND: I understand that a film is being made, based on your novel *City of Night*.

RECHY: I'm working on the screenplay now—and it's beautiful. While being faithful to the novel—all the main characters will be in the film—I'm updating the time to now. That's not difficult because I've never left that world. The main changes on the hustling scene have come about through the emergence of drugs and gay liberation.

LEYLAND: How do you feel that this happened?

RECHY: First of all drugs have changed the style of dressing. In attitudes: there's more homogeneity among subcultures now than there was in the fifties or early sixties. The gay scene is not as much of an isolated subculture now as it used to be; whereas at the time of *City of Night* it was underground; and I think a lot of the cause of that has been the exchange of drugs and styles that overlap the straight and gay worlds.

LEYLAND: What about the attitudes of hustlers now towards people they related with in sex as compared to the fifties?

RECHY: Yes, that would be the major change. Hustlers used to be "strictly straight." We weren't, of course. That was bullshit, but bullshit we were doing ourselves. But that's what was expected of us. And we wore the uniform of blue jeans, white T-shirt, and there was the myth of the hustler as straight. Gay liberation has changed that on both sides: that of the hustler and that of the client. On the hustler's side there are now four distinct breeds: one is the extremely effeminate queen and/or transsexual; second there is the androgynous young, usually blond, slender boy. This is a new breed of hustler. In my first hustling trip all hustlers were quite masculine, wanting to flex our muscles and so on. But now this young androgynous type has become very sought after. Again I think that drugs have done this in a sense, because it is a very youthful culture that is blending male and female in appearance. And it has spilled into the streets so that a large number of hustlers are this young, not necessarily effeminate, but androgynous type.

When I first came back to hustling after my years of reclusiveness in El Paso and went back to the streets, I was surprised to see this breed of hustler. And I thought: what are they doing on the streets; they will never make out. I was very isolated in El Paso after my original hustling trip. There is a third type of hustler that I'm sure has come out with gay liberation: more masculine but openly proclaiming himself as bisexual. The fourth type is still the self-proclaimed "straight."

LEYLAND: But didn't some hustlers even fifteen years ago consider themselves bisexual?

RECHY: Years ago in Hollywood, downtown L.A., Pershing Square, we were all so-called "stud" or butch hustlers with the exception of the drag queens. We would say to each other that we were straight. That was a pose.

LEYLAND: It was straight in appearance but bisexual in reality?

RECHY: Exactly! People often come looking for one of the other types now, whereas before it was just the butch stud type. A curious development has been the attitudes of the clients. They used to be more of a stereotype: close to middle age, conservative, married and totally closeted. Now some of the clients are younger than some of the hustlers; some of them are very attractive.

LEYLAND: You will be doing a program at UCLA with gay artists. Would you talk about that.

RECHY: We'll be doing it next year. We have a tentative title, "Extravagant Elegance, Sensual Sensitivity." The subtitle is "The Gay Sensibility in the Arts." I'm working on it with my friend and film critic Marsha Kinder and with Bill Moritz. It's seven evenings, and UCLA will offer it as a course. But each evening will be a separate performance. The first evening will be visual arts; the other evenings are on poetry, prose, theater, overground films, underground films, mixed gay media, which for the first time will include drag as art form. The visual arts program will be slides of painters from Michelangelo and da Vinci to contemporary painters, and we are going to have readings from Michelangelo's letters, Shakespeare's sonnets while the slides are being shown. The second half of each program will be a discussion. Critics and painters and so on will try to define what the gay sensibility is.

LEYLAND: What is the criterion for who will take part in these programs?

RECHY: You don't have to be gay. The content of every program will be gay; the works that will be exhibited and examined will be gay. The content of it is the exploration of gay art. The participants will be gay, straight, bisexual, trisexual, polysexual, pansexual, whatever. We want to open it up; we don't want it to be like a gay conference. We don't want to have any psychologists, psychiatrists, lawyers, etc. It's a celebration to open up to everybody. In the theater evening we are going to do a scene from Oscar Wilde's play *Lady Windermere's Fan,* but performed by men. It's going to explore the real beautiful aspects of gay art—and some ugly ones.

LEYLAND: What will be the role of the nongay participants?

RECHY: To see how they perceive it, how it comes across to them. In other words what we are trying to do is to see if there really is such a thing as a gay sensibility. I think there really is, quite definitely, and I think it's a very special one. I think one of the sad things is that most gay people are not aware of the specialness, the sensitivity. We are still so bound up in hatred, shame, staying in the closet. One of the main purposes of it is to display the beautiful side of gay.

LEYLAND: There's a theory going round that much gay creativity has come from the pressures of the oppression of society from outside, and that if these pressures were not there the creativity would dry up. I disagree very strongly with that theory.

RECHY: One of the theories in *The Sexual Outlaw* is that pressures have created the gay sensibility. You begin by being gay and have to be an excellent actor because you have to do two roles.

LEYLAND: But with changing consciousness over the past two or three years many gay people are not faced with exactly the same pressures, the same schizophrenia. Many people are now coming out earlier without those heavy pressures. I think a gay art can also come from that. Creativity does not always come from oppression/pressure.

RECHY: I was merely saying that a certain type of art had been produced by that. But with liberation the same marvelous dual sensibility, now freed, will produce an even more liberated art. I certainly do not think it would dry up.

LEYLAND: I think that the theory of gay creativity as springing basically from oppression is a pet theory of liberal straights who like to peg gay people into a category: "Oh, gay people are so sensitive! So creative!" This categorization is a simplification for them so that they can understand gay creativity.

RECHY: I think you're absolutely right, Winston, but I also think that that theory is correct to a point. But if you allow the theory to end there then you've trapped yourself and you end up justifying pressure and persecution on the basis of allowing the art to flourish. And that simply isn't so. The art that will be produced from homosexuals in the future will not have to deal with it.

LEYLAND: Oppressions of one form or another are still going to be coming down on gay people and straight people and creativity will continue to spring out of that. I think there will be lessening of these pressures and gay art will continue in large part as celebration. This is not to denigrate work which springs directly out of oppression. Your own novels—*City of Night, Numbers*—spring out of oppression. And such novels will continue to be important.

RECHY: Don't you think the analogy would be if you explored it from the point of any minority and the powerful, illuminating work they have produced under oppression. Incidentally, you used the word celebration. This is what I want the program at UCLA to be: a celebration. You're right Winston: sensibility is not only produced by oppression (although that has a lot to do with style), but a new kind of style will develop from it. I think some gay writers write in drag; some write in butch.

LEYLAND: I think this is especially happening in poetry. Take a poet like John Wieners. His poems of the late fifties sprang out of deep oppression and even now many of his poems spring out of the oppression he's gone through in mental institutions and so forth. His new style (his most recent poems) is changing somewhat from that, but there is that basic continuity in his writing. But there are newer younger poets writing for whom this is not the case. For instance, in John Giorno's poetry sex is a celebration, whereas for Wieners sex is often a lonely, hunting searching. How do you think the change in your sensibility is affecting your creativity?

RECHY: For me there is a beautiful abstract choreography in the sexual hunt. I know, however, that the beauty of the promiscuous sex hunt is almost balletic, symphonic; it is choreographed, it is tremendously beautiful. And I'm going to move it into the area of the art to be produced. Nevertheless, I have a love/hate relationship for the promiscuous hunt. Sometimes after a night of hustling and then moving to dark cruising alleys, I come home and literally think of nothing but suicide. Other times, when I'm caught in it, I think: "Jesus, God this is the most exciting thing in the world." So I have a vast ambivalence about it.

LEYLAND: Don't you think that promiscuity as celebration can be a revolutionary thing?

RECHY: This is one of the aspects that I'm dealing with in my new book *The Sexual Outlaw:* promiscuity as one of the few political actions that gays are taking. To me there is a lack of gay heroes and for me the promiscuous homosexuals are the heroic homosexuals. And also transsexuals and queens: the latter because it takes so much courage to come out on the street in drag. When the black woman in the bus in Alabama refused to move to the back of the bus, that was truly a revolutionary act. I think that gay people make a very strong political statement when they take the sexual revolution to the streets. That is where one is confronted with the bigotry of society and the oppressive ignorance of the law. Otherwise one would never confront them, never question them.

LEYLAND: This is course is the big bogey of conservative homosexuals.

RECHY: Yes, and aren't they odious. Like the blacks who wanted to straighten their hair. Often I'm faced with very uptight, middle-class homosexuals. I had a heavy truth once when someone said to me during one of my talks, "Look, if we move in the direction of permissiveness you are advocating, we will have sex in the streets." I thought to myself, "Don't cop out," and I said to the man, "Yes, precisely. So what?" I was questioned by several people who said, "What an outrageous thing for you to say." So I got it together in my head about sex in the streets. There's nothing wrong per se with sex in the streets. I think it's a matter of style and taste. Most people couldn't do it even if it became legal. Societal attitudes are strong enough to act as a deterrent. There's no law against painting yourself blue or yellow—but few people do it.

LEYLAND: Many conservative gay people are geared to the question of acceptance by and assimilation into straight society. Conservative gays think that public sex is outré, that it is drawing attention to oneself. I'm curious about the socioeconomic backgrounds of gay people who make it, say, in the parks.

RECHY: When you enter the park there is a spectrum from one degree to 180 degrees. My point is that it is ridiculous to outlaw sex. But one of the things about which I despair (and I've talked to Morris Kight often about this and he tells me I'm wrong) is that nothing really profound is happening any more. Sure, there are people like yourself...

LEYLAND: I think consciousness has changed in varying degrees among multitudes of gay people. For some gay people who are openly up front change is more obvious, but I think similar kinds of deep changes are happening among gay people as a whole. Deep change in consciousness has certainly only happened to a small minority of gay people in this country (perhaps 15 to 20 percent). Another change in consciousness, perhaps not as deep, has happened to perhaps another 35 to 50 percent of gay people. But I think every homosexual in this country has been affected to one degree or another by the change in climate over the past few years, even if they did not want to be.

RECHY: I hope very much that you are right because this is the sort of thing that I long for. In my vision I don't see that happening and that is one source of my despair. Winston, I see incidents like a group of five or six homosexuals going up to Griffith Park on a Sunday afternoon when everyone is cruising. They know what is happening. But this time they have gone to see it, aloof and distant and ridiculing. They drive around and yell things like, "Look at that one over there. Hi Miss Honey, don't break your heel." These comments express such a loathsome attitude toward ourselves.

LEYLAND: There is a certain amount of self-hatred in all this. And there are still elements of self-hatred, greater or lesser, among gay people. This has not disappeared with gay liberation or the change in consciousness. I just think that this self-hatred has lessened with the onset of gay liberation. Look at the situation in 1960 and compare that with the situation in 1974. In 1974 we have gay community centers, gay counseling, film groups; there are gay people expressing creativity in various fields. There are certainly more gay people into traditional life styles. Of course the fact that one is into a traditional life style doesn't mean that one is ipso facto oppressed. There are perhaps many gay people whose life style has not changed much from the fifties, but there are also large numbers of gay people who life has changed with the change in consciousness, whose creativity has been affected. Certainly mine has. And compare all this with the gay scene in 1960.

RECHY: I'm talking about what to me makes a true revolution, the kind of dynamic revolution that I would like to see happen with gay people. I agree with you about these groups and gay liberation has done some fantastic things—*Gay Sunshine, Fag Rag,* publications like that. But Winston, I'm talking about the vast majority of gay people that go to bars and cruise; they are indifferent.

LEYLAND: But they are being exposed to some of what is happening one way or another, John. Through radio, TV, magazines or whatever.

RECHY: For cops to move into a potentially violent situation in the black community there must be a good cause. They now move with some caution because blacks have protested. But cops can move into a gay area and do whatever the fuck they want and not one gay person asks, "What right do you have to do what you are doing?" I am not even talking about any vastly revolutionary act. What we do is run! I have seen two cops go into an area where perhaps there are forty gay people and hassle the hell out of these same forty people, who then stand still, frozen at the prospect of two cops. This would not happen with other minorities.

LEYLAND: I think the change in consciousness does take time. It did happen at Stonewall in 1969.

RECHY: Yes, and there haven't been any others. There was one Stonewall.

LEYLAND: You can't expect a minority which is just emerging to do as much as, say, the black minority, which has hundreds of years of community behind them.

RECHY: I'm talking about untapped energy. We could be the most powerful minority in the world because we have some of the most powerful, sensitive, creative people of any minority.

LEYLAND: We have the dual situation: on one hand a kind of defeatist attitude. Gay liberation consciousness has not yet permeated enough so that gay people in some of these circumstances will be willing to stand up. But on the other hand we do have some beautiful things happening too (community centers, etc.). So there's a kind of balance. It will take time before some of these ideas permeate to the point where people will act upon them. Ideas are being put out, action is happening through various gay groups. These things are bringing about a gradual change of consciousness. At the same time I believe there has to be a basic revolution in this country, too, in the governmental structure as a whole. And gay capitalism is nonetheless capitalism.

RECHY: But it's happening too slowly. That it's happening to some people is definitely beautiful. Gay community centers are fine, I think. But let's just say that on the battlefield we were surrendering. In the gay community when someone is busted, if everybody would pour out from an adjoining bar and say, "We're doing the same thing," then the police would be faced with a truly radical statement. Instead we run away.

LEYLAND: Perhaps you could talk a little more about your early life.

RECHY: I was born in El Paso, Texas, and went to school there. My mother was a beautiful Mexican woman whom I adored and who adored me, and my father was Scotch. Spanish is my native language and I didn't learn to speak English until I went to school. I also went to college there on a scholarship. After college I was in the army, a period that evaporates thankfully like a dream, and then I took off for New York. I had no intention of writing down my experiences. I will tell you a curious story: when I was a little kid I wanted to be a painter and I drew beautifully. I had forgotten that my mother did not throw away some drawings that I had made when I was about twelve years old. I drew this woman, obviously a prostitute, but the opposite of butch, standing under a streetlight. And I called the street "Salem," which is the exact opposite of Selma.* Much of my writing is autobiographical.

Oh, I believe in exhibitionism as art, like dancing or writing or whatever. It was beautiful to go to the beaches and go under the pier and sunbathe nude, always expecting the perfect voyeur to materialize from the shadows. There was a definite love relation that happened. But now there's so much ugly nudity on the beaches, anybody can do it. It's as if everyone wanted to get on the stage and do a ballet. And so those of us who are really elegant exhibitionists really resent the amateurs, man. You know, those that go around displaying without style— without anything to display—and the voyeurs that stand around ogling. It used to be symphonic, very beautiful.

LEYLAND: What has been the attitude of students on campuses when you lecture about homosexuality and how this enters your writing?

RECHY: The reactions have been super, Winston. I spoke to a group recently and was being brought on as the expert on male street prostitution. And I must admit I was a little uptight; it's a heavy title to hang on you, when you're going to be badgered by sociology students. I was amazed by the reaction; it was liberated and beautiful. Rarely do I meet hostility. The morning of the day I was to speak at Duke University I got up late for breakfast at the Holiday Inn where I was staying. A group of redneck businessmen were talking and I was tuning in and out, because they were talking loudly. And then they mentioned the hall where I was going to speak and they said, "Yes, and can you imagine, they expect a large crowd." And it was obvious disapproving. One of them said, "At least it's good to know who they are." I was torn between going up to them and inviting them to come listen to me and ignoring them. I don't know which was the right way. I ignored them, because I felt nothing would change.

LEYLAND: Where do you see yourself moving in your own writing?

RECHY: If I may adapt the question and say "in my own life." I would very much like to move in my life and my writing to where I would be completely free.

---

*The letters also read "males" when rearranged. —*Ed.*

Marsha Kinder, a friend of mine who knows me very well, recently read an interview with me and said, "My God, anybody reading this interview would think you are one of the most liberated gay people. And those of us who know you know that's simply not so." I don't want that kind of hypocrisy. I'm intellectually totally liberated, yet in my own life I am still ruled by all those horrible repressions and I want to shed them, believe in sexual revolution, in confronting people on the streets. But my mind is not liberated because I still play these abominable roles, although I can rationalize it. But that's the worst pitfall when you start rationalizing for yourself. So, to look at it honestly, when I hustle, I still do the same bullshit subterfuge of playing straight. And yet the rationalization is: that's why the person picked me up in the first place, so I'm fulfilling the role. But the rationalization does not hold up if you want to liberate yourself and others. Because the same radical statement that I am talking about for others is the kind of radical statement that I could make for myself on the street, when a man, say, picks me up wanting me to be straight and starts coming on with all this bullshit about my girlfriends. I could make a truly radical statement for myself and for him by saying on the spot (though I would not get paid and he would freak out; but how much further ahead I would be!): "Look man, this is a myth, a myth that's made all this bullshit possible."

LEYLAND: What do you think prevents you from doing this?

RECHY: I don't know. Images of myself...

LEYLAND: In relating sexually, do you at times put out a bisexual image?

RECHY: Yes, and that would be cool. I love beautiful women, and it's beautiful to be with them. But I'm talking about doing the most repressed number in the gay world. Playing straight.

LEYLAND: Do you verbally say you are straight?

RECHY: No, that I could not do. I go along with the assumptions and contribute to them. In hustling I'm often picked up by someone who wants me to be straight and I get the message right away. If the person says, for example, have you been married, then I get the signals. And not only will I say yes (which is not true), but I will elaborate on it and say I am living with my girlfriend somewhere.

LEYLAND: Do you hesitate to make a definite statement about your gayness, because you are afraid of a sexual rejection in this kind of encounter?

RECHY: Probably. I have on occasion made a definite statement, and the person has lost interest in me.

LEYLAND: Do you feel that most of your sexual encounters fall into this pattern?

RECHY: The vast majority of my sexual encounters are in that area. When I'm hustling virtually all are. But beyond that in the majority of the other sexual contacts I am what used to be called "trade." There are the times when I respond mutually but still guardedly. So the preponderance of my sexual experiences are on the side of assuming control and power.

LEYLAND: Perhaps you should try to search for a balance in your sexual encounters.

RECHY: I never say to people, "I am not gay." When the situation comes up and the person offers that interpretation, then I will build on it. The curious thing is that I want to purge myself of things that I don't consider liberated. I want to be really totally liberated. But those two areas are the ones that disturb me most. In the S & M area I feel the rush of power in my being the "S." I know that there's a transference of hatred to the other. I hate that. There is a similarity in hustling when one pretends to be straight, because I can tell you from my own feelings and from having hung around other hustlers as a street-friend (and other hustlers talk to each other with openness) that their attitudes are generally the same: far from affection for the client. It's a very brutal thing—hustlers talking about their clients in derisive terms, but it's very prevalent.

LEYLAND: Do you think that it's possible that one of the changes of gay liberation is that this derisive attitude may no longer be present in at least some of the "new" hustlers?

RECHY: It could be but I really don't think so!

LEYLAND: What about the androgynous hustler?

RECHY: I really don't know; but I think it's the same contempt. Sometimes on a particularly slow evening when there are ten hustlers to every client, there's an overt meanness that happens. Hustlers of all types begin hassling people driving around too long without picking anybody up. And there's a general hostility.

LEYLAND: But that's understandable! It's hardly indicative of the meanness in the hustler towards his customer.

RECHY: Yeah, right; not necessarily.... Let me tell you what happened to me recently. I was on a hustling corner; it was warm and I was showing off without a shirt. A very good looking queen in drag made a great remark about my body. I, of course, dug it, but I was also annoyed because there was somebody who was about to pick me up and she was taking up time. I mumbled something in answer to her compliment, it was just a couple of words, and I turned around. This pissed her off very much, and she said something very heavy to me. She said, "Your muscles are as gay as my drag." I was depressed for the evening; but you know, there's something to what she said in anger. Of course many bodybuilders are gay. I love the muscular aspect of myself. Yet, in effect, though different, it's similar in reversed purpose to drag. It's the opposite side but from almost the same source. The queen protects herself by dressing in women's clothes and the bodybuilder protects himself in muscles—so-called "men's clothes."

LEYLAND: In genderfuck there's not only the question of protection, there are other elements present, too. There are elements of celebration and revolution in genderfuck—an approach which goes beyond just self-protection. Perhaps the same can be true for bodybuilding too.

RECHY: As I mentioned earlier, one of the evenings of the UCLA program will include drag as art.

LEYLAND: Why not bodybuilding as celebration, as gay liberation too?

RECHY: [*Laughter.*] Oh yes, I agree. Fantastic idea. Bodybuilding as art. It's funny I haven't connected it when I do raps about it all the time.

LEYLAND: I'm curious if attitudes toward all these things are changing among the new breed of hustlers.

RECHY: There's a sort of tribe mentality with hustlers; masculine hustlers hang out together, androgynous hustlers hang out together, and so on. So I would know best about my area—and I think the attitudes remain those of contempt, hustler to client. But I don't think that the client likes the hustler much more either, finally. But remember that as in my books I'm speaking about things as they are; or as I see them, not as they should be or as I would want them to be.

PHOTO BY STEVEN ABBOTT, 1975

GORE VIDAL

GORE VIDAL was born in 1925. His maternal grandfather was Thomas Gore, the first United States senator from Oklahoma. Vidal's father was a West Point graduate and later a sub-cabinet member in FDR's administration. Gore Vidal graduated from Phillips Exeter Academy in 1943 and then joined the army. In 1946 he published his first novel, *Williwaw*. He was soon heralded as one of the most promising postwar writers. In 1953 Vidal began writing for television. In 1960 he ran for the U.S. House of Representatives from a New York district. He lost the election but ran two thousand votes ahead of John Kennedy, leader of the ticket. He currently divides his time between his homes in Italy and the United States.

Vidal has written in many forms: novels, plays, essays, film sripts. Among his best-known later novels are *Julian* (1964), *Washington D.C.* (1967), *Myra Breckinridge* (1968), *Two Sisters* (1970), *Myron* (1970), *Burr* (1975), and *1876* (1976). His plays include *Visit to a Small Planet, The Best Man, Weekend,* and *An Evening with Richard Nixon*. Four books of essays have also appeared.

TWO INTERVIEWS are printed here. The first was taped by John Mitzel (publisher of Manifest Destiny Books) and Steven Abbott in the Lounge at the Ritz-Carlton Hotel in Boston, November 4, 1973. Tom Reeves helped arrange the interview and was also present. It originally appeared in a slightly different form in *Fag Rag* 7/8 and then in the book *Myra and Gore* (Manifest Destiny Books, 1974). It is reprinted with permission.

The second interview was taped by Steven Abbott and Thom Willenbecher over the weekend of October 27, 1974, at the Plaza Hotel in New York City. It originally appeared in *Gay Sunshine* 26/27 (Winter 1975/76). Vidal revised the interview for the present anthology.

Abbott and Willenbecher wrote:

"Though he may disclaim the title, Gore Vidal is in many ways the spiritual parent of gay liberation. He was the first well-known American writer to challenge stereotypes of homosexuality, in his third novel, *The City and the Pillar,* and he did so back in 1948, when the topic was unspoken of in polite company. As a result his literary reputation suffered, and the *New York Times* refused to advertise or print favorable reviews of his novels. In addition, he was the first person to write of his own bisexuality, to do so without a hint of apology....

"After a few years' ostracism, Gore Vidal gradually settled into the role of America's chief iconoclast, a challenger of contemporary sexual, political, and cultural mores which he saw both as a residue of the Puritan ethic and as a side effect of America's worship of profitable mediocrity.... Vidal's most potent weapon is his wit: irony is the ultimate form of subversion from within, in which even the meaning of a sentence is turned against itself. What remains for us is to understand how much Vidal's weapons—irony, eloquence, and the willingness to risk one's status by challenging the powerful from within—can accomplish."

I
John Mitzel and Steven Abbott interview
GORE VIDAL

INTERVIEWER: Have allegations of homosexuality ever been used to ruin anyone in politics in your lifetime as far as you know?

VIDAL: The senator from Massachusetts, David Ignatius Walsh, tried to make my father when my father was a West Point cadet. Chased my father and his roommate, who had been down for the inauguration of Woodrow Wilson, and Senator Walsh picked them up. They were both very innocent West Pointers. My father said it was just appalling. He chased them around the room. West Point was very innocent in those days. When my father went into Roosevelt's administration, he went absolutely to pieces when he had to go before a Senate committee. I always told him that way in the back of his mind there was the memory of his bad experience of Senator Walsh. So he regarded all senators as potential rapists and pederasts. Walsh was caught during the war in a boy whorehouse, supposedly frequented by Nazi sympathizers, in Brooklyn, with a man who will be nameless—Virgil Thomson. Not together, but Virgil was also caught. One newspaper started to break the story. Walsh was chairman of naval affairs, as well as the master of Massachusetts, and he was the cardinal's business man. Roosevelt, under his wartime powers, said that any newspaper that printed this would be prosecuted and shut down. The *New York Post* printed it in the first edition, then got the word. No word ever appeared. And Walsh? Nothing ever happened to him. He was re-elected in due course. There wasn't anybody in Massachusetts from the little birds on the Common who didn't know what David Walsh was up to.

INTERVIEWER: The Jenkins thing made such an enormous scandal. At the same time you apparently have no problem.

VIDAL: I stay away from YMCA men's rooms, for one thing.

INTERVIEWER: We understand that J. Edgar Hoover actually sent him a bouquet of flowers. He was the only one in Washington who showed Jenkins any sympathy.

VIDAL: Hoover cared.

INTERVIEWER: He was helping to give Hoover work.

VIDAL: After all, I dedicated *An Evening with Richard Nixon* to "J. Edgar Hoover and . . .

INTERVIEWER: Clyde Tolson . . .

VIDAL: With appreciation."

INTERVIEWER: One thing you've said is that you didn't think that anyone was a homosexual.

VIDAL: I've always said it was just an adjective. It's not a noun, though it's always used as a noun. Put it the other way. What is a heterosexual person? I've never met one. When you say Lyndon Johnson and Adlai Stevenson behaved like two typical heterosexuals over the weekend, in their response, well, I don't know what they had in common. To me, it's just descriptive of an act.

INTERVIEWER: What about faggot or fag, the way we use it today? For example, in the title of the paper *Fag Rag?*

VIDAL: I prefer the word faggot which I tend to use myself. I have never allowed actively in my life the word "gay" to pass my lips. I don't know why I hate that word.

INTERVIEWER: I think it's because the *Advocate* and the bourgeois press has picked up on it and made it into a noun.

VIDAL: Also, I mean, historically it meant a girl of easy virtue in the seventeenth century. They'd say: "Is she gay?" Which meant: "Is she available?" And this, I don't think, is highly descriptive of anybody. It's just a bad word. You see, I don't think you need a word for it. This is what you have to evolve. These words have got to wither away in a true Hegelian cycle.

INTERVIEWER: A lot of homosexuals seem to be very concerned about whether they are called gays, faggots, fairies, or homosexuals.

VIDAL: I would give it as a general warning: it may not apply to anybody in your generation, but certainly in the case of mine that I could have been from 1948 on The Official Spokesman. But I have no plans to be so limited. I'm a generalist, and I'm interested in a great many other things. Knowing the mania of the media, they want everybody to be in a pigeonhole. Oh, yes. He's The Official Fag. Oh, yes. He's The Official Marxist. And I have never allowed myself to be pigeonholed like that. Also I don't regard myself as one thing over another. The point is, why not discard all the words. Say that all sexual acts have parity. Which is my line.

INTERVIEWER: If they're not forced.

VIDAL: Well, obviously. A voluntary act, voluntarily received, is equal to any other. And why make a fuss about what it is?

INTERVIEWER: In *Fag Rag* 5 we reprinted an article from Dwight Macdonald's old magazine *Politics,* an article by Robert Duncan called "The Homosexual in Society." Duncan used the word "jam" and I had never heard it.

VIDAL: "Jam" was a much-used word. Kind of trade, but not really trade. Pretty hard to get. Perhaps when the fact was removed the word withered away too. No one seemed to be impossible. "Jam" only referred to boys.

INTERVIEWER: Were there other words like that which have since atrophied?

VIDAL: I don't know. You'll find "jam" in *The City and the Pillar,* I think. I did a little glossary in there in my encyclopedic of World Almanac way. "Dirt" was a word; that was for a bad piece of trade. I'm supposed to have coined the phrase "Last year's trade is this year's competition." That's in *The City and the Pillar.*

I noticed it was quoted in *Fag Rag* 6. I don't think it was original with me, but I get the credit because I was the first to write it.

INTERVIEWER: Something that strikes me in the *Gay Sunshine* interviews is that at some point or other, the interviewees deal with the issue of their own homosexuality and their writing. They act as though homosexuality, the desire for sex, particularly sex with youth—which may not be at all an issue with you—is an obstacle to writing. During the period of sexual activity there is a great deal less writing.

VIDAL: I don't understand that at all. But Hemingway said something very much like that. He always liked to maintain sexual continence when he was writing seriously.

INTERVIEWER: Are you sexually active when you write?

VIDAL: The more active I am the better I write. I'm much more interested in economics and class than sex. All this is part of the middle class, part of the Puritan work ethic. You keep your seed in your bank and it collects interest; you have too many drafts on it you weaken it. This is a Protestant, work ethic, middle-class thing. It was my very good fortune not to be born middle class. So I'm at a completely different vantage point.

INTERVIEWER: Do you think you're similar to the working class, in this respect?

VIDAL: Well, that's what's always been claimed by the British, and I think so. The fact is that for us there was really no fuss about sex. You did as much as you could. I'm fascinated by this book about Vita Sackville-West and Harold Nicolson, *Portrait of a Marriage*. That's really mind-blowing to middle-class Americans. Harold Nicolson was a relentless chaser of Guardsmen and Vita Sackville-West of cunt. This is the condition of people who are not trapped into that economic middle-class tightness, and the worry of always keeping up appearances, the worry that they're always going to be "done in" by somebody. The working class, God knows, they're filled with terrible passion and prejudice, but give them a sexual act to perform that seems amusing... In Texas—that relentless Bible belt—there's nobody who's not available. It's like Italy.

INTERVIEWER: We've been discussing the issue of S & M at *Fag Rag*. How we should deal with it, etc. I have a friend from a repressed Jewish background. He's now this mad queen and has exploded—

VIDAL: That's it.

INTERVIEWER: He can't be held back. Cockrings and dog collars and the whole thing. Are there sex toy shops in Rome? And how do you contrast the sort of decadent Puritanism with sensuality—of which you've always been an advocate—in Italy?

VIDAL: The Italians are naturally sensual and opportunistic about sex. They don't fuss. That's one of the reasons why there are really no queer bars. Pornography is really outlawed, though there probably would be if the law allowed it.

INTERVIEWER: Do all middle-class men have mistresses?

VIDAL: Yeah. Till the traffic got so you couldn't get across town.

INTERVIEWER: From five to seven stuck in a traffic jam? What is your attitude toward S & M? Do you think it's only a Northern European, Anglo "vice"?

VIDAL: Doesn't seem very Latin to me. You don't see anything like that in Latin countries.

INTERVIEWER: In Greece?

VIDAL: I've spent a lot of time around Athens and in the islands and I never saw any sign of it. I don't know very much about it.

INTERVIEWER: The interviews that writers usually give to *Gay Sunshine* always seem to dwell on promiscuity. Your life seems to be very different.

VIDAL: As promiscuous as I can make it.

INTERVIEWER: Yeah, but you have more style than almost any other writer. I loved that story in one of your essays about your going to bed with Kerouac.

VIDAL: [*Laughs.*]

INTERVIEWER: So much for the "Tell—

VIDAL: "Tell It Like It Is" school.

INTERVIEWER: When I was at Boston University, Ray Mungo was a big up-and-coming star. I don't know whether you've read his books or not. Maybe he just fizzled out after Woodstock and what-not. But he had that same kind of "We're groovy. We're hip. We're with it and we smoke dope. But don't touch us on our rear ends." He finally got fucked in a hay loft in New Hampshire; it came out in his last novel. Since then, he went to India.

VIDAL: Oh dear.

INTERVIEWER: He couldn't deal with it on account of his Irish background.

VIDAL: Became very spiritual after that.

INTERVIEWER: Boston is still predominantly Irish. Even when the sex act is accomplished, I think most of the time it's not enjoyed.

VIDAL: Is that still a problem?

INTERVIEWER: It still is. Some of the working class cannot enjoy sex. Even with the desire, they don't seek to educate themselves to become expressive in sex or allow themselves to enjoy it. It's wham-bam, and they're out the door. Still.

VIDAL: The Irish are a very special case. In Ireland itself there is no sex at all of any kind as far as we've observed. They're just drunk. They don't like women at all. They're really misogynous. I think they're attracted to men, but it is much easier to go out and get drunk with a man. I know a very attractive English girl. She's *wild* about the Irish boys. She said: "To trap one into bed, you have to plan for days. You have to get him drunk enough so that he'll do it, but just before he gets too drunk and can't do it." She said: "You have to pounce at the exact moment."

INTERVIEWER: Recently I met an eighteen-year-old South Boston Irish Catholic. The amount of fear and psychic crippling in him seems great. Is it the Irish or the system?

VIDAL: A lower-class WASP boy in Virginia is totally different. And yet they have the Bible belt. They are Baptists. They believe all that hell-fire stuff. And absolutely no sexual guilt at all in the South.

INTERVIEWER: They marry and settle down.

VIDAL: They used to. I think marriage and settling down is no longer what it was.

INTERVIEWER: Children are going out now too.

VIDAL: And as children go out, there's no more need. Marriage will be all through.

INTERVIEWER: Do you have any children?

VIDAL: I may have a daughter, yes.

INTERVIEWER: We were wondering. You were very coy in *Two Sisters*.

VIDAL: Well, it's true. I don't know. It was either me or a German photographer. I did pay for the abortion. She had the baby anyway.

INTERVIEWER: You have been very open in your life in dealing with the taboo. First in *The City and the Pillar,* in many of your essays, and then with *Myra Breckinridge.* Where do you draw the line? Is the line constantly shifting? In the interview you gave to Viva you were asked: "Was your first sexual experience with a man or a woman?"

VIDAL: I think I had a very funny answer. I don't think she got it right. I said: "I was much too polite to ask."

INTERVIEWER: Were you younger than eighteen when you had your first experience?

VIDAL: Oh my God! I was eleven! And I was brought up in the South.

INTERVIEWER: You loved your father very much, didn't you?

VIDAL: I adored him, yes.

INTERVIEWER: And Hugh D. Auchincloss was your stepfather?

VIDAL: Yeah. I liked Hughdie. But he's a magnum of chloroform.

INTERVIEWER: Do you still see the Auchinclosses much?

VIDAL: I see my sister. There are so many Auchinclosses around you are bound to see some. They're always around.

INTERVIEWER: Were you an only child?

VIDAL: I was an only child until I was about thirteen.

INTERVIEWER: Even though you were not middle class, was there ever a time in that whole period that you felt you worried about your sexuality?

VIDAL: Never. Absolutely never.

INTERVIEWER: No identity crisis? No breakdown?

VIDAL: I did exactly what I wanted to do all the time.

INTERVIEWER: You were very beautiful when you were young. You're good-looking now, too, but pretty in your youth.

VIDAL: So I read in all these memoirs of my great beauty.

INTERVIEWER: Yes. Truman Capote said you took him to the Everard Baths.

VIDAL: I did take Truman to the Everard. Couldn't have been funnier. "I just don't like it." [*Mimics Truman Capote.*]

INTERVIEWER: Does Truman go to the trucks? What does he do?

VIDAL: He falls in love passionately with air-conditioning repair men. He had a tragic affair recently with an air-conditioning repair man.

INTERVIEWER: There's one thing you said about Capote's writing: "So like Faith Baldwin." If that's true about his life, he's got the inspiration.

VIDAL: I can't read him because I'm diabetic.

INTERVIEWER: Regarding youth, are you never attracted by younger people?

VIDAL: Oh, yes. I said I don't flatter the young, either as a writer or as a performer. And I don't flatter them sexually. That doesn't mean I don't like them.

INTERVIEWER: Do you enjoy being seduced as much as seducing?

VIDAL: No. I hate it.

INTERVIEWER: Getting back to the right-wing, closet, repressed mentality, we have a study group in Boston in which we've talked about repression, the matrilinear origins of civilization, your novels, Sontag, Firbank, etc. They rebroadcast *Point of Order,* and it's been playing here in theatres. The David Schine–Roy Cohn thing is intriguing. We've heard stories of them naked snapping towels in hotels. Did that come out at the time?

VIDAL: We used to sing "Come Cohn or Come Schine." Sure. [*Laughter.*]

INTERVIEWER: That it was a cover-up?

VIDAL: Senator Flanders of Vermont, noble old boy, tried to not only knock them off with it but McCarthy himself.

INTERVIEWER: The whole Army-McCarthy hearings were meant as a cover-up for this homosexual relationship?

VIDAL: Yeah. McCarthy himself was homosexual. This sort of wing of "preverts."

INTERVIEWER: Do you have a conscious feeling about your writing and politics? Do you feel you've got a political role?

VIDAL: No.

INTERVIEWER: Even though you're not in politics per se, you have a base. When I saw you on the Dick Cavett Show the other night, after you destroyed that poor Jesuit, I remarked that what's so refreshing about seeing you compared to others on the tube is that you come out with the truth very casually.

VIDAL: I'm not running for office. I don't have to worry about the unpleasant mail. I made the decision in '64 that I was not going to go to Congress. It was very plain that I would have been elected if I had run. And, I turned down, in the beginning of '68, the nomination and support for the Senate.

INTERVIEWER: You were thinking of running in '68?

VIDAL: As late as '68. This was before *Myra Breckinridge* came out. I finally told them. I said: "Look kids, I think without this book we might do it, but with this book, we won't be able to get through."

INTERVIEWER: Have you thought much about the Bicentennial and the country remembering its beginning—I know your essays in *Homage to Daniel Shays*.

VIDAL: Bicentennial? I wrote *Burr* as my meditation on the political process.

INTERVIEWER: Politically, do you see any opportunity for using the whole remembrance of the origins of the country in a political way?

VIDAL: One tactic which is useful: you can always promote radical causes under the guise of Going Back to the Constitution. And sometimes quite legitimately. The Bill of Rights is still a radical document. I find sometimes when I'm trying to be an advocate, trying to convince a really difficult audience, you can always refer back to the origins and tell them that this is the way it was meant to be.

INTERVIEWER: When you're got Daniel Shays, Tom Paine, and all the rest of them, you've got some rich potential.

VIDAL: Yes.

INTERVIEWER: What do you think of the talk show circuit?

VIDAL: There's a whole technique to it. You just have to study how to do it. Use it to your own purposes.

INTERVIEWER: How do you get through mass media with what is essentially an anti-mass message?

VIDAL: You have to become an explainer. You have to make up your mind before you go on that you are going to make the following points. Don't make too many points because they can't remember them. You are going to say: if I want to get the sex laws changed, I will then have thought it out in my head how I'll lead the conversation. It doesn't make any difference what they ask; you just go right on. "Yes, that's interesting," and go right on to the point you were going to make. It's like any other kind of skill. You have to learn how to do it. It's very useful.

INTERVIEWER: But the media itself. It's a sort of reverse from McLuhan.

VIDAL: It's better than nothing. People don't listen. All day yesterday and the day before in Chicago, little old ladies, cabdrivers who I know hate my guts, all came up and wanted to talk about the exchange with the priest on Cavett's show. They were all very pleased by it.

INTERVIEWER: Did you talk with the Jesuit [John McLaughlin, a speech writer and deputy special assistant to Nixon] after the show?

VIDAL: He told me that Walter Cronkite is a notorious left-winger.

INTERVIEWER: The nature of the bourgeois press, the very fact that they teamed you with someone like that, does this make you feel compromised having to deal with slime? That you're on a par with slime?

VIDAL: No! I'm the detergent!

INTERVIEWER: I think you did an "Inouye." You said: "Lies. Lies. Priest." You weren't on camera then.

VIDAL: No, no. I said: "You are lying, priest. Think to your immortal soul." The Brother gulped on that.

INTERVIEWER: The thing that bothers me is that every other elite—you come out of the liberal elite—in Germany, France, etc., produces leaders, phenomenal people.

VIDAL: No revolution ever came from the bottom.

INTERVIEWER: Exactly. But the United States, just in the last ten years, has had an attempt on the part of many people who come out of the elite—

VIDAL: An attempt to do what? Change things?

INTERVIEWER: Yes. From the left. We have no leadership. The media have taken every figure in the movement, just to take one example.

VIDAL: And used them up. I watched Abbie Hoffman from the beginning. I predicted the first time he appeared on the scene—at a debate between Tom Hayden and me. Abbie was in the audience. He got up and harangued. I could see they loved him on television. "Freako!" "Wild man!" I said to myself: If that man is around in three years I'll be surprised. They'll use him up. And then there will be another wild man, and he will be on a different kick.

INTERVIEWER: David Bowie now.

VIDAL: Yeah. Survival in the United States is not easy whether it is for a writer or a singer or anyone else. Certainly is a critical society. It's not easy at all.

INTERVIEWER: You didn't make the "Enemies List."

VIDAL: That's not true! I was number 212. I can't remember. I wasn't in the top twenty, which was one of their ways of destroying me.

INTERVIEWER: Have you ever had IRS, passport or FBI trouble?

VIDAL: I've been broken into twice by the FBI when I was with the People's Party. As was Spock. You can always tell because they never take anything. They should at least take the TV set, but they're so damn lazy and it's heavy.

INTERVIEWER: These are agents?

VIDAL: Yeah. Then they would go through papers, papers, papers.

INTERVIEWER: Was this under Johnson or Nixon?

VIDAL: Nixon.

INTERVIEWER: Have they ever tried to talk with you?

VIDAL: No. I am on the FBI list of people never to talk to about anything, because I went after Hoover about twelve years ago.

INTERVIEWER: Before it was fashionable.

VIDAL: Yeah. And really let him have it.

INTERVIEWER: Did you ever meet the man?

VIDAL: Yes.

INTERVIEWER: Did he look you in the eye? My brother always told me you can always tell a queer because he'll never look you in the eye.

VIDAL: Somebody was asking me. Said he thought Richard Nixon was obviously homosexual. I said: "Why do you think that?" He said: "You know, that funny, uncoordinated way he moves." I said: "Yeah. Like Nureyev."

INTERVIEWER: What was your motivation behind the Peoples' Party with Spock?

VIDAL: I didn't have any. I was just sort of riding along with it. We started the New Party in '68. The idea was simply to try and make a representative party. It wasn't worth doing. It was nothing but young group therapists who didn't believe in "elitism" or "structure." It was pointless.

INTERVIEWER: *Fag Rag* tries to see homosexuality in America at this point as being a vehicle for radical expression.

VIDAL: Yet when you get with any radical blacks or any radical anything, forget it.

INTERVIEWER: Remember the quote: "The place for a woman in the movement is on her back?" One wonders if there isn't room now for what Hofstadter did with paranoia in American politics, something to do with sexual repression. I think *Myra B.* is the tip of the iceberg.

VIDAL: There is considerable work to be done. Every intelligent person in the country knows the thing is a joke.

INTERVIEWER: I don't know. I'm very skeptical. Though I identify with your literary works, I sometimes wonder why you still have this tropism towards belief in the faith. Perhaps they could be manipulated in the right direction. When it comes to personality and style and reason and argument against the 4.4 percent and their money, you're going to lose.

VIDAL: Well, I don't know. I have seen attitudes change a good deal since I began. This magazine of yours would not have existed twenty-five years ago. I think the 4.4 percent changes in its own inscrutable way, but I do not think I believe it will be done by intelligent advocacy. I have said if it is going to change, it is going to be collapse. The system will collapse. It does not work now. The government does not work. And the economic system is not working. Something will crash. Who picks up the pieces? I would want a social democracy as my replacement. I just want to get the goddamn population down by about two-thirds. Then there's plenty of room for everybody and plenty of wealth for everybody.

INTERVIEWER: The point that continues to plague me is the lack of leadership. I do not see any positive political strategy.

VIDAL: You need a new party. You come back to it again. I made my effort along with these others in '68 and again in '72.

INTERVIEWER: But what is the base?

VIDAL: If you saw the manifesto I did ["A Dialogue with Myself," *Esquire*, October 1968], you have got to have a party of human survival.

INTERVIEWER: Regarding the issue of censorship, I'm doing an article on John Horne Burns, particularly the job the critics did on him. Did you know him?

VIDAL: Yes.

INTERVIEWER: I find in researching him that there are only three pieces still extant since his death: your piece in the *New York Times Book Review*, Brigid Brophy's piece in the Sunday *London Times* magazine, and a piece in *One* magazine, a Los Angeles–based homophile publication.

VIDAL: He was obliterated by the press.

INTERVIEWER: In rereading him, there is a certain circumspection that comes through.

VIDAL: He's being careful.

INTERVIEWER: Very careful. The homosexual passion is there, breaking through.

VIDAL: He was careful in the first one, *The Gallery*. *Lucifer with a Book*, however, is when the critics let him have it. I think *The Gallery* is certainly the best of the "war books." It was much applauded, much admired. You see, he did six or seven books before *The Gallery*. He was an awful man. Monster. Envious, bitchy, drunk.

INTERVIEWER: Another Irishman.

VIDAL: Yeah. Bitter. Which was why *The Gallery* was so marvelous. It was his explosion into humanity at a fairly late date. I think he was in his early thirties, after a half-assed career as an English teacher and writing unprintable novels.

INTERVIEWER: Have you ever seen any of the manuscripts?

VIDAL: No. But I've been told about them by Freddie Warburg who published him in England who said they were all pretty bad. They must be around somewhere.

INTERVIEWER: How did he die? I can't find that out. Was he killed?

VIDAL: No, no, no. He was drinking himself to death in Florence. Every day he would go to the Grand Hotel and stand in the bar and drink Italian brandy, which is just about the worst thing in the world. And chew on fruit drops candy. He always said that it would counteract the drunkenness. He was living with a doctor, an Italian veterinarian. They had a rather stormy relationship but nothing sinister about it. One day he was drunk at a bar, wandered out in the hot midday sun and had a stroke. Cerebral hemorrhage.

INTERVIEWER: At age thirty-seven?

VIDAL: I think he wanted to die. They really wiped him out on *Lucifer with a Book*. We were both, in 1947, the leading writers in the country. The ineffable John W. Aldridge began his career with a piece in *Harper's* magazine, out of which came his book *After the Lost Generation*. He reversed all his judgments later. He began his career as our great admirer. He discovered we were dealing with the horrors of homosexuality. He then exactly reversed himself and began to applaud the Jewish giants who are still with us today. Aldridge is nothing if not a rider of bandwagons. So Burns was absolutely at the top them. We were both admired as War Writers. To be a War Writer was pretty gutsy. You can't knock a War Writer. Then *City and the Pillar.* Then *Lucifer with a Book.* They said: "Oh, my God! What is this we've been admiring?"

INTERVIEWER: Did the straight critics pick up on the homosexual themes in *Lucifer with a Book* and *The Gallery?*

VIDAL: They got it in *Lucifer with a Book.* He hit you on the head with it.

INTERVIEWER: One never knows the mentality of reviewers.

VIDAL: We wrote differently in those days, but it was perfectly plain what was going on at that school.

INTERVIEWER: And was that reason to condemn the book?

VIDAL: Entirely. Any writer suspected of being homosexual. When Norman Mailer met me in 1950, he said: "You know, Gore, I thought you were the Devil." Just terrible but true. The only thing that they respect, that they put up with, is a freak like Capote, who has the mind of a Kansas housewife, likes gossip, and gets all shuddery when she thinks about boys murdering people.

INTERVIEWER: So Mailer went after you?

VIDAL: They all did. However, Capote never really touched on the subject. He is a Republican housewife from Kansas with all the prejudices. Just as Norman Mailer is a VFW commander in Schenectady.

INTERVIEWER: It's rather amazing that just as you were accepted, really, for something like *The City and the Pillar,* just as it was becoming acceptable to deal with homosexuality as such, you came out with *Myra Breckinridge* which even among homosexuals is controversial.

VIDAL: I always remember a remark Faulkner made about Hemingway. Faulkner was very guarded in talking about his contemporaries. He once said to me: "You know, Hemingway's problem is that he never takes chances." You have got to keep going as far out as you can, as far as your imagination will take you.

INTERVIEWER: That is the chasm I see in your life and work. While on the one hand you have a fascination with power, you know more accurately than almost any other writer or politician in America the kind of mediocrities the American electorate coughs up, quashing out any kind of leadership. On the other hand you're such an avant-garde writer, capturing the sensibility so exquisitely at any given time. You should understand that in America there is no true way of jiving them. You can't publish *Myra* without getting the housewife at the supermarket to go: No. Unh-uh. No way. Look at the job they did on Rocky when he married Happy.

VIDAL: Never underestimate their corruption. If you can amuse them, they will forgive you just about anything. And if you are a success, they will crown you.

INTERVIEWER: What kind of success?

VIDAL: Money.

INTERVIEWER: Is that why the historical novels?

VIDAL: I'm fascinated with the origins of the United States and Christianity, which were the two subjects I took on.

INTERVIEWER: Do the historical novels make more money than the earliest ones like *Williwaw* and *In a Yellow Wood?*

VIDAL: Oh yes.

INTERVIEWER: Why did you publish three mysteries in the fifties under the pseudonym "Edgar Box"?

VIDAL: I was broke. I needed money. I wrote each of them in a week. Except one of them. I wrote half of it in three days and the house burned down. I had to go back to it, and I had forgotten who was the murderer. So I had to think of a whole new plot halfway through it. Try to figure out which one I had in mind. Ten thousand words a day, seven days.

INTERVIEWER: Did you have little charts on the wall? Esther here and Warren in the window?

VIDAL: No. When you're young, it is the most amazing thing. You can do formidable things.

INTERVIEWER: Formula or formidable?

VIDAL: Formidable. Formula takes maturity.

INTERVIEWER: It seems like the other way around. It seems that someone who's such a craftsman as you would avoid formula.

VIDAL: I think you will find it takes a long time to find your tone of voice. I didn't until *Judgment of Paris*. I published five or six books before I really got it. I wouldn't say got it right, but got it accurate. I was now coming through. For us, it was very difficult to overcome Hemingway and the *New Yorker*. That style was just so oppressive. One hardly knew of anything else. Anything else sounded affected in your own voice.

INTERVIEWER: Did you know Paul Goodman in the fifties?

VIDAL: Yes. I'd see him around. I never knew him well.

INTERVIEWER: How do you measure his impact in terms of the sexual thing?

VIDAL: Well, I haven't read that diary or journals he kept or anything, but he was obviously very daring considering that he made himself the guru of the middle-brow educationalists.

INTERVIEWER: True. It was not until Sputnik that he almost nurtured his own following.

VIDAL: Yes. I was rather startled that in a way he had that much integrity. I always thought he was a bitter man. Playing up to a constituency. There is nothing worse than playing up to the young, a game I will never get into.

INTERVIEWER: Of course he was fascinated by the young. Perhaps that explains a part of his sexual fascination.

VIDAL: Yes. You can be sexually fascinated by them and still not flatter them. I think flattery had a lot to do with his sexual techniques. It has nothing to do with mine.

INTERVIEWER: One point we were quibbling about when we were doing "Some Notes on *Myra B"* was about a Senator Breckinridge—in fact you mention him in *Burr*— who was Buchanan's vice president. We had also heard that in the 1940s there was a famous transsexual—

VIDAL: In San Francisco?

INTERVIEWER: From a very rich family. She was supposedly the biggest queen in the world. And her name was Breckinridge. Is that true?

VIDAL: Well. It is true. Bunny Breckinridge. [*Laughter.*] Now this is the most extraordinary thing. I was reminded years later that I had never met Bunny Breckinridge, but that everybody that I knew had known him and talked to me about him. This was in the forties. Then it just went right out of my head, and Breckinridge came into my head. I just wanted a very solid-sounding name with lots of syllables. Myra would not be content with just being Smith.

INTERVIEWER: But the rumor was that she was related to the famous former V.P., Vice President Breckinridge.

VIDAL: Oh well.

INTERVIEWER: We figured: Vidal's into politics; he'll know that.

VIDAL: No. I didn't know that.

INTERVIEWER: It's documented, I'm told, in a book called *Queer Street, USA.*

VIDAL: About Bunny Breckinridge?

INTERVIEWER: Yes. Was she a transsexual or just a big queen?

VIDAL: Just a big queen. Very rich.

INTERVIEWER: Why did you choose not to go to college?

VIDAL: I was supposed to go to Harvard. It occurred to me. I went into the army at seventeen, got out at twenty. What was the point of going into another institution when I had already written my first novel?

INTERVIEWER: But did you know that "education" was a fraud then, too? Or just a drag on your career?

VIDAL: No. In those days we thought you could actually go to a place like Harvard and it would be worth doing. But only if you wanted to lead a conventional life and rise in a law firm or something. I had the great pleasure of lecturing at Harvard while all my classmates from Exeter were undergraduates. Greatest moment of my life, I mean I really rubbed it in. It's all been downhill since.

INTERVIEWER: What about the poetry you wrote while at Exeter? Has it ever been published?

VIDAL: I hope not. There's a book coming out about me. A professor has gone and read it all.

INTERVIEWER: I suppose literary criticism is one of the penalties for being prolific when you're young. By middle age, you have to start dealing with critical biographies.

VIDAL: Writers younger than I am like Updike and Harold Pinter. There are more books about Harold Pinter than there are about Chekhov. Most extraordinary thing.

INTERVIEWER: It's Sputnik again. It's all the college-educated *Time* subscribers who buy books now and belong to book clubs.

VIDAL: Nobody reads these books. It is make-work so you can get tenure in universities. Who's not been done from the forties? Ah, there's Vidal. Willingham. Let's do Willingham.

INTERVIEWER: I saw a Susskind show recently where he had all the old stable of Philco Playhouse writers.

VIDAL: Oh, really?

INTERVIEWER: Chayefsky. And who is the Englishman [Australian] who writes novels now?

VIDAL: Sumner Locke Eliot. A great wit. Very charming.

INTERVIEWER: Were you part of that stable?

VIDAL: Sure. I did *Visit to a Small Planet*.

INTERVIEWER: Chayevsky said he did *Marty* for $900. He wasn't bitter about it now because he's making lots of money, but the other guests did a little complaining. Now David Susskind and all the critics—

VIDAL: David was their agent.

INTERVIEWER: My impression is that you did well. *Visit* went on to become a movie and a Broadway play.

VIDAL: Yeah. Chayefsky went on. He made several movies.

INTERVIEWER: Did you make money out of your television plays?

VIDAL: For me it was a hell of a... As a writer I never seemed to be able to make more than $7000 a year, year in and year out.

INTERVIEWER: But you were published before you went and they were not.

VIDAL: Oh yes.

INTERVIEWER: They were just sort of Kitchen Writers from Brooklyn.

VIDAL: Radio men. Radio joke writers.

INTERVIEWER: You do a lot of projects. It was mentioned in *Atlantic* that you were doing a screenplay entitled *Plaza*. I looked for this and never saw it.

VIDAL: That was Robert Aldrich. Rather not a bad idea. He blew the financing. It never got made.

INTERVIEWER: Also, I read in *Life* that you were doing a novel called *Dreams*. Then I never read anything else about this.

VIDAL: I wrote part of it. I never finished it. I think it's mostly going into *Myron*.

INTERVIEWER: Concerning your relationship with Howard Austin. What is the financial arrangement and/or how will you leave your money?

VIDAL: I have lived twenty-three years with the same person. Presumably because I am older I will die first and just leave it to him. That's all.

INTERVIEWER: Do you know anything about other "gay" authors who died and left money?

VIDAL: Somerset Maugham left Alan Searle very well provided for.

INTERVIEWER: Wasn't there a big scandal with the Maugham estate?

VIDAL: Maugham was just so ga-ga. He was making trouble all over the place. He tried to cut his grandson out by saying that his daughter was not really his daughter, and she was—curiously enough.

INTERVIEWER: Gide was married. Did he have a family?

VIDAL: He had no children. I don't know where Gide's money went. Probably to Marc Allegret, the director.

INTERVIEWER: Will Capote be very rich when he dies?

VIDAL: Capote has no money.

INTERVIEWER: Really? Living at UN Plaza?

VIDAL: This is one of the reasons *why* he has no money. He thinks he's Bunny Mellon—to get back to another Bunny. He thinks he's a very rich Society Lady, and spends a great deal of money.

INTERVIEWER: Where does Auden's money go?

VIDAL: He had no money.

INTERVIEWER: He leaves an estate, though.

VIDAL: If he left $10,000, I would be very surprised.

INTERVIEWER: What will Isherwood do?

VIDAL: He would leave it to Don Bachardy, and to anyone he wants to.

INTERVIEWER: Do you enjoy the historical novel? Or is it a drudge so that you can do something mad in between?

VIDAL: No. I really like them very much.

INTERVIEWER: Among American fiction writers, who do you read for enjoyment?

VIDAL: Calder Willingham. Southern writer. Very funny.

INTERVIEWER: I couldn't get through *Providence Island*.

VIDAL: No. That's bad. But *Rambling Rose* is new and rather good. I love *Geraldine Bradshaw*. They're pussy novels, you're right. Just this terrible, relentless quest for pussy. Just full of failure, which is like life, which is what I like about it.

INTERVIEWER: Did you get through *Gravity's Rainbow?*

VIDAL: I don't think I'm going to get to that. I have tried the academic writers. There is a sort of division of literature which I cast a benign eye upon. I'm sure there is a place for it: novels which are written to be used in the classroom. Since

I think that's where the novel is going to end up, I think of myself as an anachronism, and *that* is the future. Someone like John Barth to me is just cement. Pynchon. I read *V.* Some of it is fun, but so heavy-handed. The jokes are so heavy, such awful names. Nabokov remembers him. He was in one of Nabokov's classes at Cornell. Nabokov thinks rather highly of him. Nabokov I usually enjoy, though not as much as he enjoys himself. I like old Saul Bellow. I find him cranky but true.

INTERVIEWER: Do you mind being exploited? For example, I just read Dotson Rader's new book *Blood Dues*.

VIDAL: A little cunt. A real cunt.

INTERVIEWER: In *Blood Dues*, if it had not been for you and Tennessee Williams, there would be no book, except for his bloody nose at the end.

VIDAL: I have no intention of reading that book. I read something he wrote in *Esquire* about me and Tennessee; that I had not gone to the church because I was afraid Tennessee would upstage me. Imagine a mind that would conceive that. Tennessee is one of my oldest friends. Vain as I am, that is not the sort of thing that would ever cross my mind.

INTERVIEWER: The whole Southern mentality is so foreign to me in a way. You had one foot into it. Is it easy to patronize Southern writers?

VIDAL: When I began to write, they were the center of American literature. Much overpraised. Now they're rather underpraised. And the Jewish writers came along, bringing with them their stern patriarchal attitudes.

INTERVIEWER: What is the prospect for women's liberation, gay liberation and sensuality in America?

VIDAL: I keep coming back to economics. I keep thinking about the collapse of the currency, the shortages in the world.

INTERVIEWER: It occurred to me a while ago that your whole prophecy of what is going to happen in this country would indicate that American literature as well as politics is gone, going. It has got to be replaced with something.

VIDAL: I don't think it has to be replaced with anything. American literature has always been second-rate. The schools in America, which are also second-rate, could never discuss this because their mandate rests upon pretending that since we were briefly a great world empire, therefore we were a great civilization. When you compare Mark Twain to George Eliot, or compare Dostoevsky to Stephen Crane, or poor Hemingway to Proust, my god! Henry James, a great novelist, became English.

INTERVIEWER: I think all of your work is in print except *A Season of Comfort*. This is remarkable, and proof that you are saying something. My final question is: Are queens different today in the seventies then they were in the forties?

VIDAL: Ahhh, I don't know. That's an interesting thought, though it seems to me that everything is the same always. Certain things are more open now than they were then. But they were pretty open in the sort of ghetto life of the forties. And New York, Lexington Avenue, was very royal.

INTERVIEWER: Do you keep a diary?

VIDAL: I kept one in '48. I sealed it and gave it to the University of Wisconsin with my papers.

INTERVIEWER: To be opened after your death?

VIDAL: After my death or the Second Coming, whichever comes first.

II

Steven Abbott and Thom Willenbecher interview
GORE VIDAL

INTERVIEWER: All the sex magazines have been interested in interviewing you: *Playboy, Viva,* and now *Fanny.*

VIDAL: Well, after all, I'm supposed to be the apostle of bisexuality because I said something in its favor once, and as we all know I invented homosexuality in 1948 with *The City and the Pillar.* My invention. First there was Orville and Wilbur Wright...

INTERVIEWER: ... those two fag siblings.

VIDAL: ... and then there was me. And then...

INTERVIEWER: Allen Ginsberg who invented cocksucking in 1956 and, of course, with appreciation, the tandem J. Edgar and Clyde.

VIDAL: I've been asked to do a film about J. Edgar Hoover. It's the first tempting film offer that's come my way. I plan to do it as a beautiful love story.

INTERVIEWER: Yeah. *Fag Rag* did a piece entitled "Hoover Goes Under" after his untimely demise. Are there still plans for CBS to do a film on *Burr?*

VIDAL: Yes. CBS has been following me around for three months. They're doing *Sixty Minutes* on my life and times. We've done the Italian part. Now they're shooting me here.

INTERVIEWER: Speaking of Italy, advertisements are surfacing for a new book on Italy in which you write the epilogue [*In Italy* by Roloff Beny et al., Harper & Row].

VIDAL: A beautiful book, with three kinds of paper. Very lush and decadent. They should put legs on it. It would be a coffee table. I'm afraid the epilogue is a little deflationary. As the world is coming to an end, we won't be able to look upon these beautiful scenes much longer.

INTERVIEWER: What's happening with *Sixty Minutes?*

VIDAL: I'm at their mercy. They're getting old films of me and my grandfather, Senator Gore of Oklahoma. Newsreels and home movies. Mike Wallace, of course, is doing a Hard-Hitting Interview: Wouldn't you say that you were against marriage because your mother and father did not get on? I said: No two-bit Freudianism. Spare the audience that.

INTERVIEWER: Did he ask you about "love"?

VIDAL: Yeah. I said to him, "I don't like the word love. It's like patriotism. It's like the flag. It's the last refuge of scoundrels. When people start talking about what wonderful, warm, deep emotions they have and how they love people, I watch out. Somebody is going to steal something. Romantic love as Americans conceive it does not exist. Hence, the enormous divorce rate. When sexual desire cools there's often not much left."

INTERVIEWER: What about your quarter-century living situation with Howard Austin?

VIDAL: Haven't I proved my point by living with somebody for 24 years? That's obviously not being in love. You don't live with the person you love. At least I've known very few cases of it. You live with a friend which is something quite different from having a grand passion or a love affair.

INTERVIEWER: Are they going to allow you to have the final edit?

VIDAL: I suppose not. However, when you do a tape on TV, you can tell them to fuck off, so they have to cut from that point and splice it together again. A series of sharp remarks can bring things to a halt.

INTERVIEWER: Expletive deleted. There is definitely a breach of confidence not to allow the person giving the interview to examine and approve the text. The arrangement counts.

VIDAL: Of course it counts, and the person doing the interview must know how to put it together. Everything depends on context. It's not that they mean to be malicious. They are just dumb and out of dumbness they miss things. I could do a much more devastating piece about myself than they could, and I wouldn't mind doing it. At least it would be the right kind of devastation.

INTERVIEWER: Have you written your epitaph?

VIDAL: Yes. "When I die, I'm going to take you all with me." I have thoughts about writing my last novel about the end of the world through war, famine, or nuclear contamination. In any case, how are your problems with the governor of New Hampshire and other worthies? [The governor of N.H. tried to have the gay lib paper *Fag Rag* banned. —Ed.]

INTERVIEWER: Meldrim Thompson and the *Manchester Union Libel* live.

VIDAL: A sickening newspaper.

INTERVIEWER: The *Libel*'s latest opus was a front-page editorial urging local citizens to view "The Outrage," that *Marcus Welby* show which caused a massive national gay protest.

VIDAL: The fag show about a fourteen-year-old who loses his manhood because he gets seduced ... and he wasn't even buggered, was he? I think he was just drained of his seminal juices.

INTERVIEWER: The opening scene featured a boy standing before a mirror, with either hickeys or bruises all over his torso ...

VIDAL: Oh, the poor bunny. He was chewed on, then, by this terrible attacker.

INTERVIEWER: Raped by his science teacher as the story goes.

VIDAL: Indeed. I suppose the heteros think that the back of his head will now fall off. Or that he will wear eyeliner in the gym.

INTERVIEWER: The show lent itself to the myth of child molestation and homosexuality, an atavistic dread. Though you live abroad, for a perspective on the U.S. would you elaborate on a quote from *Two Sisters* that "America's first serious novelist said that the U.S. is fit for many purposes, but not to live in. To which the nation's last serious novelist can only add 'Amen'"?

VIDAL: Did I write that? I think Hawthorne said that around the time he was our consul in Liverpool. Well I suppose one could enjoy living here, but it depends on where. Certainly New York would not be on my list. I could manage New Orleans. I used to have a lot of friends there, but the drink has gotten to them and now most of them are dead, including Clay Shaw. A gentle soul. But I think the heavy drinking would have put me under the sod, as it were, a long time ago. Los Angeles would be intolerable, and so would anywhere between. I think of San Francisco, but the weather is never really right there.

INTERVIEWER: People are being advised to stay away from San Francisco and the West Coast if they seriously value their lives.

VIDAL: Why? Because of the pollution?

INTERVIEWER: That and the earthquake.

VIDAL: Ah, yes, the earthquake. Americans must always have something to believe in. Do you know how the sodomy laws first got on the books? In the beginning, church laws proscribed all sex but had nothing in particular to say about sodomy. But according to Procopius, the emperor Justinian who was making up the law codes had a great deal of trouble with the archbishop of Constantinople whose particular pleasure was buggering boys. So the emperor outlawed such practices in his code, saying that it was against god's law and quoted scripture as best he could. He also added that, as we all know, sodomy is the principal cause of earthquakes. So I think it highly suitable that the West Coast may some day tumble into the Pacific in the name of the emperor Justinian.

INTERVIEWER: From a different historical interpretation, we understand that Justinian's wife, Theodora, who was known as the greatest cocksucker in Asia Minor, coerced her husband into the antisodomy measure.

VIDAL: Sexist talk. Anyway, it was a pure political ploy. And, of course, it stayed on the canon law books. No one would stand up to remove it, and from there it got into civil and criminal law.

INTERVIEWER: Do you think that our generation will witness the repeal of all sex laws?

VIDAL: I've been disturbed by the slowness with which legislatures around the country have reacted. They have been slow to act because people have not put the right kind of pressure on them.

INTERVIEWER: They feel that by simply declaring all such matters outside the province of the police and courts they are wholeheartedly endorsing mass orgies in the streets.

VIDAL: That's always the simplistic view.

INTERVIEWER: Exactly. In Boston, we went three months without any laws against pornograpy, yet we survived.

VIDAL: To the extent that Boston can be said to exist.

INTERVIEWER: Now the laws have been restored. *Deep Throat* has continued to play in Boston, even though it gets busted on a regular basis. It's rumored that through the efforts of the "good" Cardinal Medeiros the people who run the movie houses are going to be brought to court on special criminal charges. They may face imprisonment.

VIDAL: Under the First Amendment, you can't make any laws to ban pornography; it is not possible. But the courts, the legislatures pay no attention to the Constitution. It doesn't interest them much.

INTERVIEWER: Do you think that the recent waves of reaction have helped to stimulate the women's and gay movements, just as an upsurge of white racism brought the black movement to its feet?

VIDAL: Well, it happened for blacks. As things started to get better for them economically, their relations with whites grew worse. Newark was set afire after integration there was finally achieved. As things get better, there often develops an enormous irritability, a reaction which leads to a lot of explosions, especially toward the end of the sixties. And it may be as everything got more and more open, and as the hetero dictatorship began to loosen up a bit, the eruption began. The gay and women's movements came to life. So far I don't think the backlash amounts to much. I think it's always true that things begin to liberalize, revolutionize. Once there is an atmosphere for change, change increases exponentially, and reaction only further serves to stimulate more change. Maybe that's what we've been seeing.

INTERVIEWER: Do you think these changes or movement, for example, gay liberation, have made a lasting impact on American values?

VIDAL: I don't know. You tell me. I don't think the gay liberation movement is particularly strong. I don't think it's touched 99 percent of the people. You can go into any small town in America and the attitudes of the people there are no different from what they were in 1900.

INTERVIEWER: In the heartland of America...

VIDAL: Where the pulse beat originates. But, you know, only 3 percent of the people read books. So 97 percent never read a book. Only 10 percent read magazines—the circulation of *TV Guide* or *Playboy*. There's still 90 percent who are not reading *Cosmopolitan* on the joys of scraping your Fallopian tubes while talking to house plants. This is still unknown to them. What has happened since *The City and the Pillar,* which is how I tend to date things, which I remember rather vividly as a book that the *New York Times* would not advertise and everyone was so down on, is now very old-fashioned according to the media. Today the 3 percent who read books and the 10 percent who read magazines are used to these ideas. Not much change for twenty-six years. Eventually the pop culture does begin to trickle down, but it's awfully slowly.

INTERVIEWER: Historically, do you see social movements paralleling and reinforcing each other?

VIDAL: The women's movement has been going on since the country started. There has always been a sort of suffragette movement, at some times stronger than others. But the real impetus for that was when the 14th Amendment was passed after the Civil War, giving blacks the vote. The women quite rightly said that if the ignorant black man can vote then so can we brilliant white women. That was the big trigger. It may be that black militancy helped women's liberation, which in turn helped gay liberation by showing that people were no longer satisfied with the status quo, with the prejudices and superstitions of the heterosexual dictatorship. I think some trend is unfolding before our eyes, though I'm not totally optimistic.

INTERVIEWER: Has the gay world changed since its seminal beginnings in that riverside cabin twenty-six years ago?

VIDAL: I have noticed a very interesting change in my own lifetime. And that has been the fact that the quality of trade has fallen off. When I was young there was a floating population of hetero males who wanted money or kicks or what have you and would sell their ass for a period of their lives. Later they would marry and end up as construction workers or firemen or in the police department. And that was that. Their phase was over. But these were really all-American types, masculine in the old sense. There has emerged a new physical type who seem feminine to me, and I use the term in its old sexist sense. Very schmoo, soft shoulders, flat muscles, broad hips, high voices. Now I wonder is this your experience around Boston, which has always been a center for Irish Catholic trade? From Scollay Square they used to spread out across the country like an army with banners or shamrocks and foreskins...

INTERVIEWER: Only the Polish and Irish can be said to be intact...

VIDAL: And so perfect to the eye.

INTERVIEWER: Does this decline in trade have to do, in part, with the urbanization of society, the society becomes more powerful, the men more cerebral to rationalize—

VIDAL: Yes, but truck drivers becoming cerebral? Or day laborers? Or the average hillbilly boy from Bryant Park to Eighth Avenue? No.

INTERVIEWER: Or what are the effects of restraining the body?

VIDAL: I wonder whether the body is changing physically, whether there might be some kind of mutancy taking place, and that nature is instinctively saying that we don't need any more babies. And the men are becoming a bit less masculine and the women a bit less feminine. I don't know. I'm just guessing. Or is it something in the air which makes them play it another way?

INTERVIEWER: We'll start with norm control in sex and physical education classes.

VIDAL: It's always true in high schools, as I remember. In my youth, if the handsomest athlete was queer every boy was going to bed with every other boy; but if he wasn't, they'd all imitate him and go to bed with girls. Quite extraordinary how one or two idols would always set the tone. Dr. Kinsey noticed the same thing. He could never understand it; he was very square. There could be two high schools about thirty miles apart in the same region and consisting of students from the same economic class. One would indulge in unrestrained homosexuality, yet at the other there was almost none. He couldn't understand that. So I evolved this theory that most of the students tend to mimic the sexual tastes of the school hero.

INTERVIEWER: When was this?

VIDAL: I was about twenty-three at the time and prone to theorizing. Also, I said very vaingloriously that it is possible to make any man. I may not be the person who can do it, but someone can make him. Dr. Kinsey agreed. He said that he had met a young man in Chicago who said the same thing to him. So old Dr. K. took him up on it. Together they went to Division Street where there was a lot of action, and the young man said: now you point out somebody at random. So Kinsey pointed out some guy talking to a girl. He couldn't have been more straight looking. Our hero made the young man. Kinsey said that on three occasions he picked at random and the trick was turned.

INTERVIEWER: A wink, touch and stroke of the hand and he's yours.

VIDAL: An erection has no conscience as they used to say in the army many years ago.

INTERVIEWER: It's still around as a stiff cock, etc., though one hears such things as a civilian. But you wonder if there has been a change in people's physical construction.

VIDAL: I know at Yale they've been photographing the students naked for something like thirty years now, front and back. I think from that they might be able to come up with something. I know that they say that they are taller than they were, and I would say broader beamed.

INTERVIEWER: This probably has something to do with people toasting their toes in front of the tube during their childhood, something which began in the fifties.

VIDAL: It certainly makes for passivity. There's no doubt about that. Boys were once brought up in the back lots, playing baseball and fighting and jumping over walls and all the other things that boys did. That's an interesting thought. It's quite true. They are now brought up from babyhood staring straight ahead at commercials and eating junk food.

INTERVIEWER: And educators are making quite a stir over the drop in achievement level, especially with people now going into college.

VIDAL: Well, that of course is Dr. Shockley's theory about whites as well as blacks. Due to incontinent breeding and the fact that we are keeping alive strains that would have died at birth or soon after, a lot of weak strains are being continued. An interesting thought. But obviously a male brought up on television is going to be very different from one who was physically active and doing "manly" things.

INTERVIEWER: In other words, they are no longer stalking Division Street or Bryant Park to Eighth Avenue and selling their ass.

VIDAL: No, at best they are lying down somewhere and watching the tube.

INTERVIEWER: Or watching *Deep Throat* and reading Alex Comfort in comic book form.

VIDAL: And not having much sex. I don't think they're very sexy. I think that we were far more... Of course, it was still a great adventure with us. Things were not always as open as they are now. But we all, hetero, homo, or bi, were just obsessed. If you were in town and did not get laid every day, I mean, the spirit died. I can remember when I'd miss two days in a row, and I'd think life was over, that something terrible had happened. And I don't mean just slogging along in some domestic arrangement.

INTERVIEWER: Bond pairing with one person. Was there less talk about sex when you were younger or was the talk about the same?

VIDAL: The talk was about the same.

INTERVIEWER: Yes, but it wasn't considered a matter to write studies about.

VIDAL: Well, there was less talk in mixed company, as it were; meaning by mixed company, homo and hetero, or even hetero men and women. The talk was more euphemistic than it is now.

INTERVIEWER: In your exchange earlier this year in London with Lord Longford, you devastated the poor patriarch with a euphemistic statement: "If you don't love people sexually, you cannot love them at all." This was reprinted in the *Listener*.

VIDAL: I think that's true. If you cannot respond sexually, you cannot be close to another person. That does not mean you have to respond to everybody. To put it differently, if you always inhibit your sexual response, you will have a terrible time dealing with others in other respects. How are the Boston Irish these days now that we're on the subject?

INTERVIEWER: A lot of athletes are rumored to be available.

VIDAL: Well, athletes have always been rather more relaxed than anybody else. They are at home in their bodies. And sex, after all, is just one use of the body. They don't feel any commitment to the straight and narrow path because they have already proved their manhood on the field. Everything else they can take as a joke. Whereas the intellectual is the last person you could or would want to get into bed. Or a fag. The uptight queen.

INTERVIEWER: There a parallel to the uptightness in many of the intellectual gay movement types. The cruising scene in Boston is a lot more open than that; there nearly everyone is available at one time or another, indiscriminate promiscuity. Especially the street scene, the Fenway and the Bird Sanctuary, where the perpetual bluebird reigns...

VIDAL: Like New York's Bird Circuit thirty years ago.

INTERVIEWER: Yeah. Outside pursuit somewhat removed from New York's legendary Blue Parrot. The Sanctuary is a forest with low bushes and reeds. People enter, cruise, ball, and split.

VIDAL: And the master of the revels is Al Fresco.

INTERVIEWER: Natch! The difficulty of making it with another faggot arises in the bar scene, using booze as a crutch, consistently making the right moves at the appropriate time invariably without acknowledging what's really happening.

VIDAL: Women are actually much more interesting, because you're getting exactly the same psychic charge from a faggot, and it isn't as comfortable. The hetero in the old days was always more fun to go to bed with.

INTERVIEWER: I'm not so sure about that now. Why?

VIDAL: There was a kind of kinetic energy about it, it really could get wild. An enormous kinetic intensity, like a lightning storm, is exciting for its own sake, or, to use that word Norman Mailer always misuses, existential.

INTERVIEWER: The wildest experiences supposedly may be found in university tearooms, especially the notorious Lamont Library at Harvard. The scene there includes passing notes which outline what one is into, which for most undergrads is mutual masturbation.

VIDAL: Or belly-rubbing. What Wystan Auden called Princeton First Year.

INTERVIEWER: *The City and the Pillar* must have done wonders for belly-rubbing.

VIDAL: As *Streetcar* did for nymphomania. All of that came much into fashion.

INTERVIEWER: Let's stray over to the fashionable subject of the media. Do you think the decision to televise the House Judiciary Committee's impeachment proceedings played any part in the toppling of Tricksie?

VIDAL: Do you think it had much to do with it?

INTERVIEWER: It seems the mail that came in as soon as the proceedings got under way went from opposition to impeachment at the beginning to ten to one in favor of impeachment at the end.

VIDAL: Because of the Committee?

INTERVIEWER: Yes, and soon a number of congressional people began to reverse or reconsider their decisions when the tally was being counted up. But this prostitution was not exactly creative democracy at work.

VIDAL: I think something changed in the weather. I think the people always knew instinctively that he was a criminal. After all, we are nation of shoplifters as Napoleon said the British were a nation of shopkeepers. Americans know a crook when they see one, as they have had a lot of experience with crooks. So it was highly suitable that a nation of shoplifters should elect a criminal as their president. Only you do not get caught shoplifting. And as president, you mustn't get caught stealing money for your houses, or buying earrings for your pretty wife with money that has not been declared to the IRS. I don't think that anyone was really surprised to find out that he was a criminal. Only that he got caught.

INTERVIEWER: True, though one in five still supports the exiled emperor. When the press discerned that his fall was imminent, they got themselves busy dolling up another hero. Tweedle-Dum and Tweedle-Dee magazines had Kissinger on the cover. What would Myra say about Kissinger?

VIDAL: Well, Myra would probably find that in a sense he continued the tradition of S. Z. Sakall, known as "Cuddles," who appears as a minor actor in many films, with his heavy accent and seriously pendant jowls. So there probably isn't a need for a Kissinger figure at the moment.

INTERVIEWER: How do you see Kissinger?

VIDAL: The thing I love about Kissinger is that he has made his career out of comparing himself to Metternich. Metternich was an Austrian diplomat, an international figure, master of the Congress of Vienna. But Kissinger has never told us how Metternich's career ended. After about thirty years, the Congress of Vienna, with its balances and interdependences and linkage, was overthrown in 1848, in a spontaneous popular uprising all over Europe in which a number of crowned heads were swept away. Will Kissinger like Metternich bring on a world revolution?

INTERVIEWER: Kissinger will not last that long. He's a good liar but he doesn't have Metternich's attention for detail. Any idea what sort of hero might rush in to fill the breach, as it were?

VIDAL: It will evolve. Americans are simple and their heroes easy to design. I mean, you can invent them overnight. Look at Ford. Ford did himself in with the pardon, but before the pardon he was well on his way to being Jack Armstrong, all-American boy. The people loved him. He cooked his own breakfast and had a nice smile and a twinkle in his eye. He wasn't especially bright, but that only meant that the electorate could identify with him much more readily than with, say, the towering intellect that Kissinger has been made out to be. So through his upright stupidity he was on the way to enjoying a perfect symbiotic relationship with his electorate.

INTERVIEWER: The comparison to Ford as the man in the horror movie: the first man who sees the monster and comes rushing in to report that there's something terrible and green in the meadow, is unparalleled. A remake of *The Last Will of Dr. Mabuse*. He may have seen the monster while he was being taught by Johnson to chew gum.

VIDAL: With his foot in his mouth. But he looked all right for a couple of minutes. Had he not granted the pardon, he would have become the Leader by this point. They're all interchangeable. It is the system, not the personality, which determines the state of affairs. I was on the box with Arthur Schlesinger yesterday. Arthur said, "Well, Watergate would never have happened if we had a conventional politician in there, such as Humphrey or Muskie." And I let that go, but I'm not so sure that it would not have happened. It was due to happen. The system was so corrupt. So much money is gathered and used illegally. Something was bound to surface. It's just that Nixon was so incompetent. He did too many bad things. You see, Nixon wanted to be caught. You must remember that. From the moment he became president he had to contrive his own ruin. His character demanded this. No matter what situation he was in, no matter what peak he attained, he would contrive to get his back to the wall.

INTERVIEWER: The American public does not want to deal with the godhead as vulnerable or impotent. Witness the tepid reception to your play *An Evening with Richard Nixon*. What do you see as the most memorable character trait of Nixon?

VIDAL: He did the most extraordinary thing. It's documented on the tapes. Right after he won the great election victory, he was talking with an aide about someone in a federal bureau: "Is so-and-so a friend?" Nixon said, "Let's face it [expletive deleted] we have no friends." Now, a man who has just been elected with all those votes says "we have no friends." This means that he doesn't like the people who elected him and he knows that through trickery, through the media, through big money, through smearing his enemies, through underground dirty tricks he got the job. That to me was the tragic moment when you saw the real Nixon saying "I am not worthy, I'm a sort of Iago, I'm a Richard III. I have taken this place which is not rightfully mine." And there was a sense of not only evil, but self-perception.

INTERVIEWER: You have often said that a military dictatorship is in the offing, in the form of 100 percent Americanism, a democracy which will give people what they want, for a time.

VIDAL: Yes, I think it's possible.

INTERVIEWER: Has Watergate affected the possibility?

VIDAL: Oh, no. Watergate will not affect the chances of it coming about.

INTERVIEWER: How do you envision the next superhero?

VIDAL: Whoever becomes our next dictator will be like Arthur Godfrey—folksy and very democratic in appearance, very warm and talkative and will say a lot about how much he loves the people. He will seem all right. He will also have the full support of the Pentagon and of the big industries intertwined with the Pentagon, members of Congress who support the Pentagon. But first things will have to get unstuck.

INTERVIEWER: Due to the economy?

VIDAL: Well, people were very docile in the Depression of the 1930s. There was twenty percent unemployment, which was fantastic compared with today's figures, and there was no talk of revolution. The worst thing that happened, as I remember, is when the jobless veterans marched on Washington. That did scare the shit out of everybody. I remember riding down to the Senate in my grandfather's car with its senatorial plate, and they stoned the car on the Capitol grounds. It was my first experience with a mob. Then Douglas MacArthur dispersed them. People were very docile then, but not now. They all have Saturday night specials, and they all watch TV which has shown them all the pretty things they cannot afford, junky pretty things that they think they ought to have yet can't buy. So I think that when unemployment reaches ten or fifteen percent, they are going to go down to the grocery store with their guns and they are going to take what they want. And they are going to refuse to pay their bills. This is happening in Italy now: they refuse to pay the light bill. And it may well be that the power companies are going to have to shut down because they cannot afford to pay for fuel. With a setting like that people will not be as docile as they were in 1929. They will be militant, and therefore the military will act. But they won't act through a general. As dumb as they are, they won't be that crude. They'll use somebody like Henry Jackson to shut the door to our cage.

INTERVIEWER: Will they make use of a scapegoat? Will the industrialists come out and blame the liberals as they did in Italy in the 1920s, leading to the ascent of Mussolini?

VIDAL: Certainly they will always blame the liberals, the people who wanted to waste money on niggers and schools and things like that instead of defending the country against the international menace of communism, wherever it may show its head in any part of the world. They'll do that automatically. The blacks will probably get it too. Nobody likes them. It's fascinating to watch my Jewish intellectual friends become anti-black.

INTERVIEWER: Oh, is social acceptance still *the* issue? The Bernsteins had blacks in.

VIDAL: They have not had them in for a long time. That was 1960s chic. This year's radical chic is to light a fiery cross in Harlem.

INTERVIEWER: In the *Playboy* interview you said that you would feel "secure though uninspired" about Rockefeller as president or vice president. How do you feel now?

VIDAL: Did I really say that? I'd be inspired to real insecurity nowadays. I did not know then what I know now. I certainly knew he was bad news in New York State. I knew quite a bit about his operations in Albany. I daresay that I had said so many negative things about politicians that I should, I thought, demur on those two, Rockefeller and Muskie. Tactful, I think, is the word for it.

INTERVIEWER: Could Rockefeller be the new hero?

VIDAL: He's very much the man on horseback. I would say that of any politician who is now on the scene, he is the potential dictator. Certainly he has an authoritarian mind, loves the Pentagon, loved the Vietnam war, would double the military budget. He would never cut it, neither would Ford. If you cut it, the whole country's going bankrupt, because that is where the corporations have sunk most of their investments.

I have a theory that John D. Rockefeller, because he was suckled on mother's milk in his seventies, eighties, and nineties, attributing his long life to that, never died; that John D. Rockefeller II and John D. Rockefeller III are the same. It's the original. He is still alive at this very moment running the United States. Nelson is just one of his clones. Somewhere out there is an old man suckled on mother's milk guiding our affairs to total disaster.

INTERVIEWER: But could one individual—even the original John D.—make all that much difference?

VIDAL: Well, we're beyond leadership now. Other tides are running. Individuals are not going to make that much difference with what's about to happen. They're all interchangeable. Whoever he is, the dictator will arise by accident. History requires great change and individuals do not make that change. At least not in a period of disaster. The French Revolution just happened, you know. Nobody started it, and nobody controlled it. Then when it had run its course, Bonaparte picked up the pieces. After that an individual does have a great effect.

INTERVIEWER: How do you see sports heroes and the role of American adulation?

VIDAL: I just read somewhere, the *Miami Herald,* I think it was, that there's a book coming out on homosexuality and the baseball world. Needless to say I cannot wait for these revelations. I do remember a very funny (and it wasn't meant to be funny) interview with Joe DiMaggio talking about the young baseball players today, and the fags among them. He said: "I mean, it wasn't like in the old days. They are so ... open. I mean they hold hands right in front of you." What used to be done in a quiet corner of the shower room is now out in the open in the biggest dressing room of all. A shocking interview. Joe was scarlet. But I look forward to that. I can't imagine anyone who was not largely homosexual wanting to be a baseball or a football player, having to live with other boys so much of the time.

INTERVIEWER: Not to mention the men who are mesmerized watching athletes on television.

VIDAL: I've always maintained that this is the greatest sign of effeminacy in the male, wanting to watch other men play games.

INTERVIEWER: It's interesting that so many faggots are turned off by sports on the box.

VIDAL: It's actually fascinating. The faggots who in theory ought to like watching handsome young men playing body contact games do not like it and the heteros are just out of their minds. I guess it's the only time when the heteros may openly enjoy what they secretly dream of.

INTERVIEWER: There's obviously some sort of sublimated orgasm going on, not to bring in old Freud. But it's not like Athens where homosexuality and sports went, figuratively speaking, hand in hand.

VIDAL: No, in Athens and all those societies, people did play games until they were very old. You kept yourself up. But the American male at 25 weighs 250 pounds, is soft and paunchy and out of shape, and so identifies with the professional athletes who have to keep themselves in shape. So they are his male surrogates as well as his male lovers, in a psychic sense.

INTERVIEWER: Your essay "Pederasty, Plato and Mr. Barrett" has been sealed by the Madison Historical Society. Would you like to talk about your response to Mr. Barrett's essay "New Innocents Abroad."

VIDAL: As I remember, it was sealed for one year. My answer was irritable. I said nothing in it that I haven't said ten million times since and much better. Barrett was stupid. And inaccurate. André Gide said, "Je ne suis pas tapette, monsieur, je suis pédéraste," which was said about Capote, and not about me.

INTERVIEWER: The Catholic Church has once again begun to flex its political muscle in some states. it has managed to push through laws which completely fly in the face of the Supreme Court decision on abortion. Catholic organizations are now sponsoring a proposed constitutional amendment which would completely abolish this hard-won right. And where their efforts have proven unsuccessful, or, in the case of New York City, failed a bit, they have turned against pending gay rights legislation. Do you think that if Mother Pope succeeds in revoking the right to voluntary childbirth, that the fags will be next on the scaffold?

VIDAL: Why not? If I were dictator or president or otherwise in control of a well-run country, the first thing I would do is to forbid the Catholic Church from educating anyone. I would not allow them to have any schools as I regard their education to be inimical to the best interests of the Republic. Where the Catholic Church has dominated there has never been a democratic society. This even goes for France which is largely secular and atheistic. But nevertheless, it is sufficiently Catholic to prevent it from governing itself except as a kind of confused oligarchy. Democracy, as we know it, the modern Republic, is an essentially Protestant phenomenon. Whatever the Protestant fails at doing, the Protestant at least protests. But I would not allow any religious group to have schools. And without schools, there would be no Catholic Church in two generations because their doctrines are so insane that nobody in his right mind would accept them. Then I would tax all churches heavily. That would reduce their influence by 90 percent.

INTERVIEWER: Do you think the Church bears much of the responsibility for the current overpopulation and food crisis?

VIDAL: Yes.

INTERVIEWER: Historically, how do you see the power base of the Roman church in America?

VIDAL: I think the Roman Catholic arrivals here have not been—how shall I put this tactfully—a great addition to our Republic and its ways and customs. They bring with them a love of authority, an inability to make decisions on their own and an essential bigotry, directed specifically toward Jews and also toward the lesser breeds. It is no accident that the great support that Richard Nixon and George Wallace have is in the ethnic suburbs of the North, the Irish Catholic and Polish Catholic suburbs, just as they have the fundamentalist WASPs and other illiterates in the rural South.

INTERVIEWER: Have we not been making whipping boys out of the Irish Catholics of Boston? Are you familiar with the school situation in Boston and the opportunism of Louise Day Hicks?

VIDAL: I know about Louise Day. On the other hand, the people from Southie have a very good point aside from their native bigotry and so forth. They feel impotent and screwed by an impersonal government which won't let them send their children to the schools they want them to go to.

INTERVIEWER: And people are being bused from bad schools in black neighborhoods to bad schools in white neighborhoods.

VIDAL: Yes, as if the American public school system is any good anywhere. Wherever you go, you get a lousy education. What difference does it make if it takes an extra hour to get there?

INTERVIEWER: Additionally, in the upper-middle-class South End of Boston special experimental schools, which blacks for some reason avoid, have been set up.

VIDAL: Experimental schools. They get the blacks and then spend no money.

INTERVIEWER: Though in America all races have an equal right to illiteracy. The usual practice is to shove people through schools, willy-nilly, people who are not being educated. Those who manage to achieve their grade level are shoved into college.

VIDAL: Without ever realizing what a verb was.

INTERVIEWER: Is there a positive way of looking at that? In a vein of humor, are people perhaps concentrating more on the substance and less on the grammar? Are they discovering one another and not concentrating on mere academic aspects?

VIDAL: Oh, no. Words are words and gropes are gropes. And it's nice to be able to render a grope into words.

INTERVIEWER: Witness the recent, innumerable acts of linguistic genocide committed by the House Judiciary Committee, beginning with Rodino's "the gentle lady from New York" and leading us to the overwhelming question, "Will the president continue to offense the Constitution?"

VIDAL: "Offense the Constitution?" Oh, no. I wish I'd heard that. I didn't witness any of the hearings, I was abroad. That's very nice. That's what I call Near English. Have the immigrants done that, the schools?

INTERVIEWER: Perhaps it's the television media with pablum programming and *Time* magazine.

VIDAL: Well, *Time* magazine is more into neologisms. You know: Portly, well-educated, balding...

INTERVIEWER: And empty of content. While we're on the subject of verbiage, do you know that one of your nemeses, Truman Capote, says that he's doing a column every three weeks for the *New York Times?*

VIDAL: Oh, no. That's pure Truman. He invented it as he invents most of his conversations. The *New York Times* printed a rebuttal which went out over all the wire services, and it was very embarrassing. Poor Truman. It wouldn't be a bad idea to let him be Suzy for a while. In *Pictures from an Institution* Randall Jarrell said about Mary McCarthy, calling her Gertrude, I believe: Gertrude may not be much of a novelist, but she's a wonderful liar. That would be poor Truman.

INTERVIEWER: How do you feel your novel *Myron* is being received? *Time,* in a scatological review, uses the word "evil" thrice, and *New York* magazine claims that you do not have the courage of Myra's convictions.

VIDAL: Oh, yes. I read that. Fremont-Smith referred to *Myra* as a classic. He forgot that he used to be the daily reviewer for the *New York Times.* Originally he was horrified by *Myra B.* Obviously he's changed. Philip Roth has done a marvelous job on the *Times'* book reviewers. It started with a piece in the *New York Review of Books,* in which he went after Christopher Lehman-Haupt who then made the mistake of writing a long letter to the *New York Review.* And then Philip answered it. It was very funny. Those people are simply not competent and ought not to be doing this kind of thing. We do not want what they laughingly refer to as their thoughts on any subject. Just try and describe a book, which is difficult to do.

INTERVIEWER: We were talking about Heller's latest opus and generalizing. We couldn't understand how a reviewer could pick up a book, glance at it, write a review and then compare it to a book written in a different decade.

VIDAL: Well, you write that sort of review in advance. There are two reviews you could give it: (1) that it is not as good as *Catch-22*. That's the usual one. We all know that sequels are not as good as their originals. We all know that *Huck Finn* was much worse than *Tom Sawyer,* naturally, a great failure. So you can write that review very safely. Or (2) you just zero in and say that it has to be a very good novel because it's very long, and the author is middle-aged, Jewish, and heterosexual. These are the three most important things that you can be, the sine qua non. So how could you knock such a triad?

INTERVIEWER: We hear Mick Jagger visited you in Italy and that you cooked Irish stew for him.

VIDAL: He stayed with me three days, but I forget what I gave him. We had a cook. And he had a diamond in his tooth, which is the first thing I noticed. I said I thought he had caught something between his teeth. He said, "Yeh, it's me diamond." I said, "Isn't it uncomfortable?"

INTERVIEWER: We would venture to say that *Myron* is your most self-indulgent, though your best, book. And only you could have written it which isn't quite true of the historical novels.

VIDAL: Well, I think that. And I would say that some of the response here and there around the country, Richard Poirier and so on, is that it has to be read line by line. And, you know, readers nowadays, particularly the academics, read by the page. They figure there is not going to be much on a page anyway, so the eye zigzags down: cock, cunt, Marilyn Monroe . . . E. M. Forster. Turn the page, and so on. I work line by line, and if you miss a couple of lines you miss the point. I make little puzzles, like Agatha Christie. You know, I keep planting my clues.

INTERVIEWER: Sherman cigarette butts in Peter Sargent's ashtray.

VIDAL: Yes, remember that later, because it may be a key point.

INTERVIEWER: It looks as though *Myron* will not reach a large audience. How does that strike you?

VIDAL: Well, you do feel that you have failed when you realize people are not getting you at all. But it's ignorance which most irritates me. I've been doing interviews, eight a day, and the square ones . . . and I finally told one yesterday, who was rather bright but extremely rectilinear, that I always have to remind myself that I'm in America, and that I'm the author of a bad, dirty book like Jacqueline Susann or Harold Robbins. In Europe *Myra's* regarded rather seriously. So I take it for granted that interviewers want to discuss it seriously. Then I suddenly remember that they don't know what it is. So I have to start all over again. Explain about literature.

INTERVIEWER: Last year you talked of a way around censorship and the *Smith vs. California* decision with *Myron*, but your lips were sealed on the subject. You've taken measures to ensure that *Myron* is not banned as pornography. You've cleaned up some of the tart language.

VIDAL: Yes, I've cleaned up *Myron*. I've removed the dirty words and replaced them with clean words.

INTERVIEWER: What words?

VIDAL: Well, I thought and thought for a long time: what are the cleanest words I can find? And I discovered that I could not come up with any cleaner words than the names of the five Supreme Court justices and two other good citizens who have taken on the task of cleansing this country of pornography. I inserted the words in place of the dirty words. For example, a cock becomes a rehnquist. And a cunt becomes a whizzer white—

INTERVIEWER: After Byron White, the football hero who cracked the kamikaze code in World War II.

VIDAL: To fuck becomes to burger, and an ass becomes a blackmun and so on.

INTERVIEWER: Interesting in view of the fact that psychologists and psychiatrists from Freud to Malinowski have indicated that one can always tell what a given culture worships by determining what words are taboo. The ancient Hebrews could not take the name of the Lord in vain; for the medievals sodomy was not to be spoken of; and for us, the American pantheon consists of such deities as cock, cunt, ass and fuck. In any case, do you think *Myron* is sufficiently sanitary to get by in Drake, North Dakota?

VIDAL: In Drake, I wonder. I think they'll be upset. People will get upset as Susskind told me last night. I guess he was trying to get some conservatives on the show to debate me, and he tried to get Rehnquist.

INTERVIEWER: Our wise justice or—

VIDAL: No, the cock. And Rehnquist said no; that he never appeared on television, which is true. So that was that. Then David rang up the solicitor general, Mr. Bork, and said, "Will you appear on television with Vidal?" And he said, "I will not." And David said, "Why not?" And he said, "I do not think the solicitor general of the United States should ever become hysterical on television." And David said, "Oh, have you seen the book?" And he snapped, "I've heard about it." And David, being the *yenta* that he is, said, "What do the justices think?" And Bork said, "I wouldn't dare to mention such filth to them!" It's nice to know that in Washington there's a ticking bomb. There will come the day when someone hands Warren Burger a copy of the book as he goes into court.

INTERVIEWER: I am surprised that you or Random House have not sent the justices review copies for their judicious approval.

VIDAL: Actually I want them to change their names to what I substituted their names for.

INTERVIEWER: Do you think *Myron* will set America back on the road to rectitude?

VIDAL: Rectitude is an exquisitely chosen word.

INTERVIEWER: We have a fantasy about *Myra* and *Myron,* namely, that there will be a third book, one of those dystopic science-fiction things about overpopulation, entitled "Normy," an anagram for Myron, about this misanthropic MacDonald's chef who makes his way to power and attempts to destroy the human race through indiscriminate breeding. Myra, of course, steps in to thwart his plans, depowelling him as he emerges from the VFW headquarters in Schenectady. Is Myra still in wait?

VIDAL: Well, I don't know if there is any sign that Myra will strike again. I can't see it from here. But you can never tell. Somewhere she's rapping away. Inexorable!

INTERVIEWER: Recalling our discussion of the Everard Baths last year [*Fag Rag* 7/8], a recent issue of *Straight to Hell*, a journal on cocksucking and current affairs, documents the rumor that Truman Capote plays the part of the voyeur on his regular visits to Sauna here in New York.

VIDAL: I can't say, as I don't visit the Sauna. But I've read *STH*. Quite an imaginative little paper, as imaginative as Truman when it comes to telling stories about people. Yet I hoped that the Bob Hope story was true.

INTERVIEWER: Do you still have the tape of that evening with Mailer, Ginsberg, etc., which you described in *Two Sisters* [p. 213]?

VIDAL: Paul Bowles taped Ginsberg, Orlovsky, Norman and me. Mailer got drunk and finally just lay down on the floor. It was a hot summer night and he had his shirt off and his belly stuck out. Allen rested his bare feet on Norman's fat stomach, and said: "Of course, you know he's crazy." And then we had this long discussion about Mailer as he lay there comatose on the floor. Afterwards, I asked Paul what the tape was like. He said it made no sense at all. Every now and then you heard a screech from Orlovsky. Paul thought he was going to have a memorable piece of tape.

Also, while we're on the subject, I got a letter from Kerouac's latest biographer. He wrote me saying you'll be interested to know that I've come across a letter from William Burroughs to Jack Kerouac saying that Burroughs was coming around and would like to meet me, because he thought I was a nice-looking cat. And could Kerouac be so kind as to set this up? I didn't realize. Kerouac rang up and asked if I'd like to go to dinner with him and a friend. Burroughs was unknown then. He'd just shot his wife and I think he'd published *Junkie* under another name. So we all met down at the old San Remo in the Village. Burroughs was kind of stunned-stoned. Kerouac was stunned with drink. Strange summer night. We then went to Tony Pasteur's, a big dyke hangout. I don't know what possessed us to go there. Jack and I always sort of contemplated going to bed together, but we never got around to it. And I guess Jack did it to head off Burroughs. So he got rid of Bill at one point. By then I was well out of the idea because he was too drunk. But Jack insisted, so off to the Chelsea we went. Somebody should get a copy of the hotel register, because I think we signed our right names.

This was in the late fifties. I guess around the summer of '56. I know I was already doing television plays, because a couple of nights later Kerouac was down in the San Remo and was sitting in a corner shouting, "I blew Gore Vidal!" This was overhead by a guy named Jack Barefield who worked for the advertising agency that put the money up for CBS's *Studio One* series. I was doing a *Studio One*. And Barefield, a very nervous Southern type, said, "I just don't think this is very good publicity for you. That crazy man down there saying such things." I said, "Well, that's just Jack."

INTERVIEWER: Burroughs was in Boston recently for a poetry reading.

VIDAL: He's never said an intelligent thing in my presence. He's a bit like Andy Warhol—

INTERVIEWER: With a scissors. Have you had any contact with Warhol?

VIDAL: I don't run with that crowd. The media have made him out to be a sort of a menace, and like Norman, very obligingly, he plays the part.

INTERVIEWER: I love his so-called theory of film.

VIDAL: I asked him what was the most difficult thing about movie-making and he said, getting the film into the camera.

INTERVIEWER: Will you direct a film?

VIDAL: I've written several movies in the past.

INTERVIEWER: *Ben Hur, Suddenly Last Summer, The Best Man, Is Paris Burning?* with Francis Ford Coppola, ad infinitum...

VIDAL: *Ad Infinitum* opened in Brooklyn, RKO Albee. As for directing, I think my moment has passed. I considered it seriously a few years ago. But I think I'm too old now. You have to do it when you're full of energy. Not that directing itself takes that much energy, but dealing with the money people takes an awful lot out of you. I think I'm too old and spoiled to cope with any of that.

INTERVIEWER: Have you thought about filming *Myra* or *Myron?*

VIDAL: I never saw the first film of *Myra.* Judging from the reviews, I was fortunate. They never used my script.

INTERVIEWER: Unfortunately. I read the script last month in Madison when I was reviewing your papers. The memorable episodes involved Myra as various stars: Bogart, Julie Andrews (*The Sound of Music*), James Mason (*The Seventh Veil*), Ingrid Bergman (*Joan of Arc*), Garbo (*Camille*), culminating with Myra as Queen/King Kong to Rusty's Fay Wray. Would you like to see a film of *Myron?*

VIDAL: Yeah, but it would be kind of tricky; it would probably include a lot of literary foreplay, all that stuff about a film within a film and never getting to the point. Things of which the French are so fond. But I would fancy a film of *Myron,* possibly starring Woody Allen. Or Tricia Nixon.

INTERVIEWER: In *Myron* there is the view that Hollywood has definitely altered our concept of ourselves. It seems to say that if Myra could go back in history and change several aspects of *Siren of Babylon* and thereby manage to save Hollywood, that history itself would be altered. Going back to the past to change the future which is now the present. Surely this is all jest. But do you see more hope of changing society through the film than through the printed word? And, secondly, do you think that to be the goal of any conscientious filmmaker?

VIDAL: No. I don't think that any film nowadays can have the slightest influence in the way those films had when everybody went to the movies. The equivalent today would be the TV commercials.

INTERVIEWER: An industry where some of our most creative people master the art of subliminal seduction.

VIDAL: Yeah. A television series, maybe. I'm sure that *All in the Family* and *Mary Tyler Moore* have had more impact on American mores. But you won't see the impact for ten to twenty years, the same way as you did not see the influence of Hollywood in my generation.

INTERVIEWER: What about your fascination with George Arliss?

VIDAL: Everything I've ever wanted to be, he's played: The Green Goddess, Disraeli, Cardinal Richelieu, oh my god, did I love that. He only had one expression which I always admired. You know I hate actors who have lots of expressions. He had just one. The eyebrows would lift, and he would look with absolute disbelief at what was going on around him whether the scene called for it or not. You could see plainly he did not know what was going on. Oh, he was great.

INTERVIEWER: How was your generation influenced?

VIDAL: Mailer, for example, is still playing John Garfield. I mean he'll never really play anyone else. That's in his head, though he sometimes attempts Bogart and tries to shift around. We all have these mythical figures in our heads. That was the first thing that really compelled our imaginations. But it is no longer film, nor will it ever be, because the film speaks only to specialized audiences. I can't imagine a nation changed by Ingmar Bergman. So few people go to see him.

INTERVIEWER: Our generation appears to be influenced by Mick Jagger, David Bowie, Elton John's androgyny or bisexuality.

VIDAL: Well, when Jagger came to stay with me I got the impression that he was a rather shrewd, very intelligent, rather donnish businessman who really is mostly hetero and square. And then from somewhere inside himself he throws this switch and suddenly goes into this bisexual number. I said, "I think you are getting away with murder with this bisexual number." He giggled.

INTERVIEWER: We have been working on a piece involved with the nexus between Jagger and the gay sensibility. We concluded that Jagger is basically hetero, but his appeal to homo vis-à-vis hetero is dissimilar.

VIDAL: This travesty number has been going on forever.

INTERVIEWER: You said to *Playboy* that you wrote first to create a work of art and secondly to change society.

VIDAL: Yes, and not necessarily simultaneously.

INTERVIEWER: You told *Fag Rag* last year that as an artist you do not have a political function. Has your feeling changed? What are your latest feelings now that you have published *Myron?*

VIDAL: Well, I don't think it does, overtly, no. But I've always said over and over again that the one immutable law of physics is that there is no action without a reaction. So therefore anything you set into motion will lead to some response, though you cannot calculate what it will be. It could be political, social or what have you. Obviously there will be something. Some waves will be made by what one throws into this vast sea.

INTERVIEWER: Critics expect writers to improve with each work. This is certainly good reason to live abroad. How do you see your work? Do you feel your best work lies ahead?

VIDAL: Oh, God, I don't know. I would doubt it only because you cannot do good work without a future sense of time. And I have no sense of future time. I don't think Western Civilization as I've understood it and cared for it will continue. I don't really in my mind's eye see the human race in existence for another hundred years, right or wrong. When you feel like this, it makes it very difficult to create a work of art because I think the principal impulse to create is the will to make something permanent, even though you know that from the standpoint of eternity, nothing is permanent. But certainly in terms of the generations of man, as the Bible would put it, you do have a sense of continuing and addressing future generations. And so you will not become entirely extinct because of what you have wrought. Well, if you don't have that sense or if you are fairly convinced that there is going to be no future either for the written word as you practice it or for the human race as such, well, this sort of takes the moxie out of you. And I don't think that I'm the only one to feel this. I think that the deterioration in all the arts that we see now is a sign of this.

INTERVIEWER: You wrote, "You have nothing to say, only to add" [*Two Sisters*, p. 16].

VIDAL: I said it to Dwight Macdonald.

INTERVIEWER: About the decline in the condition of the arts?

VIDAL: They are being destroyed from the inside by the practitioners. Music which is made up of silences, pictures which are at random and are made to fall apart, sculpture that sings to you, writing that is intercut with words found at hazard. This is the general direction in all the arts.

INTERVIEWER: How do you see the continuing demise of the novel and the status of literature in academia?

VIDAL: It seems to me there are only two survivors: the type of novel that is written by a Harold Robbins or an Erica Jong for a general public, books with lots of violence, not too many big words, books for those who are bored with television, extolling the virtues of citizenship and virility. The others are written within and for the universities, dull books written to be taught in class as examples of experimental technique, to keep people busy deciphering the allusions. Barth and Pynchon, those people. I would say that apart from TV, the universities have been the worst thing for literature. But Literature with a capital L has gone the way of Andy Hardy and Louis B. Mayer.

INTERVIEWER: The former junk dealer turned mogul. In 1968 you said to a *Boston Globe* reporter that your life was your business.

VIDAL: I'm personal in an impersonal way.

INTERVIEWER: Now that several scholarly reviews of your work have come out, how does it feel to be officially regarded as part of the literary tradition?

VIDAL: A prize for endurance. Not to be taken seriously.

INTERVIEWER: Perhaps Modern Library or someone will come out with paperback editions of your works for undergraduate courses, with a few changs to accommodate the new generation.

VIDAL: Such as printing ironies in red, major points in boldface type and figures of speech in brackets.

INTERVIEWER: It's been nearly thirty years since you published your first novel. You've been saddled with a number of alliterative labels: Bernard Dick's Apostate Angel, the Permissive Puritan, and soon, presumably, the Pontifical Pederast and Clairvoyant Catamite. How do you respond to the media image in capital letters of GORE VIDAL?

VIDAL: There is no such person. One becomes a fictional character in other people's work. Actually, I have been for some years, secretly, of course, Lon McAllister, star of *Home in Indiana* (1944).

PHOTO BY SAM SHAW

TENNESSEE WILLIAMS

TENNESSEE WILLIAMS (Thomas Lanier Williams) was born in Columbus, Mississippi, in 1911. One of America's foremost playwrights, he achieved his first successes with the productions of *The Glass Menagerie* (1945) and *A Streetcar Named Desire* (1947; Pulitzer Prize). In these plays as in many of his later works, Williams explores the intense passions and frustrations of a disturbed and frequently brutal society. An eloquently symbolic poet of the theater, he is noted for his scenes of high dramatic tension and for brilliant dialogue. He is perhaps most successful in his portraits of the hypersensitive and lonely Southern woman, clutching at life, particularly at her memories of a grand past that no longer exists.

His later plays include *Summer and Smoke* (1948), *The Rose Tattoo* (1950), *Cat on a Hot Tin Roof* (1955; Pulitzer Prize), *Sweet Bird of Youth* (1959), *Night of the Iguana* (1961), *In the Bar of the Tokyo Hotel* (1969), and *Small Craft Warnings* (1972). His one-act plays were collected in *27 Wagons Full of Cotton* (1946) and *The American Blues* (1948). He has also written four collections of short fiction: *One Arm and Other Stories* (1948), *Hard Candy* (1954), *The Knightly Quest* (1969), and *Eight Mortal Ladies Possessed* (1974); two novels: *The Roman Spring of Mrs. Stone* (1959) and *Moise and the World of Reason* (1975); two collections of poems: *In the Winter of Cities* (1956) and *Androgyne Mon Amour* (1977); and a film script based on two of his short plays, *Baby Doll* (1956). His autobiography *Memoirs* was published in 1975. Tennessee Williams' *Letters to Donald Windham 1940-65* appeared in 1976.

THE PRESENT INTERVIEW was taped in New York City at the Hotel Elysee in October 1976 by George Whitmore. It originally appeared in *Gay Sunshine* 33/34 (Summer/Fall 1977). From 1974 to 1975 Whitmore was a contributing editor to *The Advocate,* where his column on literature appeared regularly. He resigned in protest over its publisher's comments on the gay liberation movement (see *Gay Sunshine* 24). A freelance writer, poet, and playwright, he has also been active in New York gay organizations for some time. His most recent book of verse, *Getting Gay in New York,* was published by the Free Milk Fund Press in 1976. His play *The Caseworker* premiered at Playwrights Horizons in New York in spring 1977. He has authored a biographical study on Thoreau, *Friendship in New England,* and contributes verse and criticism to a number of gay publications. His essay on "Living Alone" was published in the Karla Jay-Allen Young anthology *After You're Out.*

The *Gay Sunshine* article on his work to which Tennessee Williams refers at the beginning of this interview was published in issue 29/30 (Summer/Fall 1976). The views in that article were solely those of the writer and were not those of *Gay Sunshine* or its editor.

George Whitmore interviews
TENNESSEE WILLIAMS

WHITMORE: What have you been doing the past couple of weeks? I know that you've been in a lot of different places, seeing a lot of different plays.

WILLIAMS: I was in Philadelphia this last weekend. I've just come back from Key West and San Francisco.

WHITMORE: What was showing in Philadelphia?

WILLIAMS: They had two productions there. One was with Shirley Knight. I'm particularly interested in her for a long play of mine called *The Red Devil Battery Sign,* which is going to be performed in London, I think.

WHITMORE: When?

WILLIAMS: I think around the first of the year is what they're aiming at, and she'd be wonderful in it. Then they were also doing, at Temple University, a production of *Camino Real.*

WHITMORE: How was that?

WILLIAMS: Beautifully done, especially the Kilroy.

WHITMORE: Who directed it?

WILLIAMS: Rick Winter was the name of one of them. He's gay and he's married, to a young man who's working with him on the show. His base used to be San Francisco.

WHITMORE: Do you think the play will come back from London?

WILLIAMS: Oh I think so, eventually. It's safer in London right now, for one thing, because it's much easier in London to raise money on a serious play than it is in America, than it is in New York. And the material is somewhat dangerous in America right now because it could be interpreted as an attack on the "corporation" . . . the military . . .

WHITMORE: The military-industrial complex?

WILLIAMS: Yes.

WHITMORE: Was that a problem in Boston?

WILLIAMS: Yes, I think it was the unspoken problem, the one they didn't mention.

WHITMORE: I heard so many rumors about the rest of the problems.

WILLIAMS: There were many problems. One was that the script was not yet ready and the other was Claire Bloom. She was miscast—an excellent actress but miscast in that. All of us hope that it will be much better received in London. Gene Persson, who was coproducer of *This Is,* which was done at ACT [American Conservatory Theater] in San Francisco last year, is going to produce this in London. He hopes to get Shirley Knight, to whom he was formerly married, for the leading feminine role.

WHITMORE: Are you disappointed with Broadway?

WILLIAMS: I don't care *where* the plays are performed. I don't care if they're performed in a 99-seat house like the Showcase in San Francisco. I don't care if they're performed off-off-Broadway. It's just as exciting and important. I just prefer that they be my recent work, not my old work—these old chestnuts like *The Glass Menagerie* that couldn't offend anybody's maiden great-aunt.

WHITMORE: How do you feel about these revivals?

WILLIAMS: Oh, I'm very gratified by them because they show the plays have continuing interest to the public. Virtually all have been well received and well reviewed, and they show the plays have longevity....

I picked up a copy of *Gay Sunshine* [GS 29/30] saying that plays such as *Streetcar,* and virtually all of my plays, were really lies because they were about homosexuals disguised as women, which is a preposterous allegation and a very dangerous one. It's dangerous to the whole art, to all the written arts. It won't hold water; it don't stick, it just can't stick. So I wrote them back a very temperate but strong letter [GS 31] explaining that in my own particular case I have found no difficulty whatsoever in identifying totally, but not with transvestites. I don't understand transvestites or transsexuals. They are *really* outside my understanding.

WHITMORE: You knew Candy Darling fairly well, didn't you?

WILLIAMS: Candy Darling was an angel. She was a transvestite, yes, but she was . . . just a very sweet person. I didn't quite understand her, and I don't understand most transvestites. I think the great preponderance of them damages the gay liberation movement by travesty, by making a travesty of homosexuality, one that doesn't fit homosexuality at all and gives it a very bad public image. We are *not* trying to imitate women. We are trying simply to be comfortably assimilated by our society.

WHITMORE: Well, that would be a moderate view.

WILLIAMS: Would it? Eventually we don't want to feel self-conscious, we don't want to be discriminated against.

WHITMORE: I think most radical gay liberationists, most movement gay liberationists, would say that transvestites are offensive to women, are mocking women, and they are very much against transvestitism.

WILLIAMS: I think they make a mockery of the female sex, yes. And I happen to . . . be partial to them, not sexually, but as people.

WHITMORE: Transvestites?

WILLIAMS: No, women. . . . But I found this article outrageously obtuse and dangerous because it's imitating exactly a certain kind of chauvinistically male attack that gay playwrights have been receiving.

WHITMORE: It disturbs me because it shows me a gay person attacking you on the same basis that straight critics have.

WILLIAMS: They're not attacking me anymore on that basis. They've stopped that, they've quit that, they've gone beyond that.

WHITMORE: You gave an interview in the *New York Times* when the *Memoirs* came out, and you articulated very well how you felt about writing about women and that you could write about women and not transvestites.

WILLIAMS: I can get just as much satisfaction, if not more, writing about a love affair between a perfectly normal man and a perfectly normal woman, as... Well, I never tried really, there's never been any reason for me to write a play about a love affair between two men unless you can interpret that between Skipper and Brick in *Cat* as a love affair, and it's legitimately interpretable that way.

WHITMORE: Why haven't you done it yet?

WILLIAMS: I've done these stories, and I've never had any embarrassment about doing it, never tried to disguise my homosexuality.

WHITMORE: I was very surprised to see some of the dates on the stories where you were writing more openly than almost anybody else was, in fiction. Why not on the stage?

WILLIAMS: There would be no producer for it.

WHITMORE: Now?

WILLIAMS: Oh yes, now there's a surfeit of them. It's become a cliché.

WHITMORE: So you are simply not interested in doing it at this point?

WILLIAMS: I'll do what interests me at this point.

WHITMORE: And you're not interested in writing about it?

WILLIAMS: Maybe tomorrow; at the moment I'm not engaged in that—oh yes, I am: *The Wild Horses of the Camargue,* a play I started in France. There's a great deal to do with a relationship between a tyrannical older man and a very beautiful younger man who is not really a homosexual but who is enslaved by the older man. The Camargue is a section of southern France, an estuary of the Mediterranean. And I've gotten all but one or two key scenes of that written. I've only written what I've wanted to write about, never hesitated to write about anything. I observe certain... delicacies, because I always think the theme of the play, if it's important, should not be impeded by fending people right off by a tangential thing like the precise sexual orientation of characters; in fact I don't think there is such a thing as a precise sexual orientation. I think we're all ambiguous sexually.

WHITMORE: I think for a number of reasons we plunk down on one side or the other.

WILLIAMS: Yes. In practice, yes. But I find it increasingly unimportant.

WHITMORE: You've written about all sorts of "deviant" themes though.

WILLIAMS: I wouldn't stop at anything. Why would I?

WHITMORE: Why should this be exempted?

WILLIAMS: I don't know. I don't understand that man's point of view. In my letter I said that I'm sure that my arguments will not at all dissuade you from your point of view, but I hope they will warn critics on gay magazines in general not to imitate the chauvinistic attitudes that we've had to combat as gay playwrights in straight critics.

WHITMORE: Simply because we're gay playwrights.

WILLIAMS: Everybody knew I was a gay playwright. Many, many years ago *Time* was the first publication to spell it out, that I was homosexual. I didn't give a damn.

WHITMORE: I don't think Albee has ever, to my knowledge, publicly stepped toward any kind of disclosure, and yet he suffered the same way you did simply for the fact that... people did know.

WILLIAMS: I don't think Albee sneaks around corners much. If he wanted to write about two men I think he would have; he's very stubborn.

WHITMORE: I wonder why major playwrights aren't interested. Do you have any idea?

WILLIAMS: They have important things to say, and they want to say them to a large public. Their message is not pertaining simply to sexual orientation. Like *Cat on a Hot Tin Roof* had a great many important things to say about society. The mendacity, in general, of society. That was what I wanted to get across, not the precise sexual identification of these two men.

WHITMORE: Well of course when anybody writes about heterosexuals, there are a lot of sexual relationships that you don't have to deal with because the audience simply takes them for granted. Just as a general question, if X playwright with a certain large audience were going to write about two homosexuals as the protagonists of a play, what special problems would that playwright have to approach in terms of the audience? Is it still a shocker to the extent that it throws everything off?

WILLIAMS: The male, the straight male members of the audience would be bored and just as hostile as ever. Women... would be intrigued. Of course women have always been intrigued by the grace and the style of the gay man.

WHITMORE: I think women appreciate ambiguity.

WILLIAMS: They sense it, they like it; it charms them frequently....

WHITMORE: There seems to be a gay theater developing, on the order of the way the black theater developed in the sixties—specific little theaters, generally in the cities. Now, for the first time, there is an opportunity to write for a gay audience, as opposed to a general audience, which has always been your audience.

WILLIAMS: Do you expect to find a gay audience providing commercial support to the theater?

WHITMORE: No, as a matter of fact it's been the opposite. The gay audience supports Broadway, it supports certain performers, it goes to the ballet...

WILLIAMS: It goes to the popular successes.

WHITMORE: But there are gay people who are concerned with theater specifically. It's happening in New York in a few places now. It seems to me there's a great struggle to make these works... not gay.... They start out with a gay premise... but to give those works a general impact, for them to be about something other than homosexuality. Do you think that's the major problem with writing about homosexuality, writing with gay characters? If you were going to write for a gay audience, what sort of problems do you think you would face?

WILLIAMS: I would be narrowing my audience a great deal. I wish to have a broad audience because the major thrust of my work is not sexual orientation, it's social. I'm not about to limit myself to writing about gay people.

WHITMORE: What's happened in the past few years is that some of us are trying to define ourselves as gay people politically, not only sexually.

WILLIAMS: You know, in my experience I've discovered that some of the most politically reactionary people in America are gays. Oh, they *love* William Buckley, it's the masochism in them.

WHITMORE: An innate masochism?

WILLIAMS: Innate? In any case it is quite conscious. In most of the porno gay films you see now people are being subjected to horrible masochistic acts. It's just revolting.

WHITMORE: Do you think this is slave mentality?

WILLIAMS: I think it's the result of centuries of being treated brutally. They've identified themselves with the masochistic object, and they have to be liberated from that. But right now a lot of them are Buckleyites, the exact opposite of revolutionaries. What should happen is, the gay lib movement should consolidate with the other lib movements—the women's lib movement, and particularly with the revolutionary movements which are nonviolent—and become a single thrust toward emancipation in America. I wish that the gays would get away from riding around in Cadillac convertibles, especially the fat ones that look like travesties of Mae West, and just camping it up on the streets in public view. They make the whole homosexual thing seem ridiculous. Homosexuals are not like that. They're indistinguishable from the straight man, except that the have more sensibility and they are more inclined to be good artists.

WHITMORE: Why do you think that is?

WILLIAMS: Because they have greater sensibility, and because they've *had* to develop a greater sensibility because they have been rejected.

WHITMORE: So it's a matter of being more introspective?

WILLIAMS: Yes. They look deeper into themselves, are deeper into the human heart. Men are all caught up in the competitive rat race—normal straight men, I mean. They lose all sensibility and become like so many big, overgrown pigs rushing for first place at the trough.

WHITMORE: But we know a hell of a lot of competitive gays who pick up the whole game.

WILLIAMS: They imitate the worst aspects of that—their opposites.

WHITMORE: So on one hand we see the fat cat driving around in the convertible, and on the other hand we have the transvestite—

WILLIAMS: Doing the same goddamn thing but dressed up like Mae West.

WHITMORE: Where would the general bulk of the gay people be? We can't generalize and say all gay people are politically reactionary, can we?

WILLIAMS: No, we can't. There's too many of them. They should all be behind the legitimate revolutionary movements.

WHITMORE: Does any kind of theater have a place in that?

WILLIAMS: Oh yes. All good art is essentially revolutionary, in the wide sense of revolutionary. "Revolutionary" is a misunderstood word.

WHITMORE: I'm trying to get a little more specific. If we're going to have a gay community that has a revolutionary thrust to it, should we be concentrating on agit-prop theater—or propagandistic or street theater?

WILLIAMS: Well that is never art really, if it's strictly that. It has to be implicit; revolution is implicit; not explicit, but woven into the fabric of the work.

WHITMORE: Give me a few examples of plays that you have written.

WILLIAMS: Revolutionary plays? Every goddamn one of 'em.

WHITMORE: Let's have a few examples. *Camino Real* I can pick up on right away.

WILLIAMS: Oh, definitely. *Cat, Streetcar,* name me one that isn't . . . *Sweet Bird of Youth,* with Boss Finnley and all his cohorts. Now let's get down to the less well known ones like *Gnädiges Fräulein*: that is the artist in combat with the indifference of society. The artists, specifically the painter, working in a revolutionary form. Maybe it's stylistically revolutionary, still it's revolutionary. And he is going contrary to society.

WHITMORE: All of your protagonists go counter to society.

WILLIAMS: They do indeed.

WHITMORE: Is Blanche a revolutionary?

WILLIAMS: Blanche? Indeed she is. In a small Southern town like Laurel, Mississippi, to live such a life is totally revolutionary and totally honest. She was oversexed, she dared to live it out, without harming anybody.

WHITMORE: I never thought that that's like the character you wrote about in "Miss Coynte of Greene," the woman who went to bed with blacks for the rest of her life.

WILLIAMS: Oh yes.

WHITMORE: Is that consciously Blanche in any way?

WILLIAMS: Blanche? Heavens no! I don't think Blanche had any black fetish, do you?

WHITMORE: No, but it's a comparable situation—a small town—

WILLIAMS: But Blanche was hung up on blue-eyed boys. They reminded her of her young husband, whom she inadvertently forced to suicide.

WHITMORE: Who was homosexual.

WILLIAMS: Whose death she had to atone.

WHITMORE: I think that Blanche is an incredibly strong person.

WILLIAMS: She was demoniacal. She was a tigress, yes. She had the strength to take on the whole society of Laurel, and she also had the strength to take on Kowalski. When she was thrown out, the story calls for her to go to an asylum, yes. But her fantasy world was probably an improvement on her real world.

WHITMORE: I think that in most people's minds, in most audience's minds, and maybe this is because of the way she's been played so often, she's looked upon as frail, a delicate creature—

WILLIAMS: Oh, that's a misinterpretation. Her circumstances were adverse, yes. Society made them that way.

WHITMORE: So if your garden-variety women's liberationist were to criticize that play I think she'd probably say, "Blanche loses in the end. She doesn't have a chance. The playwright has stacked the cards against her." I don't happen to agree with that, but—

WILLIAMS: What's a person to answer these people when they start saying you're a goddamn liar, all your works are lies.

WHITMORE: Now, as a gay person and an artist who has developed a certain kind of sensitivity, like we just talked about, one that many gay people have—

WILLIAMS: They do have a special sensitivity as a rule. But you can find some gay people that are amazingly imitative of callous elements of society, socially callous elements.

WHITMORE: I think you said something in the *Memoirs* about men who cruised all their life with wolfish eyes. Is that the kind of personality you're talking about?

WILLIAMS: Men who don't fall in love but just go for one-night stands and bar pickups, they get wolfish looking, you can see it in their eyes. Their eyes lose a certain . . . humanity, because they only want the brutal sexual act. It's equally brutal with men who continue to pursue woman after woman. There's not that much difference.

WHITMORE: Is that the only way your homosexuality translates into your art, because you've become a more sensitive person through introspection . . . through what I call "our oppression as a group," our being left out, etc.? Is that the only way it's translated? Because you haven't translated it thematically in your plays.

WILLIAMS: Let me try to follow what you're asking. State it once more.

WHITMORE: I started in as a gay playwright, and in the first few plays that I wrote said, "All right, I'm a gay playwright, I'm also a very political person." This is before I had characters or anything to deal with, and I said, "I want to write something about gay people. I want to write about my experiences as a homosexual."

WILLIAMS: Did you want to write exclusively about gay people?

WHITMORE: No, because I don't think that's a theme. I don't think homosexuality is a theme to write about... I think *love* is a theme.

WILLIAMS: Love. The specific gender doesn't matter.

WHITMORE: For me, starting out to do that, there were several ways that I could see immediately, how I could translate my experience as a homosexual into my work. For one thing, I would want to write about men loving men. I've done so, and I think it's worked. It hasn't worked for a general audience. What I'm asking is, has your homosexuality translated generally because you're a sensitized person because of your homosexuality?

WILLIAMS: I have within me, as you have within you, male and female components. Everybody has. Somebody put it very well in Washington. A cousin of mine came to see the play, it was *Out Cry*. He said, "This is a play about *animus*," which is the male spirit, "and the *anima*," which is the female spirit. Those are the two characters. We all have both in us. One may take over in the way we live, or the other may take over. But all of us contain both.... We omitted the androgyne, the one between. I think I have in me all three genders.

WHITMORE: The thing that interested me when I started rereading things a couple of weeks ago was that, like the story "Two on a Party," everything thematically gay in that story is integrated into everything else. It's all of a piece. You've never written a play like that.

WILLIAMS: I've been very anxious to write a film of "Two on a Party." I think it would make a great film. I want it to be done by Paul Morrissey. He is a great artist. He could be even greater if he divorced himself from so much camp. Camp is fun though, I enjoy camp. I think it's an important element of American humor. It's an outlet for us. We can't be serious all the time. We need the... diversion of camp.

WHITMORE: In *Small Craft Warnings,* when you bring gay characters onto the stage—

WILLIAMS: Quentin delivers, from the literary point of view, the most eloquent speech in the play. He's not the most interesting character, but he delivers the best-written speech, the most eloquent speech.... A wonderful character is the leading woman, Leona. She's a faggot's moll. She's going back to it. She found more satisfaction. She's gay, wouldn't you say? She's not a lesbian, but she's a faggot's moll. She prefers the company of faggots, and says so quite often. And she adored her younger brother, who was gay.

WHITMORE: We have two gay characters onstage that are perfectly credible to me, and then we have Leona—

WILLIAMS: But one was a cynical character. He had wound up as a cynical character through social pressures and isolation, and he had been twisted into a man who just takes pleasure in one-night stands and who will even reject a trick if he discovers the trick responds to him.

WHITMORE: Which was a really chilling thing.

WILLIAMS: And I am attracted to the Gothic in the chilling.

WHITMORE: The thing that disturbed me, and it disturbs me because I thought you were making a statement, is that Leona says, in response to him, "I've seen the gay life and I've seen how sick it is, the sadness and the sickness of it." I felt that was a pretty bald statement about gay life.

WILLIAMS: Well it's no longer necessarily that way. I think we're back in the Chekhovian era of the sexual revolution.

WHITMORE: Tell me about that.

WILLIAMS: Chekhovian—where he was predicting, and people were sad, they were lost, they were living for a future that would happen after they were dead. For things would be so much better in the years that followed. Unfortunately they weren't; they turned more reactionary. Things turned into a bureaucracy— the monolithic bureaucracy. Communism as it's known now was to undergo a revolution. It's only waiting for the siege to turn into a normal form of socialism.

WHITMORE: I think Leona is a terrific character. I think she makes a totally stark, bald statement about gay life that you don't—

WILLIAMS: She's commenting upon it as it is now.

WHITMORE: Well don't you think that it's an awful stereotype?

WILLIAMS: Her statement... did she make a statement? She had just been rebuffed by this swine that she lived with who stepped on her at night when she passed out on the floor. She is in a shattered state. She's bound to make bitter statements.

WHITMORE: But that's the world that she's going to re-enter when she packs up her trailer.

WILLIAMS: Yes. She'll have no longer any sexual commitments.

WHITMORE: But it's a world that she sees as sad and sordid.

WILLIAMS: But she feels at home in it. Because she offered them something.

WHITMORE: I understand *that* completely. The thing that bothers me about the speech is that it's a statement about gay life that seems to be a fairly stereotypical view of it and it's one of the only ones you've ever made.

WILLIAMS: People so wish to latch onto something didactic; I do not deal with the didactic, ever.

WHITMORE: That's why the speech stuck out for me, because it seemed—

WILLIAMS: Well, you were looking for it.... Chekhov was probably gay. But he was very ill, and whether or not he practiced his sexual inclination... if you were to look at early pictures of him you would see that he was a very beautiful man with a very sensitive face that you were not likely to encounter among straight men.

WHITMORE: There's a new book out about Gogol—Simon Karlinsky's *The Sexual Labyrinth of Nikolai Gogol* [Harvard University Press].

WILLIAMS: I don't know Gogol's work. I know Gorky's work.

WHITMORE: One of the major points is how misogynistic Gogol's work is. Not necessarily misogynism, but antimarriage.

WILLIAMS: Sexually where did he stand?

WHITMORE: Well, it's a very interesting story. He was gay but not actively. His priest told him he must not do it and must fast to exorcise it. And he fasted himself to death.... Just one more in the line of martyrs....

I want to talk about *Out Cry* because I didn't quite understand what you were getting at technically. It's written differently. I wonder if you would talk about what new directions you're taking in terms of form.

WILLIAMS: More and more adventurous I think. Of course I'm sixty-five and a half years old, and most of my youthful energies have already poured into work. What I have left I must conserve and use carefully, in shorter forms. I no longer feel any pressure to conform to any convention. I write more and more just for pleasure, for my own satisfaction.... You still want to know why I do not write a gay play, don't you? I don't find it necessary. I could express what I wanted to express through other means.

WHITMORE: I have my own theories about gay sensibility but they would probably bore you to tears.

WILLIAMS: I'm interested to hear about them. I think we're in agreement on the subject. Gays are forced to accept those few who are reactionary—an increasing few.

WHITMORE: I do think that a credible gay character on the Broadway stage would be somewhat revolutionary in itself.

WILLIAMS: Oh it would indeed, hasn't yet occurred.

WHITMORE: We've had terrible things like *Find Your Way Home*.... I wonder if the general audience can see the humanity in a gay character when it's in front of them.

WILLIAMS: Yes, they're ready for it now. Well... the men still regard homosexuals as a threat, because their wives are too readily infatuated by attractive homosexuals... such as I [*Laughing*].

WHITMORE: You left a lot about your life in the theater out of the *Memoirs*. Are you going to write something more?

WILLIAMS: Yes. If I ever write again about my life. I'm supposed to do a text for a photo-biography. And when I get other things out of the way I hope to do the text of it. Then I'll have an opportunity to write more about a lot of things. I won't deal so much with my sexual life, that's been pretty thoroughly dealt with. I don't want to be identified as a writer of such-and-such a sexual inclination. I think gay writers have to cease to be known simply as gay writers; they must be admitted into the total of writers, without any special label attached to us, if *Time* magazine and news publications will permit it.

WHITMORE: I don't think we have very much to say about it as soon as it's known we're gay.

WILLIAMS: The primary concern of this world right now should be overpopulation.

WHITMORE: I worked for Planned Parenthood for a number of years, so I'm on your side.

WILLIAMS: Oh yes, it should be planned—limited and planned. It's so hard to reach India...

WHITMORE: *Iguana* is opening in New York this month, I understand.

WILLIAMS: *Eccentricities of a Nightingale,* too.

WHITMORE: Is that the one Michael Kahn is directing?

WILLIAMS: No, Edwin Sherin is directing *Eccentricities of a Nightingale.* It opens at the Morosco. The other one, *Iguana,* is with Richard Chamberlain, Sylvia Miles and Dorothy McGuire.

WHITMORE: Have you seen that production?

WILLIAMS: I saw it in California. It was quite extraordinary. I saw it in L.A.

WHITMORE: How do you feel about *Sweet Bird of Youth,* with Irene Worth?

WILLIAMS: Oh, the woman was extraordinary. I think the boy was much underestimated.

WHITMORE: You were satisfied with him?

WILLIAMS: Christopher Walken was marvelous, much underestimated.

WHITMORE: Maybe I just had a faggot's reaction to the part, because I found him very very unattractive.

WILLIAMS: His face is very very sensitive and beautiful... and sensual. His body is getting a bit overblown but not in an ugly way.

WHITMORE: I thought he was terribly miscast.

WILLIAMS: I preferred him to Paul Newman, despite Paul's musculature.

WHITMORE: I think Irene Worth's performance was such a miracle that I didn't see anybody else on stage at all.

WILLIAMS: Yet when it was obligatory that Walken had a scene he played it beautifully. He's a great actor. She wanted him; she wanted to do it in England but she would not do it because they didn't want him. She chose to stay and do *The Cherry Orchard* rather than do it without him.

WHITMORE: You mentioned one new play that you are working on. Are there any others?

WILLIAMS: Any other plays? No. I'm writing a novel.

WHITMORE: Where will it take place?

WILLIAMS: On an island called Isla de la Boca. It's off the coast of Bolivia.

WHITMORE: About the *Memoirs.* My response and the response of a lot of people I talked to (when I reviewed it I got a few letters about the review) was that they loved it, not only for all the other reasons—that it was your life and that they were interested in it—but because they were so sympathetic toward your coming-out story, the way you treated your sexuality. It meant so much to them to see something in print about that.

WILLIAMS: Oh, I have an avalanche of mail; I think everybody gay in America must have written me.

WHITMORE: That's what I wanted to ask you. How was the response from gay people?

WILLIAMS: Oh everybody was delighted. And many wrote. Very few straight men.

WHITMORE: I felt that you were shabbily treated by the *Times* and a few other reviewers.

WILLIAMS: I don't remember. I didn't get any very *bad* notices. The *Times* is not predisposed toward homosexual writing.

WHITMORE: To what extent do you think your critical reception, when it's been bad, has been because you are gay?

WILLIAMS: I don't know how to measure.

WHITMORE: I wouldn't know how to measure either. I can see with Albee because it's well documented—the critical reception to *Virginia Woolf* from the newspapers to the magazines.

WILLIAMS: It's a huge success nevertheless.

WHITMORE: I still think a number of theatergoers buy the proposition that there are four men on the stage. It's been stated again recently, as a matter of fact I think in the *Village Voice* about a year ago.

WILLIAMS: The *Village Voice* is sort of pseudo-intellectual, isn't it?

WHITMORE: I think so. There were reviews of plays by Maugham, Coward and I think a play of yours, where the critic came out with the thing about "gay writers can't write about women."

WILLIAMS: Very few of the sexually straight writers can write about women.

WHITMORE: But there have been great women written by straight men.

WILLIAMS: Madame Bovary. Now let's look at that. Flaubert was asked, "Who is Madame Bovary?" He said, "Madame Bovary, c'est moi."

WHITMORE: Well Blanche DuBois isn't you, is it?

WILLIAMS: Mostly. I draw all my characters from myself. I can't draw a character unless I know it within myself.

WHITMORE: I'm surprised that you say that, because you said in some interview in *Time* that you had taken her from another person.

WILLIAMS: I used her mannerisms and her appearance; I can't use my own appearance!

WHITMORE: A couple of months ago I came across an article about William Inge. I think Robert Brustein wrote it. He said that in all of William Inge's plays the major theme is the emasculation of the vital protean man by the homebody woman and seemed to imply that Inge had this one theme because he was homosexual.

WILLIAMS: I think maybe it was true of his family life. He made a desperate effort to make the heterosexual adjustment, through an actress whom I know, and he could get an erection touching her breasts. But as soon as he tried to penetrate her sexually the erection collapsed.

WHITMORE: Did he have any "gay life"?

WILLIAMS: Yes. Enormous. I was in Chicago with *Iguana*, staying at the Blackstone. He came up to my room. But I had a friend there. He just got in bed with us.

WHITMORE: The reason I brought up Brustein was because the tone and temper of his article were so similar to others that postulate a homosexual conspiracy to distort reality in the theater.

WILLIAMS: Brustein is ruthless. I don't feel temperately about this man. I'm too old to be afraid of him. Despicable! He is despicable beneath contempt.

WHITMORE: Do you think there is any such thing as a homosexual conspiracy in the theater?

WILLIAMS: In England, under H. M. Tenner, the theater was dominated by great homosexual talents. H. M. Tenner was one of the leading producers of London's West End theater. And I think Binky Beaumont did exercise a considerable tyranny.

WHITMORE: When was this?

WILLIAMS: In the forties and fifties. And I think the theater was, in London, dominated by homosexuals, mainly because they offered the most talent. They don't anymore.

WHITMORE: Of course there are innumerable homosexual producers in New York.

WILLIAMS: Probably. I don't know. I'm not interested in the sex lives of producers. They're not attractive enough to interest me.... And I don't go to bed with actors who are in plays of mine. Any other ones that are attractive, yes.

WHITMORE: Here's something out of left field. Can you compare the performances of Donald Madden to Michael York's?

WILLIAMS: Both great but why compare them?

WHITMORE: Did you write for Donald Madden?

WILLIAMS: I have written plays for him. I wrote *In the Bar of the Tokyo Hotel* for him and Anne Meacham. He was the first one I thought of when *Out Cry* was revived in Chicago. There's nothing homosexual about the personality of Donald Madden.

WHITMORE: So I've heard.

WILLIAMS: Michael York has a charming androgynous quality.

WHITMORE: I think Michael York appeals across the board to everybody.

WILLIAMS: To women and men . . . to women and gay men.

WHITMORE: Whereas Newman probably appeals to everybody.

WILLIAMS: Newman has a very definite consciousness of his gay appeal. Whether he's bisexual I don't know. At least one eminent writer claimed that he was. I disregard such charges. I heard the most unattractive man, in San Francisco, claim that he was cruised by Marlon Brando and that he put him down, rejected him. And this was when Marlon Brando was around twenty.

WHITMORE: Well, there are so many stories about Montgomery Clift.

WILLIAMS: Montgomery Clift was gay. Everybody knows he was. There was nothing effeminate at all about him. A very hairy chest, which I find unattractive. A strange boy: it was hard to relate to him. He'd rush up to you very affectionately and hug you, and then all of a sudden he'd vanish and sit brooding. A very tortured man.

WHITMORE: I don't really know much about his private life.

WILLIAMS: Very few people did except Kevin McCarthy.

WHITMORE: I wonder if Kevin McCarthy's out. I wonder if we could print his name. I don't think he would pick up *Gay Sunshine*.

WILLIAMS: I don't think he would sue, do you?

WHITMORE: Do you think you're going to revive *Out Cry*?

WILLIAMS: It opened in San Francisco just recently, in a small theater, 99 seats, called the Showcase—wonderful manager, Lyle Leverich. There were two very fine actors in it.

WHITMORE: How was it received?

WILLIAMS: Oddly enough it got an excellent notice from the man I was most afraid of. The other notice I haven't seen yet.

WHITMORE: Have you had a chance to see much theater lately?

WILLIAMS: Oh, *No Man's Land* has opened. I want to see it again; I've seen it twice before.

WHITMORE: What did you think of it the times you've seen it?

WILLIAMS: It's my favorite play. *A Chorus Line* is very good of course. It wouldn't have seemed good a few years back. A great thing that's showing is *Threepenny Opera*, the greatest production of it I've ever seen. I saw the '55 production, eight times, but I prefer this.

WHITMORE: Why?

WILLIAMS: It was so magnificently stylized. Every gesture, every move was calculated. It was German expressionism at its highest.

WHITMORE: You said you were writing shorter forms. *Out Cry* seemed to me to be different because there were Pirandellian aspects that weren't so marked in other things you've done.

WILLIAMS: It was not influenced by Pirandello. In the period in which I wrote it I was undergoing some very traumatic experiences and I didn't know the borderline between reality and fantasy. I've tried to read Pirandello, and he translates so badly that very few things are readable. I just can't read it.

WHITMORE: Has your work changed because of experimentations in theater in the sixties?

WILLIAMS: No. I wasn't aware of what was going on in theater in the sixties. What's going on now doesn't interest me that much. Once in a while something does, like *No Man's Land.*

Biography of Winston Leyland

BORN IN Lancashire, England, in 1940 of English and Scottish ancestry, I came to live in the United States (Rhode Island) at the age of twelve with my family. High school and some college on the East Coast. B.A. in philosophy; M.A. in medieval history from UCLA (1970). I was ordained Catholic priest by Cardinal Cushing in 1966 but left structured religion two years later because of the Church's position on Vietnam, ecclesiastical fascism in general, and my own increasing radicalism. I've been involved full time in the Gay Liberation Movement since 1970: editor of *Gay Sunshine* journal from 1971 and publisher of Gay Sunshine Press books. Editor/contributor to the two gay literary anthologies *Angels of the Lyre* (1975) and *Orgasms of Light* (1977). I see Gay Sunshine Press as a catalyst in the evolving Gay Cultural Renaissance and myself as deeply involved in that process.

In the fall of 1977 I visited Brazil and met with many writers and artists, as well as being interviewed myself in several Brazilian journals. The material I gathered is included in the anthology of Latin American gay literature published by Gay Sunshine Press in 1978.

PHOTO BY STEVEN LAFER, SAN FRANCISCO, 1978

This edition is published in paper wrappers; there are 500 hardcover copies of which 26 are lettered (A to Z) and signed by the editor. Five numbered *hors de commerce* hardcover copies are specially bound, signed by the editor and several interviewees.